Workflow in the 2007 Microsoft Office System

David Mann

Apress®

Workflow in the 2007 Microsoft Office System

ISBN-13 (pbk): 978-1-59059-700-2

ISBN-10 (pbk): 1-59059-700-1

Printed and bound in the United States of America 9 8 7 6 5 4 3

Lead Editor: Jonathan Hassell
Technical Reviewer: George Hatoun
Editorial Board: Steve Anglin, Ewan Buckingham, Gary Cornell, Jason Gilmore, Jonathan Gennick, Jonathan Hassell, James Huddleston, Chris Mills, Matthew Moodie, Dominic Shakeshaft, Jim Sumser, Keir Thomas, Matt Wade
Project Manager: Sofia Marchant
Copy Edit Manager: Nicole Flores
Copy Editor: Liz Welch
Assistant Production Director: Kari Brooks-Copony
Production Editor: Kelly Winquist
Compositor: Susan Glinert
Proofreader: Lori Bring
Indexer: Joy Dean Lee
Artist: April Milne
Cover Designer: Kurt Krames
Manufacturing Director: Tom Debolski

Distributed to the book trade worldwide by Springer-Verlag New York, Inc., 233 Spring Street, 6th Floor, New York, NY 10013. Phone 1-800-SPRINGER, fax 201-348-4505, e-mail `orders-ny@springer-sbm.com`, or visit `http://www.springeronline.com`.

For information on translations, please contact Apress directly at 2855 Telegraph Avenue, Suite 600, Berkeley, CA 94705. Phone 510-549-5930, fax 510-549-5939, e-mail `info@apress.com`, or visit `http://www.apress.com`.

The source code for this book is available to readers at `http://www.apress.com` in the Source Code/ Download section. You will need to answer questions pertaining to this book in order to successfully download the code.

To my family

Contents at a Glance

Contents

PART 2 Having an Out-of-the-Box Experience

PART 3 ■■■ Teaching Your Workflow to Dance

Foreword

On behalf of the engineers on the Microsoft Office and Windows Workflow Foundation teams who spent over three years building workflow into the 2007 Microsoft Office system, I would like to thank you very much for your interest in Microsoft Office and workflow. I am pleased to recommend this book to you as a roadmap and tutorial for getting started designing and building workflows for Microsoft Office.

While we've prebuilt the most common review and approval workflows into Microsoft Office, I know well that we did not scratch the surface of all the important processes that organizations will need to build as they modernize the *way* their information workers get their jobs done. That is because a primary goal in building workflow into Windows SharePoint Services and Microsoft Office was to provide a platform for developers to build a wide range of People-Ready Processes. When I say *People-Ready Process,* I mean to emphasize Microsoft Office's focus on *human*-centric workflow scenarios—those business processes that will reduce clutter in your inbox, help you track and correlate information automatically, and hopefully help you get home to your family a bit earlier each day.

Speaking of saving time, David Mann has done a heroic job of synthesizing large volumes of information into a well-organized reference for developers and IT administrators alike. I would particularly commend his focus on connecting the topics in this book to real-world scenarios, which makes the technical information even more valuable. In many cases, such as his primer on writing workflows for mobile devices, he explores new scenarios that can be built on the Microsoft Office platform that go beyond our out-of-the-box feature set—but are quite doable if you follow his step-by-step instructions.

Although this is a comprehensive book about the workflow features in Microsoft Office, it's not the only reference that you will need as you build your own workflows. I would encourage you to also consult the Microsoft Office developer resources available on MSDN (`http://msdn.microsoft.com/office`), especially the SDKs for Windows SharePoint Services and Microsoft Office SharePoint Server.

George Hatoun
Program Manager for Microsoft Office
Microsoft Corporation

About the Author

DAVID MANN is the principal architect for portal and collaborative solutions at Anexinet, a Microsoft Gold-Certified partner headquartered in Philadelphia. Anexinet provides solutions for customers spanning the entire Microsoft stack. Dave has been working with portal, information worker, and content management technologies for just shy of 300 years (OK, really for 12 years). He has designed and delivered solutions for Fortune 500, international conglomerates, small family-run businesses, and everything in between—always with a focus on end users and making their lives easier.

Dave can be reached at `dave@kcdholdings.com` or `www.kcdholdings.com`.

About the Technical Reviewer

GEORGE HATOUN is a program manager on the Microsoft Office User Experience team. For the 2007 Microsoft Office system release, he defined Office workflow engine requirements and the integration of Windows Workflow Foundation into Windows SharePoint Services. He worked closely with customers and IT departments to understand how workflow in Microsoft Office could improve their efficiency. George has been working on collaboration products at Microsoft for over a decade, including seven years on Microsoft Office. His previous roles at Microsoft include lead program manager for Outlook Express and MSN Explorer. George holds a BA in computer science from Rice University. He lives in Bellevue, Washington, with his wife Angela, where he enjoys kayaking, snowshoeing , and hiking in the great Pacific Northwest, and traveling abroad when the weather there is not so great.

Acknowledgments

First of all, I'd like to thank the Academy...

But seriously, this book would not have been possible without the help, support, prodding, and gentle nagging of some good people at Apress. Jon, Sofia, Liz, Kelly—thank you for your feedback, your comments, and for putting up with a manic first-time author. Thanks, too, to my boss Paul for giving me time to write and helping to keep me moving forward.

Without the input, help, and guidance of my technical reviewers, this book would not have been possible. George, thank you for your insightful comments; they helped keep things on track and helped me fine-tune the direction and contents of the book as the beta evolved. Eilene, although you came on late in the project, your help was outstanding. I couldn't have wrapped my head around some of the final pieces without your help.

Last but most importantly, thank you to my family. You guys are the best. Lil: what can I say, I couldn't live without you. K-Man: Keep doing your best—you'll be amazed at what you can accomplish. You're a smart, funny, and caring young man, and I'm proud of you. C-Note: You're a wonderful person—kind, caring, and smart. Keep reaching for your dreams and never let anyone tell you what you can't do. I'm proud of you. D: You work harder than anyone I know—not bad for a five-year-old. You're an amazing kid. Someday we'll talk and I'll tell you all of this. I can't wait.

Finally, a request to you, my reader: please support autism research and autism awareness. It's an epidemic that is stealing our future. Thank you.

PART 1

A New Beginning

I'll be the first to admit it—I never read the first chapter of a technical book. Introductions are often boring and rarely contain much useful information.

I'd like to ask your indulgence here, though. Read the first two chapters that make up this part. As the author, I'll admit to being biased, but I think there's a lot of good information in these chapters. We're going to be wading deep into new waters as we progress through the later chapters and it's important that everyone speak the same language and start from the same base.

Chapter 1 is an introduction to all things workflow and then an overview of Windows Workflow Foundation and Workflow in the 2007 Microsoft Office System. It provides information that lays the foundation for what we will cover later.

Chapter 2 covers establishing our environment. It talks about all of the pieces and how to get them installed and configured properly. Chapter 2 then wraps up with an overview of the scenarios we are going to cover later in the book. If you're going to skip a chapter, skip this one. Naturally, as the author, I hope you don't, but, hey, you paid for the chapter whether you read it or not. Also, don't blame me if something doesn't work for you later—everything you need to get things working properly is covered in Chapter 2.

That's it, so let's get started...

CHAPTER 1

Introduction

Imagine waking up one morning and finding everything you knew, or thought you knew, had been flipped over 180°—the sun was green, the sky orange, and you were suddenly no longer a seasoned computer professional but instead a 10-year-old kid sitting in elementary school again. That's kind of how most of us felt when we sat down in front of Office 2007 for the first time—or the first few dozen times.

It's a whole new ballgame.

Once the shock begins to wear off, however, you can see some glimmer of hope. Things are different, certainly, but not so different that you can't function. There are some interesting new kids on the block but most of your old friends are still around—just pimped out in some fancy new clothes. You still use Word to produce documents, Excel to crunch numbers, and SharePoint to collaborate and share content. They just look and act a little differently.

Hopefully, that's where you are when you start reading this book. Are the Office 2007 client applications different from what came before them? Yes, absolutely. Is the Office 2007 System—server and client—better than what came before? Again, the answer is a resounding *yes.*

Continuing on with my somewhat lame analogy, Workflow is just one of those new kids on the block. Workflow is the kid who somehow makes everything else better. Sure, you've got an Xbox 360, but the new kid has the wireless controllers and the big-screen HD TV to play it on. Could you play Xbox before? Sure. But once you've sipped from the fountain, there's no going back. Workflow is the same way. There's very little in Office 2007 Workflow that you couldn't do before, either manually, with a third-party product, or with a homegrown solution. Office 2007 Workflow just makes it all easier, faster and better in every way—*everything tastes better on an Office 2007 workflow...*

Introducing Workflow

All bluster and pontificating aside, Workflow truly is the single most exciting new feature in Office 2007. It is, perhaps, not as immediately noticeable as the changes to the client interface, but it is going to have the most impact on business productivity.

Note One thing that is important to understand early on is that we're talking about workflow in the Office 2007 System—this includes both the client products typically referred to as "Office," as well as the server products—primarily SharePoint.

You would think, perhaps, that Workflow is new technology Microsoft has developed to fill what had been a huge hole in the Office system. In reality, though, Workflow is as old as the hills. It existed before computers were invented and will exist after your souped-up gaming rig has been replaced with something that makes the HAL 9000 look like the ENIAC.

■Note Before going any further, I'd like to make sure that we are all on the same page with regard to the definition of workflow. After all, the rest of this book is going to be about workflow so we should get a definition out of the way right here at the beginning. *Workflow* is a term that means different things to different people. For our purposes, we'll start defining the word by breaking it down:

> *work*: a task to be completed
>
> *flow*: a process

We'll add one other important aspect and that is a *goal*. Every workflow has an identified end result it is targeted to achieve. So, our full definition of workflow is as follows: *the process that defines and controls the completion of one or more tasks in order to bring about the realization of an identified goal*. The key parts of this definition are "process," "tasks," and "identified goal." Everything else typically associated with workflow—notification, reporting, tracking, escalation, etc.—merely support the process and the realization of the goal.

Before computers, workflows were handled manually, usually by a secretary or low-level manager. For example, back in the dark ages (i.e., when I was in college in the '80s) the secretary of the MIS department for the college played the role of what we now call the workflow engine. She would take in documents and manually deliver paper copies to professors or computer operators for review or approval. She had a separate calendar on her desk where she would write herself reminders to follow up on documents and remind people to review them in a few days. To remind people, she would walk to their office and talk to them, talk to them in the hallway, or place a note (an actual physical piece of paper—gasp!) in their mailbox. For what we now call long-running workflows, she had a tickler file—a collection of file folders in a filing cabinet into which she would place copies of documents that she needed to do something with at some point in the future. Every Monday morning she would check the tickler file for the current month to see if there was anything she needed to act on. If there were, she would pull out the paper copy and route it or act on it appropriately. The system worked great—with only the occasional hiccup when she was out sick—until she and her husband moved out of state. Suddenly, the entire department fell apart for a few weeks while the new secretary got up to speed on the system. Documents didn't get circulated, people felt out of touch, and work fell through the cracks. It was really ugly for about a month. Then the new secretary had a handle on everything; she had learned the process and caught up on everything that had fallen behind. All was right again with the world.

A computer's role in workflow is merely to automate that manual process. Like most other computerized processes, the computer isn't doing anything that couldn't be done by a human being, as you saw earlier. It is just doing it more quickly, efficiently, and without cigarette breaks. You also don't have to worry about the computer moving out of state. However, in a sense, something is missing from computerized workflows—human intelligence and adaptability.

Until HAL is installed in your office, computers can only follow a prescribed series of steps. Those steps can be flexible and account for many exceptions and situations within a process, but they will not replace a human being's capability to adjust for a new situation. For example, Nancy (the original secretary from my college) knew that a certain professor would not be at work the day after his alma mater won the NCAA basketball championship and so she had to not only cancel all of his classes, but also follow up with the department head for approval on a document due back to the president of the college that day. While not impossible, computerized processes generally don't account for sudden, unplanned, celebratory drinking binges. Keep that in mind as you plan and execute your workflows.

So, trips down memory lane aside, where are we? At a high level, we know that workflows automate a business process, handling all touch points, routing, escalation, and so forth. Office 2007 fits into this picture as the tool used by most workflow participants to interact with the workflow. This chapter presents some theory on workflow as well as architectural details and some high-level information on how workflows are implemented in the new Office system.

A WORKFLOW BY ANY OTHER NAME...

Business process management. Business process automation. In most cases, these terms are just fancy names for a workflow. Somewhere, someone decided that *workflow* just didn't sound impressive enough, so they coined a new set of terms. When you break it all down to its core, though, it's just workflow.

Workflow Scenarios

Still staying at a high level, workflow basically comes in two flavors:

- *Human-centric*: People are the primary participants and completers of tasks.
- *Machine-centric: Computers* are the primary participants and completers of tasks.

There will almost always be some mixing of human versus machine participation in a workflow, but we classify them based on who does *most* of the work.

Starting with the machine-centric, the following are both examples of machine-centric workflows:

- *Assembly-line robotics,* for example, assembling cars. This is a workflow because there are tasks to be completed (rivets, welding, electrical connections, etc.) and they must be completed in a certain order (you can't install the seats before the floor) in order to achieve a goal (a new car). Human beings do not get involved in most of this work because we are too slow and it is dangerous.
- *Credit card approvals for online purchases.* This is also a workflow because there are tasks (verify card number, verify address, check credit limit, etc.) to be completed in a certain order (you need to verify the account number and access the account before you can verify the billing address) to achieve a goal (sell a product). Human beings do not get involved in this process for fraud-prevention reasons and because we are too slow—imagine what Amazon's sales would look like if a human being had to review and approve every transaction.

These examples are very different and yet both fit well within our definition of a workflow. Similarly, these are machine-centric workflows for different reasons, but at a very basic level it is because the process can be defined and codified to a degree that does not require human intervention. All seats are riveted to the floor in the same way for a given car. All credit card transactions are approved following the same well-defined set of rules and conditions. There is no reason for a human being to be involved for any reason other than exception handling—which brings up a good point. Most machine-centric workflows exist because the process can be defined well enough for someone to write code to enforce the process. However, no matter how well defined the rules and process are, there must *always* be a final piece to handle unplanned-for conditions. That final step is usually to stop and pass the process off to a person to take care of the problem—whatever it may be. A well-written machine-centric workflow will always have this step for unforeseen circumstances because there is no way to code for the unknown.

Human-centric workflows are different—they *start* with preparing for the unknown and support the human participants in whatever tasks they need to perform in order to complete the process. Human-centric workflows generally need some sort of advanced reasoning, comparison, or abstract thinking that cannot be codified. Also common to a human-centric workflow is some sort of approval decision. Whether for accountability or opinion, many human-centric workflows include a step where someone makes a judgment call on whether to proceed. The following are examples of human-centric workflows:

- *Document approval*: The stereotypical human workflow example. No two documents are alike. Each requires advanced reasoning and a high level of abstract thinking in order to be approved. In the vast majority of scenarios, there is no way this can be fully automated.

- *Design approval*: Machines cannot assess aesthetics. For example, there is no way for a computer to determine which of three designs is best suited for a web site, a brochure, or some other marketing material.

- *Document translations*: Machines cannot yet capture all of the nuances of human language. This requires a human being who understands context, cultural implications, and often very precise domain-specific knowledge.

Most human-centric workflows are similar to these examples. Machines are involved for the routing, storage, and notification of task assignments—in effect, the mechanics of the process—while humans are responsible for the actual work performed at most of the steps. In some cases, machines may play a bigger role; for example:

- *Retrieving data* from external sources to augment information contained in a Workflow step. During a purchase requisition workflow, for instance, the computer may retrieve purchase history, budget, and other information to provide additional data to the person responsible for approving the purchase request

- *Automated document creation* based on content supplied during the workflow steps. A scenario for this would be where a salesperson supplies information via a workflow form as part of a sales order workflow and the computer automatically creates a contract document based on a template prefilled with the appropriate details and then routes that document for approval.

- *Automated document manipulation*, for example, removing macros from Word documents before they are circulated for approval to combat the spread of viruses.
- *Process automation* based on information supplied during the workflow. An example of this is the creation of Exchange and Active Directory accounts as part of a new employee workflow.

These steps, however, are still typically secondary to the human tasks in the process. The machine is still following a prescribed set of steps in support of, or based on, the human pieces of the process.

Human-centric workflows are the focus of Workflow in Office 2007. Office is a human-productivity tool and so this makes perfect sense. Office is all about documents (*documents* in a generic sense as this includes not only Word documents but also Excel spreadsheets, PowerPoint presentations, InfoPath forms, etc.). These documents are often referred to as the *payload* for the workflow; they are the chewy nougat at the center. The whole reason the workflow exists is to move this payload through a process.

■ **Note** All of this *machine-centric* and *human-centric* talk makes me feel like I'm in a bad *Terminator* sequel—*T99: Rise of the Workflow*. Since we're focusing on Office 2007 Workflow, which is all about human-centric processes, I'm going to drop the human-centric bit from here on out. Just remember that there is a whole other world of workflow out there that has very little to do with documents and people. When we talk about Windows Workflow Foundation later in this chapter, we'll revisit this dark side just a little bit.

Types of Workflow

Workflows fall into one of two broad types, based on how the tasks are processed:

- *Sequential workflows*: Typically depicted as a flowchart, in which the process has a beginning, a prescribed path (which could include parallel branches, criteria-based branching, and loops, but is nonetheless a defined path) and an end. Figure 1-1 shows a generic example of a sequential workflow. It includes most of the typical structures found in a standard flowchart. Starting from the top, it is possible to trace the execution logic from beginning to end without much knowledge of even what the process represents.
- *State machine workflows*: State machines are a significantly different beast from sequential workflow and often harder to bend your mind around. They are, however, much better at modeling complex human activities. Essentially, a state machine is based on the concept of conditions and transitions. A *condition* is a set of circumstances that indicate the current status or situation of the process being modeled. Events occur and cause a *transition* from one condition to another. Unlike sequential workflows, there is no prescribed path through the workflow. Instead, the path taken by the workflow is determined by the events that occur as the workflow is processing. Figure 1-2 shows a generic state machine workflow.

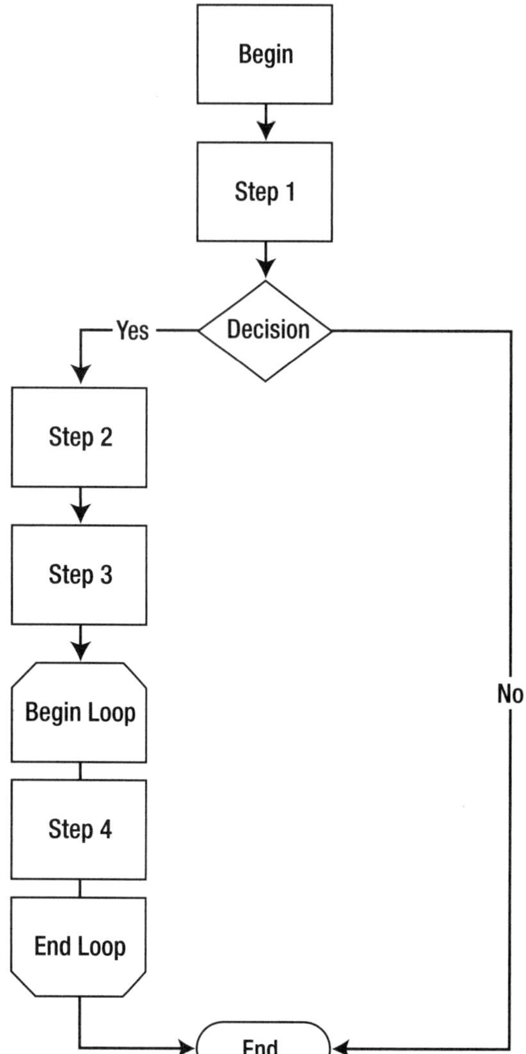

Figure 1-1. *A generic sequential workflow has a prescribed path through the process.*

Looking at Figure 1-2, you can see that on the one hand, the representation of the workflow is much simpler; there are only two structures—states and events. On the other hand, the process seems more complex because there is no way to start from the beginning and step through to the end—there is no prescribed path to follow. Office 2007 supports either type of workflow. We'll cover each in more detail and with concrete examples in the next sections.

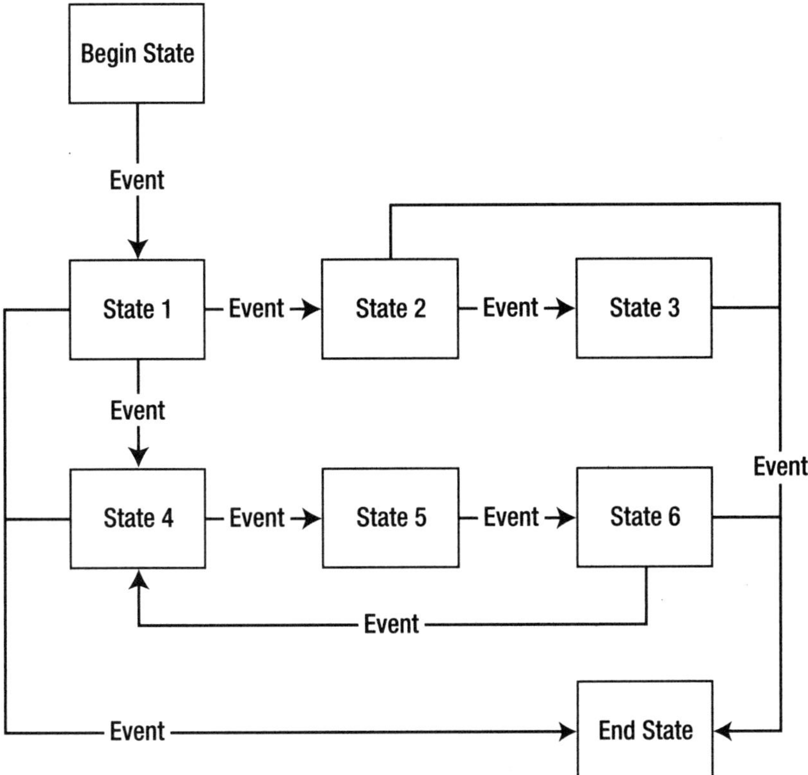

Figure 1-2. *A generic state machine workflow*

Sequential Workflows

As alluded to earlier, and as indicated by the name, sequential workflows follow a sequence of prescribed steps to move from beginning to end. They are easy to understand and follow when presented graphically; consequently, most people start their exploration of workflows with sequential workflows.

For those of you old enough to remember life before event-driven programming, sequential workflows are like the first programs you learned to write in high school or college—linear. They started, did something in the middle, and stopped. You could read from line 1 of the source code all the way through to the end and get a good understanding of what the program did without much (or any) jumping around. There were likely conditions and branches that might send the code down one path or another, but it was all laid out cleanly and in a way that was easy to step through. Sequential workflows are like this.

One key tenet of sequential workflows is that the participants do not typically determine the next step in the workflow. Each participant merely indicates to the workflow engine that they have completed their step. They may or may not have any knowledge of what happens after they have done their task. As I have said before, there is a prescribed path to the sequential workflow so the workflow engine determines the next step in the process based on how it was constructed. The workflow engine is in control.

A sequential workflow works very well in many scenarios you are likely to encounter when implementing Workflow in Office 2007:

- Approval
- Translation
- Feedback
- Collaboration

Most of these scenarios, however, can be generalized into a single category known as *basic routing*, in which documents need to be moved from one person to another. Each person reviews the document and passes it along either with or without adding or changing some content. A sequential workflow handles that scenario very well.

Unfortunately, most business processes are not quite that simple. Sequential workflows are not well suited to modeling complex business processes. They begin to break down with the introduction of significant exception handling, multiple (often arbitrary) execution paths, and nontrivial external factors. In these scenarios, it's time to explore state machine workflows.

State Machine Workflows

Revisiting my programming analogy, state machines are to workflow what object orientation is to programming—a way to simplify the development of something that is complex. As mentioned before, only two elements make up a state machine:

- *States*: A condition that represents the current status of your workflow
- *Events*: Responsible for managing the movement of your workflow from one state to another

Therefore, the definition of a state machine workflow is simply the identification of the possible states and the allowable events that signal a transition to and from each state.

To help understand this better, let's look at an example. A common workflow scenario in Office 2007 will be the approval of a document, so we'll explore a state machine implementation of an approval workflow. Figure 1-3 shows a basic document approval process as a state machine. Not counting the begin and end states, which are really just labels for the diagram and will not actually be developed as part of our workflow, there are three states:

- *DocumentSubmitted*: A document is in this state from the moment the workflow is initiated until the moment someone approves or rejects the document.
- *DocumentRejected*: A document is in this state when the reviewer has rejected it.
- *DocumentApproved*: A document is in this state once someone has approved it.

and three events:

- *OnDocumentSubmitted*: This event occurs when the workflow is initiated. The handler for this event will need to determine who needs to approve the document and notify them in some way that there is a document awaiting their review.
- *OnDocumentRejected*: This event occurs when the reviewer rejects the document. The handler for this event will need to notify the author that their document was not approved.
- *OnDocumentApproved*: This event occurs when a user approves the document. The event handler for this event will need to perform any finalization tasks for the workflow.

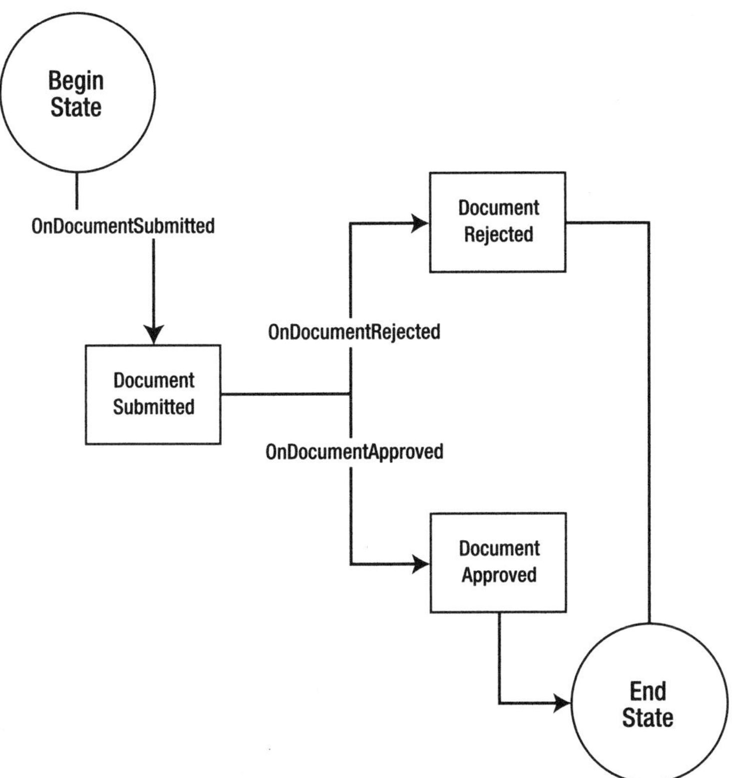

Figure 1-3. *A simple state machine for document approval*

State machine workflows can be used for any scenario you are likely to encounter in Office 2007. As shown earlier, even the simplest workflow can be handled by a state machine. But the real power of a state machine comes in handling complex scenarios. To help you understand this, the next section will look at a single scenario modeled as both a sequential and a state machine workflow.

Sequential vs. State Machine: A Workflow Smackdown

If each style of workflow can handle any scenario we are likely to encounter in our Office 2007 Workflow lives, how do we know which style to use in a given scenario? We already know that simple workflows can be modeled as either sequential or state machine, so the answer there is really whichever model you are more comfortable with. Complex scenarios are a different story, however. I've stated a few times that state machines are more suited to complex scenarios, but there is nothing inherent to Workflow in Office to stop you from handling complex scenarios with a sequential workflow. I'll show you an example of a complex scenario modeled as both sequential and state machine to help you grasp why a state machine is a better choice for complex situations.

First, let's present our scenario. We'll start with the same basic scenario we saw earlier for the state machine—document approval. While not uncommon, a simple scenario such as this is not typical. More common is a situation in which complexity is added in the form of requirements like those listed here:

- The document is time-sensitive so approvals need to happen in a timely fashion or be escalated to another approver.
- There are multiple potential approvers of a document, each with their own area of focus. For example, a document might need approval from several departments.
- Not all reviewers are created equal—some reviewers can trump another's approval or rejection with their own super-approval or super-rejection.
- There are levels of approval, occurring either in series or parallel. What happens when a document is rejected by a second-level reviewer—does it go back to the first level, back to the original author, or continue on for a final review?
- A document requires a subset of the reviewers to approve or reject it before it moves on or falls back. For example, a document is sent to five reviewers and requires any three of the five to approve it before it can be published.
- The document is modified by one approver—does it go back to the original author, start the workflow over again, or just continue on?

For our scenario, we're going to take on just a few of these additional complexities. Our approval is going to require the fourth and fifth items from the previous list. Figure 1-4 shows our process modeled as a sequential workflow. As you can see, even a process that is only slightly more complex gets unwieldy in a sequential model.

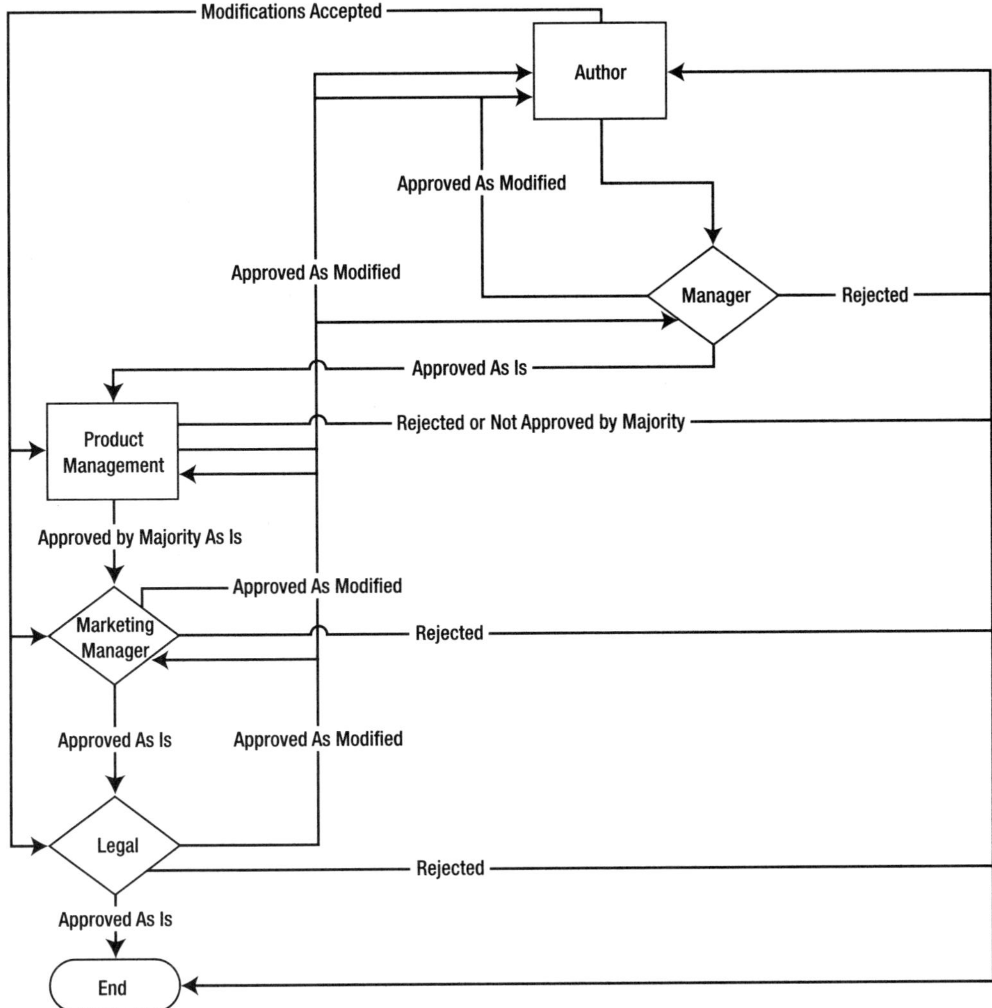

Figure 1-4. *A complex process modeled as a sequential workflow*

Looking at Figure 1-4, we can describe the process as follows:

1. An author creates a document and initiates the workflow.
2. The manager reviews the document and takes one of three paths:
   - *Rejects document outright*: The document is returned to the author as rejected.
   - *Approves document but makes some modifications*: The document is returned to the author with suggested modifications.
   - *Approves document as is*: The document moves on to the Product Management step.

If the document is returned to the author with suggested modifications, the author can accept the modifications, in which case the document moves on to product management, or else reject the modifications, in which case the document dies.

3. Product management has the same three options as the manager—reject, accept as modified, or accept as is. The only difference here is that anything except *rejected* requires a majority of the Product Management Committee. If less than the majority of the committee approves or approves with modifications, the document is returned to the author.

4. The Marketing Manager and Legal steps are similar to the Manager step as well, except that if they reject or accept with modifications, they can opt to send it back to anyone in the process earlier than them—depending on what their objection or suggestion is related to.

Figure 1-4 is not the easiest process to follow. It loops back on itself, branches multiple ways, and generally is difficult to understand. The process depicted is not really that complex and yet the representation is quite complex. The code to implement this process will be equally intricate. It must account for many situations and track the current status of the document through a maze of possibilities. Making this situation worse is the fact that if this process needs to change in the future, making any changes will require someone with significant knowledge of how the process was coded in the first place. None of this makes for a good situation.

Now let's take a look at the same process modeled as a state machine. Figure 1-5 shows this same process.

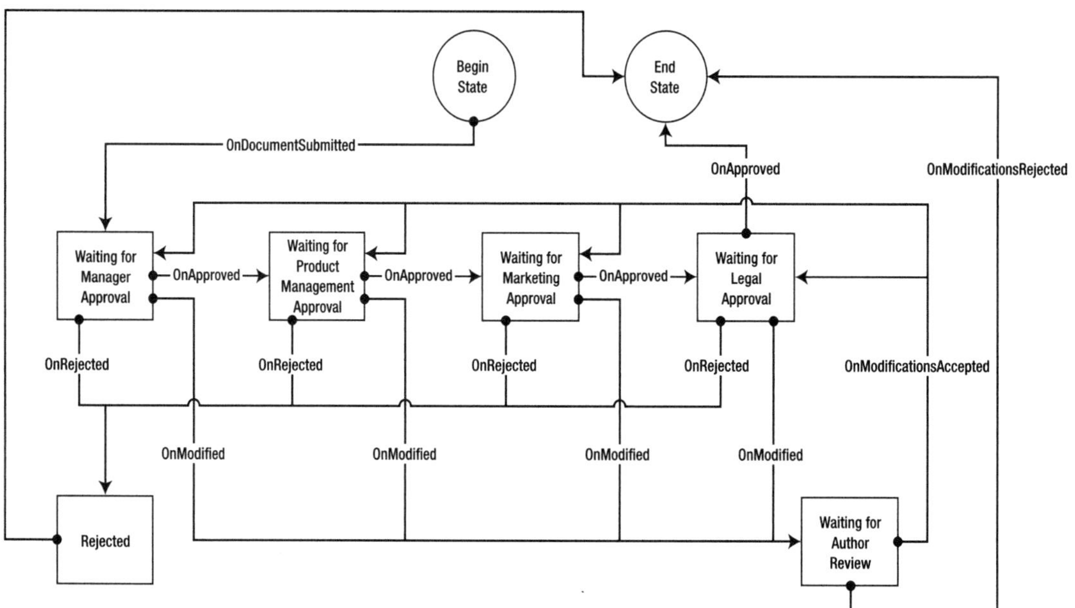

Figure 1-5. *A complex process modeled as a state machine*

At first glance, Figure 1-5 may not seem any simpler. However, once you come to grips with how state machines are modeled, it is much easier to understand. Remember, too, that this is only a somewhat more complex process—fortunately, however, a state machine workflow does not get progressively more complicated as the process it models does. In many ways, once you get over the initial learning curve, very, very complex state machines are not much harder to follow than simpler ones. Take a few minutes to review Figure 1-5 and you'll begin to see what I mean. You'll notice that there are five states (excluding the placeholder begin/end states):

- Waiting for Manager Approval
- Waiting for Product Management Approval
- Waiting for Marketing Approval
- Waiting for Legal Approval
- Waiting for Author Review

and six events:

- OnDocumentSubmitted
- OnApproved
- OnRejected
- OnModified
- OnModificationsAccepted
- OnModificationsRejected

Each participant in the workflow has the same options as in the sequential model. However, looking at Figure 1-5, you can see that it is easier to follow—each state has a set number of events that it supports to transition to or from another state. Future modifications are simply a matter of adding new states or events and updating which are supported at each part of the workflow. The object-oriented nature of a state machine workflow brings all of the same benefits to our workflows as it does to our programs—modularity, ease of maintenance, isolation, and so forth.

As we progress through the book, we'll look at examples of both state machine and sequential workflows. However, we're going to begin our exploration of workflows in Office 2007 with sequential workflows for three reasons:

- Sequential workflows are what most people think of when they think about workflow. They are simpler to understand and so we can focus our time on understanding Workflow's tools and constructs in Office 2007 rather than a new processing paradigm.
- The out-of-the-box workflows (detailed in Chapter 3) are all sequential models.
- The SharePoint Designer—the software formerly known as FrontPage (presented in Chapter 4)—only supports the creation of sequential workflows.

As we delve deeper into Workflow in Office 2007, we'll revisit state machines and see the power and simplicity they bring to a complicated process.

Workflowasaurus: Workflow in the Pre–Office 2007 Mesozoic

With a pretty good understanding of workflow now under our belts, it's time to start honing our knowledge of Office 2007. Before we start, however, you need to understand a bit about where I'm coming from. I alluded earlier to the fact that the lack of workflow has been a huge hole in the Office System for quite some time. Does this mean that the work didn't happen, or that it didn't follow a process? No, naturally not. What it means is that until now, the solution was harder than it could have been. Before Office 2007, workflow in an Office environment was handled in one of three ways:

- With a third-party tool
- With custom code
- As a manual process

Of the three of these possibilities, the last is by far the most common. People route paper copies of documents or email electronic copies. Just last week I spoke to two clients about their processes. Both use folders with the tabs marked as "Return to <*Name*>" to make sure that the document inside eventually made it back to the author. In one case they placed sticky notes inside the folder with the document listing the names of the people who had to review it. In the other case, they just sent the document out and hoped it made the appropriate rounds. The apparent benefit—the cost of implementing this "solution" is zero—is more than outweighed by the ongoing costs of lost productivity and incomplete, incorrect, undocumented, and inconsistent processes. The amount of time, paper, and network or email storage wasted routing, tracking, and following up on documents in a manual process is staggering. In addition, in today's ever-more-regulated business environment a good automated workflow implementation can help ensure regulatory compliance that could save millions of dollars in legal fees, penalties, or settlements.

For those companies that implemented some sort of automated workflow process, most were homegrown solutions. While certainly better than a fully manual process, the time, effort, and cost spent developing, managing, and extending this solution often reduced its business value to a marginal sum. True, the compliance benefits were still there—if the developers did their jobs right—but the costs were often immense.

Finally, workflows built using a third-party tool—and there are many—were often nearly as costly (or in some situations more costly) than a homegrown solution. The benefits of support, reliability, and compliance were usually better than in the homegrown solution, but again, the costs were often a fairly high barrier to entry. Compliance benefits were generally very good and solid, but there's still that niggling little detail of cost.

Windows Workflow Foundation and Workflow in Office 2007 allow you to take care of all of the same compliance issues but at a software cost that is easier for most companies to handle—free (well, at least for the workflow engine). Yes, there is still development, configuration, and administration that needs to happen, but that's no different than any third-party solution and better than a homegrown one. Add to that the tight integration with the most popular productivity suite on the planet, the tight integration with SharePoint, and a few other bells and whistles and you'll begin to understand why the 2007 Microsoft Office system is rocking the workflow world.

■ **Note** In Chapter 9, we'll burn a few cycles on integrating Office 2003 with our Office 2007 Workflow experience. We won't come close to the full-blown Office 2007 experience, but we'll at least make Office 2003 a player in the game.

Ladies and Gentlemen...Windows Workflow Foundation

The core of every workflow in Office 2007 is the Windows Workflow Foundation (WF). WF is part of the .NET Framework 3 that also includes the Windows Presentation Foundation and the Windows Communication Foundation. WF consists of

- A collection of classes and objects that form the in-process workflow engine
- Add-on designers for Visual Studio 2005
- A programming model for delivering workflow-enabled applications

In the rest of this chapter, we focus on the core workflow engine provided by WF. The other two aspects will be covered throughout the book as we discuss various development tasks and scenarios.

■ **Note** Workflow in Office 2007 is deeply intertwined with the new Office servers and the significant changes that have been made to the Office client applications. While this book is not an authoritative source for either the Office servers or the Office client applications, a brief overview of the salient points of each is provided later in this chapter.

Windows Workflow Foundation Architecture

The workflow engine part of WF is responsible for providing several core services to all workflows built utilizing Windows Workflow Foundation. These services are classified into several categories. Figure 1-6 shows a high-level view of the WF architecture. To better understand the architecture of Workflow, we'll discuss each piece of Figure 1-6 in the following sections.

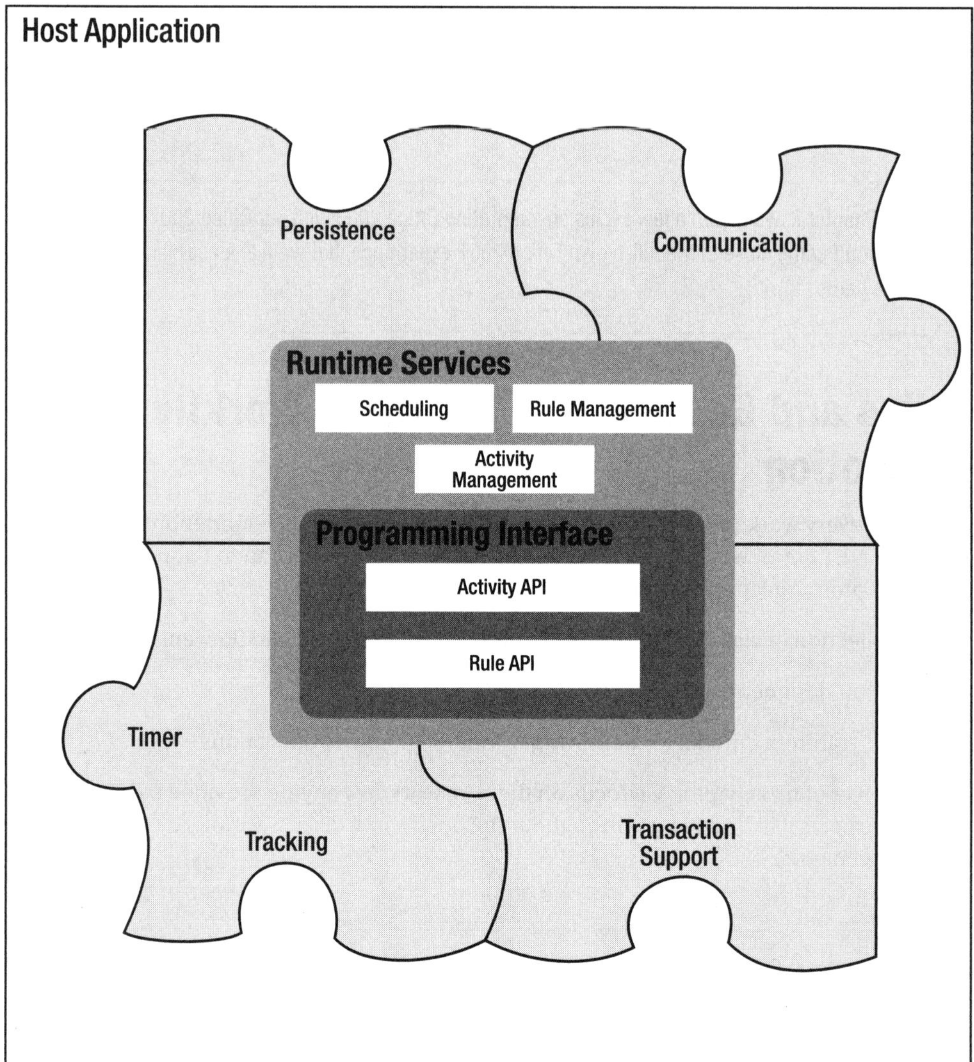

Figure 1-6. *The Windows Workflow Foundation architecture*

Host Interface

One thing that it is important to understand about WF is that it is not directly executable. It is designed only to exist within another process. That *other process* is called the *host*. For Office 2007, the host is SharePoint. We'll talk more about the host functionality provided by SharePoint later. For now, it's only important to understand the concept of a host and the role it plays in our workflows. For more information on workflow hosts, see the sidebar "Every Party (Workflow) Needs a Host."

■Definition A *host* is an executable process that serves as the interface between the workflow engine and workflow participants. The host provides common mechanisms for all WF workflows to provide core services.

WF provides a common set of interfaces that allows hosts to directly interact with the core engine. Specific implementation details are left up to the host. As shown in Figure 1-6, the services provided by the WF host interface are like sockets that a specific host application can plug into. The services provided include

- *Persistence*: Even if the various human participants in a workflow responded immediately to notifications and dropped everything to complete their workflow tasks, each workflow would still be considered a *long-running process*. Let's face it, from the computer's point of view, wetware is slow. Combine the fact that people are rarely able to respond to workflow tasks immediately with the fact that some workflows are by nature going to require days, weeks, or months (the design and approval of a new multimillion-dollar widget is not an overnight process) and we could have a major problem on our hands. If the server processing our workflow had to keep all of the details concerning each running workflow in memory, it would soon run out of memory. Furthermore, if all the details about a workflow are stored in memory and the server were to go down for any reason, all of the workflow information would be lost. To get around these problems, WF provides for workflows to be stored and unloaded from memory in the middle of processing. As WF is meant to be hosted inside another application, it does not specify precisely how the information is persisted; it merely provides a mechanism for signaling when the workflow details need to be dehydrated and stored or rehydrated and activated (for details on dehydration/rehydration, see Chapter 9). Each workflow host determines the specific storage mechanism appropriate for its workflows and responds accordingly when signaled by WF. So, for example, one host may store its information in a set of XML files, while another may write them to a set of tables inside a database. In Office 2007, our workflow host is SharePoint, and it stores persistence information in SQL Server.
- *Timer*: It is not uncommon for a workflow to wait for a specified interval before proceeding. For example, a workflow may wait three days and then send out a reminder for a task that has not been completed. It may then wait an additional two days and then escalate the task assignment to a manager. In some cases, this delay information may need to be persistent as well. A typical Windows timer would not serve in all cases because it would not survive a system restart. Each workflow host must be able to specify how it handles delays and other time-based events. WF, therefore, needs to provide a mechanism for each host to implement its own Timer subsystem but still hook into the core workflow processing.
- *Communication*: Each host implementation for WF is going to require a different mechanism for communicating messages (events, information, etc.) from the core workflow engine to the specific host implementation or from the host implementation back into the core. If the WF were to limit communications to only one channel, it would severely limit the flexibility of the platform. For this reason, WF provides a communication interface that can be extended to support whatever mechanism is required by each individual host—from web services to Microsoft Message Queue (MSMQ)-style messages to whatever is required by the host implementation.

- *Tracking*: As workflow is the representation of a business process, it is not at all unusual for the business to need to monitor the progress of a workflow. Companies may need to know where in the process each workflow is at a given point in time. Similar to the Timer process, the details of how this information is stored and retrieved could depend on a number of factors. It would be impossible for the developers of WF to predict each case in advance. Instead, they provide an event system inside WF that raises events during the course of a workflow. Each host implementation is responsible for responding to or ignoring those events as it deems appropriate.

■ **Note** Unfortunately, SharePoint does not implement the Tracking provider from WF and does not support third-party tracking providers. It does implement various types of reports and status windows but nothing as extensible as what would be possible were this interface supported. If we need to track our workflow progress, we will need to handle all of that manually.

- *Transaction support*: Transactions in a workflow can be a tricky thing. Some workflows will require full rollback and transaction isolation functionality whereas others will require no transactions. Every workflow is going to be different. WF therefore can't be all things to all workflows. Instead, it supports a transaction interface that allows the host to determine how to handle transactions. Workflow merely signals when transaction functionality is required and lets the host do the rest.

EVERY PARTY (WORKFLOW) NEEDS A HOST

Much like a host at a party, a workflow host is responsible for the entire experience of its guests. In this case, those guests are the workflow activities as well as the end users. As mentioned earlier, WF by itself is simply a set of objects that expose functionality. It does not expose a user interface (UI) that would allow you to create a workflow, manage a workflow, or respond to workflow events or notifications.

That is all the job of a workflow host. The host presents the interface and the functionality that allows

- Document owners to select and assign a workflow to a document
- Administrators to manage and track workflows
- End users to receive notifications of workflow events that concern them
- End users to update the status of tasks assigned to them

Important tasks of a workflow host include

- *Security*: WF is a generic engine. There is no way that the developers at Microsoft could write a security model into a workflow engine that would suit every application's needs. This is left to the host to implement as it needs to. Some hosts will require no security; others will require Department of Defense–level security. Most will be somewhere in between.

- *User interface*: Similar to security, building one all-encompassing UI into the WF engine would be a nearly impossible task. It would mean that the UI would need to be so generic as to be almost useless, or else that the process of customizing the UI be so open-ended and flexible that it would be exceedingly difficult to work with. So the UI is left entirely to the host developer.

There is nothing in WF that would stop you from writing your own host. Microsoft wholeheartedly supports and encourages this, and WF contains a wealth of information and processes to simplify this task. Unfortunately, writing a workflow host is well beyond the scope of this book.

■ **Note** For information and resources on writing a workflow host, you can visit `http://wf.netfx3.com`.

The next version of SharePoint is a workflow host and for our purposes will serve all our needs nicely. Any customization work that we need to do can be handled with custom *activities*, which will be covered in more detail in Chapter 5.

■ **Definition** An *activity* is a discrete unit of functionality used to build a workflow. Send Email, Create Task, and Write to Log are all examples of potential activities. We'll look at activities in much greater detail, and even build one of our own, in Chapter 5.

Runtime Services

The next set of services provided by WF that we're going to discuss are Runtime Services, shown as the first interior box in Figure 1-6. Unlike the host interface in Figure 1-6, this layer of functionality is isolated from the world outside of WF and will be identical for all hosts and workflow implementations. This layer provides the core services that allow individual workflows to execute. It includes these services:

- *Scheduling*: The Scheduling service is responsible for controlling the runtime execution of activities. It determines when each activity runs.
- *Activity Management*: This service provides the functionality for execution of activities—event management, exception management, transaction management, tracking, and persistence. As necessary, this service interfaces with the host interface layer services.
- *Rule Management*: WF provides for the external application of policy to a workflow via a rules engine. Rules will be addressed in greater detail in Chapter 8.

Programming Interface

The final layer of Figure 1-6 that we need to discuss appears in the innermost shaded box—the programming interface. As workflow developers, this is the functionality that interests us the most; it allows us to write our own custom activities that do what we need. This is the primary means of developing a highly custom workflow. Most of the rest of this book covers the programming interface.

■**Note** One final item to be aware of with regard to WF is that it can support machine-centric workflows as easily as it supports human-centric workflows. We talked earlier about the distinction between these two types of workflows and discussed how most of this book will focus on human-centric workflows. I just want to make sure that you remember that WF is not limited to only human-centric workflows.

Office 2007 Workflow Technology

So far, we've been talking about workflow in a generic sense, with little if any specific references to Office 2007. That trend stops here. We've covered all of the basics, and everyone should have a pretty good idea of what workflow is, the different types of workflows available, the benefits of workflow, and so forth. From here through the end of the book, we're all about workflow specifically in the Office 2007 system.

Before we get started, you need to understand the Workflow-specific features and additions in the Office 2007 system. We're not going to cover them in painful detail—we'll touch on the various aspects in more detail as we cover topics throughout the rest of the book—for now we're just going to talk about them at a fairly high level so everyone has a basic understanding. Because we're only covering the Workflow-specific features of Office 2007, this should not be considered an exhaustive dissertation on Office 2007. For a more detailed look at Office 2007 in general, or any specific topic not related to Workflow, you'll need to look elsewhere.

■**Note** There will be plenty of books on Office 2007, some good, some not so good. The pundits will heap praise and scorn on Office 2007, sometimes at the same time. Just about the only thing you can say with *absolute certainty* about Office 2007 is that it will not be a nonevent. For my thoughts on some of the various Office 2007 books that come out both before and after this one, please visit `www.kcdholdings.com` and peruse the book lists.

We'll start with the Office 2007 client applications and then cover the server-side elements of the Office 2007 System.

Introducing the Office 2007 Client

Unless you've been living under a rock (what a strange expression!) for the last several months, you have likely heard all of the chatter about the new UI in the Office 2007 client applications. It is different, I'll grant you that. But once you get used to it, you look at Office 2003 the way a Ferrari owner looks at a minivan—*I'm not going near that...* While we won't specifically walk through the new interface, we will see various parts of it as we explore Workflow.

The full list of Office 2007 client applications is stunningly impressive:

- Access
- Business Contact Manager
- Communicator
- Excel
- Groove
- InfoPath
- OneNote
- Outlook
- PowerPoint
- Project
- Publisher
- SharePoint Designer
- Visio
- Word

Fourteen applications that do just about anything you need, short of laundry and grocery shopping. Wonderful, simply wonderful; no wonder Microsoft has such a lion's share of the productivity suite market. However, and I hate to rain on your parade, but the most important thing to realize about the Office System is that not all of the client applications are created equally. In the client-side world of the Office System, there are

- The Fabulous Four: Word, Excel, PowerPoint, and Access
- Outlook
- A young upstart known as InfoPath
- A bunch of other applications

Please understand that this is not a slight on those "other applications." I love OneNote—it's probably my most-used Office application. I use Project frequently, and Visio, Publisher, and the SharePoint Designer are all great at what they do. However, none of these "others" gets the new UI in this release. Personally, I can see why and it makes sense to me—these applications fall into one or more of several exception categories:

- They are not part of what most people use in Office.
- They are more specialized in their focus than the rest of Office.
- They are not document-centric (*document* in a generic sense of a cohesive file that is easily portable and shared among multiple users).
- They are focused on developers.

Having the two UIs presents a problem in a workflow scenario, however. As mentioned earlier, some of the new constructs in the Office UI are intended to inform users of workflow information, for example, the tasks assigned to them. This works beautifully if the document they are working with sports the new UI. But what if it doesn't? Presumably, this is only a significant problem in Publisher, Project, and Visio as the rest of the "others" are not so file-centric. However, from a workflow point of view, there are two very different experiences:

- If the user opens a Word document in Word 2007, they will be informed of their workflow tasks. The new UI will inform them of the task and support them in managing and completing that task.
- If the document they open, however, is a Project plan, or a Visio or Publisher file, they will receive no indication in the client itself that they have to review and approve that document—even if they open the file in the 2007 version of the program.

Workflow builders and administrators will need to keep this fact in mind and must be sure to support these other file types as special cases should the need arise in their environment. Presumably, a future release of Office will at least partially remedy this situation.

Workflow Features in the Office Client Applications

Hidden among the myriad changes to the Office 2007 client applications are a handful of features that impact our workflows. We're going to touch on them briefly here. As mentioned previously, we'll drill into them in more detail as we step through the examples and scenarios later in this book.

Business Bar

First and foremost among these elements is a construct known (during the beta cycle, at least) as the *Business Bar*. The Business Bar integrates the client application with a Microsoft Office 2007 SharePoint Server (MOSS) that is storing the document.

Realizing that there are multiple ways for a user to get access to a document (through email, through a browser, through the Office client, etc.), Microsoft has made sure that users will still be aware of workflow information by placing it directly within the client application itself. If a user has a task assigned to them for the current document, the Business Bar will be shown just under the Ribbon. It will contain information regarding workflow tasks related to the currently opened document. Figure 1-7 shows an example of the Business Bar displaying information about a pending workflow task as well as a notification about editing the document.

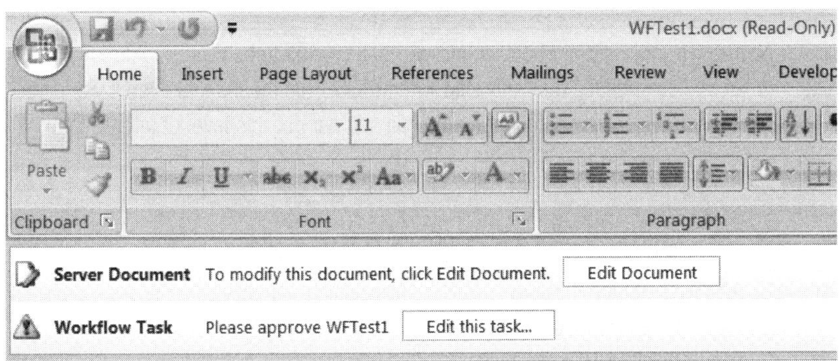

Figure 1-7. *The Business Bar shows information about pending workflow tasks so the user always knows what they need to do.*

Clicking the Open link on the Business Bar will present the user with information related to the workflow task they have been assigned and give them the opportunity to directly complete and modify that task. The user's experience will depend on which components of the Office 2007 System are installed in their environment.

- Clicking the Edit this task button will launch a browser. The task information will be presented as an ASPX page, as shown in Figure 1-8. This is the only option available if only WSS is installed.

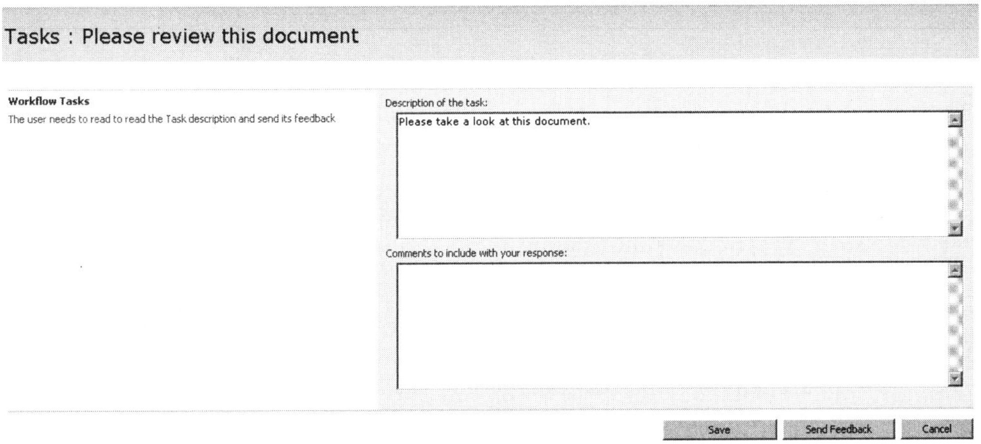

Figure 1-8. *The Workflow information dialog box shown as an ASPX page*

- We have not discussed the new part of Office 2007 known as the Forms Server. However, it is part of the 2007 Office System and is responsible for converting InfoPath forms to HTML. MOSS ships with core components of the Forms Server that allow for the conversion of our Workflow forms (even if the full Forms Server is not installed). In this case, the workflow task information will be presented as a form in a dialog box, seamlessly displayed by the Office client application as though it were a native dialog box. An example of this is shown in Figure 1-9. We'll cover the Forms Server in much more detail in Chapter 7.

■ **Note** There is another component of MOSS that allows our workflow forms to be rendered directly in the Office client applications—a set of web services that *only* ship with MOSS. This means that even if you install the full Forms Server in an otherwise WSS-only installation, you will still not get this level of integration.

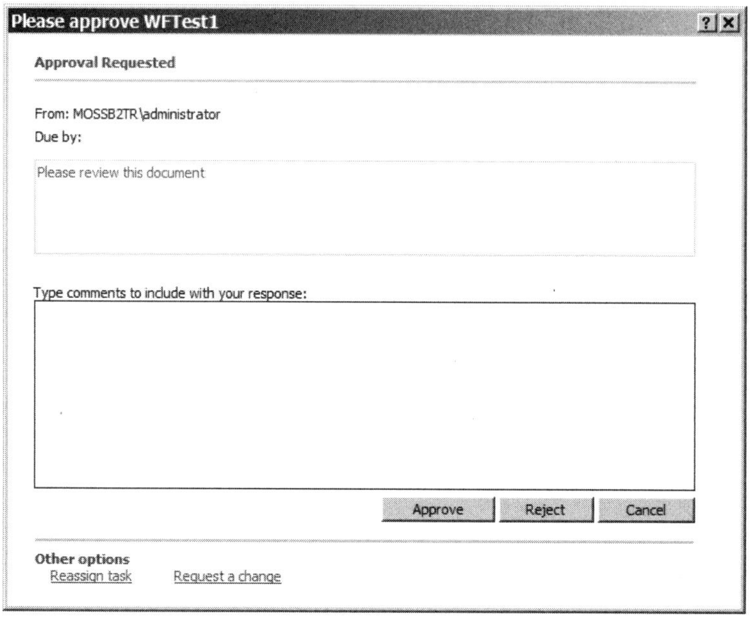

Figure 1-9. *The Workflow information dialog box shown utilizing the new Office 2007 Forms Server*

If the Office Forms Server is not installed in the environment, then the only option available to us as Workflow Builders and Administrators will be the ASPX forms.

File Menu Integration

OK, so technically there is no *File* menu anymore—another one of those little changes in the Office client applications that will take a little getting used to. In place of the File menu, we now have a construct known (again in beta-terminology) as the *Office Button.* Clicking the Office Button will reveal what is effectively the old File menu on steroids, as shown in Figure 1-10.

We'll see the Workflow features of the Office Button in action later as we walk through the various scenarios (although you can get a sneak preview of some of the functionality in Figure 1-10).

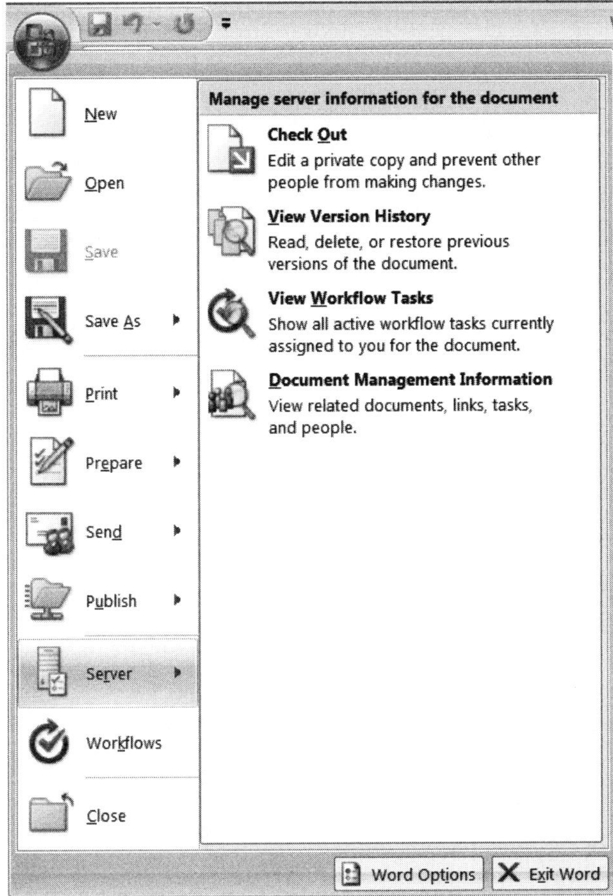

Figure 1-10. *The new Office Button menu replaces the File menu and provides access to Workflow functionality right from within the Office client applications.*

Outlook

Outlook is likely the most often used Office client application. It's typically the first application opened in the morning and the last closed at the end of the day. Wouldn't it be nice if we could get our Workflow information to show up in Outlook, too? With a lead-up like that you shouldn't be surprised to find out that the level of integration between Outlook and SharePoint has gone through the roof in the 2007 release.

Sticking just with the Workflow-related aspects, the main thing we're looking at is that our Workflow tasks will now show up in our Outlook task list. But it gets even better—the synchronization is two-way. If you edit the task (mark it as complete, etc.) in Outlook, the change will be reflected in the SharePoint task list. Figure 1-11 shows the same Workflow task we saw in Figures 1-8 and 1-9 as an Outlook task.

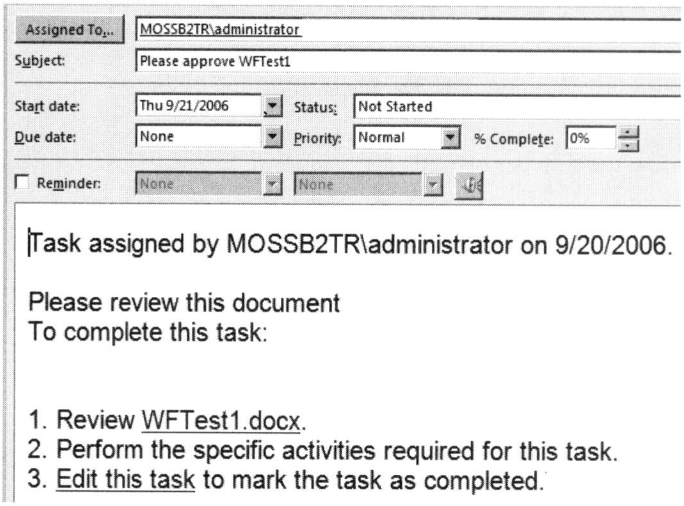

Assigned To... MOSSB2TR\administrator
Subject: Please approve WFTest1
Start date: Thu 9/21/2006 Status: Not Started
Due date: None Priority: Normal % Complete: 0%
Reminder: None None

Task assigned by MOSSB2TR\administrator on 9/20/2006.

Please review this document
To complete this task:

1. Review WFTest1.docx.
2. Perform the specific activities required for this task.
3. Edit this task to mark the task as completed.

Figure 1-11. *A Workflow task synchronized into Outlook*

■ Note Later in the book, we'll make use of this two-way functionality to get our Workflow tasks to be accessible from a mobile device.

Microsoft Office SharePoint Designer 2007

No, this is not another client application; it is simply FrontPage renamed and all spruced up. There is some new functionality added that impacts Workflow. The SharePoint Designer includes a wizard interface that allows power users to build a workflow without writing any code. It's called the Workflow Designer and we'll cover it in detail in Chapter 4.

Introducing the Office 2007 Servers

The changes that have been made server-side in the Office 2007 system are, in my opinion, even more significant than the client-side changes. Not all of them will impact our workflows, and they won't be as noticeable to most users, but to a company as a whole they offer much, much more. As before, this section will barely scratch the surface of the new features and functionality. I will cover only those elements that are relevant to Workflow.

Microsoft Office SharePoint Server 2007/Windows SharePoint Services v3

We'll start with the biggie—you can't do workflow right in Office 2007 without doing SharePoint. The next version of SharePoint contains significant changes and will have the most impact on our workflow world. Dozens of books on SharePoint 2007 will flood the market. Hundreds of white papers will be written covering the details of specific features—even the most seemingly insignificant. Thousands upon thousands of blog entries will be written with tips and tricks on how to work with the new features. We're going to cover the couple of items that relate directly to Workflow. Trust me, this barely scratches the surface of the new SharePoint.

■ **Note** Before we really begin, a quick word about SharePoint. First and foremost, there really is no product known as *SharePoint.* What people refer to as *SharePoint* is really two distinct products—just as in the last version. First there is Windows SharePoint Services (WSS). This product is free and forms the basis for the next product, Microsoft Office SharePoint Server (MOSS) 2007. WSS ships as part of Microsoft's server products (Windows Server 2003, Longhorn, etc.). MOSS, on the other hand, is a separate product and is not free. It extends WSS in several important ways, primarily due to its lineage—it is a combination of the old SharePoint Portal Server and Microsoft Content Management Server products. When I refer to *SharePoint,* I mean both products. If I'm talking about just one product, I'll call it be name.

We will discuss the specific feature breakdowns of the two SharePoint products in Chapter 3 when we discuss the out-of-the-box functionality of Workflow in Office. For now, a high-level overview of the differences between the two products follows.

WSS is a platform component central to all of Microsoft's collaborative applications. The functionality provided by WSS includes

- Document management
- Core collaboration
- Core Workflow capabilities
- User management
- Security

As stated previously, MOSS is built on WSS. In the future, more and more Microsoft products will build on this base and extend it for their own needs. Microsoft has already announced that future versions of many of their products will utilize WSS as their core collaboration platform. MOSS is simply the first product to build on that base. The additional functionality provided by MOSS includes

- Enterprise content management—drawing on its Content Management Server heritage
- Business Intelligence capabilities
- Expanded search and management functionality
- Integration with line-of-business applications
- Internet publishing

Workflow Features in WSS and MOSS

SharePoint (remember, that means both WSS and MOSS) contain a host of new features that impact our workflows and allow us to build robust, Workflow-enabled applications. Many of them are incidental to Workflow itself, since they are more focused on SharePoint as an application platform and as a robust product. We'll touch on the two most significant of these features here and cover them all in later chapters as we walk through our scenarios and examples.

Content Types A *content type* in the next version of SharePoint is a means of packaging functionality and metadata into a single manageable and deployable unit. Content types are focused on the developer's mantra of *write-once, use-often*. Because we define the functionality, features, and information in one place, it can be managed centrally. That's the *write-once* part. The *use-often* comes in when you deploy the content type and associate it with multiple lists. Each list gets the full power of the content type without having to define it over and over again. Changes made to the single central copy can be immediately reflected in the lists that use it.

■ **Note** Rather than typing "lists and document libraries" repeatedly here, I'm just using *lists* in a generic sense. In SharePoint 2007, the distinction between lists and document libraries blurs considerably. Document libraries are merely specialized lists with some additional functionality.

A related benefit is the fact that in the 2007 release of SharePoint, lists can contain more than one type of item. By storing multiple types of documents in a single document library, we can reduce the complexity of our sites, for both administrators and end users. For example, a site dedicated to a specific project can now contain a single document library that houses all of the documents related to that project—designs, requirements, status, project plans, etc. Within a list itself, content types show up on the *New* menu, as shown in Figure 1-12, which show two new content types—*Expense Report* and *Status Report*.

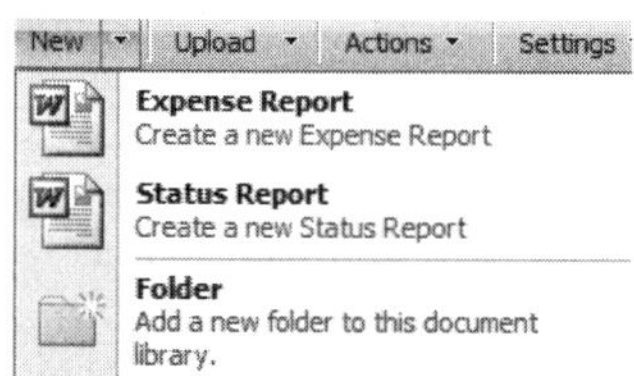

Figure 1-12. *Content types are a powerful new feature in SharePoint.*

Now that you have a basic understanding of what a content type is, let's talk a little about what you can put into a content type. The answer is just about anything you would need to:

- *Metadata*: Each content type can contain any number of columns of any data type available in SharePoint. By adding the content type to the list, you can automatically add the columns.
- *Policy*: Each content type can have its own information management policy defined and enforced.
- *Workflow*: Content types can carry with them their own workflows to enforce business policies specific to the content type. This is obviously the part that interests us the most.
- *Document Information Panel*: Each content type can define a custom form to be displayed in the Business Bar within the Office client applications. This form can be used to keep users informed or to collect information from them.

By default, SharePoint ships with a single content type per list, but it is certainly possible to create your own and add them to your lists as necessary to meet your requirements.

Note For lists of resources that cover creating content types, please visit `www.kcdholdings.com`.

An example here will help clarify the power of the new content types feature. In SharePoint 2003, each list contains one type of information—announcements, links, events, etc. Each document library contains one type of document—contracts, status reports, budget reports, etc. If you need to store multiple types of information and documents, you're forced to create a list for each and put them all in the same site. Although this is certainly better than simple file shares, it is nonetheless problematic. Each site contains the full definition of lists, which means that initially you had to create them all each time, or use site or list templates. In either event, each site still contains the full definition of the list and because each list can only effectively contain a single type of content, you have multiple lists to manage.

Six months pass and you've created dozens or hundreds of sites, each containing your multiple lists. Suddenly the business need changes and you need to start tracking additional information. You need to add one column to every list on every site. Because each list contains its own copy of its definition, you need to manually or programmatically change each.

Ugh.

Now let's look at this using content types in SharePoint 2007. Instead of having to create multiple lists to store all of the various types of content, you can centrally create a content type for each type of item that you need to store and add them to a single list on each site. Not only is your site design easier and cleaner for the end user, but six months, or six days, down the road, you've built hundreds of sites utilizing your new content types. So when the business needs change, you make the necessary changes to the single centralized content type, push those changes out to all lists using the content type, and all is right with the world. It's time for happy hour.

Perhaps this is a *little* more work up front to identify and design the content types, but the payoff in the long run is more than worth any extra initial effort.

Content types are one of the strongest additions to the next release of SharePoint—regardless of whether you are looking from a Workflow point of view. The ability to wrap our business needs up into a nice, neat package and deploy that package as a unit across multiple sites, but still manage it centrally, is quite powerful.

Note It doesn't have to be the case, but to my mind, content types are most useful with documents.

Features While customizing a site definition in SharePoint 2003 was possible, it wasn't exactly the easiest thing in the world. Even seasoned veterans would not look forward to opening `ONET.xml` or `Schema.xml` and wading through line after line of raw XML. In SharePoint 2007 this task is considerably less onerous because site definitions are now broken apart into *Features*.

A Feature is essentially a package of functionality that can be developed, deployed, managed, and activated as a unit. Once deployed to a server, Features can be turned on or off for individual sites.

Features are certainly used for more than Workflow in SharePoint 2007, but from a Workflow point of view, Feature packaging is a useful means of encapsulation and deployment. As you'll see in Chapter 6, we will package our custom workflow into a Feature and deploy it to our SharePoint server.

Microsoft Office Forms Server 2007

Another big addition to the Workflow family is the Forms Server. This Office 2007 server is responsible for dynamically generating HTML forms for data collection. This is going to come into play in two primary ways with regard to Workflow:

- As a mechanism for displaying and collecting information intrinsic to our workflow. We've already seen this use of the Forms Server in action. Flip back a few pages to Figure 1-9. The Workflow task information dialog box shown earlier is an example of a dynamically generated form using the Forms Server delivered right in the Office client applications. The integration with the Office 2007 clients is impressive—it looks like an integrated piece of the application.
- As documents stored in a SharePoint List, forms can have their own workflows assigned directly to them. The possibilities for this scenario are practically limitless. Any form used in your business can be delivered via the web and have a Workflow associated with it. When an instance of that form is submitted by a user, the workflow can automatically begin the appropriate business process.

There is naturally a lot more to this server than that, and the use outside Workflow is equally as important. For now, however, we'll leave it at that. We'll cover the Forms Server in more detail in Chapter 7.

The Cast of *Ben-Hur*

Well, no, not really. There are really only five user types that come into play in a workflow:

- *Initiator*: This is the person who originates or kicks off a workflow. Typically, this will be owner or author of the document or list item but it doesn't have to be. Anyone with sufficient privileges can start a workflow on an item.
- *Participant*: This person receives the tasks of a workflow and completes them.
- *Server administrator*: The server administrator is responsible for establishing and maintaining the environment in which the workflows operate. Primarily this means installing workflows on the server so that they are available to individual sites.

- *Site administrator*: The site administrator is responsible for associating our workflow with a specific list or document library. Often, this will be the same person as the server administrator, though it does not have to be.
- *Builder*: This role is tasked with creating new workflows. This role could alternately be named *designer* to cover the declarative workflows created with the SharePoint Designer (covered in Chapter 4) but for simplicity's sake, I'll just stick with builder.

The majority of this book focuses on the builder and two administrator roles. The initiator and participant roles are typically end user focused (though certainly at one point or another, both administrators and builders will find themselves as participants in a workflow). The primary audience for this book is not end users, so we will not spend a lot of time on those roles. As we walk through examples in the later chapters, however, we will step through the end-user experience. Among other things, it is important for builders and administrators to walk the proverbial mile in the end user's shoes if we are going to create and support an efficient workflow system for them.

Key Facts Summary

That wraps up our whirlwind introduction to Workflow, WF, and Workflow in Office 2007. We've covered a lot of ground pretty quickly. Here's a quick review of what we've seen:

- Terminology: A few key terms were presented in this chapter:
  - *Workflow*: The process that defines and controls the completion of one or more tasks in order to bring about the realization of an identified goal.
  - *Payload*: The document or other piece of content that a workflow is assigned to. For example, in an instance of an approval workflow, the document that a reviewer must approve or reject is called the payload.
  - *Host*: The interface between the workflow engine and workflow participants.
  - *Activity*: A discrete unit of functionality used to build a workflow. *Send Email, Create Task*, and *Write to Log* are all examples of activities.
  - *State*: In a state machine workflow, a condition that represents the current status of the process.
  - *Event*: In a state machine workflow, the action responsible for managing the movement of our workflow from one state to another.
- Windows Workflow Foundation, part of .NET Framework 3.0, is the basis for Workflow in Office.
- SharePoint is a Windows Workflow Foundation *host*.

- Despite all of the fun that could be had with a WWF acronym, the preferred acronym for Windows Workflow Foundation is simply WF. Somehow the World Wildlife Fund is drawn into the fight and even Microsoft doesn't mess with the Panda. I'm still on the lookout, though, for a Windows Workflow seminar that calls itself "SMACKDOWN"!
- Windows Workflow Foundation provides a pluggable architecture to facilitate specific implementations of the following services within each workflow host:
  - *Persistence*: Management of long-running processes
  - *Communications*: Integration of myriad disparate components through a common communication subsystem
  - *Tracking*: Monitoring workflow progress in real time (unfortunately, this is not supported in SharePoint)
  - *Transaction support*: The ability to commit or roll back workflow actions as a unit
  - *Timer*: Support for delay or time-triggered processing
- Office 2007 focuses on human-centric workflows, as opposed to machine-centric workflows. Windows Workflow Foundation, however, supports either.
- Office 2007 supports both sequential and state machine style workflows.
- The primary Office client applications (what I termed the Fabulous Four—Word, Excel, PowerPoint, and Access, plus portions of Outlook) support Workflow through a variety of customizations and user interface constructs.
- Some of the new aspects of SharePoint that support Workflow are content types and Features.

Sample Office 2007 Workflow Scenarios

To help everyone understand Workflow in Office 2007 better, straight from the home office in Ottumwa, Iowa, here is my list of the top-10 scenarios best suited to Workflow in Office 2007:

1. *Document lifecycle*: Controlling a document from creation to archiving to destruction.
2. *Document translation*: In our increasingly global economy, support for multiple languages is a business necessity.
3. *Feedback*: Submitting an idea (list item or document) for review and formal or informal suggestions for improvement (as opposed to approval).
4. *Collaboration*: Working with a team to build a document collectively.
5. *Design approval*: Whether for a web page, a brochure, a logo, or some other type of marketing material, aesthetic reviews and feedback are an integral part of this creative process.

6. *Form processing*: Forms strongly imply a process. Any electronic form that generates a discrete document can likely be routed and processed by a workflow. Though certainly not limited to these types, here are a few examples of forms that would lend themselves well to Workflow:

   - Requisition forms
   - Expense reports
   - Travel requests
   - Timesheets

7. *Web content management*: Moving content from concept to publication is often a precise and intense process requiring multiple levels of review and approval. Often, in highly regulated environments, there are prescribed steps to follow prior to publication.

8. *Knowledge management*: Maintaining a knowledgebase is an increasingly important part of corporate life. The ability to have multiple people submit content is often one way to improve the relevancy and quantity of information available. However, without a process to manage those submissions, the knowledgebase will quickly become overgrown and unwieldy.

9. *Document approval*: Not quite as formal or involved as a whole document lifecycle process, this is just a simple review and approval.

10. *<Insert Your Favorite Scenario Here>*: I'd like to say I was being considerate of my audience and letting them supply an entry to this "Top-10" list that met *their* needs, but the truth of the matter is that I got stumped at 9. Somehow, though, a "Top-9" list just doesn't sound right. So go ahead and supply your own entry for number 10.

Summary

I'll close out this chapter with a quick synopsis of a conversation I had with my CTO and one of our salespeople. We were discussing a few projects we were either bidding on or had recently won. After I had mentioned Workflow as an option for the first three brought up, they both asked me what was up with this sudden Workflow-based approach. The end result of our little tangential conversation was a realization that Workflow represents one third of all business applications. Think about it this way: nearly every business application ever written consists of only three things:

- Data storage
- Data presentation
- A business process

Every application differs somewhat in the degree of complexity involved in each of these areas, but any way you slice it, Workflow is roughly 30 percent of every business application. You've been writing Workflow applications for years likely without ever realizing it. Wait and see how much easier your life is going to become.

CHAPTER 2

Getting Started

Before we can begin building a workflow, we need to get our environment set up. This chapter is going to cover everything we need to get that taken care of. Yep, I know, it doesn't sound that exciting. Nonetheless, it is important. As I said in the introduction to this part, if you feel some pathological need to skip a chapter, this is the one to skip. I'd recommend at least skimming it, though, just to make sure that you've got everything covered. The chapter is pretty short and I'm not going to insult your intelligence by walking you through each installation. I'm going to discuss all of the prerequisites and talk about the part they play. I'll cover any *gotchas* and just generally make sure that everyone gets started out correctly. If something doesn't seem to be working properly as you go through the examples later in the book, check back here to see if you missed some configuration step.

Also in this chapter I'll briefly walk through the scenarios that will be covered in the subsequent chapters. Because this technology is brand-new, having all of the scenarios covered in one place will help you get a sense of what is possible with the technology.

Setting Up the Environment

The first thing we need to do is get our environment established. Anyone familiar with SharePoint 2003 development won't find this very different. There are just a few new things to take care of. For the rest of you, this is all new so I'll cover things in enough detail to get you going without padding out the book with mindless step-by-step directions to install everything. I've taught classes to fifth graders on how to install their operating systems. They need step-by-step directions. I'll assume most of you are not fifth graders (no offense to fifth graders...).

Note This chapter is going to cover setting up a development environment—D-E-V-E-L-O-P-M-E-N-T—not a production environment. There are many, MANY, additional steps you will need to take to set up a production environment. Some of the shortcuts and configuration options I recommend here would make a network admin shudder and a security analyst crawl up in a fetal position and whimper. Please, please, please do not rely on this chapter for your production setup. Every production setup is different so you need to work out the details on your own. At most, look at these instructions as a starting point.

First let's take a look at the pieces we need. Table 2-1 covers the software requirements for our little excursion into Workflow.

Table 2-1. *Software Prerequisites for Developing Workflows in Office 2007*

Component	Version	Notes
Windows SharePoint Services	2007	Core component, which will be installed for you if you install MOSS. If you're installing MOSS, you don't need to install this.
Microsoft Office SharePoint Server (MOSS)	2007	SharePoint Server, including Forms Services. If you're installing this, you don't need to install WSS separately.
Windows Server	2003, with Service Pack 1 or better	
.NET Framework	2.0	Provides the primary .NET runtime and development components. You will be prompted to install this by the 3.0 Framework if it is not already installed.
.NET Framework	3.0	Provides core WF components.
Visual Studio	2005	Development environment.
Workflow Extensions for Visual Studio 2005		Workflow extensions for Visual Studio. Contains the Workflow Designer elements and supporting libraries (like IntelliSense).
Office client applications	2007	For the examples in the book, you'll need the SharePoint Designer, Word, Excel, and InfoPath.
Office System XML Code Snippets	2007	Not technically required, but we'll be making use of one of the snippets in Chapter 7.
WSS and MOSS SDKs		Reference material. Part of the MOSS SDK is some material that used to be called the Enterprise Content Management Starter Kit. It contains excellent samples, white papers, and information on development in SharePoint 2007, including Workflow. Again, not technically required but we'll use them heavily and the value they provide is huge.

Note A list of current prerequisites, including links to download them (where available), is available at `www.kcdholdings.com`.

One thing that you'll notice as being conspicuously missing from this list is a database. While you could install a full version of SQL Server (SharePoint requires SQL 2005 or SQL 2000 SP3a or better), we're going to let the SharePoint installer install SQL Server 2005 Express Edition for us. This isn't a production environment, and our usage will be limited to a single user (you) and low volume. Naturally, I would never recommend SQL Express for a production environment but for our purposes it will work out nicely.

Caution When you install Visual Studio you will be given the option of installing SQL Express. Don't. Let SharePoint install the database.

The software requirements in Table 2-1 are a little daunting. Am I telling you that you need to install all of this on your development machine just to get started? Well, the answer is really "It depends." If all you want to work with are the out-of-the-box features and you don't want to do any custom coding, you won't need Visual Studio or the Workflow Extensions. If you're not going to be using Forms Services and some of the other MOSS features, you won't need that component. Otherwise, you pretty much need everything.

I can hear your reaction already:

YOU: Dave, that's an awful lot to install on my machine just to play around with a new technology. I have real work I have to do. I can't risk my machine being taken out of commission.

ME: Yep, it's a problem, all right.

YOU: So what's a poor workflow developer to do?

ME: Virtualize...

Seriously, I strongly recommend that you look into one of the virtual machine products available on the market for your development efforts—both for Workflow in Office 2007 and just general development. See the sidebar "Virtual Reality" for more information. Little if anything in this book will presume that you are working in a virtual environment as opposed to a "real" one; nonetheless, I strongly recommend it as the benefits are tremendous and the downside is pretty minimal.

Looking back at Table 2-1 you'll see that I am freely mixing client and server elements. As this is a development environment, we are going to be installing everything on a single machine. It just makes things easier. Again, this would not be the case for a production environment, or even your test/QA environment. But for development, it works just fine.

VIRTUAL REALITY

Virtual machine technology is the greatest thing since sliced bread and that Internet fad we all keep talking about. Why? Because it is, trust me. For our purposes, it allows us developers to have a separate environment for every project we work on. We can configure a base environment with all of our usual tools and make a copy of this every time we need to start a new project. We can then customize each separate environment exactly as we need to *for that project*.

Customized environments is only the tip of the iceberg. Also of tremendous value is the ability to stop a project in the middle, save everything exactly how you need it, and pick it up again months later with everything unchanged. A quick list of other benefits to virtual machines for development includes

- *Sandboxing*: The ability to quickly set up a test environment completely independent of your standard environment.
- *Testing*: Using a virtual environment allows you to simulate multiple operating systems/software version combinations all on one physical machine.
- *Rollback*: If you're about to press the button on a potentially risky piece of code that could bring your entire machine to its knees, you can do so without fear in a virtual environment. If things go south in the proverbial handbasket, a quick file copy gets you back up and running in very little time—even less time if you use undo disks.

That's a very tiny look into the benefits. There are many more, but those are the biggest ones to me.

All it costs is a little performance (virtual machines are generally a little slower than their physical counterparts) and disk space, but that's pretty cheap these days anyway. There are licensing implications to this, naturally, but MSDN Universal and a Microsoft Gold Partnership help there. Not having the intelligence of Einstein, the wisdom of Solomon, and the patience of Job, I generally don't try to understand Microsoft's licensing plans. I periodically check with a Microsoft rep or someone from a license reseller to make sure I'm OK. You'll each need to wade through your own licensing situation and make sure you're covered. As a general rule, you'll need a valid license for every piece of software you install and, in the case of server products, at least one Client Access License. Microsoft typically has trial versions available for most of their products so that is worth looking into—it gets you typically 4–6 months of coverage.

Different virtual machine products have different features and you'll need to find the one that works best for you, your style, and your company. Personally, I've always used Microsoft's Virtual PC product, but I have heard people rave about VMware as well. You can choose whichever product suits you best. The benefits of a virtual environment remain, regardless of which product you use.

As promised, I'm not going to lead you through each and every step of each and every installation—that would just be too painful. I will, however, point out a few caveats and other important things to take into consideration as you go through the setup process. Table 2-2 lists this information.

Table 2-2. *Information and Recommendations for Setting Up Your Workflow Development Environment*

Element	Detail
Hardware	More is better—especially memory. You're going to be running some heavy-duty server applications, so the most hardware you can afford to throw at this, the better. Memory is critical. I do all development in a virtual machine on my laptop, which has 2GB of RAM. I typically allocate about 1200–1500MB to the guest OS and things move along pretty well. A nice, fast hard drive is also important. Also, if you're using a virtual environment and have multiple hard drives available, store your virtual hard drives on a different physical hard drive from your host OS's system files to avoid contention.
Windows Server 2003	You must be using the NTFS file system. Use the Convert utility rather than reinstalling if you need to fix this.
Windows Server 2003	You'll need IIS and ASP.NET 2.0 installed.
Web server	Configure IIS 6.0 to run in worker process isolation mode, which is the default unless you've upgraded from IIS 5.0.
Web server	Enable ASP.NET 2.0 in IIS (from a command line: `aspnet_regiis -i`).
Email	We are going to be using Outlook 2007 and email notifications, so I suggest you install the POP3 and SMTP components of Windows Server 2003. You could connect to external providers, but then you are tied to them. Running it all locally makes you completely independent—and mobile.
Security	This is the part that will make your security and network administrators cringe. My advice is to violate every password requirement known to man—use a short, simple password that is easy to remember and type, and use the same password for every account. This *is* a development machine and it shouldn't be on your production domain anyway so the risk is minimal.
Updates	After installing each component (OS, Office, WF, etc.), check for and install any updates.
User Accounts	Create several user accounts ahead of time. As you configure SharePoint you can assign them various levels of access. This makes it easy to test various users as you try out the different scenarios in the book. I usually give my users clever names like *Admin, Reader1, Reader2, Author1*, and *Author2*, but those may be too esoteric so feel free to use whatever names you want.
Visual Studio	Don't install SQL Express.
MOSS or WSS v3	Select to install on a single server.

■ Note Everything here assumes you are running your development environment on Windows Server 2003. At the time of this writing, Longhorn Server is still in beta. There's enough new stuff going on to worry about in Office 2007 without throwing a beta operating system into the mix. I strongly recommend not running on Longhorn until it ships.

Other than the few things listed in Table 2-2, all of the installs are pretty vanilla. There are a few particulars with getting things installed in the right order. I recommend the following:

1. Install and configure Windows Server 2003. Use NTFS for your file system. Make sure the email (POP3 and SMTP) and web server components (IIS, ASP.NET 2.0) are installed and configured, and then connect online and install all of the latest patches and service packs.
2. Enable ASP.NET in IIS (`aspnet_regiis.exe -i`) and the IIS Manager Management Console.
3. Make sure IIS is configured to run in worker process isolation mode.
4. Create all of the user accounts you'll need—for both users and service accounts. Remember: Use short, simple, common passwords. For user accounts, I typically do this through the POP3 console so I can create mailboxes and user accounts in one fell swoop. Two accounts that I always create are an SPAdmin account, which I configure as the SharePoint administrator, and SPService, which I use for all service accounts (job servers, application pools, database access, etc.). This is a development environment, so this simple, albeit extremely unsecure, approach is OK.
5. Install the .NET Framework (2.0 and 3.0) components next. Again, after these are installed, connect online and download any updates.
6. Install MOSS or WSS v3. Select Basic for the installation type to install all components on your single machine.
7. Run the SharePoint Configuration Wizard to configure your environment.
8. Install Visual Studio 2005.
9. Install the Office 2007 client applications. As mentioned previously, for the examples in this book, you will need the SharePoint Designer, Word, Excel, and InfoPath.
10. Install the Workflow Extensions for Visual Studio 2005.
11. Install the various SDKs, Code Snippets, and various other nonrequired elements from Table 2-1.
12. Finalize your MOSS or WSS v3 configuration through Central Administration:
    - Configure incoming and outgoing email settings for your environment.
    - Configure Workflow settings—all options should be set to Yes.
13. Connect online and install all service packs and updates.

For each installation step, just run the component's setup program (as appropriate). Unless otherwise noted, you can accept all of the setup program defaults, or whatever installation settings you typically use. If you have the hard drive space and are using a virtual machine, it wouldn't hurt to make a quick backup copy of the virtual machine files after steps 5 and 7. It only takes a few minutes and you don't need to keep these backups; just use them as a fall-back as you go through the process in case something goes awry. Once you have completed step 12, you can delete these interim backups.

So there you have it. Our development environment is all set up and ready to go. If you're running in a virtual environment, there's only one more step and it's an important one: back up your virtual machine file. Do it right now. Do not pass Go, do not collect your $200. Burn it to DVD (you'll likely need to compress it first) and store the DVD somewhere safe. When (not if, *when*) something goes all FUBAR ("fouled" up beyond all recognition), all you'll need to do is copy the image file back from the DVD and you'll start all over again right here.

Scenarios in This Book

In a futile attempt to make this book somewhat coherent, all of the scenarios and examples in the book are going to be related. Some of the chapters will build on a previous one, though this won't always be the case. In any event, all of the examples will center around a fictitious company. I placed all of the samples in the context of a single company so that they should be a little more relevant. I tried to pick realistic business problems, although they are somewhat stilted because my main goal is to help you understand the material.

So, without further ado...

Welcome to KCD Holdings

The premise behind all of the scenarios presented in this book is that you are a new employee of KCD Holdings in the not-too-distant future. KCD Holdings is an international conglomerate formed by purchasing other, smaller companies and streamlining their operations to reduce costs, improve efficiency, and improve profits. You have been hired to expand the company's portal and collaboration functionality for use by the Global Marketing department.

To get a feeling for the possibilities offered by a consistent, enterprisewide implementation of the 2007 Office System, imagine that you have arrived at the office on your first day and need to fill out all of your typical first day paperwork—tax forms, direct deposit forms, benefit forms, and so forth. Typically, this is a manually intensive operation—get out your blue or black pen and prepare to do a lot of writing.

You'll find, though, that KCD is anything but typical.

Imagine your surprise when you arrive and find only a single piece of paper awaiting you. The HR administrator explains that everything else is done electronically. This single piece of paper is simply your agreement that your digital signature is legal and valid for all company-related documents on which it is used. Still a little skeptical, you sit down at the conference table and sign the paper. Once you hand the paper back to the HR administrator, she hands you a smart card and explains how to use it. She shows you how to log into a computer using it and how to digitally sign documents.

Over the course of the next few hours, you read the documents and fill out the forms that constitute typical new employee paperwork. After you have finished with each document or form, you sign it with the digital certificate from your new smart card. As you progress through the documents, you notice a few things. First of all, you never have to enter information twice. Once you've put your address on the W4, it automagically appears on all subsequent forms in the appropriate place—same thing for your Social Security number, date of birth, and so forth. You begin to get the feeling that there's a lot happening under the covers here:

- As you are filling out the forms, you notice that new documents and forms are showing up in your list. For example, on the payroll form you checked the boxes for 401(k), life insurance, and the Section 125 plan. After you submit the payroll form you notice the following new documents in your "to do" list:
    - 401(k) enrollment
    - Life insurance details and beneficiary designation
    - Section 125 claim instructions
- Each document in your list has a "status" associated with it: Incomplete, Submitted, Under Review, Approved, Rejected, Posted, etc. Some of these statuses are changing apparently in real time as the result of the actions of others somewhere in the background. You made a mistake on a few of the documents and they are showing back up in the list flagged as *Requires Attention.*

You notice that all of the documents you are accessing are coming from KCD's New Employee Orientation portal, which also includes links to information about the company and other things of interest to a new employee. The portal itself looks vaguely like the SharePoint Portal Server that was used at your last job. But there's more to it than that. It acts like your previous portal the same way a Model T acts somewhat like a Formula 1 racecar—they both perform the same basic job but are light years apart in how they achieve their goal. This entire experience is more like your previous portal and document experience after it has been given enough steroids to disqualify it from any professional sporting event for the rest of time.

After all of the administrivia is finished, you finally meet your new boss for lunch and you nonchalantly bring up the new portal and the entire new hire process. She chuckles and says "*You ain't seen nothin' yet.*" She then proceeds to fill you in on some of the details:

- KCD has been a part of an early adopter program for the Office 2007 wave of products. Timing worked very much in their favor as they were preparing to upgrade the majority of their systems anyway.
- Beginning with the private alpha build of the Office 12 System, KCD began planning for and preparing to upgrade all of their applications.
- Over the last 18 months, they have been upgrading their internal systems. While not all systems are upgraded yet, the HR portions are done and are jokingly referred to as their "Shock and Awe" campaign for new hires.

You stare at her a little dumbfounded. That was all Office? She smiles knowingly... the Shock and Awe campaign claims another victim.

Business Value of the Office 2007 System

After picking your jaw up off the floor, you continue your discussion with your boss. She moves away from the technical details and fills you in on the business reasons for the investments they've made. Early in 2005, KCD found itself struggling. As a large company formed by an aggressive purchasing schedule, they were suffocating under the weight of their multiple, disparate internal systems. The volume of information that had to be stored, tracked, and acted upon was growing exponentially. They couldn't keep up. A few high-profile failures had focused attention of the entire senior management team on the value of information and the importance of process.

Your boss found herself in a unique situation and she took full advantage of it. Working closely with a consulting partner, her team mapped out a strategy to upgrade all of their critical internal systems to the latest product releases, including beta products, where possible, for proof-of-concept projects and eventual deployment. An overall, process-driven, service-oriented architecture was designed for all of their internal systems, and each piece of the puzzle was plugged into the architecture as time and resources have permitted. The benefits to the company have been many, including

- A single, global portal environment for all of their information and multiple user bases (employees, partners, customers). Because of this:
    - Content is now created, managed, and secured in one place and with one paradigm.
    - Duplicate content is eliminated.
    - Content publishing now pushes content to their public web sites as appropriate from a single source.
    - Defined policies now control all aspects of the content and document lifecycle, information rights management, and records management.
    - IT needs only to support a single technology base.
    - Users have a single experience for all content management, searching, and consumption.
    - Training costs have dropped significantly.
- Fully mapped and documented processes. This allowed the company to investigate and study what they did and how they did it. They could eliminate inconsistencies, inaccuracies, and bottlenecks. Common processes were implemented across departments to eliminate duplication. The user experience was streamlined and implemented in a consistent manner to reduce training and support costs and also make employees more efficient.
- Transparent access to their business data through scorecarding, aggregated data views, and reporting.

Workflow is the glue that ties all of their systems together. Your boss explains how even outside the Office 2007 pieces of the company's new infrastructure, Workflow enforces their processes and streamlines their operations. Because they built all of their processes in Windows Workflow Foundation, their human- and machine-centric processes were built utilizing the same technology. This reduces their costs, simplifies their environment, and allows for reuse of the various components they developed.

Your job is to extend this architecture into the last department of the company that is not currently using it—Global Marketing. Although this department is taking advantage of some of the new architecture, such as document and content management, it is not making use of Workflow elements specific to their processes yet. Their processes have been all mapped and designed to fit into the overall architecture. It is now up to you to implement the solution.

Good luck. As always, if you or any member of your team are captured or killed, the Secretary will disavow any knowledge of your actions.

Scenarios in the Chapters

Table 2-3 provides a quick overview of the scenarios covered in each chapter of the book to help you understand how everything ties together.

Table 2-3. *Scenarios Used in Each Chapter of the Book*

Chapter	Scenario	Overview	Products Utilized
3	Monitoring Marketing Campaigns	Using nothing but the out-of-the-box capabilities of MOSS, develop a workflow based on a sample template to handle document review and approval.	MOSS
4	Product Launch Campaigns	Building a new workflow using the SharePoint Designer. Functionality includes these steps: Collect Feedback, Review and Approval, and Notification. Participants review material, provide feedback, and verify details. Other participants are notified but provide no feedback or approval.	SharePoint Designer, MOSS, WSS v3
5	Removing Macros	This chapter does not include a full workflow as it is focused on building activities. The scenario focuses on removing macros from Office 2007 documents.	Visual Studio, MOSS, or WSS v3
6	Removing Macros	A sequential workflow that uses the custom activity built in Chapter 5.	Visual Studio, MOSS, or WSS v3
6	Preventing Outdated Tasks	A state machine workflow to ensure that task assignments are current and accurate.	Visual Studio, MOSS, or WSS v3
7	Global Marketing Campaigns	Custom forms used to modify workflow processing. This scenario is duplicated using InfoPath forms and ASP.NET forms.	Forms Services, MOSS, WSS v3, InfoPath and ASP.NET forms, Visual Studio
8	External Ruleset Management	Similar to Chapter 5, this chapter does not really implement a workflow scenario. Its primary purpose is to build a custom activity. It has a workflow at the end, but it's just there to see our new activity in action.	Visual Studio, MOSS, or WSS v3

■ **Note** I know you haven't backed up your virtual machine file. Don't say I didn't warn you...

Summary

There you have it—short but sweet. The bulk of this chapter is geared toward making sure that you get your environment set up correctly. We covered all the elements that are necessary to build our development environment as well as some pointers on getting things set up correctly. Finally, we went through an overview of the scenarios that will be presented in later chapters and discussed the business benefits our fictional company is getting from their investment in the Office 2007 System.

Next up, we start looking at specific workflows and the functionality they provide. See you in Chapter 3.

PART 2

Having an Out-of-the-Box Experience

Now it's time to get our hands dirty. All of the introductory material is out of the way and we can finally get our hands around the product. Part 1 introduced workflow concepts in general and Windows Workflow Foundation (WF) in particular. It also covered some of the important changes to the Office system that will impact workflow and showed how to set up your environment.

This part walks you through the capabilities and features of Workflow in Office 2007 that become available to you as soon as you install and configure the product—no code required. As you'll see, you can do a lot with this out-of-the-box functionality.

Chapter 3 introduces and provides details on the workflows that ship with MOSS. We take a look at how administrators should configure these workflows and what situations the workflows were designed for. Finally, we take a walk in a participant's shoes and get an understanding of what their experience will be like.

In Chapter 4 we build our first workflow. Nothing too exciting yet—we still stick with the out-of-the-box capabilities. However, in this chapter we fire up the SharePoint Designer and build a customized workflow to solve a specific business problem at KCD Holdings. We go through the process of building our workflow and deploying it to the server, and take a brief look at the administrator and participant experience.

Let's get started...

CHAPTER 3

Using the Default Workflows

MOSS ships with a number of preconfigured workflows out-of-the-box. WSS ships with only one. Each workflow provides immediate value, and also serves as a sample for developers who need to create their own workflows.

The MOSS workflows are more interesting and a bit more relevant in a document scenario than the WSS workflow. However, the one WSS workflow is intriguing as it is fairly generic, though still quite useful across multiple scenarios. This chapter explores the default workflows and the experience they provide to end users.

The first thing that it is important to understand is that, just like the previous version of SharePoint, WSS is the core product and MOSS extends it. From a Workflow perspective, this means that both products provide the same basic experience and core capabilities for participants, administrators, and builders. MOSS just provides more capabilities on top of that base. Not taking into account the Forms Services (which we'll cover in a bit), there is nothing in MOSS that you couldn't build yourself in WSS. The extra out-of-the-box workflows in MOSS are just part of its value.

The Out-of-the-Box Workflows

To get an understanding of what is available in SharePoint out-of-the-box, take a look at Table 3-1. It lists all of the out-of-the-box workflows and provides a brief description of each.

Table 3-1. *Default Workflows Available in MOSS and WSS*

Workflow Name	Available In	Description
Three-State	WSS, MOSS	Used to track and move list items through a series of states. Can be configured to react differently at various stages.
Approval	MOSS	Routes a document for approval. Approvers can approve or reject the document, reassign the approval task, or request changes to the document.
Collect Feedback	MOSS	Routes a document for review. Reviewers can provide feedback, which is compiled and sent to the document owner when the workflow has completed.

Table 3-1. *Default Workflows Available in MOSS and WSS (Continued)*

Workflow Name	Available In	Description
Collect Signatures	MOSS	Gathers signatures needed to complete an Office document.
Disposition Approval	MOSS	Manages document expiration and retention by allowing participants to decide whether to retain or delete expired documents.

As you can see in Table 3-1, the default workflows in MOSS are geared toward typical document management tasks, and the WSS workflow is a generic, list-targeted workflow. While they may not suit every need, all these workflows are a good start and can be implemented immediately as a complete process to meet many organizations' immediate concerns. In a moment, we'll walk through a scenario solved entirely with one of the default MOSS workflows. First, though, let's take a quick look at the WSS default workflow.

WSS Workflow: Three-State

As implied by the name, this workflow handles the movement of a list item from an initial state, to a middle state, and ultimately to a final state. All transitions are triggered by the completion of workflow tasks. At each transition, the workflow can be configured to automatically send an email to the appropriate user notifying them of the task assignment.

The perfect example for using this workflow is a help desk scenario. When a problem occurs, a help desk ticket is created and the information for it is stored as a list item. When each help ticket is created, it is assigned an initial state of *Active*. By configuring the workflow (the term is *associating*—we'll examine the process shortly when we explore the MOSS workflow in detail), you can control what happens when the list item is created. In all cases, a workflow task will be created and you can specify the person to whom that task should be assigned. Optionally, you can choose to have the server send that person an email and specify the details of that email message.

Continuing on, you can configure the workflow to control what happens when the user marks their assigned task as complete (which causes the list item to transition to its middle state). Again, a task is going to be created and you can specify the details of that task. Also as before, you can indicate whether you want an email to be sent to the person to whom the task is assigned and configure the details of that email.

When the second user completes their task, the list item is automatically set to its final state and the workflow is complete.

In order to function, the list to which this workflow is associated must have at least one Choice field with at least three potential values from which to choose. If you attempt to associate the workflow with a list that does not meet these requirements, you will get an error, like the one shown in Figure 3-1, and the OK button on the form will be disabled, preventing you from submitting the form.

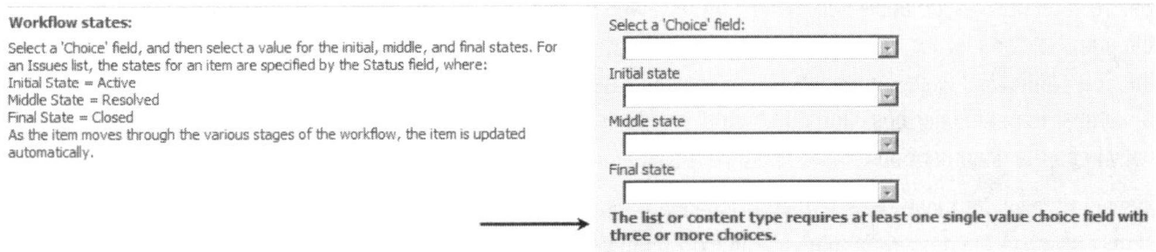

Workflow states:

Select a 'Choice' field, and then select a value for the initial, middle, and final states. For an Issues list, the states for an item are specified by the Status field, where:
Initial State = Active
Middle State = Resolved
Final State = Closed
As the item moves through the various stages of the workflow, the item is updated automatically.

Select a 'Choice' field:

Initial state

Middle state

Final state

The list or content type requires at least one single value choice field with three or more choices.

Figure 3-1. *The Three-State workflow will only work on a list with a Choice field type.*

Note This workflow only supports three states. If the Choice field you designate has more than three possible values, you can still only specify a beginning, middle, and end state. Figure 3-1 also shows the interface that allows you to select the List field and specify the values for each of the three states from those available within that Choice field.

The Three-State workflow is interesting because it is a good example of codifying a generic process but still providing a workflow that can be easily applied to multiple situations. It places only one significant requirement upon the list to which is applied—the need for a Choice field with at least three values. While we haven't gotten to workflow forms yet (that's not until Chapter 7), this workflow is also a great example of a pretty complex workflow form delivered via ASP.NET.

Next up, we'll take a more detailed look at one of the out-of-the-box MOSS workflows.

MOSS Workflow: Document Approval

Document approval is a fundamental problem for information workers. Multiple ad hoc methods of tackling this problem have been created. Some are manual; some are automated. Some utilize a third-party solution, some utilize homegrown solutions, and some are cobbled together from available functionality within Office. In any case, the problem being addressed is similar to the scenario we'll investigate here.

Scenario: Monitoring Marketing Campaigns

Mary works in the Global Marketing department of KCD Holdings. She is responsible for posting the results of marketing campaigns at biweekly intervals and a final summary document at the conclusion of each campaign. These documents are known as CEBs—Campaign Effectiveness Briefs. The intention is to closely monitor the effectiveness of each campaign and allow KCD to take steps to increase the effectiveness of a campaign if necessary. In addition, the final summary of the campaign's effectiveness allows KCD to continuously improve by learning from the past.

Before each CEB can be published, it must be reviewed by Mary's boss, the director of Global Marketing, as well as the product manager for the particular product being marketed by the campaign. Currently, Mary emails a draft of the CEB around and waits for results. As you can imagine, this is not a very effective process. It is up to Mary to remember to remind her boss and the product manager to provide feedback, and when they do, she needs to manually keep the document up to date and if necessary circulate another draft for additional review.

It is not unusual for these CEBs to be published late, not due to any incompetence or inactivity on Mary's part, but simply because the process is manual and extremely time consuming. The whole Global Marketing department needs the information in these CEBs in order to do their jobs. Everyone is frustrated when the documents are published late, and Mary bears the brunt of this frustration.

Your job is to automate this process and help Mary out. The primary goal is to increase the timeliness of publishing the results documents. KCD has been unable to reliably fine-tune their marketing campaigns in mid-stream due to a lack of information. Although there are no hard-and-fast numbers to support it, there is anecdotal evidence and a general feeling that the campaigns are not as effective as they could be.

It's still your first day on the job (see Chapter 2 if you missed the introduction to KCD Holdings and this whole scenario is making very little sense to you). As your boss had explained, your job is to help KCD automate the processes in their Global Marketing department. This problem has been identified as a high-profile, relatively straightforward problem to be solved. It is therefore considered a perfect candidate for the first process to be automated. The process itself is pretty simple. Success in improving the CEB publishing process will go a long way toward eliminating the resentment various key members of Global Marketing have had toward IT for wanting to meddle in their department. Success here will convert Global Marketing to a believer and make the rest of your work much easier—good luck, Agent 86.

After talking to Mary, you've got a good understanding of the business needs for the situation. In short, the process is as follows:

1. Mary creates the CEB on Monday morning.
2. Mary emails the CEB to her boss, the director of Global Marketing, for review.
3. If the director approves the CEB, he emails Mary back or tells her in the hallway that she can send the document to the product manager.
4. If the director makes changes, he emails the document back to Mary with his notes and comments. Mary reviews and updates the CEB document and then emails it to the product manager.
5. If the product manager approves the CEB, she also sends an email back to Mary. Mary now emails the document to all of Global Marketing.
6. If the product manager makes any changes, she emails the document back to Mary. Mary reviews and updates the CEB, emails it back to the director for review, and the whole process starts over again.

In the past, people have complained about not being able to find the CEBs in their email Inbox. Similarly, the director and the product manager have complained that having multiple copies of the CEB document show up in their inboxes as new drafts are circulated is confusing. They never know which copy is the correct one.

Being a MOSS 2007 guru, you immediately recognize this as an opportunity custom-made for a document library and a simple workflow. You assure Mary that you will be able to help her.

We're going to explore the process of configuring one of the out-of-the-box workflows to solve this problem. All of the out-of-the-box workflows (and really *all* workflows) will be configured in a similar manner. After the workflow is configured, we'll walk through the end user's s experience using the workflow.

Solving the Problem: The Workflow Administrator's Role

To begin with, the CEBs belong in a document library. Email is a bad mechanism for delivering mission-critical content. You connect to the Global Marketing site on the KCD intranet and create a document library to store the CEBs.

■ **Note** In a real production system, the CEBs would likely be a candidate for a content type. There are numerous other settings, such as versioning, permissions, and so forth, that would need to be taken into consideration. For this simple scenario, let's skip all this and put the workflow directly on the document library.

After creating the new document library, you need to configure the workflow settings. The process to do this varies depending on whether this is your first workflow for the document library or whether you have previously configured workflows to be available in the document library. In either case, the process begins the same: From the toolbar inside the document library you select Settings ➤ Document Library Settings and in the resulting screen, select Workflow Settings in the Permissions and Management section.

Now the process changes slightly. If this is not the first workflow instance on the document library, you'll see a screen similar to the one in Figure 3-2. It allows you to either change (or remove) an existing workflow instance, add a new one, or view workflow reports (we'll cover workflow reports in Chapter 9). If this *is* the first workflow instance on the document library, you will be taken directly to the Add a Workflow screen, shown in Figure 3-3. For the CEB process, if you are shown the screen in Figure 3-2, just click the Add a workflow link to proceed to the next screen.

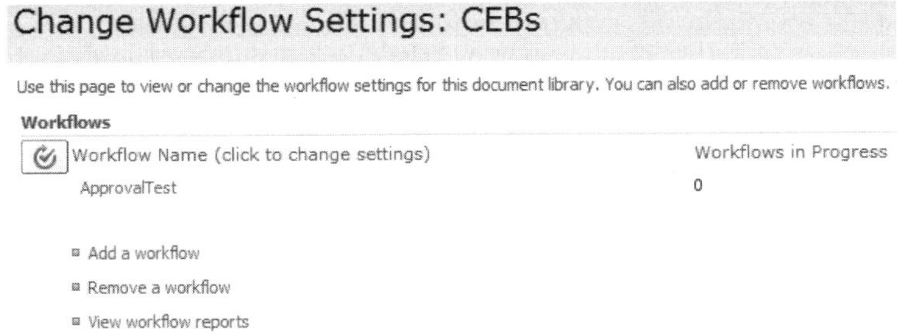

Figure 3-2. *If you already have workflows in a document library, this screen allows you to change them or add a new workflow.*

Add a Workflow: CEBs
Use this page to set up a workflow for this document library.
Workflow
Select a workflow to add to this document library. If the workflow template you want does not appear, contact your administrator to get it added to your site collection or workspace.
Select a workflow template:
Approval
Collect Feedback
Collect Signatures
Disposition Approval
Description:
Routes a document for approval. Approvers can approve or reject the document, reassign the approval task, or request changes to the document.
Name
Type a name for this workflow. The name will be used to identify this workflow to users of this document library.
Type a unique name for this workflow:
Task List
Select a task list to use with this workflow. You can select an existing task list or request that a new task list be created.
Select a task list:
Tasks
Description:
Use the Tasks list to keep track of work that you or your team needs to complete.
History List
Select a history list to use with this workflow. You can select an existing history list or request that a new history list be created.
Select a history list:
Workflow History
Description:
History list for workflow.
Start Options
Specify how this workflow can be started.
Allow this workflow to be manually started by an authenticated user with Edit Items Permissions.
Require Manage Lists Permissions to start the workflow.
Start this workflow to approve publishing a major version of an item.
Start this workflow when a new item is created.
Start this workflow when an item is changed.
Next
Cancel

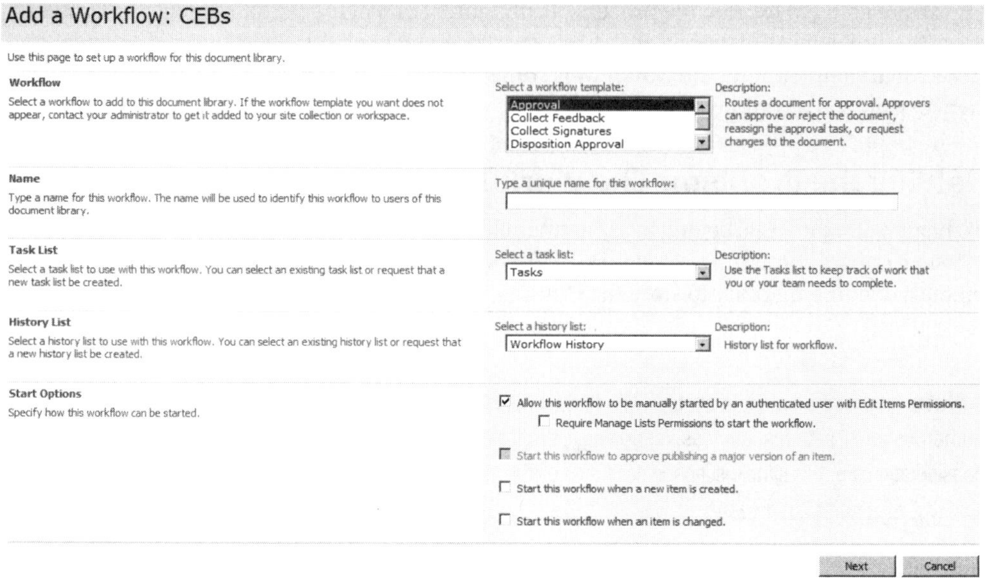

Figure 3-3. *Configuring one of the out-of-the-box workflows is a simple matter of filling in a form in the document library settings.*

Regardless of how you arrived at it, the Add a Workflow screen (shown in Figure 3-3) allows you to specify how the workflows that are available on your site will be customized to meet your particular needs. Finishing the setup of the workflow for the CEB process is fairly straightforward. On the Add a Workflow screen there are six basic settings to configure. Table 3-2 gives details on each of these settings as well as the value to provide for our CEB workflow.

Table 3-2. *Configuring the Add a Workflow Screen for the CEB Process*

Option	Setting for CEB Scenario	Notes
Workflow	Approval	In this section at the top of the screen, you will see the default workflows listed. Each custom workflow represents an instance of one of the available templates. Later in the book we will create new workflow templates and deploy them so that they show up as available templates in this list.
Name	CEB Approval	Each workflow instance must have a distinct name. While any name is permissible here, it is important to remember that this is the name that will be shown to end users, so it should be short but descriptive.

Table 3-2. *Configuring the Add a Workflow Screen for the CEB Process*

Option	Setting for CEB Scenario	Notes
Task List	Tasks	Presumably, all workflows in Office 2007 are going to create and assign tasks to participants. To accomplish this, a SharePoint list needs to be designated as the task list for each instance of a workflow, including our CEB Approval instance. Depending on your needs, you can either select an existing list from the drop-down or choose to have a new list created. Having a unique list for each instance keeps things cleaner, but it does create a number of potentially extraneous lists. Having all workflow tasks in one list is not as straightforward, but it keeps down your list count. For our purposes here, select the option to use the existing task list.
History List	New History List	The history list for a workflow does exactly what the name implies—it stores a record of the activities and actions taken by the workflow instance and its participants.
Start Options	Manual	The Start options allow you to specify the conditions and circumstances that allow your workflow instance to be kicked off. The basic options are Manual: A user needs to step through the UI and choose to kick off this workflow. You can further fine-tune the setting to indicate which permissions the user must have in order to be able to start the workflow. You can require either Edit Items (the default) or Manage Lists. New Item Created: The workflow is kicked off whenever a new item is added in the document library. Item Changed: The workflow is kicked off whenever an item is updated in the document library.

Because Mary needs to specify the appropriate product manager for the particular CEB, we'll have her start the workflow manually.

This first screen in the process of configuring a workflow will be exactly the same for all workflows. The information you provide here is used to create the new workflow instance. Click the Next button at the bottom of the screen to continue customizing our new workflow instance. The screen that appears next, shown in Figure 3-4, will be unique to each and every workflow template. While the specific options available on this second screen will be different for each workflow, the general gist of the next screen will be similar. This second screen is used for configuring each instance of the workflow by providing values for the settings the workflow requires in order to execute. In some cases, this will simply be the names of the people to assign tasks to. In other cases, there may be significant additional metadata that must be provided in order for the workflow to process. The ultimate decision for this lies with the builder.

Customize Workflow: CEB Approval
OK Cancel
Workflow Tasks
Specify how tasks are routed to participants and whether to allow tasks to be delegated or if participants can request changes be made to the document prior to finishing their tasks.
Assign tasks to:
All participants simultaneously (parallel)
One participant at a time (serial)
Allow workflow participants to:
Reassign the task to another person
Request a change before completing the task
Default Workflow Start Values
Specify the default values that this workflow will use when it is started. You can opt to allow the person who starts the workflow to change or add participants.
Type the names of people you want to participate when this workflow is started. Add names in the order in which you want the tasks assigned (for serial workflows).
Approvers...
Assign a single task to each group entered (Do not expand groups).
Allow changes to the participant list when this workflow is started
Type a message to include with your request:
Due Date
If a due date is specified and e-mail is enabled on the server, participants will receive a reminder on that date if their task is not finished.
Tasks are due by (parallel):
Give each person the following amount of time to finish their task (serial):
Day(s)
Notify Others
To notify other people when this workflow starts without assigning tasks, type names on the CC line.
CC...
Complete the Workflow
Specify when you want the workflow to be completed. If you do not select any options, the workflow will be completed when all tasks are finished.
Complete this workflow when:
Following number of tasks are finished:
Cancel this workflow when the:
Document is rejected
Document is changed
Post-completion Workflow Activities
Specify the actions you want to occur after the workflow has been successfully completed.
After the workflow is completed:
Update the approval status (use this workflow to control content approval)
OK Cancel

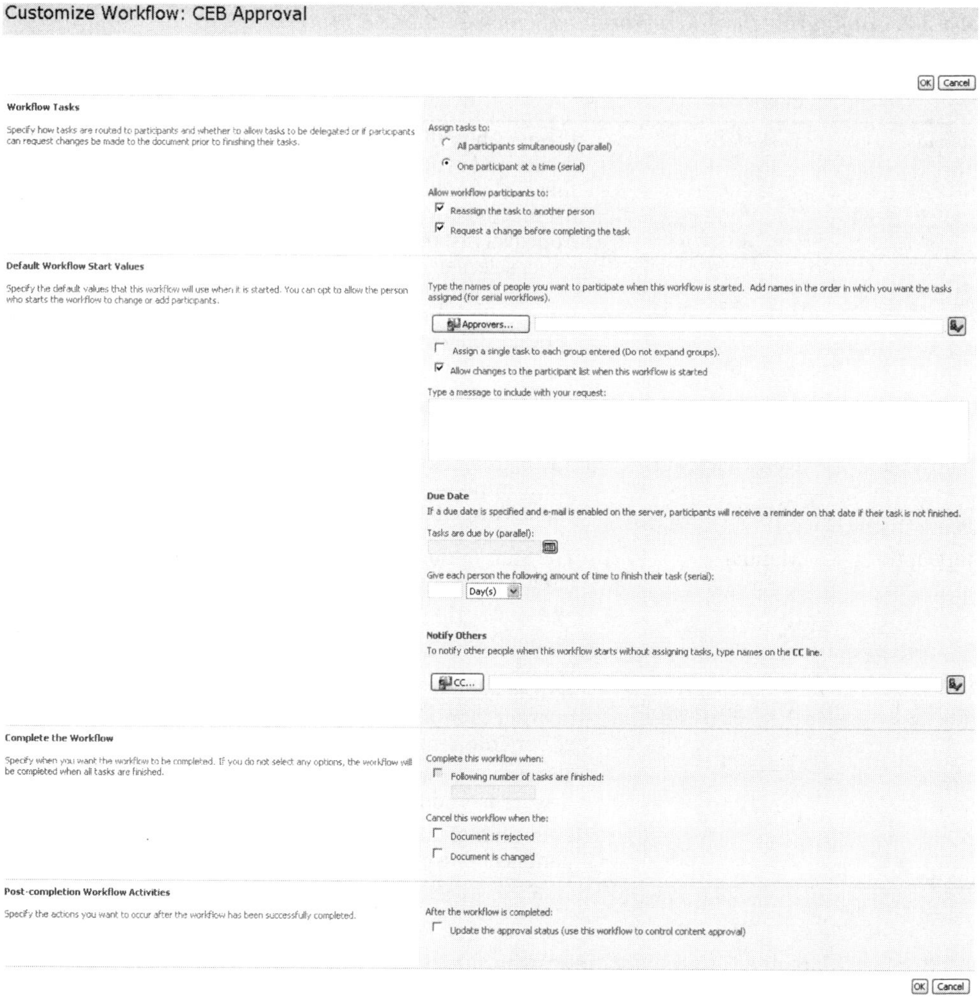

Figure 3-4. *The second screen in creating a new workflow is used to supply metadata for the specific workflow instance.*

Table 3-3 gives the details for each option on this second screen, along with the values to provide for our CEB scenario.

Table 3-3. *Configuring the Customize Workflow Screen for the CEB Process*

Section	Option	Setting for CEB Scenario	Notes
Workflow Tasks	Assign Tasks To One Participant at a Time (serial)	Checked	This option allows you to specify how tasks are assigned. For our purposes, we want to make sure that the director of Global Marketing is assigned the review task before the product manager. In the case of the other option (parallel), all participants would be assigned their tasks simultaneously.
Workflow Tasks	Allow Workflow Participants To Reassign the Task to Another Person	Unchecked	Allows participants to delegate tasks. For the CEB process, the director must review each document. Business rules prohibit this from being delegated.
Workflow Tasks	Request a Change Before Completing the Task	Checked	If the director requires that changes be made to the document, he can request that Mary make these changes and then resubmit the document for approval.
Default Workflow Start Values	Approvers	*<two valid usernames in your environment>*	Since we've opted for a serial assignment of tasks, it is important that the names entered here be in the proper order—the first person named will receive their task first and the second will receive their task when the first is done.
Default Workflow Start Values	Assign a Single Task to Each Group Entered	Unchecked	With this box unchecked, any Active Directory, NTLM, or SharePoint groups entered will be expanded and each member will receive a task assignment. If the box is checked, a single task is assigned and any member of the group can complete it.
Default Workflow Start Values	Allow Changes to the Participant List When This Workflow Is Started	Unchecked	If this option is checked, the person manually starting the workflow will be given the opportunity to modify the approvers. For the CEB process, this is disallowed by a business rule.

Table 3-3. *Configuring the Customize Workflow Screen for the CEB Process (Continued)*

Section	Option	Setting for CEB Scenario	Notes
Default Workflow Start Values	Message	Please review this CEB	Allows you to enter a customized message or instructions to participants for this instance of the workflow.
Default Workflow Start Values	Due Date	Give each person two days to complete their task.	
Default Workflow Start Values	CC	*<blank>*	This option allows you to specify other users who will be notified that a task has been assigned, though they will not be assigned a task.
Complete the Workflow		All unchecked	This section allows you, as the workflow administrator, to define certain conditions that can cause your workflow to end prematurely—that is, before all of the tasks have been completed. For more information, see the sidebar "Short-Circuiting Your Workflow."
Post-Completion Workflow Activities	Update the Approval Status	Checked	This setting allows you to have your workflow control the document or list level approval for the document (if content approval is enabled). In our case, we will be enabling Content Approval on the CEB document library and will use it to make sure that users will not be able to see the CEB until it has been approved.

SHORT-CIRCUITING YOUR WORKFLOW

Typically, you will want your workflow to complete the whole business logic—after all, that's why the logic exists. However, in some cases, your business logic will define circumstances under which the process needs to stop immediately. As each one of these situations will be unique to your particular business case, there is no way for the default workflows to account for all potential situations. Instead, the default workflows give you the option of stopping your workflow in response to a number of situations:

- *A certain number of tasks are completed*: In some cases, your business logic may dictate that not all users need to complete their tasks. Typically, this will be the case in, for example, an Approval workflow in which only a majority of participants need to approve the document. Once that majority of participants have approved of the document, the document is considered *Approved* and so there is no reason for the other participants to compete their tasks. This option allows you to account for this situation.

- *Document is rejected*: If one of the participants rejects the document, you would likely not have later participants in the process continue to review a document that has already been rejected.
- *Document is changed*: Again, if the document is changed by one participant, there is no way for the workflow to route the document back to earlier participants. In this case, those earlier participants reviewed one version of the document, but it is not the same version as the one that completes the workflow. This could cause significant problems.

Regardless of the reason that the workflow is ended early, the end result is the same: the workflow history list is updated and the current outstanding tasks are marked as complete (and therefore removed from users' task lists, the notification areas of the Office client applications, etc.).

Once you have configured these options, click OK and you're done. The CEB Approval process is now automated and ready for use by Mary.

REMOVING A WORKFLOW

While we're looking at the out-of-the-box functionality, let's take a quick little side trip into some additional administrative functionality: removing a workflow. It is important to note, however, that this functionality will be the same regardless of whether it is an out-of-the-box workflow or one of our custom workflows.

From the Change Workflow Settings screen (shown earlier in Figure 3-2) for any list or document library, click the Remove a Workflow link. You will be taken to a screen similar to the one shown here:

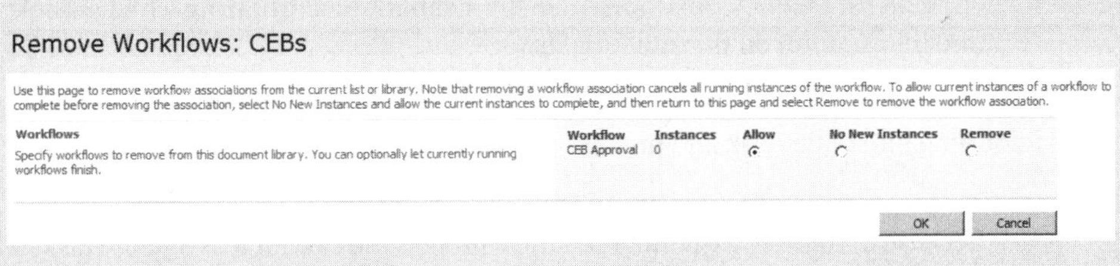

Remove Workflows: CEBs

Use this page to remove workflow associations from the current list or library. Note that removing a workflow association cancels all running instances of the workflow. To allow current instances of a workflow to complete before removing the association, select No New Instances and allow the current instances to complete, and then return to this page and select Remove to remove the workflow association.

Workflows

Specify workflows to remove from this document library. You can optionally let currently running workflows finish.

Workflow	Instances	Allow	No New Instances	Remove
CEB Approval	0	◉	○	○

OK | Cancel

At the right of the screen are a few columns. The first lists the available workflows. The Instances column lets us know how many instances of this workflow are *currently* running on items within the list or document library. The other three options are presented as radio buttons, allowing us to indicate whether this workflow should be allowed to remain unchanged (the default), whether it should be immediately removed and all instances canceled (the right radio button, Remove*)*, or whether existing instances should be allowed to finish running but no new instances started (the middle column, No New Instances).

In a production environment, in most cases your choice will likely most often be the No New Instances option.

There's just one more setting to change before our workflow is complete. If you recall from our earlier discussion, we are using the workflow to control the content approval setting for the document, so we need to change the configuration to require content approval. It is perhaps a bit unintuitive, but the option for this is in the Versioning settings for the document library.

Change that option and that's it—the CEB Approval workflow is complete and ready to be demonstrated to the users.

Showcasing the Solution

Mary is naturally quite surprised to hear that you are ready to show her your solution so quickly. She is a little skeptical but agrees to set up a meeting with her boss and a few of the primary product managers who are most often involved in reviewing and approving the CEBs.

The End User's Experience

When you arrive at the conference room, you explain the new process to everyone before walking them through a sample. The process will now work as follows:

1. Mary still creates the CEB on Monday morning. The way she creates the document remains the same.
2. Instead of emailing the document to her boss, Mary connects to the Global Marketing department site and uploads the document to the new CEB document library.
3. Once the document is in the library, Mary manually kicks off the workflow and specifies the appropriate product manager. For now, Mary's work is done.
4. Mary's boss has a task assigned to him to review the CEB. There are two ways he can be notified of this new task, besides navigating to the site and seeing it:
    - Assuming he is synchronizing the task list with Outlook, he will see the task assignment right in his Outlook To-Do Bar. See the sidebar "Synchronizing with Outlook" for more information on this functionality.
    - Assuming that outbound email is configured on the server, he will receive an email informing him of the task and providing links to the task.
5. Mary's boss can choose to approve or reject the document or request changes from Mary. Because of the way we configured the workflow, he cannot reassign the task to someone else.
6. When Mary's boss approves the document, the appropriate product manager receives a notification of the document that is awaiting his review. He has the same options as Mary's boss.
7. Once the document is fully approved, it will be automatically flagged as *Approved* and therefore available to users with at least Reader access to the CEB document library.

To help everyone understand the power and simplicity of this new process, you explain what each of the participants will experience in the brave new world you've created for them.

SYNCHRONIZING WITH OUTLOOK

While this functionality is not directly related to Workflow, it is so useful, and likely to be used for most of our workflows, that it is worth covering here. What I'm talking about is synchronizing a SharePoint list with Outlook so that the information is accessible (and manageable) in either application.

For our workflows, this will most often take the form of synchronizing Workflow task lists with Outlook so that the tasks show up on our To-Do Bar. The process to set this up is astoundingly simple:

1. Navigate to the SharePoint list that you wish to synchronize.
2. From the Action drop-down, select Connect to Outlook, as shown here:

3. In the dialog box that appears, click the Advanced button.
4. In the SharePoint List Options dialog box, change the Folder Name to **CEB Tasks** and click OK.
5. Click Yes.
6. Outlook will open, automatically configured to maintain a two-way synchronization with the SharePoint list on the server.

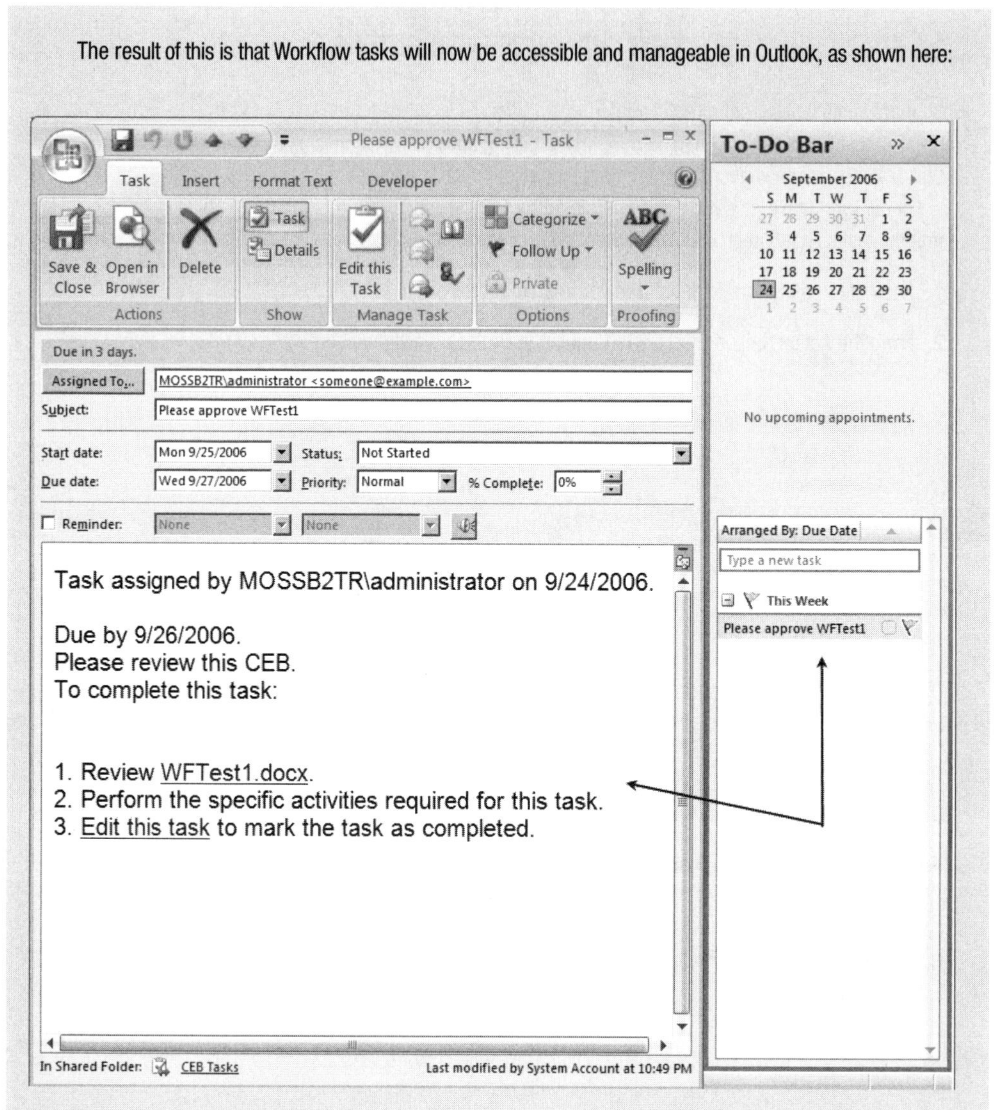

The Document Owner's Experience

Mary begins her Monday like any other—she collects the information necessary to produce a CEB. Today it is for the Ultra-Widget II product marketing campaign that has been running for the last six weeks. Once she has collected the raw information necessary to produce the document, she fires up Word 2007 and begins typing away.

Note The experience detailed here is the same regardless of who initiates the workflow. It does not have to be the official owner of the document. Anyone with sufficient privileges can start a workflow (as specified in the workflow association form).

When the document is complete, Mary saves it and uploads it to the CEB document library on the Global Marketing site. As mentioned previously, if this were a real production system the experience would be slightly different because we could take advantage of the new content types feature in SharePoint, but that's unrelated to Workflow and for now we're going to keep things simple. So far, the experience has not been any different for Mary. But here's where the fun begins.

After uploading the document, Mary runs her mouse over the document name in the document list and selects Workflows from the drop-down menu, as shown in Figure 3-5.

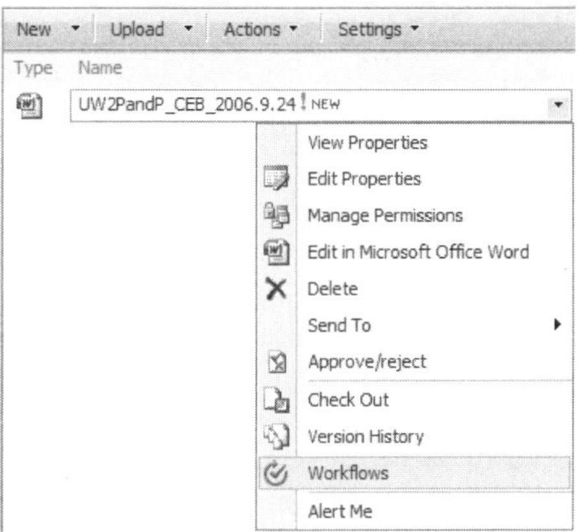

Figure 3-5. *The document drop-down menu has been expanded in SharePoint 2007 to include new functionality—including the Workflows option we're interested in here.*

The screen that comes up next (shown in Figure 3-6) lets Mary choose which workflow she wants to use. This screen also shows information on currently running and completed workflows, if there are any. Mary chooses CEB Approval Workflow and is shown a screen that allows her to customize this instance of the workflow (Figure 3-7).

In our scenario, Mary needs to specify the appropriate product manager for the UltraWidget II product line. This person needs to approve the CEB document before it can be published. Other information to be supplied on this screen includes a message to be included with the emails and task assignments. This message will be the same for all approvers. Mary can also customize the number of days each approver will get to review the document as well as any other people who should be notified of the tasks. Notice that each field on this screen is set to the default values we set up as the administrator when we added the CEB workflow to the CEB document library. Mary does not need to change any of these options so she can just click the Start button.

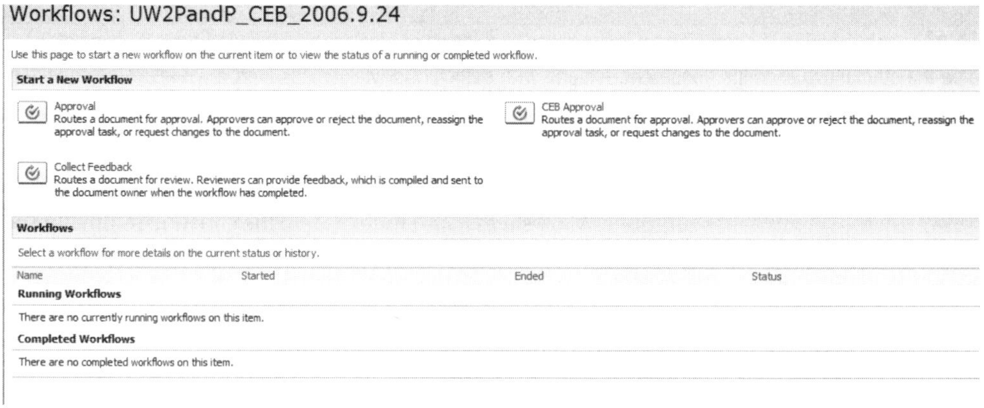

Figure 3-6. *The Workflow screen for our document library shows workflows available to be started, as well as information on currently running and completed workflows, if there are any.*

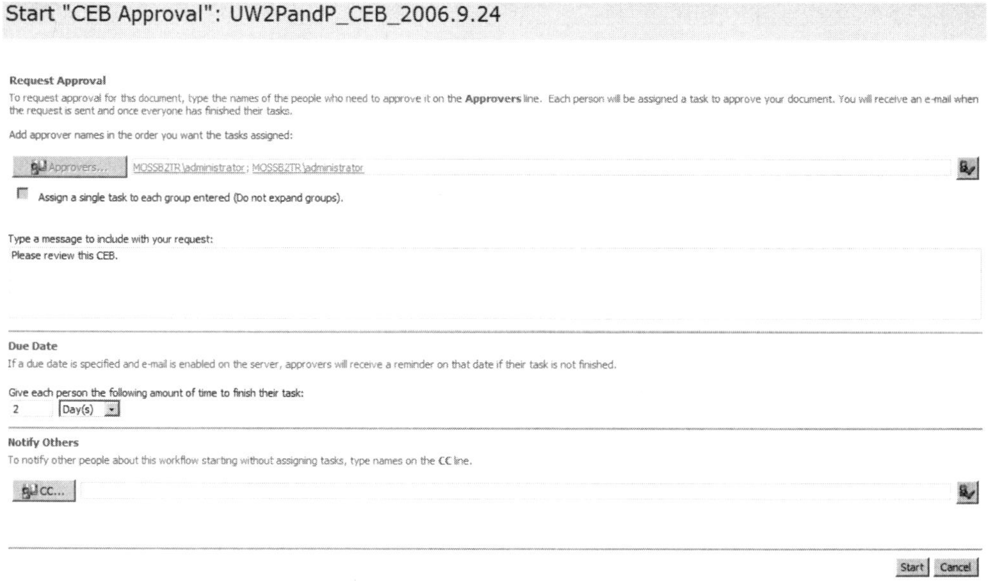

Figure 3-7. *This screen allows the person starting the workflow to specify the parameters for the workflow.*

The MOSS server will whir and pop in the background for a few seconds as it starts the workflow. Then Mary will be shown the document library screen listing all of the available documents, as shown in Figure 3-8. One thing to take note of is the new CEB Approval column that has been added to the view. This column is added the first time a particular type of workflow is run for a document shown in that view. The column is named for the workflow, so in our case it is CEB Approval. The column shows the current status of the workflow where applicable.

Figure 3-8. *The CEB Approval column shows the status of our workflow for the CEB document.*

As the originator of the workflow, Mary receives an email informing her of the successful initiation of her workflow process. The email lists the name of the document, the participants of the workflow, and other relevant details. The email also includes a link to allow her to view the current status of the workflow. This link takes her to a screen (shown in Figure 3-9) that shows the details of the workflow running on her document. From this screen, she can see a concise view of all tasks assigned and their current status. She can also see the entries from the workflow history list, cancel the workflow, or view workflow reports.

■ **Note** The Workflow Status screen is also available by navigating through the SharePoint site. Open the list or document library that stores the document, select Workflows from the drop-down menu for the document, and then click the name of the workflow in the list of running workflows. You'll arrive at the same screen as shown in Figure 3-9.

Workflow Status: CEB Approval

Workflow Information

Initiator:	MOSSB2TR\administrator	Document:	UW2PandP_CEB_2006.9.24
Started:	9/24/2006 11:17 PM	Status:	In Progress
Last run:	9/24/2006 11:17 PM		

▫ Cancel this workflow

If an error occurs or this workflow stops responding, it can be terminated. Terminating the workflow will set its status to Canceled and will delete all tasks created by the workflow.
▫ Terminate this workflow now.

Tasks

The following tasks have been assigned to the participants in this workflow. Click a task to edit it. You can also view these tasks in the list Tasks.

Assigned To	Title	Due Date	Status	Outcome
MOSSB2TR\administrator	Please approve UW2PandP_CEB_2006.9.24 ! NEW	9/26/2006	Not Started	

Workflow History

▫ View workflow reports

The following events have occurred in this workflow.

Date Occurred	Event Type	User ID	Description	Outcome
9/24/2006 11:17 PM	Workflow Initiated	MOSSB2TR\administrator	CEB Approval was started. Participants: MOSSB2TR\administrator, MOSSB2TR\administrator	
9/24/2006 11:17 PM	Task Created	MOSSB2TR\administrator	Task created for MOSSB2TR\administrator. Due by: 9/26/2006 11:17:51 PM	

Figure 3-9. *The Workflow Status screen is always available to show the progress of a process.*

Mary's work is now mostly done. She can monitor the process via the Workflow Status screen shown in Figure 3-9.

The Workflow Participant's Experience

Our workflow was configured to run serially, so this means that all participants will receive their tasks in the order in which their name appears in the Approvers list. The first participant in our workflow is Mary's pointy-haired boss, the director of Global Marketing. Continuing our walkthrough, we find him at his desk hard at work on his morning Sudoku puzzle and drinking his third cup of coffee. He is just beginning to wonder whether everyone has completed their TPS reports when his Outlook toast pops up informing him that he has a new email message. Like a little kid at Christmas, he switches over to Outlook to see what the email fairy has sent him. He sees a message similar to the one shown in Figure 3-10.

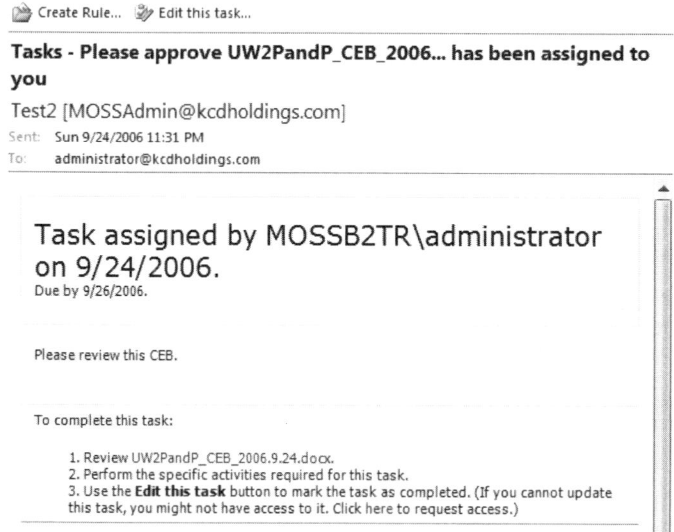

Create Rule... Edit this task...
Tasks - Please approve UW2PandP_CEB_2006... has been assigned to you
Test2 [MOSSAdmin@kcdholdings.com]
Sent: Sun 9/24/2006 11:31 PM
To: administrator@kcdholdings.com
Task assigned by MOSSB2TR\administrator on 9/24/2006.
Due by 9/26/2006.
Please review this CEB.
To complete this task:
1. Review UW2PandP_CEB_2006.9.24.docx.
2. Perform the specific activities required for this task.
3. Use the Edit this task button to mark the task as completed. (If you cannot update this task, you might not have access to it. Click here to request access.)

Figure 3-10. *SharePoint sends out an email notification of new task assignments for the out-of-the-box approval workflow.*

Drat. Now he's got work to do. It doesn't look too bad, though. The email fairy has kindly given him an Edit This Task button at the top of the email message that he can click to see more information on the task that has been assigned to him. When he clicks the button, a new screen (shown in Figure 3-11) pops up on his desktop. It gives him more details on what he needs to do and when it has to be completed by. It also includes a link to the document he must review.

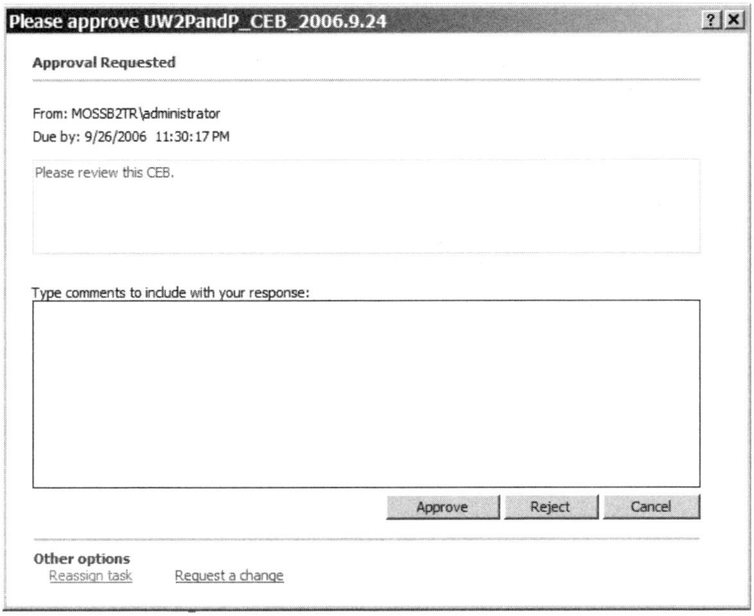

Please approve UW2PandP_CEB_2006.9.24

Approval Requested

From: MOSSB2TR\administrator
Due by: 9/26/2006 11:30:17 PM

Please review this CEB.

Type comments to include with your response:

Approve | Reject | Cancel

Other options
Reassign task   Request a change

Figure 3-11. *The task information screen provides details on the work that needs to be completed.*

From this screen, he is given several options:

- *Approve*: After reviewing the document he can click this button to give his blessing to the document and pass it along to the next person in the process. He can fill in comments if he has anything to say about the document or his review. These comments will be persisted with the document and available to other participants in the workflow.
- *Reject*: If after reviewing the document he decides that it is wholly inaccurate, unnecessary, or for some other reason should not be published, he can click the Reject button. As before, he can supply comments to explain his choice. Rejecting a document immediately ends the workflow.
- *Reassign*: This is usually the pointy-haired boss' favorite option. Selecting this option allows him to give the work to someone else. Unfortunately, this option is annoyingly unavailable to him—he keeps clicking on it, but nothing happens (remember, when we configured the workflow, we turned this option off). If we had allowed this option, he would be presented with the form shown in Figure 3-12.
- *Request Change*: If after reviewing the document he decides that the document needs some revision before he approves it, he can select this option. The screen for requesting a change is shown in Figure 3-13.

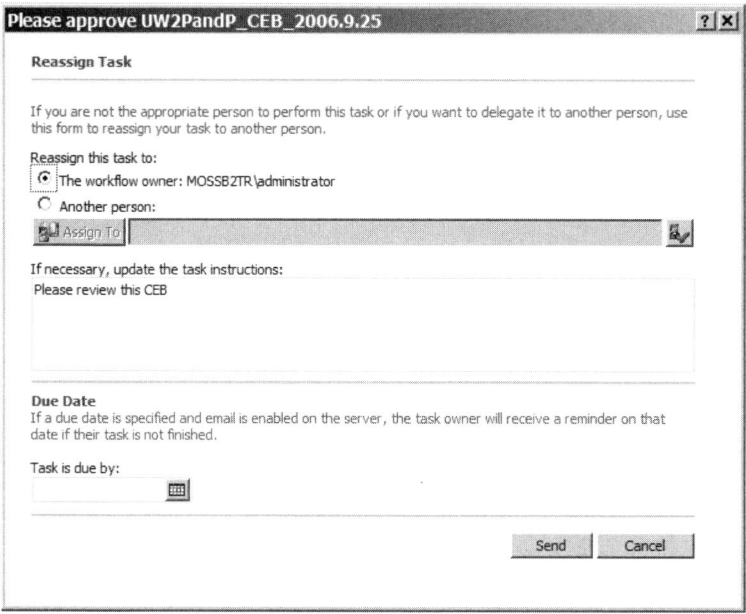

Figure 3-12. *If the workflow is configured to allow this option, participants can choose to assign a task to another user.*

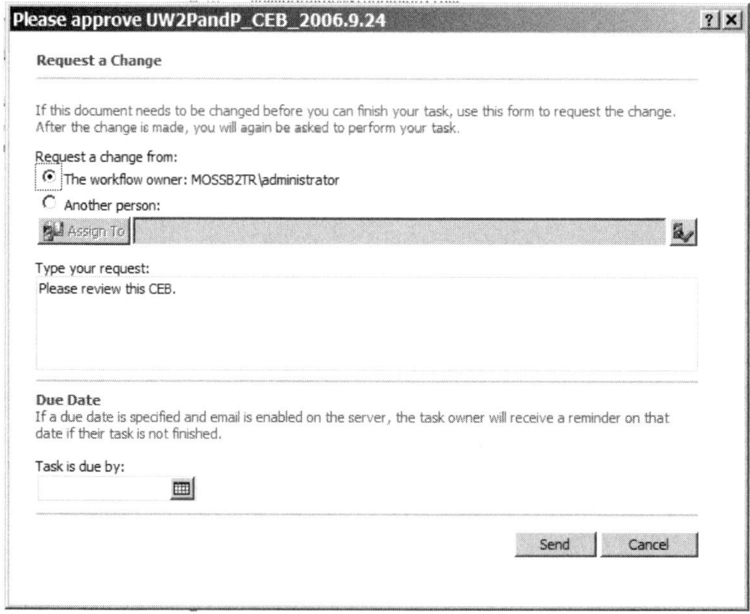

Figure 3-13. *Workflow participants can ask for a change to the document from either the person originating the workflow or anyone else.*

The director of Global Marketing reviews the document and decides that everything in the CEB looks OK. He clicks the Approve button and happily goes back to his puzzle.

Unlike the pointy-haired boss, the product manager for the Ultra-Widget II product is hard at work. He is already browsing the company portal and completing other work when he notices that the CEB document for his product has been posted (he can see the document even though it is not approved because he has permissions to approve documents in this document library). He clicks directly on the link to the document and opens it in Word. He has not seen the email yet and is not aware (yet) of the task that has been assigned to him. He just knows that the document pertains to his most important product.

Because he is interacting with the workflow through a different mechanism than that used by the director of Global Marketing, his experience is slightly different. The end result is the same, but the interface is integrated directly into his Office client, in this case Word. When the document opens, he sees the document, as expected, but he also notices something new just below the Ribbon.

What he sees, shown in Figure 3-14, is called the *Business Bar*. It is responsible for ensuring that users who interact with a document that is part of a workflow directly through the client application are still informed of relevant tasks assigned to them. In this case, the product manager sees that he has a task assigned to him to review and approve the CEB he currently has open. Clicking the Edit this task button will take him to the same screen the pointy-haired boss saw back in Figure 3-11.

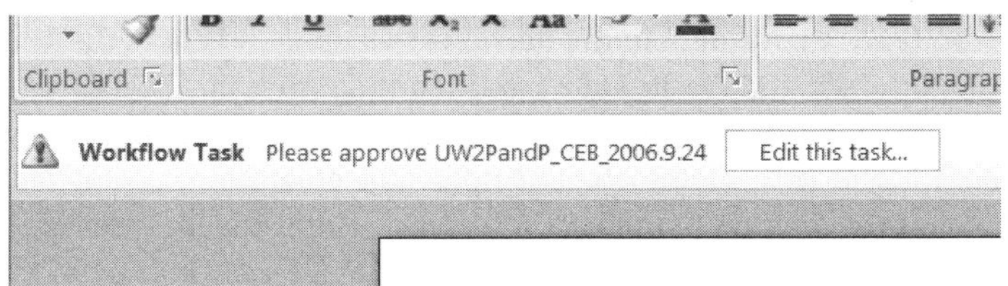

Figure 3-14. *Users opening documents in the Office 2007 client applications are still informed of workflow tasks via the Business Bar.*

Keeping the user informed regardless of their access method is part of the benefit of Office 2007. Rather than forcing the user into one method of access, Microsoft has let the application do the heavy lifting and kept the user experience as simple and streamlined as possible. In each case in our story, the Workflow forms were rendered via the Forms Services component and shown directly in the Office 2007 client application—either Outlook or Word.

Returning to our Newbery Award–winning story, the product manager reviews the CEB document and realizes that Mary might be using the wrong figures for the number of responses received to the campaign. He clicks the Request a Change link, fills out the form he is presented with (shown back in Figure 3-13), and clicks Send.

Back at Mary's desk, she receives an email informing her that the product manager has requested a change. From the email, Mary can see the details on the request that the product manager entered into the Comments section. She can also click the Edit this task button to access the other task information and the document itself, as shown in Figure 3-15.

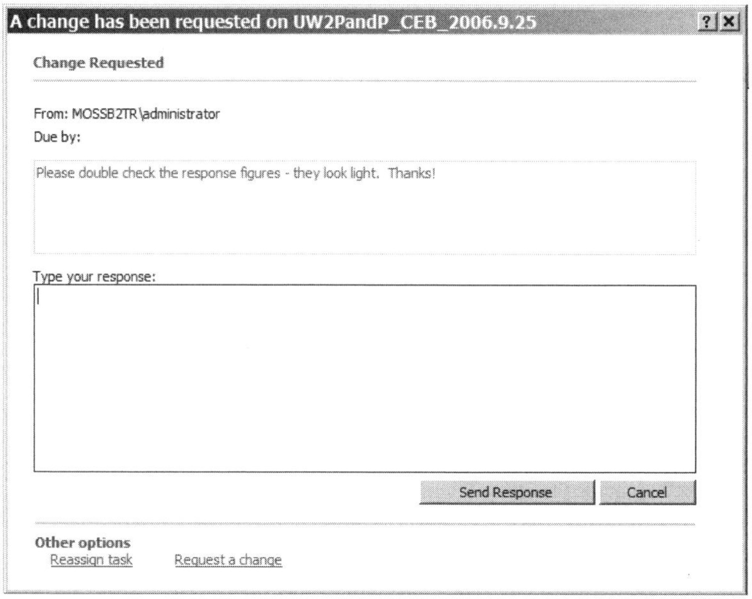

Figure 3-15. *The task screen when a participant has requested a change to a document*

Mary updates the document, types a comment in the Response section, and clicks the Send button. The workflow automatically updates its status and sends another notification to the product manager that a task has been assigned back to him. Again, he receives this notification both via email and directly in the Word client when he opens the document.

In the event that he already has the document open in Word, he can still check for tasks assigned to him. Clicking Office Button ➤ Server Tasks ➤ View Workflow Tasks brings up a dialog box similar to the one shown in Figure 3-16. It lists and provides access to all incomplete tasks for the current user (for the current document).

■ **Note** The Server Tasks menu option is only available for documents that were opened from a SharePoint server.

The product manager again reviews the document and everything looks OK this time. He approves the document. As this step is the end of the workflow, Mary, as the person who originated the workflow, will receive an email that the process is complete. The email, shown in Figure 3-17, provides details on the workflow—including the change request—and provides her with a link to view the workflow history.

The workflow history is the same Workflow Status screen we saw back in Figure 3-9 and provides details on every task and action taken during the course of processing this instance of our workflow. The primary difference now, of course, is that the workflow is complete so much more information is provided.

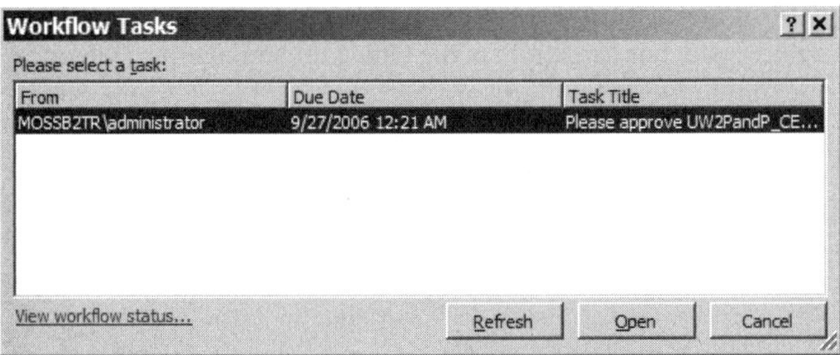

Figure 3-16. *Users can view workflow information on demand by accessing this dialog box through the Office Button menu.*

CEB Approval has completed on UW2PandP_CEB_2006.9.25.

MOSSAdmin@kcdholdings.com

Sent: Mon 9/25/2006 12:26 AM

To: administrator@kcdholdings.com

CEB Approval has completed on UW2PandP_CEB_2006.9.25.

CEB Approval on UW2PandP_CEB_2006.9.25 has successfully completed. All participants have completed their tasks.

Approved by MOSSB2TR\administrator

Change Requested of MOSSB2TR\administrator by MOSSB2TR\prodmngr
Please double check the response figures - they look light. Thanks!

Finished by MOSSB2TR\administrator
Sorry about that! These are the correct figures.

Approved by MOSSB2TR\prodmngr

View the workflow history.

Figure 3-17. *The final email received by the person who started the workflow contains a summary of the process.*

With the workflow complete, the CEB document is flagged within the document library as *Approved*. This has the effect of making it visible to all users with at least Reader access to the CEB document library. The process is now complete. We have moved a CEB document from conception through to publishing all with a simple, out-of-the-box workflow.

Permutations = Power

There are many, many possible variations of this process. Our first scenario showcased the out-of-the-box functionality but barely scratched the surface of what's possible. The options available in MOSS and WSS are quite powerful and let you construct a solution that meets just about any need. Other possible elements of our CEB Approval workflow, all of which are out-of-the-box functionality not requiring any code, would include elements such as the following:

- *Starting workflows from within the Office 2007 client applications*: Figure 3-18 shows the Workflows option dialog box, which is available on the Office Button menu. While the Workflows option is only available for documents opened from a SharePoint server, selecting it will bring up a screen similar to what you have seen before that lets you choose which workflow to start. Figure 3-18 assumes that MOSS and Forms Services are available. WSS alone or combined with Forms Server cannot deliver this level of integration. In that case, the dialog box would open in a browser.

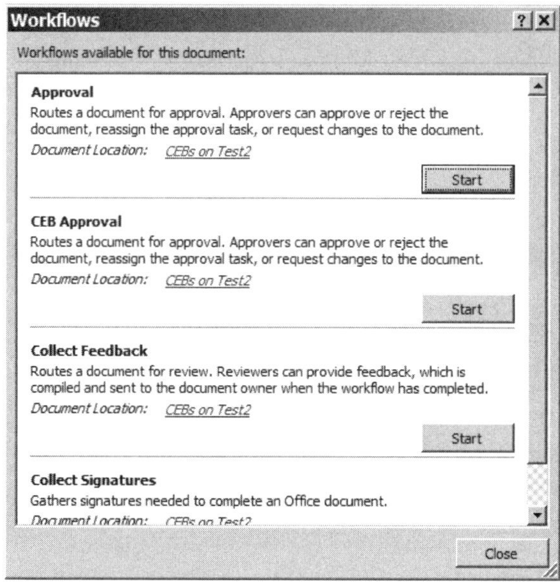
Workflows
Workflows available for this document:
Approval
Routes a document for approval. Approvers can approve or reject the document, reassign the approval task, or request changes to the document.
Document Location: CEBs on Test2
Start
CEB Approval
Routes a document for approval. Approvers can approve or reject the document, reassign the approval task, or request changes to the document.
Document Location: CEBs on Test2
Start
Collect Feedback
Routes a document for review. Reviewers can provide feedback, which is compiled and sent to the document owner when the workflow has completed.
Document Location: CEBs on Test2
Start
Collect Signatures
Gathers signatures needed to complete an Office document.
Close

Figure 3-18. *Office 2007 is flexible enough to allow users to start workflows from right within their Office client.*

■ **Note** This level of integration with the Office client applications is only available with MOSS. Even installing the full-blown Forms Server with a WSS installation won't get it for you. The web services that enable the integration only ship with MOSS.

- *The ability to assign workflow tasks to external users*: In some cases, there may be people (clients, partners, contractors, etc.) who need to perform a task as part of your process but who do not work for your organization. Naturally, as users outside of your environment, they do not have access to an internal SharePoint site that contains the documents and other workflow information. Fortunately, SharePoint will allow you to assign tasks to these users. What it does, however, is delegate the task to the workflow originator in lieu of the actual external user. The external user will receive an email with the document attached, asking them to review the document and send their feedback to the workflow originator. An example of this email is shown in Figure 3-19. The workflow originator receives the email, shown in Figure 3-20, informing them of the task assigned to the external user. When the external user completes the task, they email their feedback to the workflow originator, who can then complete the task in SharePoint on their behalf. One thing that is important to note is that the external user can be using any Simple Mail Transfer Protocol (SMTP)-compliant email server and client to receive their notification. It does not *have* to be Outlook or Exchange.

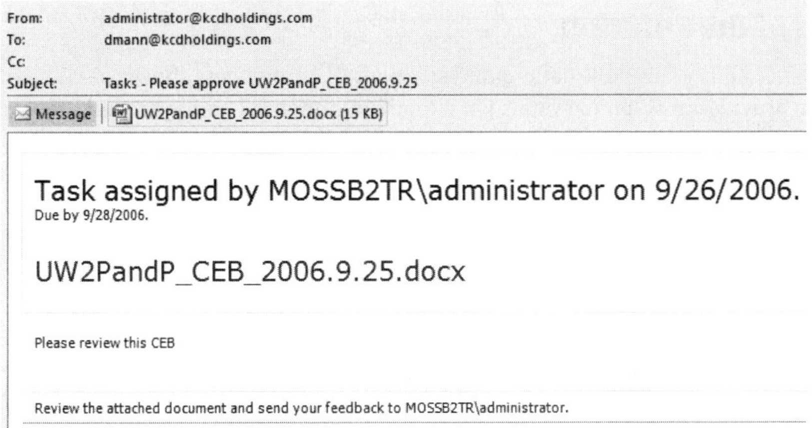

Figure 3-19. *External users receive an email with the document attached if they are assigned workflow tasks.*

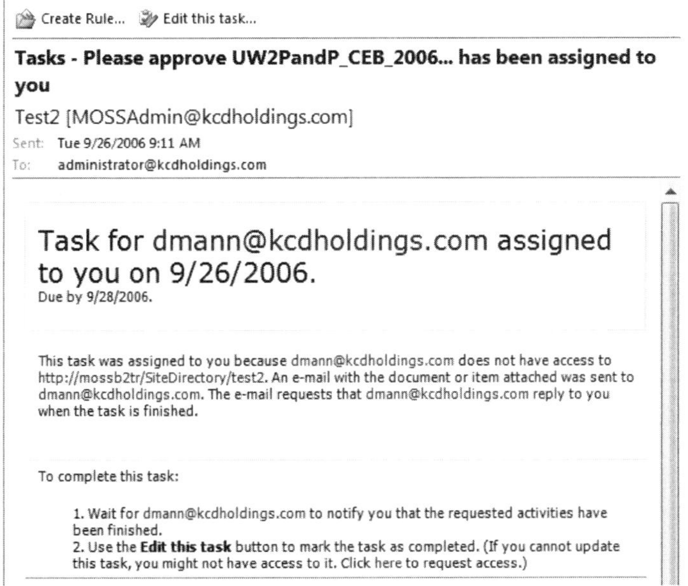

Figure 3-20. *The workflow originator is sent an email notifying them that they have been delegated responsibility for a task assigned to an external user.*

The task created will show that it has been assigned to the workflow originator on behalf of the external user.

■ **Tip** External users are typically not going to have entries in your Active Directory tree. In order to assign tasks to them, you will need to enter their name as a valid email address (e.g., `dmann@kcdholdings.com`) instead of as a domain name (e.g., `KCDHoldings\dmann`).

Benefits of the Solution

Although this is a fairly simple situation (and solution), it nonetheless showcases the power of Workflow to provide considerable value. For a total investment of perhaps 15 minutes on your part, you have now saved Mary, her boss, and numerous product managers countless hours of time and improved their ability to respond to and fine-tune their marketing campaigns. Over the course of time, the return on investment on this effort is going to be phenomenal. Here are just some of the benefits that will be realized as a result of your efforts:

- All steps of the process are logged and auditable.
- The process always follows the same series of steps.
- All communication about the process is handled automatically via email by the system but the document is not routed in this way. However, if a participant is browsing the site and opens the document in Word (or Excel or PowerPoint) they will still be notified of the pending workflow tasks. Email is an unreliable communication medium, so even if the email is not delivered, the important information—the document and the task information—is still available via MOSS.
- There only exists one copy of the document—it is stored centrally in the CEB's document library. Remember that prior to this workflow, copies of the document were routed via email and no one was ever sure which copy was the most current. Now, the single current copy (plus any historical versions if versioning is enabled) is stored centrally on the server.

Perhaps most important, you have a new *champion* in the Global Marketing department. From this point forward, Mary will sing your praises to anyone in the department who will listen. No longer will IT be seen as trying to meddle in Global Marketing. You will now be viewed as a partner who can help streamline their operations, saving them time, money, and frustration.

Not bad for a 15-minute investment.

■ **Note** As mentioned previously, this process could be streamlined further by making the CEB a content type and associating the content type with the document library. Our workflow could then be attached to the content type, rather than directly to the document library. However, this would only really change the way Mary creates the document and not the workflow process itself. To keep the focus on workflow, I have avoided this additional complexity.

Workflow in Previous Office Versions

Before closing this chapter on the out-of-the-box capabilities of Workflow in Office 2007, I would be remiss if I didn't at least mention the experience for users of previous versions of Microsoft Office. Typically, Microsoft has what they call their *Good, Better, Best* scenario for the interaction of various Office versions with SharePoint.

Note While neither stratification covered in this section is strictly a Workflow phenomenon, it is nonetheless relevant to our experience. We are, after all, users of Office and so all of the good and bad baggage comes along for the ride.

For Office 2003 with SharePoint 2003, this breaks down into the following:

Good = Office 2000. Users of Office 2000 have a minimum level of integration with SharePoint. This integration is limited to basic file input/output (I/O) operations and the ability to receive alert emails in Outlook.

Better = Office XP. Office XP improves on the integration capabilities of Office 2000 and adds the ability to import and export information between SharePoint and Excel. In addition, document properties and metadata are viewable from Office XP for documents stored on a SharePoint site.

Best = Office 2003. Office 2003 continues to build on the integration capabilities of previous versions. In addition, Office 2003 offers a tightly integrated experience through the use of task panes. End users can interact directly with SharePoint in many ways without leaving their Office client application.

For Office 2007, this breakdown steps up a notch and morphs slightly. In my mind, the integration experience for the various Office clients is now more like *Barely Acceptable, Acceptable,* and *Phenomenal*:

Barely Acceptable = any version of Office prior to Office 2003. Office XP and Office 2000 will be able to open and save files from the SharePoint site. That's about it. To my mind, if your organization is still using these versions of Office with no plans to upgrade, then moving to the next version of SharePoint as your collaboration platform makes little sense. It would be like buying a sports car and then only driving it to the grocery store at 15 miles per hour.

Acceptable = Office 2003. With some development effort, the integration of MOSS/WSS v3 and Office 2003 can be improved considerably. There are still some issues to be overcome, and some items that cannot be overcome, but this experience is closer to the ideal state. See Chapter 9 for information on improving the integration between Office 2003 and the next version of SharePoint—strictly from a Workflow point of view.

Phenomenal = Office 2007. No surprise here. The capabilities of the Office System are only fully realized when you have all of the pieces working together. And the experience here is a gigantic leap forward. As I've said before (and will say again), once you've sipped from the fountain, there's no going back...

Again, these breakdowns are not limited to the Workflow experience. They are, however, part and parcel of what our end users will experience as they interact with our workflows and so you should keep them in mind. As mentioned earlier, we'll burn a few cycles in Chapter 9 looking to improve the integration of Office 2003 with the Office Workflow Experience (not to be confused with the Jimi Hendrix Experience). We won't bring Office 2003 up to the same level as Office 2007, but we will smooth out some of the rough edges.

Summary

We covered a fair amount of ground in this chapter even though we never left the default capabilities of the products. As we progress through the book we'll build on this foundation, extending the products to their limits to drive significant value. To wrap up this chapter, here are some important things to remember:

- Workflow is available in both WSS v3 and MOSS. Other than the Forms Services elements, the capabilities are identical.
- MOSS provides five sample workflows out-of-the-box—WSS v3 provides one.
- While not required, the Forms Services component of MOSS provides significant improvement to the user experience—especially in the area of integration directly into the Office client applications.
- We created our first workflow in less than 15 minutes and without writing a single line of code. For basic processes, it really is that easy.

In the next chapter, we'll still be sticking with the out-of-the-box features, but we'll build a custom workflow. We'll use the SharePoint Designer to construct a new workflow to meet another business need for the Global Marketing department of KCD Holdings. We'll touch on both the building of the workflow and the deployment to the server.

CHAPTER 4

Using the SharePoint Designer

Until now, we have been working strictly with the out-of-the-box features and capabilities of SharePoint. We have reviewed the changes in Office 2007 both from the client and server sides; we have examined workflow in a generic sense and then drilled into the details of the Windows Workflow Foundation. Finally, we examined the roles of the two primary participants in workflows, participants and originators, as we walked through an instance of one of the default workflows.

Now we can get our hands dirty. This chapter begins our discussions on development of new workflows in Office 2007. We're going to start with no-code workflows so we're still not in full-bore developer mode; however, we are beginning to cover customized solutions so it kind of counts as development. In any event, it is a good first step in understanding the full capabilities of the product. We'll pull the gloves off after we're done with this chapter and foray into full-tilt-boogie coding.

Introducing the SharePoint Designer

No, don't worry; Microsoft hasn't introduced yet another client application. This is merely FrontPage in new clothing. In reality, the name change is simply a reflection of the fine-tuning of Microsoft's strategy for non-IT-built web initiatives. FrontPage has been Microsoft's premier web-site coding and development tool for power users. It offers nondevelopers powerful tools to design, code, deploy, and manage their web sites. FrontPage has a long history but recently has been focusing more and more on SharePoint. This trend continues in Office 2007.

Deserved or not, FrontPage has a bad reputation among the ranks of professional developers. Like many other arguments in the IT industry, the battle cries between FrontPage aficionados and those who eschew its reputation for code mangling and being too much of a black box have approached religious zealotry. Those of us in the SharePoint space have had to strike an often uneasy truce between these two camps. Our views on the pros or cons of FrontPage have fallen by the wayside as we had to learn that FrontPage was a necessary tool in our arsenal. We learned tricks and workarounds for dealing with the *ghosted* versus *unghosted* issue and code mangling, and we learned to love the Data View web part.

Whatever your personal views on this argument, if you want to play in the SharePoint sandbox the SharePoint Designer is going to be in your future. Fortunately, Microsoft has made significant strides in eliminating the most serious problem many people have had with FrontPage in SharePoint development—namely that the *ghosting* issue is largely rendered toothless in the next version of SharePoint.

As this is a book about Workflow, we're going to focus in on only those aspects of SharePoint Designer that are relevant to Workflow. This means we'll be spending all of our time on a new feature in FrontPage/SharePoint Designer called the Workflow Designer.

Overview of the Workflow Designer

The primary purpose of the Workflow Designer is to build new workflows from preexisting activities. According to Microsoft, the primary audience of the Workflow Designer tool is non-IT department power users. While I understand this, I feel that Microsoft is selling the tool short. This tool, like any other, is used to accomplish a certain task. Although the tasks handled by the Workflow Designer are somewhat limited in this version (for example, no support for state machines and no arbitrary branching, or `goto`), there are still a wide range of scenarios at which it excels. Look for the capabilities of this tool to be expanded in future versions.

So, limitations aside, the tool handles certain tasks well and should be used by anyone who needs to accomplish those tasks. You could use other tools to accomplish the same thing, but in some cases this tool happens to be the most efficient. Again, there are other tools, and über-developers may look down their noses at FrontPage and use Visual Studio instead. Although this is certainly possible, the rest of us will be sitting at a bar somewhere while they manually step through all of the tasks that the Workflow Designer did for us automatically.

So, marketing focus aside, if you need to work with SharePoint and workflows, you will at one time or another use this tool. Whether you are in the IT department; whether you are a power user, administrator, or über-developer; or if you need to build a basic workflow from preexisting activities and attach it to a single list or document library, you should use this tool.

Like much of the SharePoint Designer, the Workflow Designer presents you with a wizard-type interface in which you proceed through a number of steps to design and deploy your workflow. This approach takes the complexity out of building workflows. It extends the underlying user-empowerment design goal of SharePoint by taking certain tasks out of the hands of the IT department and placing them in the hands of users.

Later in this chapter, we'll walk through the process of building a workflow in the SharePoint Designer. First, though, we need to examine a few core concepts and details about the process.

■ **Note** In order to design workflows in SharePoint Designer, you need to have the .NET Framework 3.0 installed on the client machine.

Steps

A workflow built with the SharePoint Designer (SPD) consists of one or more *steps*. Each step defines the conditions and actions that control the activities of that step. For example, a step in an approval workflow might be as follows: "If the cost is greater than $10,000, assign a task to the department manager to review and approve." In the Workflow Designer, the steps of your workflow are shown as a list on the right side, as shown in Figure 4-1.

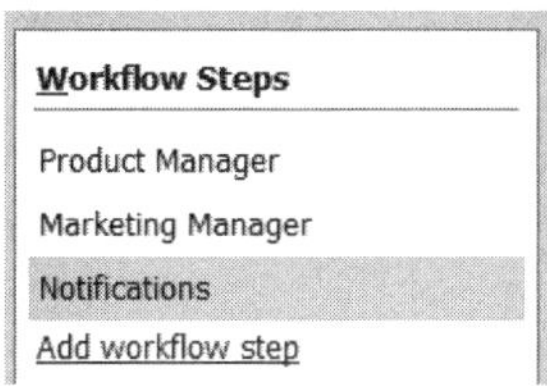

Figure 4-1. *Steps are the core building block of a workflow in the Workflow Designer.*

Each step is made up of zero or more *conditions*, which determine whether the step processes or simply proceeds to the next step. If a condition is met, then the actions for the step are executed. Conditions and actions are discussed next.

Note In case you're wondering, each workflow can hold a lot of steps—I don't know exactly how many; I stopped adding steps when I got to 300. If you are creating a workflow in SPD that has 300 steps, you really ought to have your head examined. Visual Studio would be a far better tool for a workflow that is so complex. Unfortunately, I can see a power user somewhere implementing their 248-step workflow and feeling very proud of themselves. Quietly, very quietly, drag them out behind the shed and beat them with a copy of this book. If you need to, buy a second copy explicitly for this purpose—my publisher and I won't mind.

Conditions

Conditions are the circumstances that signal that this step of the workflow should execute. Conditions allow your workflows to contain some logic and determine at runtime whether the actions for that step should execute. This is useful for situations where your workflow is not always a straightforward process but needs to branch based on some value provided by the originator or some value of the payload.

Definition *Payload* refers to the document or list item that our workflow is acting upon.

The Workflow Designer in SPD ships with a number of default conditions out-of-the-box. Table 4-1 provides details on the out-of-the-box conditions. It is also possible to extend the Workflow Designer by adding custom conditions; we'll cover that process in Chapter 9.

Table 4-1. *Default Conditions Available in the SharePoint Designer*

Condition	Description
Compare *<List name>* Field	Allows you to specify a value for a column in the list this workflow is attached to. If the payload item has that value in the specified column, then this step will process.
Compare Any Data Source	Allows you to specify a set of values to be compared. Each value can contain either a hard-coded value or a lookup to another list on the site. See the section "Workflow Lookups," later in this chapter.
Title Field Contains Keyword	Allows you to specify a value to look for in the Title column. If the current list item has that value in the title, then this step will process.
Modified in a Specific Date Span	Allows you to specify begin and end dates for when the list item was modified. If the current list item was modified within this span, then this step will process.
Modified by a Specific Person	Allows you to specify the name of a person. If that person modified the list item, this step will execute.
Created in a Specific Date Span	Same as Modified in a Specific Date Span but works off the list item creation date.
Created by a Specific Person	Same as Modified by a Specific Person but works off the original list item creator, not the last modifier.
The File Type Is a Specific Type	Allows you to specify a certain type of file. If the file payload matches this file extension, the step will process.
The File Size in a Specific Range of Kilobytes	Allows you to specify a range of kilobytes. If the file payload falls within this range, the step will process.

■ **Note** The specific conditions available for each step depend on the SharePoint list that the workflow is attached to. If the list permits attachments, then the two file-based conditions (file type and file size) are available. Otherwise, they are not.

Conditions can be stacked, so that you could specify a compound condition such as "Modified by a certain person, before a certain date and the Title field contain certain keywords." To do this, simply select additional conditions from the drop-down list.

■Note All compound conditions are "and-ed" together. To create "or" conditions, you need to specify what the Workflow Designer calls "else-if" conditional branches.

You add an else-if condition by clicking the Add "Else-If" Conditional Branch link in the Workflow Designer. You set up the else-if condition in exactly the same way as you would a regular condition. The only difference is that at runtime, the else-if branch will be evaluated only if the parent condition evaluates to false. If the parent condition evaluates to true, then the else-if condition will never process. We'll see this later in the chapter when we build our own custom workflow.

It is also possible to set up a step with no condition. In this case, the step would always process. Use this if the actions in the step should be executed for each instance of this workflow, regardless of any other factors. There are countless cases where this would be necessary, including the following:

- Logging the initiation, conclusion, or an internal milestone of a workflow
- Notifying the originator of the initiation, conclusion, or an internal milestone of their workflow
- Requiring all documents in the workflow to pass legal review before being published

To set up a condition-less step, simply add an action to the step but no condition. Actions are covered next.

Actions

An *action* is what happens in a workflow step. If the condition(s) for a step are evaluated and indicate that the step should process, then the actions set for that step are the tasks that will be executed.

Actions can be either serial (each action happens after the preceding action has completed) or parallel (all actions happen simultaneously). Serial actions are the default and are useful when actions must follow a process and are dependent on the completion of a preceding action. Parallel actions are useful for notifications or when there is no dependency between actions. To switch between serial and parallel, click the drop-down arrow located at the right side of the condition branch and select either Run All Actions in Sequence or Run All Actions in Parallel. Figure 4-2 shows this menu.

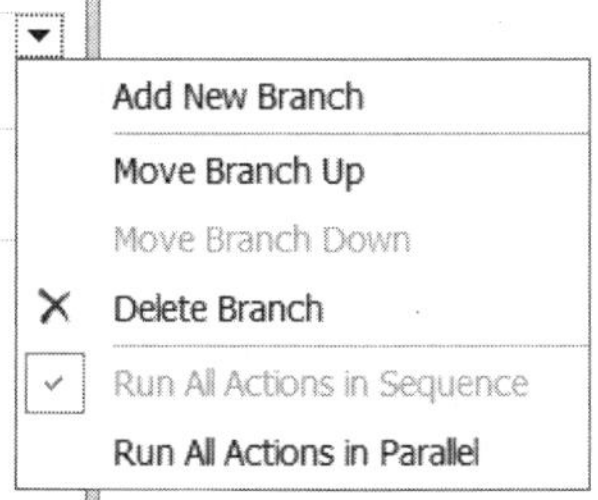

Figure 4-2. *Actions can be run either in sequence or in parallel.*

Unfortunately, the only indication of how actions are processed in the regular user interface (UI) is a single word. As shown in Figure 4-3, *then* indicates serial; *and* indicates parallel. This is not the easiest difference in the world to spot and it will likely cause some consternation as you work through your processes.

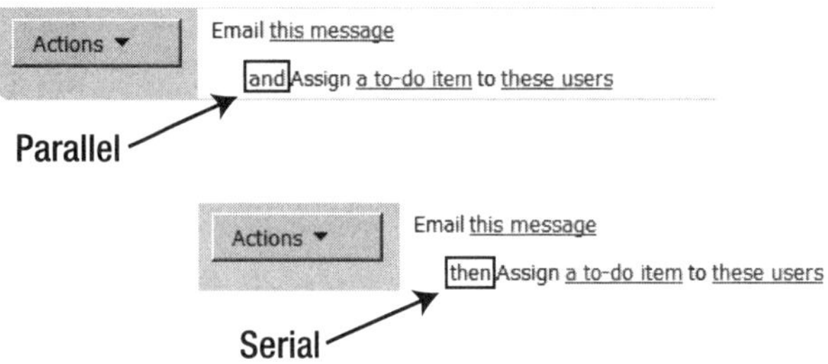

Figure 4-3. *Checking whether your actions happen in sequence or parallel is a matter of looking at one word in the UI.*

Table 4-2 shows the default actions available out-of-the-box.

Table 4-2. *Default Actions*

Action	Description
Add Time to Date	Allows you to work with date values and store the result in a variable. You can add (or subtract, by indicating a negative value) time (minutes, hours, days, months, or years) to a specified date and store the result in either an existing variable or in a new variable created in this step.
Assign a Form to a Group	Launches a custom wizard that allows you to easily build a form to collect information from users. The wizard is similar to the Variables Editor discussed in a moment. You can indicate which users are assigned the survey as part of the configuration for this action.
Assign a To-Do Item	Launches a dialog box that allows you to specify the parameters for creating a simple task for a specified user.
Build Dynamic String	Configure this step to create a string value and assign it to a variable. The string value can contain values retrieved from the current workflow instance by using lookups. We discuss lookups later in this chapter. The variable used to store the string value can be either preexisting or created as part of this action.
Check In Item	Checks in an item so other users can edit it. You can specify Current Item or provide a column name and value to identify which item to check in. Also allows you to specify a check-in comment, which can be either hard-coded or set via a workflow lookup.
Check Out Item	Checks out an item so other users cannot edit it. You can specify Current Item or provide a column name and value to identify which item to check out.

Table 4-2. *Default Actions (Continued)*

Action	Description
Collect Data from a User	Creates and assigns a task to the specified user. Tasks are used to collect specific information from the assigned user or to have the user complete a process. The ID of the task is stored in a variable so that the information from that task is available later in the workflow via a workflow lookup. Configuring this action will launch the custom task wizard, which is similar to the Variables Editor discussed in a moment. This action is similar to the Assign a To-Do Item action, but allows you to collect information for later use instead of just creating a task.
Copy List Item	Creates an exact duplicate of an existing list item in a different list on the current site. You specify both the source and destination lists. You can specify Current Item or provide a column name and value to identify which item to copy.
Create List Item	Creates a new list item in any list on the current site. You specify the list as well as values for all necessary columns. Values can either be hard-coded or based on a workflow lookup.
Delete Item	Deletes an item from a list on the current site. You can specify Current Item or provide a column name and value to identify which item to delete.
Discard Check Out Item	Pretty self-explanatory, but this allows you to undo the check-out of an item. All changes to that item will be lost.
Do Calculation	Performs a simple calculation (plus, minus, multiply, divide, modulo) with two values, which you can either specify or base on a workflow lookup. The results of the calculation are stored in a variable. Typically, this variable would be one created specifically for this workflow.
Log to History List	Allows you to write an entry to the designated history list for this workflow instance. You can use either fixed text or a workflow lookup value (but not both) as the text to be written.
Pause for Duration	Allows you to specify that the workflow should suspend processing for a time period you specify (in days, hours, and minutes) when you configure this action.
Pause Until Date	Similar to the previous action, except that you configure a specific date on which to continue processing the workflow.
Send an Email	Sends an email when it is executed. The action can be customized to specify the recipient, CC, subject, and body of the message. Each of these fields can be either hard-coded or based on formulas, lookups, or workflow variables.
Set Content Approval Status	Allows you to specify the current status of the payload item. You can also specify comments, but keep in mind that those comments will be the same for every instance of this workflow unless you use lookups.
Set Field in Current Item	Allows you to set the value of a specific column in the payload item to a specified value. You can specify this value with either fixed text or a workflow lookup value (but not both).

Table 4-2. *Default Actions (Continued)*

Action	Description
Set Time Portion of Date/Time Field	Similar to the Add Time to Date action, except that you specify a specific value for hours and minutes (i.e., not a relative time—plus 5 minutes from when the action executes) and store the results in a variable.
Set Workflow Variable	Sets a variable for this workflow to a specified value. The value can be either hard-coded or set via a workflow lookup. You can reference a previously created variable or create a new one.
Stop Workflow	Causes the workflow to stop processing. You can specify text to be logged to the history list with either fixed text or a lookup.
Update List Item	Updates one or more existing columns in one or more lists. You can specify the list(s), the column(s), and the value(s). You can also specify Current Item to indicate the item that triggered the current workflow instance.
Wait for Field Change in Current Item	Pauses the workflow until the specified column for this item from the attached SharePoint list equals the value specified. The value can be hard-coded or based on a workflow lookup.

Variables

In discussing actions and conditions, we have several times referenced workflow variables. Workflow variables are no different from other programming variables—they store a value (or values) for later use. They can be set by the workflow originator when they initiate a workflow, set as part of a task assignment during a workflow step, or set programmatically by the workflow itself. They are useful for collecting and storing values for use later in the workflow.

At the bottom of every screen in the Workflow Designer wizard is the Variables button. This button provides access to the Variables Editor, as shown in Figure 4-4.

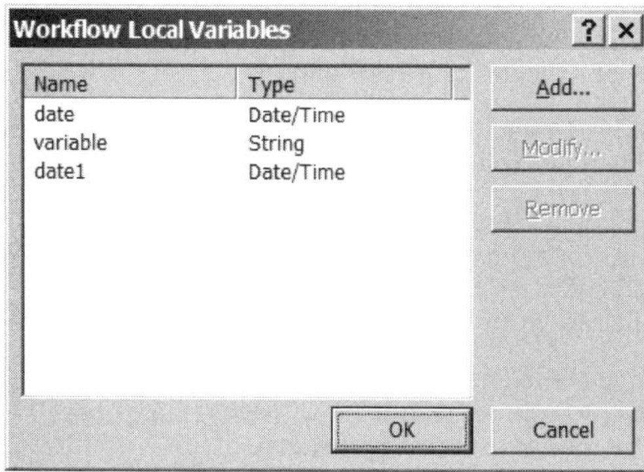

Figure 4-4. *The Variables Editor allows you to quickly and easily create variables to store values used by your workflow.*

When you click the Add button, you are presented with a dialog box that allows you to specify the name and data type of your new variable. Figure 4-5 shows this dialog box.

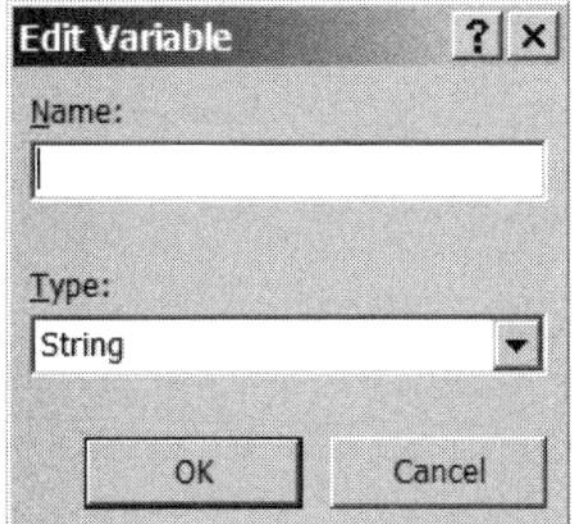

Figure 4-5. *The Edit Variable dialog box allows you to specify the details of your variable.*

The Workflow Designer provides a number of data types to customize the data collected:

- Boolean
- Date/Time
- List Item ID
- Number
- String

The only one from this list that you may not recognize is the List Item ID. It is used to store a globally unique identifier (GUID) for a SharePoint list item.

Workflow Lookups

As we've already indicated, values for actions, conditions, and variables can be hard-coded or based on other values located elsewhere. To retrieve a value from somewhere else, you need to make use of a workflow lookup. A workflow lookup is available any place you see the function button:

In general, a lookup is useful to refer to or retrieve another value. This value could be from another list on the site where users store content or a value retrieved from the payload for the current workflow instance. But perhaps a more useful situation would be to provide for central configuration of variables. For example, if you create a hidden list and store values in there for things like

- Delay time before escalation
- Threshold values for approvals
- Values for routing

you can then reference these list items from any workflow on the site and be certain of utilizing the correct value. If the value needs to change, you can make the change in one central place. As an example, suppose sales orders require approval from a branch manager if they are greater than $10,000; you can specify the $10,000 in this configuration list. If later the threshold changes to $15,000, you need to make the change in only one place, instead of any workflow that may reference that value.

To configure a lookup, click the function button. You will be presented with a screen similar to the one shown in Figure 4-6.

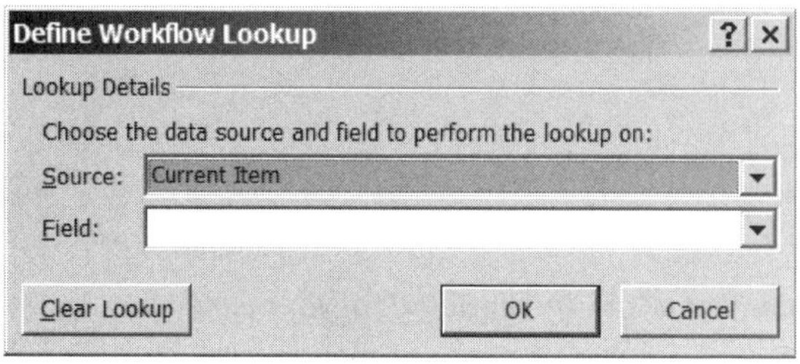

Define Workflow Lookup

Lookup Details

Choose the data source and field to perform the lookup on:

Source: Current Item

Field:

Clear Lookup | OK | Cancel

Figure 4-6. *Workflow lookups are a powerful mechanism for retrieving data from external sources.*

The Source drop-down lets you select the item you want to retrieve a value from. Lookup values can be retrieved from one of three places:

- *Current Item* gives you access to item that the workflow is currently acting upon.
- *Workflow Data* gives you access to the variables that have been set up as part of this workflow.
- Select another list on the site to get access to items from another list.

Regardless of what is selected for the Source drop-down, you then need to specify the field or variable that you want to retrieve a value from. The Field drop-down contains all of the possible choices from the selected source. If you selected Current Item or another list, the Field drop-down will contain the available columns. If you selected Workflow Data as the source, then the Field drop-down will contain the available variables.

If you select another list as the source, you need to specify the particular item from the selected list that you want to retrieve a value from. To facilitate this, the dialog box will change to look as shown in Figure 4-7.

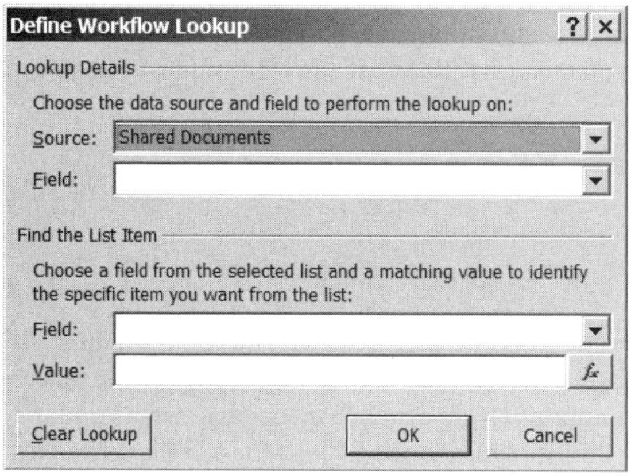

Define Workflow Lookup

Lookup Details

Choose the data source and field to perform the lookup on:

Source: Shared Documents

Field:

Find the List Item

Choose a field from the selected list and a matching value to identify the specific item you want from the list:

Field:

Value: *fx*

Clear Lookup | OK | Cancel

Figure 4-7. *Defining a workflow lookup allows you to specify the specific list item you need to retrieve a value from.*

The bottom portion of the dialog box now allows you to supply a field and a value. This enables you to specify the filter criteria to identify the specific item that you wish to retrieve a value from. Select a field from the chosen list and specify a value. The lookup will use these entries to select which item from the source list to use to retrieve the lookup value.

The Clear Lookup button will reset all of the drop-downs to their default blank values to let you start over again.

Initiation

The Initiation button at the bottom of the Workflow Designer allows you to create a custom Workflow form. We haven't covered Workflow forms yet (we dive into those in Chapter 7), but at a high level, forms allow you to collect information from the various participants in your workflow. This button in SPD allows you to specify the data that you need to collect from the person who starts an instance of your workflow on a particular payload. This form is called the initiation form—hence the name on the button.

Clicking this button will present a simple wizard-type interface that will step you through the process of indicating the information you need to collect. We cover the information types supported for initiation form fields in a moment. We'll create an initiation form later in this chapter and you'll see that the process is pretty straightforward.

Check Your Workflow

The Check Workflow button at the bottom of the Workflow Designer window does just that—it checks your workflow for errors. When you click on it, a message box pops up that says "The Workflow contains no errors"—at least, that's what you want to see.

If your workflow does in fact contain errors, they will be indicated in one of two ways:

- In the Workflow Steps pane on the right side of the screen, the step(s) that contain errors will have an indicator next to the step name, as shown in Figure 4-8.
- The particular condition or action will be highlighted with asterisks, as shown in Figure 4-9.

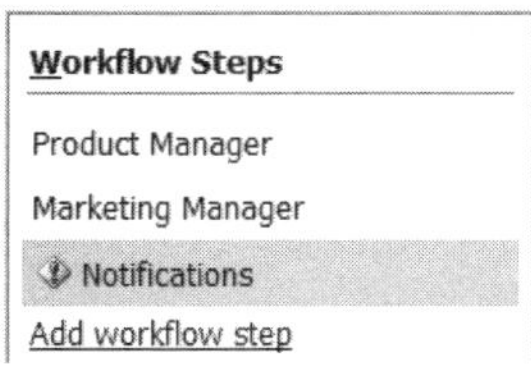

Figure 4-8. *Errors are indicated in the workflow steps by a small icon next to the step name.*

Figure 4-9. *The specific location of the error is highlighted with asterisks.*

Information Types

Workflows in SharePoint Designer support the use of a number of different types of information in a number of different places. We saw the brief set of data types supported by workflow variables earlier. The following list provides details on all of the information types, including where they are usable and a screenshot of the UI that each renders:

- *Single Line of Text*: Presents the user with a textbox they can enter characters into. In the custom task wizard, this can be configured to require a value. In the initiation form, you can only specify a default value.
  - Usable on an initiation form and for task assignments
  - Interface rendered:
- *Multiple Lines of Text*: Allows the user to enter multiple lines of freeform text. In the custom task wizard, you can control whether it can include HTML markup and other rich text, whether the field is append-only, and the number of lines to display. In the initiation form, you can only specify a default value.
  - Usable on initiation form and for task assignments
  - Interface rendered:

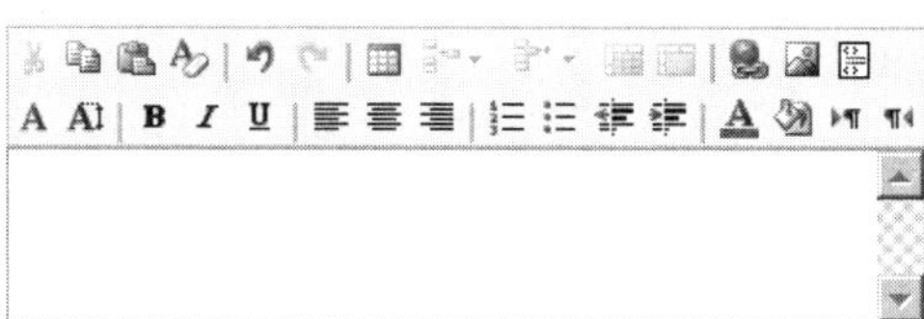

- *Number*: Presents the user with a space in which to enter a number. In the custom task wizard, you can control the formatting (number of decimal places, display as percentage, etc., as well as specify a minimum and maximum value). In the initiation form, you can only specify a default value.
  - Usable on initiation form and for task assignments
  - Interface rendered:
- *Currency*: Similar to the Number type, but also presents you with a currency-type drop-down list for supporting international currencies.
  - Usable for task assignments
  - Interface rendered:

- *Date and Time*: Presents the user with an interface to specify a date/time combination, including a pop-up calendar. Allows you to specify the display format—Date only or Date and Time.
    - Usable on initiation forms and for task assignments
    - Interface rendered for date and time:

      12 AM 00

    - Interface rendered for date-only:

- *Choice*: Presents the user with a list of options to choose from. Allows you to specify the display format (radio button, drop-down list, or checkboxes for the custom task wizard; only radio buttons or drop-down list for the initiation form). The custom task wizard also allows you to specify whether the user can supply their own value and whether blank values are permitted.
    - Usable on initiation forms or for task assignments
    - Interface rendered for drop-down:

      2

    - Interface rendered for checkboxes:

      1
      2
      3

    - Interface rendered for radio buttons:

      4
      5
      6

- *Yes/No*: Presents the user with a checkbox to flag the variable or field either *on* or *off*.
    - Usable on an initiation form or for task assignments
    - Interface rendered:

- *Lookup*: Allows you to add a workflow lookup. See the earlier section on lookups for details. In this situation, you specify the list and field you want the user to select a value from when they fill out the form. The form presents the values from that field as a drop-down list for the user to select from.
    - Usable for task assignments
    - Interface rendered:

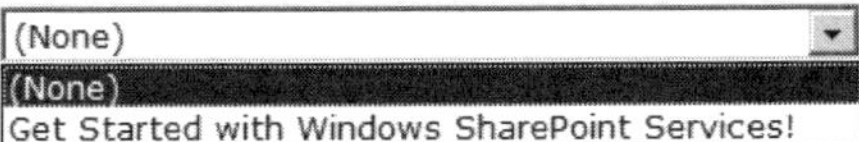

- *User*: Presents the user with a control to allow them to enter usernames. Also includes functionality to verify usernames and to select names from the user profile store.
  - Usable for task assignments
  - Interface rendered:

- *Hyperlink or Picture*: Presents the user with an interface to enter a hyperlink to another resource or the URL of a picture. Provides the capability to browse the site in an open-file dialog box to locate the resource or picture. The user can also enter a description of the resource. Also provides a facility to test the link. Allows you to specify default values for the URL and the text as well as whether blank values are permitted.
  - Usable for task assignments
  - Interface rendered:

Type the Web address: (Click here to test)
http://www.example.com
Type the description:
Example

- *Calculated*: Allows the workflow builder to set the value of one variable based on a formula, which could include values of other fields.
  - Usable for task assignments
  - No interface rendered

Each information type is configured slightly differently, depending on the details of each type. For task assignments, there is an additional screen in the wizard used to define them that lets you customize each information type. A sample of this screen is shown in Figure 4-10. In this case, the screen is for configuring a multiline field, though the screen for other field types will be similar. The Variables Editor (discussed earlier) supports only simple information types so there is no additional customization screen.

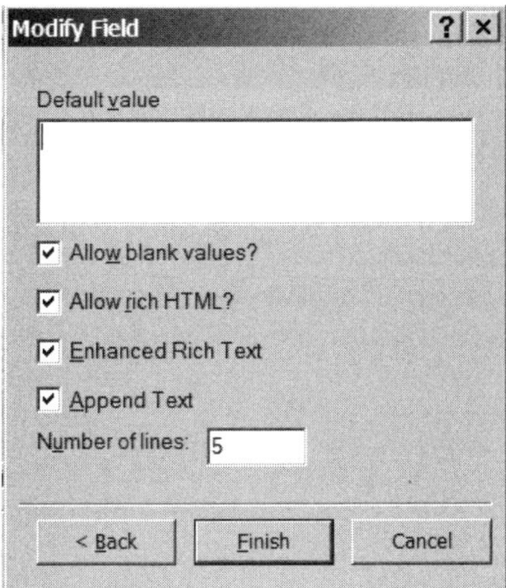

Figure 4-10. *The final screen of the task assignment wizard will vary based on the information type selected.*

Workflow Forms

One more point about workflow forms here before we leave them until Chapter 7: after you specify the fields for the information you need to collect for either task assignments or initiation forms, SPD automatically generates an ASP.NET form for you. This ASPX file is stored and deployed with your workflow automatically. If you would like to edit this ASPX file before deploying it—perhaps to add some user instructions or some other content—you can edit it right in SPD and it will be deployed with your workflow. One thing to keep in mind, however, is that if you make changes to one of the ASPX forms manually and then go back into SPD and edit the form there (either the initiation form or one of the task forms for a To-Do item) all of the changes you made manually will be lost because SPD will re-create the form from scratch.

■ **Caution** Be careful when you are editing the ASP.NET form that you don't inadvertently change any of the Workflow-specific elements or code. I recommend only working in Design view for these pages.

Constructing a Workflow with the Workflow Designer

In this exercise, we are going to build and configure a workflow from preexisting actions. We will use the SharePoint Designer to build and deploy our workflow. Let's begin by setting up the situation.

The Scenario: Product Launch Campaigns

For this exercise, you are going to work closely with the marketing director in the KCD Holdings Global Marketing department. As director of the Global Marketing department she has a number of marketing managers reporting to her. Each marketing manager typically handles the details of a specific product launch. In the past, product launches have been difficult and intensive processes involving multiple emails, phone calls, missed deadlines, and an excessive amount of manual tracking. Over the last several months, the director has worked to identify the core tasks that need to be completed in order to ensure a smooth and successful product launch. After she has explained the details to you, you tell her she is faced with two choices:

- She can oversee each product launch herself and make sure everything is completed properly.
- She can create a workflow that embodies all of the steps and tasks that have been identified and let the workflow enforce the process.

Considering that the various member companies that comprise KCD launch an average of three new products every month, she decides that the second option is probably the right way to go (besides, choosing the first option would mean working many late nights and missing all of those *MacGyver* reruns). After she shows you her Richard Dean Anderson shrine, you tell her that this workflow is something she can build herself, but that you'll help her out this first time because you happen to think that *Stargate SG-1* is a pretty decent show, too.

KCD's intranet already has a section dedicated to Global Marketing. The Global Marketing page has a document library dedicated to marketing plans so you don't need to worry about establishing space in which to work. All you need to do is set up the workflow process and attach it to the document library.

SETTING UP THE ENVIRONMENT

Before we can begin setting up our workflow, we need to make sure that our environment is set up properly. The first step is perhaps somewhat obvious, but I'll mention it anyway: we need to have our SharePoint site set up and our task lists created.

For this exercise we are going to use the standard TeamSite site definition. This contains a document library and a task list, which for this scenario, is really all we need. Naturally, in a production environment, we would use a custom site definition with content types, lists, and document libraries related to other aspects of product marketing. To keep things simple and focused on Workflow, we'll just use an out-of-the-box site definition.

If you do not already have a site suitable for use, go ahead and create one. Once your SharePoint site is created, you need to decide on how the tasks your workflow creates are going to be stored. As discussed in Chapter 3, all workflow tasks are created in standard SharePoint task lists. If your workflow is going to store its tasks in a unique list, you need to create that list before starting to design your workflow. If all of your workflows in the site store their tasks in a central list, you need to make sure that you have access to that list before beginning.

To follow along at home, you'll also need to create a document library named *Marketing Plans*. This is the document library that we'll add our workflow to. If you don't want to create a new document library, you can just use the default Shared Documents library on the site.

Going Through the Steps

Now that we know the background scenario for our exercise, we are ready to begin designing our workflow. In this section, we will step through the process to build, configure, and deploy our workflow.

At a high level, the process we need to enforce is as follows:

1. A marketing manager creates a draft marketing plan.
2. The marketing manager sends the plan to the product manager to review and verify product details and specifications.
3. After the product manager approves the specifications, the following things need to happen simultaneously:
   - The external advertising agency needs to be notified of the upcoming marketing effort and provide feedback on the planned budget.
   - The manufacturing coordinator needs to be notified of the upcoming marketing effort and approve of initiation and other dates based on current production schedules.
4. After all these steps have been completed, the plan is submitted to the marketing director for final departmental approval.

At any stage of this process, the plan can be returned to the originating marketing manager for modifications. Figure 4-11 shows this process.

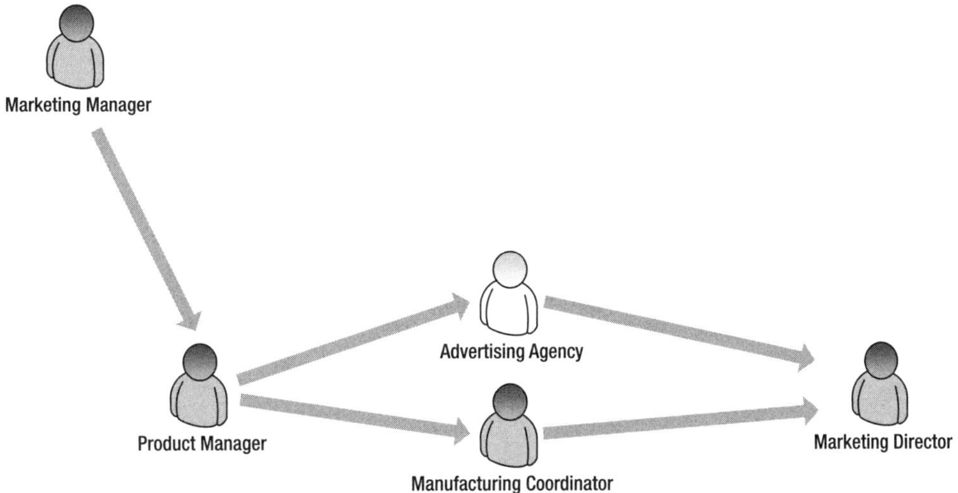

Figure 4-11. *Overview of the approval process for a KCD Holdings product marketing plan*

With our site and task list created and an understanding of what processes we need to enforce with our workflow, we can now begin designing our workflow.

Defining Our Workflow

The first thing we need to do is get our environment set up and create our workflow. This step will connect to the site that will run our workflow. We will also name our workflow and set up some basic variables.

To complete this task, we need to

1. Open the SharePoint Designer.
2. Open your SharePoint site by clicking File ➤ Open Site and typing in the URL for your SharePoint site (without the page name)—for example, `http://intra.kcdholdings.com/sites/marketing/products/UltraWidget2`.
3. Once the site has loaded, launch the Workflow Designer. From the top menu, click File ➤ New ➤ Workflow.
4. The Workflow Designer will load and you will see the Define Your New Workflow screen, as shown in Figure 4-12.

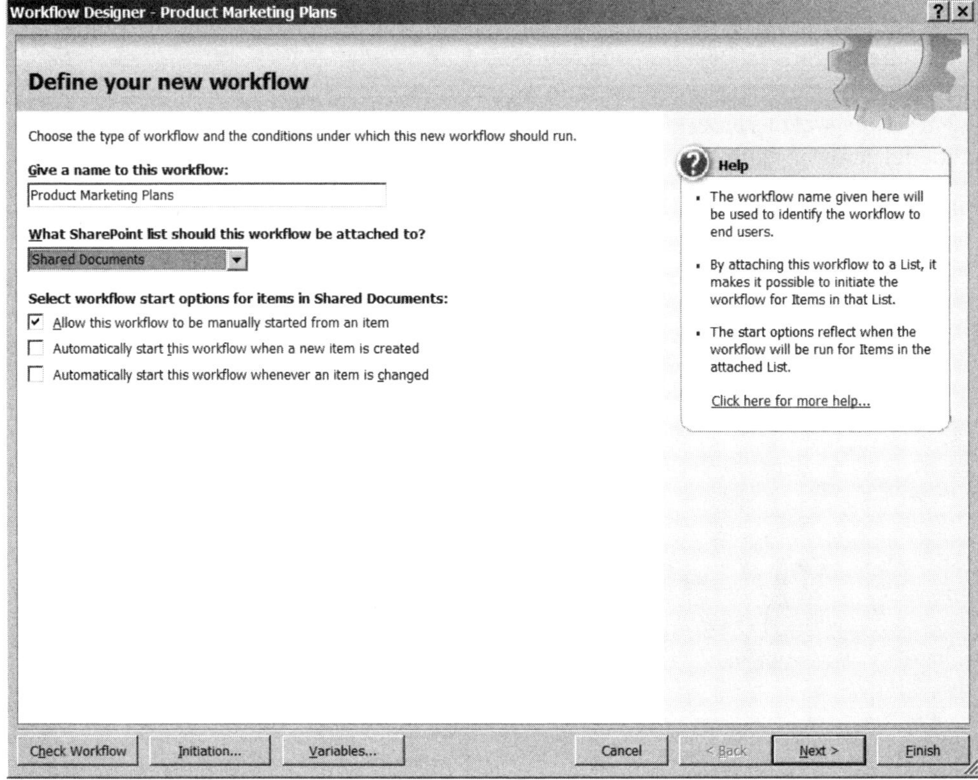

Figure 4-12. *The Workflow Designer is a wizard-based tool to walk you through the steps of creating a workflow.*

This screen allows us to set up the basic details for our new workflow. Table 4-3 details each of the options and how we need to set them for our workflow. Configure these options as indicated and then click Next.

Table 4-3. *Basic Settings for the KCD Holdings Marketing Plan Workflow*

Item	Description	Setting for Product Marketing Plan Workflow
Name	Pretty self-explanatory, but just make sure the name is unique and descriptive. This is what will be presented in the UI for originators and recipients	Product Marketing Plans
What SharePoint List Should This Workflow Be Attached To?	This is the list from our SharePoint site where the payload documents or list items will be stored.	Marketing Plans (or for this walkthrough, any valid document library on the site)
Allow This Workflow to Be Manually Started for an Item	Indicates whether or not originators will have the option to initiate this workflow from the Start a New Workflow screen.	Checked
Automatically Start This Workflow When a New Item Is Created	Indicates whether this workflow should be automatically initiated whenever a new item is added to the attached list.	Unchecked
Automatically Start This Workflow Whenever an Item Is Changed	Indicates whether this workflow should be automatically initiated whenever an item in the attached list is modified.	Unchecked

Setting Up the Initiation Form

Before we get into defining our workflow, we must collect some information from the marketing manager when they initiate the workflow in order to allow the workflow to process. For this exercise, this includes

- The name of the product the marketing plan relates to
- The specific subsidiary that creates the product
- The budget allocated for this marketing campaign
- The proposed launch date for the marketing campaign

We briefly discussed initiation forms earlier. Setting up the fields for the form is a simple matter of following the steps of a wizard. Click the Initiation button at the bottom left of the screen and then click Add to set up the fields as shown in Tables 4-4 through 4-7.

■ **Note** In reality, some of this information could likely be retrieved programmatically from the payload document itself. However, this would require custom code, and for now we're focusing on just the capabilities available in no-code workflows built with the SharePoint Designer.

Table 4-4. *Configuration Settings for the Product Name Field of Our Initiation Form*

Item	Value
Name	Product Name
Information Type	Single Line of Text
Default Value	*<blank>*

Table 4-5. *Configuration Settings for the Subsidiary Field of Our Initiation Form*

Item	Value
Name	Subsidiary
Information Type	Choice (menu to choose from)
Choices	KCD Widgets Ltd. (UK) KCD Widgets, Inc. (US)
Default Value	*<blank>*
Display As	Drop-down Menu

Table 4-6. *Configuration Settings for the Budget Field of Our Initiation Form*

Item	Value
Name	Budget
Information Type	Number
Default Value	0

Table 4-7. *Configuration Settings for the Launch Date Field of Our Initiation Form*

Item	Value
Name	Launch Date
Information Type	Date and Time
Display Format	Date Only
Blank default Value	Selected
Use Date and Time of Item Creation as Default	Unselected
Default Value	Unselected

When you have set up the variables, your Workflow Initiation Parameters screen should look like the one shown in Figure 4-13.

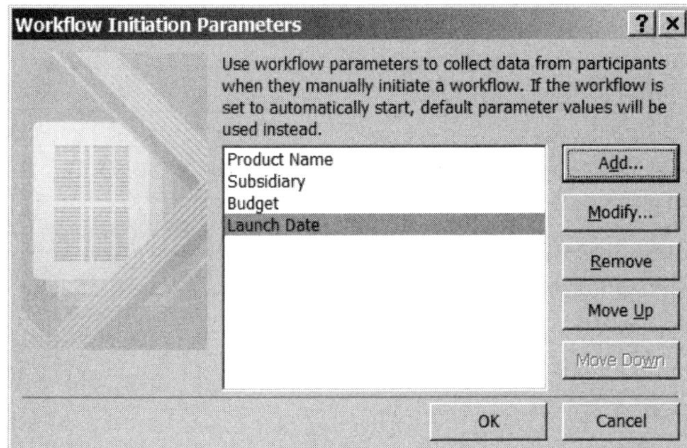

Figure 4-13. *Parameters configured properly for the KCD Marketing Plan example*

Click OK to close the Initiation window and return to the Workflow Designer.

Building the Workflow Steps

With the basic workflow settings in place and the initiation form created, we can now begin creating the steps our workflow requires. This exercise requires three steps:

- Product Manager
- Notifications (to advertising agency and manufacturing coordinator)
- Marketing Director

Step 1: Product Manager

This step will notify the product manager that the marketing plan for one of their products needs to be reviewed. The next screen allows us to specify the details of each step of our workflow.

To complete this part of the exercise, follow these steps:

1. Click on Step 1 in the Workflow Steps list on the right side of the screen and we'll begin customizing this step.
2. Rename the step to **Product Manager**.
3. Click the Conditions button and select Compare Any Data Source to set up our first condition. A sample is shown in Figure 4-14.

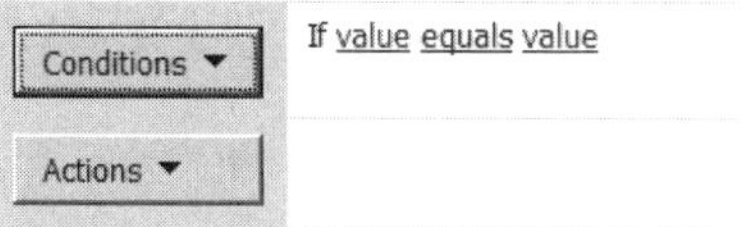

Figure 4-14. *The Compare Any Data Source condition allows you to specify values to determine whether the step will process.*

4. Click on the first Value link and then click the function button that appears next to the field to define the condition.

5. Select Workflow Data from the Source drop-down and Initiation: Subsidiary from the Field drop-down in the Define Workflow Lookup dialog box (shown in Figure 4-15) and then click OK.

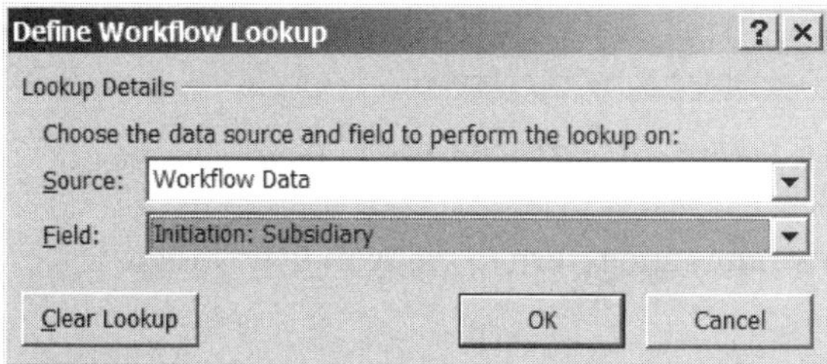

Figure 4-15. *The completed workflow lookup for our first workflow step*

6. Click on the second Value link and type **KCD Widgets, Inc. (US)** in the textbox that appears. It is important that this value match exactly the value you typed in the Subsidiary Initiation Form drop-down list.

7. Click the Action button and select Send an Email. You may need to click on the More Actions option to view the full list of available actions.

8. Click on the This Message link to open the Define Email Message dialog box.

9. In the To parameter, type **ProdMngrUS@kcdholdings.com** (or a valid email address on your development machine).

10. Configure the Subject parameter by clicking the function icon to the right of the field and selecting

    - Source: Workflow Data
    - Field: Initiation: Product Name

11. For the body of the message, enter the information shown in Figure 4-16.

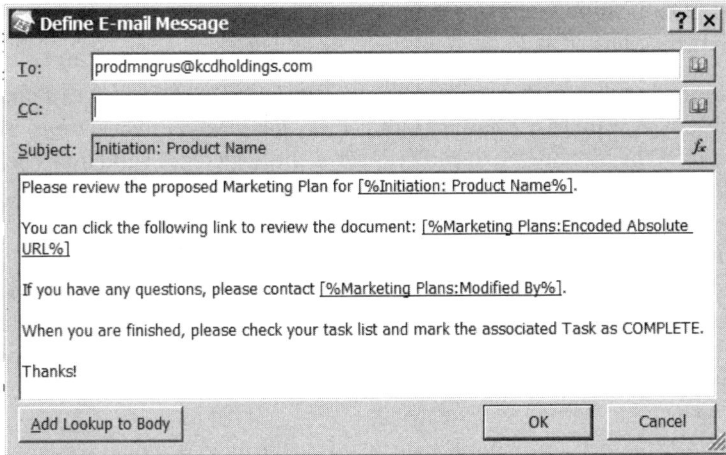

Figure 4-16. *Configuring the email message that will be sent as part of our workflow*

The information in brackets can be automatically entered by positioning the cursor in the proper place and clicking the Add Lookup to Body button. Select the following Source and Field combinations:

- [%Initiation: ProductName%]
  - Source: Workflow Data
  - Field: Initiation: Product Name
- [%Marketing Plans: Encoded Absolute URL%]
  - Source: Current Item
  - Field: Encoded Absolute URL
- [%Marketing Plans: Modified By%]
  - Source: Current Item
  - Field: Modified By

12. Click OK to close the Define Email Message dialog box.
13. We need to wait until the product manager has completed their task, so we'll assign them a To-Do item. The To-Do item action will automatically pause the workflow until the item is completed. To add another action to this step, click the Actions button and select More Actions from the drop-down.
14. In the Workflow Actions dialog box, select the All Actions category and then select Assign a To-Do Item.
15. Click on the A To-Do Item link in the action.
16. In the first screen of the custom task wizard, click Next.

17. On the next screen, name the To-Do item **Review Plan (US)**, enter a description of **Please review the Marketing Plan**, and then click Finish.

18. Click the These Users link in the action and select the ID for the US product manager (or whichever user you want to use as the product manager in your environment) from the list of users. Click the Add button to add the user to the Selected list and then click OK to close the dialog box. The actions for this condition are now complete.

If the subsidiary company was not KCD Widgets, Inc. (US), then the only other choice is KCD Widgets, Ltd. (UK). To finish setting the proper product manager, we need to add an else condition. We do not need to set a condition for this branch—this will ensure that the action associated with this branch will always execute if the preceding branch's action does not.

Here are the steps to follow to set this up:

1. Click the link Add "Else If" Conditional Branch link on the main Workflow Designer screen.

2. Repeat steps 7 through 18 except

   - Enter **ProdMngrUK@kcdholdings.com** for the To parameter in step 9.
   - Name the To-Do item **Review Plan (UK)**.
   - Assign the To-Do item to kcd\ProdMngrUK in step 20.

3. The first step of our workflow is now complete. Our Workflow Designer should look similar to Figure 4-17.

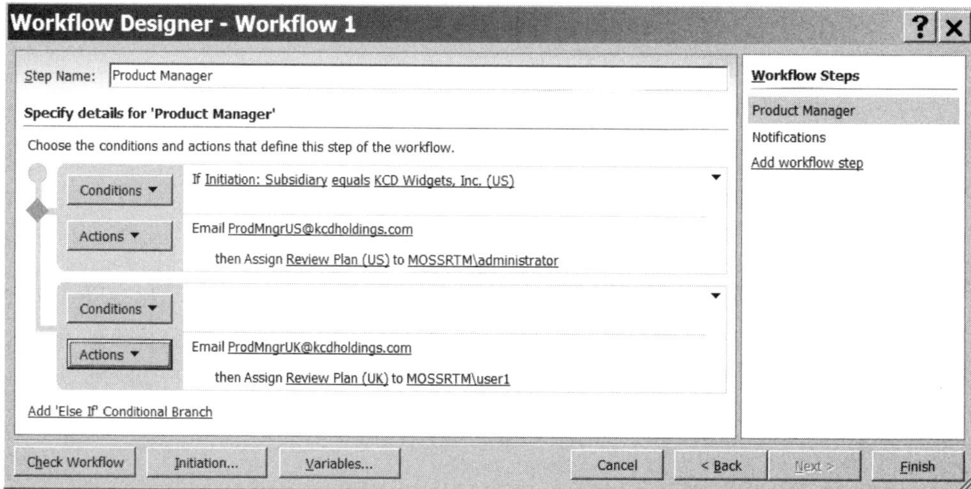

Figure 4-17. *When completely configured, step 1 of our workflow should look similar to this.*

That takes care of the first step in our workflow. We can continue with the subsequent steps.

Step 2: Notifications

This step will notify the advertising agency and manufacturing coordinator that a marketing plan needs to be reviewed. These tasks will happen in parallel.

To complete this part of the exercise, follow these steps:

1. Click the Add Workflow Step link in the Workflow Steps section on the right side of the screen.

2. Rename this step to **Notifications.**

3. Since we will not reach this step until the appropriate product manager has approved the specs and marked their To-Do item as complete, we can safely execute the actions for this step without checking a condition.

4. Click the Actions button and select Send an Email.

5. Click the Actions button again and select Send an Email a second time.

6. Click the small arrow at the top-right corner of the Condition/Action box and select Run All Actions in Parallel from the drop-down menu (as shown in Figure 4-18) to make sure the two emails are sent simultaneously.

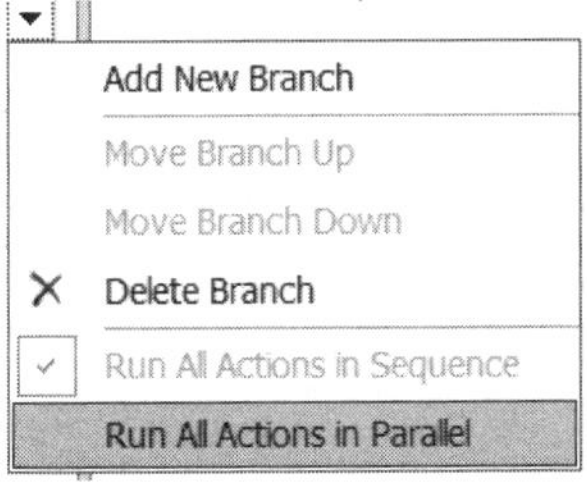

Figure 4-18. *We want all of our notifications to go out simultaneously.*

Note that the Actions text now reads ***and** Email this message* as opposed to the original ***then** Email this message.* This is how we can be sure that the actions will happen simultaneously. Remember, unfortunately, it's just that one-word difference.

7. Click on the first This Message link and configure the fields as shown in Figure 4-19.

■ **Tip** To actually test this workflow later, you'll want to send it to an email address you can receive mail on.

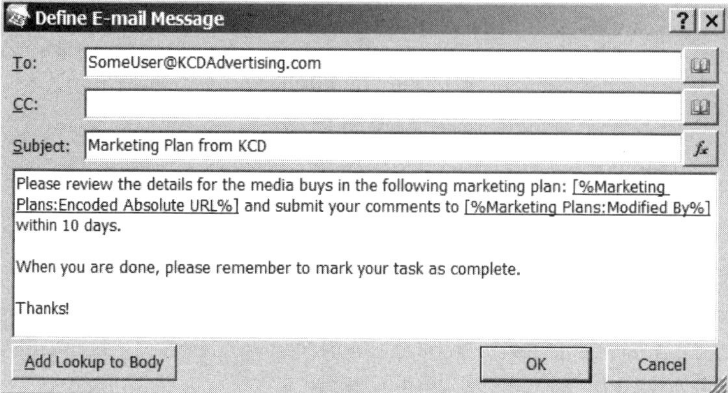

Figure 4-19. *Configuration settings for the email to the advertising agency*

8. Click on the second This Message link and configure the fields as shown in Figure 4-20. Again, set the email address to one you can monitor.

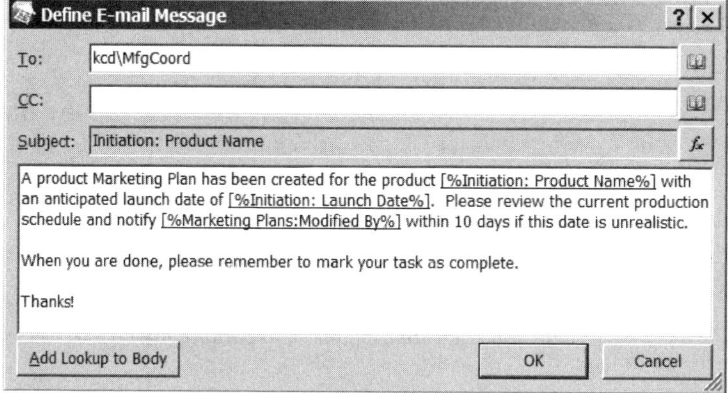

Figure 4-20. *Configuration settings for the email to the KCD manufacturing coordinator*

9. To cause the workflow to pause until the advertising and manufacturing people have completed their work, we want to assign a To-Do item to each of them. We stepped through the process for this earlier, so I'll just give you the details this time around and let you fend for yourselves:

    - Assign a To-Do named **Verify Media Buys** to `SomeUser@kcdadvertising.com`.
    - Assign a To-Do named **Verify Production Schedules** to kcd\MfgCoord.

■ **Tip** Remember, when you are assigning To-Do items and sending emails, you'll need to make sure that the accounts and email addresses you use are valid in your environment *and* ones that you can monitor.

The second step in our workflow is now complete. The Workflow Designer screen should now look similar to Figure 4-21.

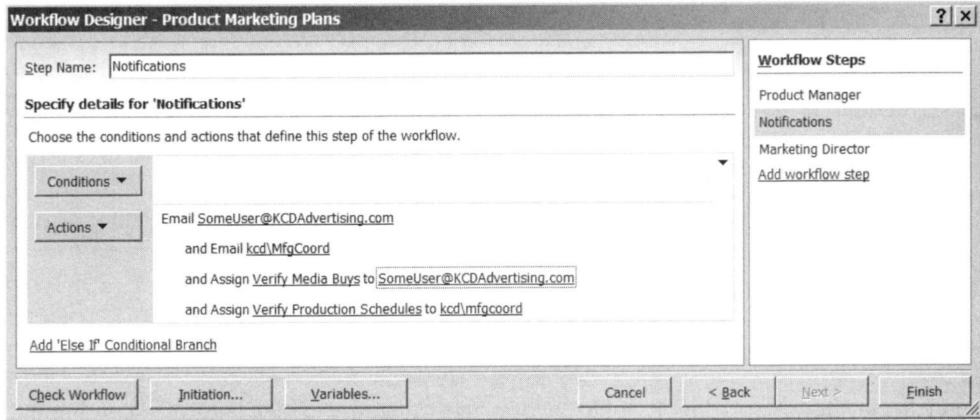

Figure 4-21. *The completed step 2 for our workflow*

Step 3: Marketing Director

This step will notify the marketing director that the marketing plan for a product is complete and ready for final approval. This step won't execute until the To-Do items in the previous step have been completed and we want it to execute every time. All of the tasks you'll need to complete for this step have been covered earlier in this chapter, so I won't spoon-feed you directions. At a high level, the tasks are

1. Create a new workflow step called **Marketing Director**.
2. Configure the step to not wait for a certain condition to be met (hint: configuring this is actually *not* doing something as opposed to doing something).
3. Configure this step to send an email to the marketing director. Include the name of the product in the body of the email as well as some text describing what is going on, as well as a link to the document.
4. Configure this step to assign a To-Do item to the marketing director to have them review the plan. Have this action execute at the same time (parallel) as the email action.

When you are done, step 3 should look like Figure 4-22.

Our sample workflow exercise is now complete. In a matter of minutes, using nothing but out-of-the-box features, we have completed a workflow that supports the required business process. All we need to do now is deploy and test.

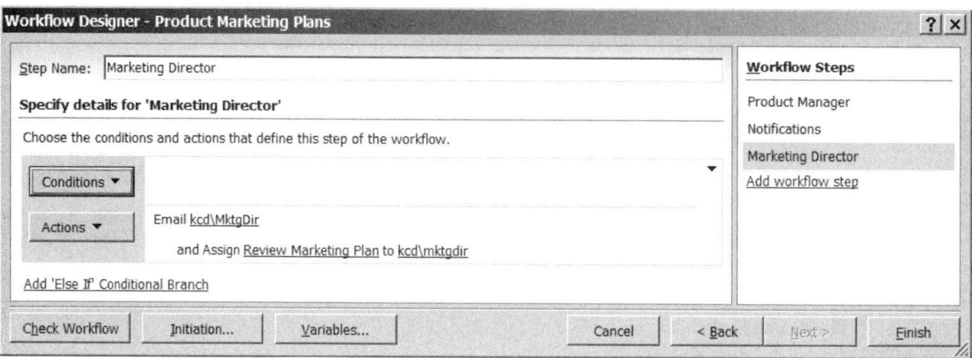

Figure 4-22. *Step 3 in our custom workflow*

Deploying Our New Workflow

Before deploying our workflow, it would behoove us to make use of the Check Workflow button. Go ahead and click it. If you typed everything correctly, you should get a message box telling you that your workflow contains no errors. If you don't get this, go back and check that you've completed each step correctly.

Now we're ready to deploy. You might want to pause here for a minute and get yourself a drink and snack before beginning this next part of the process because it's a doozy and you won't want to stop in the middle.

All ready now? Good. To deploy our workflow, simply click the Finish button in the Workflow Designer. The SharePoint Designer will validate our workflow, build the initiation form, and deploy the files to the SharePoint site. When it is finished, it closes the Workflow Designer and returns you to SPD.

Man, that deployment was hard work. Go ahead and take another drink now. You've earned it.

Drum roll please... Congratulations, you've just created your first Office 2007 Workflow.

Testing 1, 2, 3...Testing 1, 2, 3

Before we can really say that we're done, we need to test our workflow. This will give you the opportunity to see how your workflow looks, too. To get started, fire up a browser and navigate to the site you deployed the workflow to (the same URL you specified when you opened the site in SPD). From here, navigate into the Marketing Plans document library and upload a new document.

Once the document is in place, run your mouse over the document name and select Workflows from the drop-down menu. Near the top of the next screen, in the Start a New Workflow section, will be a listing of the workflows that are available in this document library. You will likely have two default workflows (Approval and Collect Feedback) plus our custom workflow (Product Marketing Plans), as shown in Figure 4-23.

Go ahead and click our workflow name to get it started. The first screen you'll see (shown in Figure 4-24) is the initiation form that SPD created for us based on the fields we specified. Fill in some test values for each field and click Start.

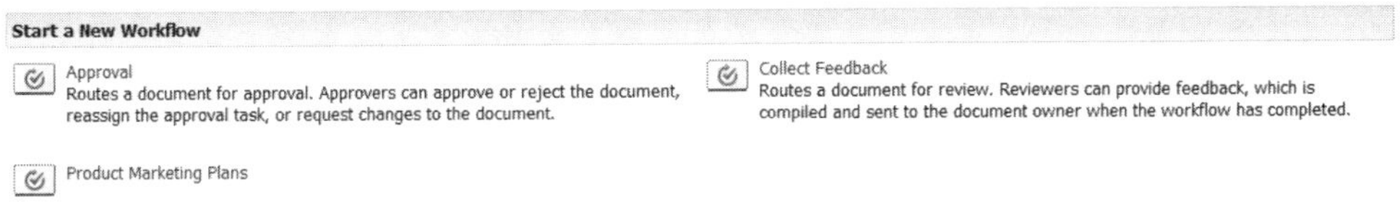

Start a New Workflow

Approval
Routes a document for approval. Approvers can approve or reject the document, reassign the approval task, or request changes to the document.

Collect Feedback
Routes a document for review. Reviewers can provide feedback, which is compiled and sent to the document owner when the workflow has completed.

Product Marketing Plans

Figure 4-23. *Our custom workflow is available in the list of workflows to start on our document.*

Product Marketing Plans
To initiate Product Marketing Plans, click Start.
Product Name:
Subsidiary:
Budget: 0.00
Launch Date:
Start Cancel

Figure 4-24. *SPD automatically created this initiation form for us based on the fields we specified.*

Our workflow will start and we will be returned to the view of our document library, as shown in Figure 4-25. You'll also notice in Figure 4-25 that a new column has been added to this view. The column is named for our workflow—Product Marketing Plans—and contains the current status of our workflow; in this case, it is currently In Progress. This column is added to the default view the first time a new instance of a workflow is added. Any documents or list items that have run or are running this workflow will show their status in this column.

Marketing Plans
New Upload Actions Settings

Type	Name	Product Marketing Plans
	WFTest1 ! NEW	In Progress

Figure 4-25. *The default view of our document library shows the current status of our workflow.*

If you recall, the first step of our workflow checked whether the subsidiary was US or UK and then sent an email and assigned a task to the appropriate product manager. If you check the email for the account you set up as the product manager, you will see our email sitting there. A sample of this email is shown in Figure 4-26. Notice that the workflow lookups we added to the body of the email message have been replaced with the appropriate information.

Back in the browser, if you check the task list, you will see a new task created with a name of Review Plan (US) and assigned to the account you set up for the US product manager. Figure 4-27 shows this task as well as the Complete Task button that's provided to allow us to indicate when the task is finished. Go ahead and click the button now.

From: MOSSAdmin@kcdholdings.com
To: administrator@kcdholdings.com
Cc:
Subject: UltraWidget III

Please review the proposed Marketing Plan for UltraWidget III.

You can click the following link to review the document: http://mossb2tr/spd1/Marketing%20Plans/WFTest1.docx

If you have any questions, please contact MOSSB2TR\administrator.

When you are finished, please check your task list and mark the associated Task as COMPLETE.

Thanks!

Figure 4-26. *The email sent by the first step of our workflow has the appropriate information for this instance and this payload.*

Title:	Review Plan (US)
Description:	Please review the Marketing Plan
Related list item:	WFTest1

Complete Task | Cancel

Figure 4-27. *The task created by our workflow*

You can click through the tasks and emails that are sent by the other two steps in our workflow. You'll notice that each step only executes when the tasks (To-Do items) from the previous step have been marked as complete. In the case of the third step, it only executes when *both* tasks from step 2 have been marked as complete.

Notice, also, that the status of our workflow back in the document library stays as In Progress until the last task—assigned to the marketing director—is marked as complete.

So there you have it. In just a short amount of time, we've built and tested a custom workflow using nothing but the out-of-the-box capabilities of SharePoint and the SharePoint Designer. Before we close up shop on this functionality, there are a few things you should know:

- There is *no* way to save your in-progress workflow in SPD. Once you start, you need to deploy it in order to save your work. Don't ask me why—that's just the way it is.

- As I said before, SPD is great for what it is intended for. However, it is not, repeat not, going to meet all of your needs. For pretty basic, straightforward workflows attached to a single list or document library, it is a great tool. It does have some pretty significant limitations in this release, though. My recommendation is to familiarize yourself with the tool first on some basic test balloons before you try to tackle something more complex. Make sure that it is the right tool.

- With that said, if it *is* the right tool, it *will* save you lots of time.

- There is no way to do escalation, parallel branches, or other more advanced workflow constructs with this tool.

Summary

For the seriously time-pressured among us, here is the abridged version of this chapter. For more information on any of these items, you ought to at least skim the chapter. Thanks.

- In Office 2007, FrontPage has been rebranded as the SharePoint Designer.
- The Workflow Designer in the SharePoint Designer follows a wizard-based process to allow nontechnical users to build workflows.
- Workflows are built as a collection of steps.
- Initiation forms allow you to collect information from an originator of your workflow and use it later in the workflow to do conditional routing, updating lists, and so forth.
- The Variables Editor walks you through the process of adding variables to store values used elsewhere in the workflow.
- Conditions control which steps, or which parts of steps, are processed.
- Actions are the meat of the workflow; they're what the workflow does.
- The SharePoint Designer ships with certain out-of-the-box actions readily available to cover many situations you are likely to encounter.
- The Workflow Designer works directly with a single list on a single site. It is not intended for creating workflows that are to be deployed to multiple lists or sites. (This is not to say that you can't make that happen; it's just not what the tool does well.)
- Workflow lookups allow you to retrieve information from other lists in your site or from variables set as part of your workflow.

Here's some food for thought:

- The SharePoint Designer is good but it still requires a client install and a fairly knowledgeable power user. It would be interesting to build a purely browser-based interface for building very basic workflows. There has also been some discussion in the community about building a workflow designer right into the core Office applications via a task pane. I'll post some thoughts on my web site and point you to some of the discussions elsewhere in the community. I'd love to hear your thoughts on this.
- The Workflow Designer is built for simple, single-path workflows. For example, there is no way to automatically escalate a workflow to another user if one user doesn't complete their assigned task within a certain period of time. Yes, there are two delay-type actions, but they are going to block your whole workflow and prevent any additional steps from processing, even if the user does complete their task in the time allotted. You could probably cobble something together but it wouldn't be pretty. It would be an interesting discussion on how to make it work easily. Visit me at `http://kcdholdings.com` if you have ideas and would like to discuss them.

PART 3

Teaching Your Workflow to Dance

This just keeps getting better and better. So far we've covered some introductory material and then the out-of-the-box capabilities of SharePoint and the rest of the 2007 Office System. Now it's time to take things to a whole new level.

Beginning in this section we start to flex our development muscles. In Chapter 5, we build custom activities and explore the power and flexibility these new components bring to our programs. In Chapter 6 we finally build our own workflows. We look at both sequential ("flowchart") workflows as well as state machine (um... "not flowchart") workflows. Chapter 7 covers everything we need to know to introduce custom InfoPath and ASP.NET forms to allow users to interact and customize our workflows. Chapter 8 explores the Rules engine and builds a custom solution that allows us to manipulate rules externally and use them to modify the processing of our workflow.

These chapters form the core of the book. Everything that precedes them is laying the foundation. Everything after them is icing on the cake. Take your time going through the material. Honestly, none of it is that difficult technically, but there are lots of moving parts. Try to ignore all of my annoying tangential comments and you'll be fine. Have fun—things get interesting now.

CHAPTER 5

Activities

As the more astute among you will have already guessed, this chapter is all about activities—what they are, how they work, what's available, and how to build our own. We'll cover the out-of-the-box activities provided by the Windows Workflow Foundation (WF) that are usable from our Office workflows, as well as the activities that are added with SharePoint. Finally, we'll end the chapter with a review of the activity architecture as well as a walkthrough of building our own custom activity.

So, jumping right in—activities, what are they? Simply put, activities are the building blocks of a workflow. Generically, an activity is just a component—no different than any other .NET custom control.

At a very high level, two types of activities can exist within WF, whether they are built by Microsoft, third parties, you, or your Aunt Matilda: simple activities or composite activities.

Note Microsoft is lumped in with the rest of us (yes, even with your Aunt Matilda) when it comes to activity development. All of the default activities that ship with WF or SharePoint were developed using the same framework that we're using. There's no secret-squirrel, magical API for Microsoft activities.

Simple Activities

The term *simple* here does not imply that these activities are not complex. *Simple activities* could require months of design and thousands of lines of code. Simple here means only that the activity does something (and typically only *one* something). For instance, sending an email is an example of a simple activity. It is an atomic unit of functionality. Although it could be broken down into various subtasks (set To address, set email subject, set email body, etc.), those are merely steps within a single functional unit of sending an email.

Note For simplicity's sake (no pun intended) and because simple activities are far more common than composite activities, the *simple* prefix is typically dropped. It is assumed that if you say just *activity* you are referring to a simple activity.

Although there is nothing explicitly in the WF framework that prohibits the inclusion of multiple tasks within an activity, adding multiple tasks would be bad form. So, for example, having a single activity that sends an email and creates a SharePoint list entry would be too much in a single activity—even if those two tasks "always" occur together. If it were necessary that both of these tasks succeed or fail together, they could be wrapped in a transactional context activity (see the activity breakdown later in this chapter for further details) by a workflow builder. As a writer of a simple activity, our job is to write single task–based components. Our mantra is *do one thing and do it well.*

So, all pontificating aside, we know what activities are in a theoretical, bore-your-audience-at-a-cocktail-party kind of way, but still nothing concrete. Some examples will help bring things home. The following are all examples of specific simple activities:

- Send email
- Invoke web service
- Execute code
- Create task
- Delay

That should wrap things up pretty nicely. We now know what activities are: units of code that perform a logically atomic task. The only real question left to round out our definition is, just what can that task be? The answer: anything your business requirement needs it to be. Really. If your business requirement—whatever that may be—can be expressed in code and executed on a computer, that's your activity. There is no reason that any of the following couldn't be coded as custom activities:

- Insert or delete a database row
- Send or wait for a fax/SMS message/email/voicemail
- Send a control sequence to a piece of robotic equipment
- Record an input from a piece of test equipment
- Open or close an electrical circuit
- Erase the high scores from your MAME arcade cabinet

Specifically in the Office 2007 space, the following are additional examples of potential custom activities:

- Create WSS site
- Create WSS alert
- Strip macros from Office 2007 documents
- Replace document style sheet in new XML file formats
- Convert document to PDF or XPS (Microsoft's XML Paper Specification)

Some of these activities exist already; others are just waiting for you to code them.

Composite Activities

Typically, *composite activities* act as containers for other activities. These other, or child, activities are not typically included as part of the composite activity built by the developer. Instead, they are usually added by the workflow builder at the time they are creating a new workflow. Unlike simple activities, composite activities don't do anything. OK, that's not precisely true; composite activities are used to control the flow of the process being enforced by the workflow or perhaps do some processing either before or after its child activities run, so they do something. It is not, however, a typical task that would be listed as a step of a workflow. So, in a sense, a composite activity doesn't really do anything, but rather it controls and augments how other activities do their things.

■ **Note** Similar to the guideline of a simple activity only performing one task not being enforced in WF, there is nothing in the WF Framework that explicitly dictates that a composite activity not perform any tasks. It's just a good convention to follow.

By way of example, the following are all composite activities that ship with WF:

- Parallel
- ConditionedActivityGroup
- Replicator
- IfElse

Details on these and other default activities are provided later in this chapter. For now, it is important just to know that each of these activities is designed to control how their child activities are processed.

Building composite activities will not be as common a task as building simple ones. This is merely because there are not as many different needs or options for controlling workflow processing as there are for performing actual tasks. Building a composite activity is also a fundamentally different process than writing a simple one. The bulk of this chapter will focus on simple activities. We'll circle back around at the end of the chapter and cover the creation of a sample composite activity.

Out-of-the-Box Activities

As you've seen, there are very few limitations on what your custom activity can be or do. The sky's the limit. Before you take off, however, it might be a good idea to get an understanding of what already exists—no sense reinventing the wheel. As I mentioned before, WF ships with certain out-of-the-box activities. SharePoint adds more. So before you start creating your activity masterpiece, you might want to see what Microsoft has already given you. Your idea may have already been taken, or at the very least there may be something you can inherit from to get you part of the way. Either way, the next two sections will cover the known world. Where you go from there is entirely up to you.

WF Activities

While WF is primarily an engine and does not provide a lot of extended functionality out-of-the-box, it does include a number of core activities. These activities are provided as part of the base WF platform and are therefore available to every workflow built on top of the platform.

A total of 31 activities ship out-of-the-box with WF. To me, only 20 are of real use to us when we're developing workflows in Office 2007. More than 20 will work in Office workflows, but I honestly don't see them as being useful for most of the situations that you will find yourself in. Table 5-1 provides the name of each of the 20 as well as a description of the functionality provided and, where appropriate, an example of where the activity might be useful to you. Note that this table is intended to give you an overview of these default activities and not serve as an exhaustive reference.

■ **Tip** Additional information on the full list of default activities can be found at Microsoft's WF site, `http://wf.w3fx.com`.

Table 5-1. *Activities from the Windows Workflow Engine That Are Useful in Office Workflows*

Activity	Description	Thoughts on Usage
Code	Allows you to add custom code to your workflow. This code can be Visual Basic .NET or C#.	This activity is a catchall; it can be used to execute any server-side code your workflow requires. Calling web services, instantiating and using objects, and executing inline code are all valid uses of this activity.

Table 5-1. *Activities from the Windows Workflow Engine That Are Useful in Office Workflows (Continued)*

Activity	Description	Thoughts on Usage
ConditionedActivityGroup (CAG)	The CAG is a control mechanism for a workflow. It allows you, the workflow builder, to specify a group of activities that will execute based on certain conditions. The CAG is different from a simple *if-else* or *while* activity in a couple of key ways. First, the CAG itself has a `UntilCondition` property that controls the processing of the CAG and therefore all of the activities that it contains. Second, each activity contained within the CAG gets a `WhenCondition` property added to it that specifies the condition under which that individual activity executes. This combination of conditions can be combined to create an extremely powerful, complex workflow operating off conditions not known until runtime. The third difference is that the CAG can contain multiple child activities, unlike the while activity, which can only contain one child (yes, you could make that one child a composite activity, but...). The CAG activity is quite advanced and entire chapters of WF books will be dedicated to it.	
Delay	Allows you to pause your workflow. Useful if you need to have your workflow stop executing until a certain time.	If your workflow needs to execute a process that consumes a large amount of server resources, you may want to delay that execution until after business hours.
EventDriven	Enables your workflow to process based on events.	Necessary for state machine workflows to handle transitions between states based on events and also for enabling workflow modifications. (We cover state machines in Chapter 6.)

Table 5-1. *Activities from the Windows Workflow Engine That Are Useful in Office Workflows (Continued)*

Activity	Description	Thoughts on Usage
EventHandlingScope	Like the EventDriven activity, this one is necessary to enable workflow modifications.	
FaultHandler	Allows your workflow to handle errors. This is a composite activity that serves as a separate branch of your workflow that executes if an error is encountered. We cover fault handling in workflows in Chapter 9.	
HandleExternalEvent	Used for indicating which events are handled by various states in a state machine workflow.	
IfElse	Allows your workflow to branch conditionally.	Useful in a scenario such as when your approval workflow requires a department manager's approval if the dollar amount is under $10,000 but a vice president's signature if the amount is over that.
InvokeWebService	Enables your workflow to call an external web service and wait for a response.	Useful in a scenario where you need data or functionality available from an external system that exposes a web service interface.
Parallel	This composite activity is a container to hold other activities and allows your workflow to branch into multiple independent operation streams. This activity will wait until all branches complete processing before continuing.	Useful in a situation where your workflow needs to complete several long-running tasks. Rather than wait for each to be completed before starting the next, this activity allows you to execute them all at the same time. Can also be used to introduce timeouts and escalations into your workflow.

Table 5-1. *Activities from the Windows Workflow Engine That Are Useful in Office Workflows (Continued)*

Activity	Description	Thoughts on Usage
Replicator	Another container activity, the Replicator can hold only one other activity—though that one activity could be another container such as a Sequence or Parallel. The Replicator allows your workflow to repeat its set of child activities with the number of repetitions not being known until runtime.	Useful in a scenario such as one where your workflow needs to collect approvals for a proposal. The specific approvers and the number of approvers will vary from proposal to proposal depending on which technologies are used and which departments are affected. The Replicator will allow you to build that approver list at runtime and execute the approval process the appropriate number of times.
Sequence	This activity is similar in form to a Parallel activity in that by itself it does nothing—it is merely a container for other activities. In this case, it controls the execution of its child activities, causing them to be performed in a series. As serial execution is the default for workflow execution, this activity is only useful as a container object. It allows you to place several activities in situations (such as inside a Replicator activity) where only one activity is allowed.	
SetState State StateInitialization StateFinalization	These activities are only useful for state machine workflows. They allow you to control the *state* of your workflow. More on state machines in the next chapter.	
Suspend	The Suspend activity pauses the execution of your workflow and optionally passes an error message back to the host (SharePoint). Workflow execution can be resumed from the host.	

Table 5-1. *Activities from the Windows Workflow Engine That Are Useful in Office Workflows (Continued)*

Activity	Description	Thoughts on Usage
Terminate	This activity causes the immediate cessation of all workflow activity—your workflow just stops running. Similar to the Suspend activity, an error message can be provided back to the host application. Unlike the Suspend activity, this activity makes it impossible to restart a workflow.	
Throw	This activity allows you to explicitly invoke an exception, which should then be handled via a Fault Handler activity. This is functionally equivalent to the C# `throw` statement.	Useful in a scenario where your workflow accepts external input and expects that input to be within a certain range. If the received input is outside that range, you can throw an exception and let the Fault Handler catch and handle the error.
While	Another flow-control activity. This activity allows your workflow to loop through, and continue looping through a series of activities so long as a certain condition is met.	

Caution Officially, only four of the standard WF activities are supported:

- Code
- ConditionedActivityGroup
- Sequence
- Replicator

I'll admit to being puzzled by this. The IfElse activity isn't supported? Not to mention While, Delay, Parallel, and Terminate? If the FaultHandler activity isn't supported, why is there a Fault Handler view on our workflow? As near as I can figure, the official documentation is lagging behind the product itself. Various Microsoft people I've spoken with confirm that this list of supported activities is from very early in the product development process and needs to be updated. So I've left the full list intact in Table 5-1. At one point or another, I've worked with each of the activities and haven't run into any problems. Perhaps there is some esoteric issue that will raise its ugly head in certain scenarios and I'm just not testing those scenarios. Keep that in mind as you go, but I think you'll be all right.

For the record, the 11 activities that I disregard are

- CallExternalMethod
- CompensatableSequence
- Compensate
- InvokeWorkflow
- Listen
- Policy
- SynchronizationScope
- TransactionScope
- WebServiceFault
- WebServiceInput
- WebServiceOutput

SharePoint Activities

With 20 of 31 out-of-the-box activities available to us, you might wonder what's left. What else do we need? The answer is that we need SharePoint-specific functionality (and, believe it or not, we need the ability to send an email—a conspicuous hole in the default activities list). SharePoint ships with a number of activities out-of-the-box to provide SharePoint-specific tasks. We can make use of these activities in our custom workflows. Table 5-2 provides details on the additional 22 SharePoint activities—each with a brief description (although most are pretty self-explanatory). Table 5-2 brings our total count of available activities up to 42—not too bad for an initial release (and perhaps a little significant if you're a Douglas Adams fan). Once the vibrant third-party component community kicks in, this number will explode.

■ **Note** If you can't see these activities, you need to add them to the Toolbox. I recommend creating a new tab called something clever like *SharePoint* to place them all in. Right-click on the new tab, select Choose Items, select the Activities tab, and add a reference to the `Microsoft.Sharepoint.WorkflowActions` assembly from the `\Program Files\Common Files\Microsoft Shared\Web Server Extensions\12\ISAPI` folder. Now you'll have a whole slew of new activities to play with.

Table 5-2. *Additional Activities Added by SharePoint*

Activity	Description
CompleteTask	Facilitates the closing of a workflow task. Allows you to specify the final status of the task.
CreateTask	Enables you to create a new workflow task—bet you never would have guessed that one.
CreateTaskWithContentType	The same as the previous item, except that you can also specify a content type for the task. Among other things, this enables the task to be opened with a specific form.
DelayFor	Allows you to pause your workflow for a specified number of days, hours, and minutes. This composite activity is just a glorified wrapper around the default Delay activity. It adds the ability to specify a comment that is logged at the beginning of execution and also one logged at the end of execution (via the `EnterComment` and `ExitComment` properties), although you need to do this in code as those properties are not exposed in the Properties window.
DelayUntil	Similar to DelayFor except that you specify an absolute end date as opposed to a relative one. The time cannot be set through the Properties window, but can be set to any valid Date/Time value in code.
DeleteTask	Um... deletes a workflow task? Good guess. You specify the `TaskId`.
EnableWorkflowModification	Used to enable a workflow modification form at the specified point in your workflow. The modification form is available within the scope prescribed by the activity.
InitializeWorkflow	Allows you to specify a method to be fired off to initialize your workflow. Similar to a Code activity, except that it has a `CorrelationToken` property. We'll talk about correlation tokens in the next chapter.
LogToHistoryList	Permits your workflow to explicitly write an entry to the SharePoint list designated as the history list for the running workflow instance. Because this list can be set at the time of workflow association, there is no way to know its identity at design time.
OnTaskChanged	Allows your workflow to subscribe to an event raised when the specified task is modified—either by the user or programmatically. You can specify a custom event to be fired when this activity triggers. This activity also contains a custom property for both `BeforeProperties`—which records the state of the task prior to the change—as well as `AfterProperties`—which contains the sate after the change.

Table 5-2. *Additional Activities Added by SharePoint (Continued)*

Activity	Description
OnTaskCreated	Similar to the previous item, but triggered when the event is created.
OnTaskDeleted	Also similar to the previous item, but for task deletion.
OnWorkflowActivated	This activity *must* be the first activity in every one of our SharePoint workflows and will in fact be automatically added when you create a new SharePoint workflow class. Facilitates the establishment of various aspects of our workflow.
OnWorkflowItemChanged	Like the OnTaskChanged activity, receives an event when an item is modified. Allows you to execute code in response to this event. Also contains both `BeforeProperties` and `AfterProperties` properties.
OnWorkflowItemDeleted	Similar to the OnTaskDeleted activity but for a workflow Item.
OnWorkflowModified	Works in conjunction with the EnableWorkflowModification activity. Receives an event when the workflow modification is actually implemented.
RollbackTask	Allows your workflow to undo a workflow task.
Sendemail	Pop quiz! You have to guess what this one does...
SetState	Not to be confused with the state-machine-based activity of the same name, this one is used to specify the current processing status of a workflow. This status is shown in the column added to the default view when an instance of the workflow is run for the first time. Default potential values are specified in the `SPWorkflowStatus` enumeration, although you can specify your own custom values.
SharepointSequentialWorkflowActivity	This is the base activity from which our SharePoint workflows derive. We can't add it to one of our workflows, so you can just delete it from the Designer.
UpdateAllTasks	Allows for batch processing of workflow tasks. You can specify the new property values via the `TaskProperties` custom property.
UpdateTask	Modifies the properties of a single task.

Tip One more set of activities that bears looking into before you begin developing your own are those available on Microsoft's Workflow site: `http://wf.netfx3.com`. In addition to hosting an ever-growing library of activities this site is an invaluable resource to activity and Workflow developers. Check it out, contribute some ideas or code, and keep checking back. It's well worth the effort.

Building a Custom Simple Activity

So, now that we have an understanding of what is available to us out-of-the-box, it's time to talk about building custom activities. If activities are the building blocks of a workflow, then developing custom activities is like making your own Lego blocks in the exact size, shape, and color that you need.

We're going to start with a simple activity and then at the end of the chapter build a composite activity.

WHY WRITE CUSTOM ACTIVITIES?

The question was posed to me: why should we write custom activities? The default Code activity allows us to write any custom code we need. This inline code is compiled into our workflow assembly so there's no performance reason to write custom activities. So why bother with the extra hassle of packaging, deploying, and maintaining a separate activity if we can just put the code directly into our workflow?

It's true; not every bit of custom functionality should be turned into a new activity. So how do we know when to write an activity and when to use inline code? The answer requires a little forethought, a little experience, and a small leap of faith. The forethought comes in identifying the right custom activities. You need to know your organization and its business, and you need to think about the types of functionality that happens frequently. For example, if your organization utilizes Microsoft CRM it would not be unreasonable to assume that at some point more than one workflow is going to need to get information from CRM or provide information to CRM. So a set of CRM activities would probably make sense.

Now here's where the experience part comes in. Rather than write a whole set of activities to get/set every possible piece of data in CRM, you should try to abstract the functionality and develop only two CRM activities—one to get data and one to set data. All of the specifics of what data to get/set can be configured via activity properties. Now instead of dozens of CRM activities, we have just two that should suffice for the majority of our needs. Understand, though, that there will be situations where these two do not fit the bill. You then have a decision to make: do I write a third activity or do I handle that one-off with inline code? It depends on the situation and the need. There is no right or wrong answer, provided that you think about it and don't just blindly follow one path or the other.

So finally, the leap of faith. You need to trust that your knowledge of the business (validated by the businesspeople or not) is sufficient. You need to trust that the business needs will not change significantly in the immediate future (if your old CRM system is being replaced by Microsoft CRM in two weeks, don't plan on spending three weeks writing a CRM activity to work off the old system). You need to trust that your coding skills are sufficient to write a robust, reusable component. You need to trust that the other developers in your organization will use your activities.

Here are a few general rules to keep in mind when deciding what functionality to make into a custom activity:

- It should be functionality that will be used more than once in a single workflow or used in multiple workflows.
- It should be written as generically as makes sense to facilitate reuse without making specific instances of the activity overly difficult to configure.

- It should be configurable through properties so that individual instances of the activity can be customized to do what they need to do.

- It should be as atomic as makes sense. Don't lump functionality together in a single activity even if they "always" go together. A good way to think about this is, "How would I explain this to my manager?" In the CRM example earlier, a GetCRMData and a SetCRMData activity make sense, even though each is composed of perhaps dozens of subtasks (connect to CRM, authenticate, pass parameters, query data, etc.). The get/set boundary is a good, logical breakdown for the functionality.

Organizations should look to develop a solid library of custom activities over time. The ability to easily develop custom activities is one of the strongest features of WF, and smart companies will carefully build on this strength.

Like other components, activities must meet certain requirements. In this case, those requirements are specified by WF—the engine that drives the workflow. Primarily there are two major requirements placed on every activity:

- *An entry point*: Each activity must have an `Execute` method that can be called by the WF host.

- *Notification of completion*: Each activity must inform the host when it has completed its tasks. The host can then continue with the next step of the workflow.

There are other optional elements—related to the presentation of the activity in the Visual Studio Designer and Toolbox, and also validation of activity properties. We're going to cover most of the elements that make up an activity as we progress through this chapter, so before we get started we need to talk a bit about the structure of an activity.

An activity is more than a single class. In fact, a complete activity is made up of seven separate classes:

- *Activity Definition*: The *guts* of the activity; controls what the activity does and what properties it exposes. This class contains the `Execute` method called by the workflow host. This class is required.

- *Activity Toolbox Item*: Used in Visual Studio to display the activity in the Toolbox and control the events when the activity is dropped onto the Designer.

- *Activity Designer*: Used in Visual Studio to control the behavior and structure of the activity at design time in Visual Studio.

- *Activity Validator*: Handles verification of activity properties and environment to ensure that they are configured properly at both design time and runtime.

- *Activity Theme*: Also used in Visual Studio, this time to control the color and other appearance elements of the activity as it is rendered in the visual designer. I don't see this class as being overly useful unless you are rehosting the Designer in another application.

- *Activity Serializer*: Provides for custom serialization in case your activity makes use of objects that the default serializers cannot process.
- *Activity Code Generator*: Allows you to inject custom code during compile-time code generation.

As indicated, only the first class, the Activity Definition, is required. All of the other classes are optional but can be used to enhance your activity in a variety of ways. If you don't include them, Visual Studio will use default functionality. As we build our sample activity throughout the rest of this chapter, we're going to make use of the first five elements from the previous list. I don't want to belittle the remaining two, but honestly, I don't see them being used much for our Office workflows. They're a little more hardcore than we typically need to get in the Office world.

Scenario: Removing Macros

Like many other companies, KCD is concerned with viruses and other nasty things that go bump in the night. They have a corporate policy against macro-enabled documents, and for documents produced internally, they have things under control. However, it is not easy to enforce externally as they deal with a large number of external partners and customers, many of whom can post documents on KCD's customer or partner extranets.

Because all documents are stored inside their MOSS document management system, this seems like the perfect place to take steps toward alleviating the problem. You have been asked to prototype a solution. After kicking around various options, your recommendation is to produce a single workflow activity that will remove macros from all Office 2007 documents it processes. This activity can be used in workflows that kick off automatically for any document posted to one of the externally available document libraries.

Now that we know what we are building, we can begin. The rest of this chapter is going to walk you through the process of building and deploying the custom activity described in the "Removing Macros" scenario. Rather than build the traditional Hello World–type activity, we're going to build one that actually has some value. Among other things, this will help you understand the value of activities, and you'll see what goes into making a real-world solution to a business problem.

The activity we'll build is going to work with a few new features of the Office 2007 System, namely SharePoint v3 document libraries and the new XML file formats. If you are unfamiliar with the new XML-based file formats introduced with Office 2007, see the sidebar "Party Like It's 1997..." for a quick introduction.

PARTY LIKE IT'S 1997...

For those of you who are old like me, you'll remember when Microsoft introduced new Office file formats back with Office 1997. It was a bit painful for a while—you would produce a document or a spreadsheet and send it to someone to review and they wouldn't be able to open it. You would have to save it back to the old format and send it to them again. Certainly not a difficult task, but an annoyance nonetheless and, after doing it a few dozen times, a major annoyance.

Office 2007 again introduces new file formats. It's going to be painful again for a little while. Unlike before, the new file formats are now set as the default format for saving files. That's going to make things worse. Like before, Microsoft is introducing an update for older versions of Office that will allow them to work with the new formats. This time around, however, that update will allow older versions of Office to both read *and* write the new formats. That should make things a little bit easier on everyone.

All of that is interesting, but what do the new formats mean to us as developers? Simple. The new file formats, as I've mentioned, are all XML based. This means that working with them is no different than working with any other XML file. Reading and writing Office files can now be done with familiar XML tools and code. The DOM, XPath, namespaces, and so forth will become even more critical to understand. As developers, the new XML file formats open up a whole new world for us.

For our custom activity, the most important aspect of the new formats we need to understand is the concept of a *package*. Quite simply, a single Office document is in reality not a single, monolithic, binary file anymore. From a user's point of view, nothing is different—they will see one file, and they will interact with one file and never know the difference. As developers, however, we are aware that the single file that looks like an Office document is actually a collection of individual files, packaged and compressed (using the familiar ZIP algorithm). The constituent files that make up the ZIP package represent the elements of the file—styles, content, properties, markup, and so forth. Each of those components is stored in individual XML files within the package—and are therefore called *package parts*. Besides those that I just mentioned, other package parts include images, embedded objects, attachments, and macros. The XML-based parts can be extracted from the package and worked with just like any other XML file. To help facilitate this, Microsoft has introduced a new set of packaging APIs to allow us to work with the new packages.

One final element you should understand is the concept of *relationships*. Rather than dictating naming standards or other rules to define what each part is, and how it interacts with the other parts, relationships are used to define parts and their connections to each other. A part with a relationship type of *style* to the main document content is going to define the stylistic elements for the document. Similarly, a part with a relationship type of *vbaProject* is going to represent the macros contained within the file. We'll be making use of these relationships in our activity.

That's a five-paragraph overview of an element that will have entire chapters devoted to it in other books. It's enough of the important stuff that you can understand the code we'll write in a bit, but is by no means an exhaustive reference. If you'd like to read more, please visit `www.kcdholdings.com` and peruse the list of resources there.

Setting Up the Environment

First, we need to set up our project and explore the activity environment inside Visual Studio, so go ahead and create a new project. The Workflow Extensions for Visual Studio has added a number of project templates to the standard New Project dialog box specifically related to Workflow. We're going to make use of only one of them here: the Workflow Activity Library. Select Workflow for the Project Type and then select Workflow Activity Library for the Template. For this example, I'm going to call the project **KCD.SharePoint.Activities**.

The Visual Studio IDE will open up, looking much like it does for any project we create. The IDE opens up in Design view, which we don't need right now, so you can go ahead and close it.

There are a few steps to walk through to tweak our project before we start coding:

1. In the Solution Explorer, right-click on the `Activity1.cs` file and select Rename from the context menu. Rename the file to **MacroStripperActivity.cs**. Click Yes when you're asked whether you want to rename all references to `Activity1`.
2. In the Solution Explorer, expand the References list and notice the additional assemblies that have been added for our activity:
   - `System.Workflow.Activities`
   - `System.Workflow.ComponentModel`
   - `System.Workflow.Runtime`

   Each of these namespaces provides functionality we need in our activity.
3. Add references to the following assemblies:
   - `WindowsBase`: This one should be near the bottom of the .NET tab in the Add Reference dialog box. It provides access to the packaging APIs to work with the new file formats.
   - `Microsoft.Sharepoint`: Browse to `\Program Files\Common Files\Microsoft Shared\Web Server Extensions\12\ISAPI` to add this one. It gives us access to the majority of the SharePoint APIs.
4. Examine other aspects of our project inside the Solution Explorer. Note that all other aspects of the project are the same as any other class library project in Visual Studio 2005.

Coding the Activity

Continuing on with the process of building our custom activity, it's time to start writing code. We'll be adding code initially to the `MacroStripperActivity` class. This is our Activity Definition class—as I said before, the only one actually required for a valid activity. We'll add the other supporting classes to our activity as we go.

Let's get started:

1. Open the `MacroStripperActivity.cs` file in Code view.
2. Take a minute to review the code provided for us by the template. There are a few items to take note of:
   - The `using` declarations give us access to the necessary components of the WF engine without having to supply the fully qualified name. There are seven declarations related directly to a workflow project, as shown in Listing 5-1.
   - Our namespace declaration defaults to the name of the project. If you're following along at home, my namespace is `KCD.SharePoint.Activities`.
   - Our class declaration itself: `public partial class MacroStripperActivity: SequenceActivity`. Notice that we inherit from the `SequenceActivity` base class. Honestly, I'm not sure why the template is set up that way. Go ahead and change that to inherit just from `Activity`.

Listing 5-1. *The Seven Namespaces Used for Most Workflow Projects*

```
using System.Workflow.ComponentModel.Compiler;
using System.Workflow.ComponentModel.Serialization;
using System.Workflow.ComponentModel;
using System.Workflow.ComponentModel.Design;
using System.Workflow.Runtime;
using System.Workflow.Activities;
using System.Workflow.Activities.Rules;
```

As mentioned earlier, the WF engine is going to be looking for an `Execute` method in our activity to use as its entry point. This is the method that will be called by the engine when our activity is started. The method stub is not provided for us, so we need to add it ourselves.

3. Add the code from Listing 5-2 to our class file.

Listing 5-2. *A Syntactically Correct and Complete Execute Method—It Just Doesn't Do Anything!*

```
protected override ActivityExecutionStatus Execute ➥

(ActivityExecutionContext context)
{
    return ActivityExecutionStatus.Closed;
}
```

Technically, this is the shortest custom activity you can build. It will compile, you can add it to a workflow, and it won't throw any errors. It won't do anything, but it is technically complete. All we've done is provide the required entry point (the `Execute` method) so that the WF runtime can start our activity and then immediately tell the runtime that we are done.

Six statuses are available within the `ActivityExecutionStatus` class referenced in Listing 5-2:

- *Canceling*: Some occurrence during the activity's processing has caused the activity to cancel. Indicate to the runtime that we are canceling.
- *Closed*: The activity has finished its work and the runtime can now proceed with the next activity. This is typically what will be returned during the course of normal processing.
- *Compensating*: The activity is rolling back changes. This status won't be used very often in our Office workflows.
- *Executing*: Return this status to indicate to the runtime that we've initiated some asynchronous tasks or kicked off some child activities and are now signaling that the runtime can proceed to the next step. Note that when the child activities or asynchronous tasks are complete, you'll need to tell the runtime with the `CloseActivity` method of the `ActivityExecutionContext` object. We'll see this in action later on when we build our composite activity.
- *Faulting*: Some occurrence during the activity's processing has caused an error. Indicate this to the runtime.
- *Initialized*: The activity is instantiated and ready to execute. This is an internal status and we will never use it in our code.

Naturally, looking at Listing 5-2, anything we need our activity to do will have to happen before the `return ActivityExecutionStatus.Closed;` line.

To get our activity to actually do what we need it to do, we need to add quite a few lines of code. The next few steps, and their accompanying code listings, take care of this—line numbers are provided for reference only.

■ **Note** If you'd rather not type in all of this code, you can download the source files for this activity from `www.kcdholdings.com`.

---

4. Add some directives at the top of the class to get shorthand access to the namespaces we need, as shown in Listing 5-3.

   Listing 5-3. *Our using Statements*

   ```
   using System.IO;
   using System.IO.Packaging;
   using Microsoft.SharePoint;
   using System.Xml;
   ```

5. The next code we need to type in is shown in Listing 5-4. It fills out the `Execute` method by preparing things for the call to the `RemoveMacros` method, which actually does the work of taking out the macros:

   - Line 1 retrieves an `SPFile` object representing the payload for the current instance of the workflow.
   - Lines 2 and 3 grab some values we'll use later.
   - Lines 4 through 7 check that the payload is a macro-enabled file in one of the new file formats. If it is, we continue processing. If it is not, we skip to the end and just return our status of Closed; our work here is done.
   - The switch statement in lines 11 through 24 sets the file extension for the macro-free file type that corresponds with the macro-enabled file that is the payload.
   - Line 27 sets a custom property so that we can get at this information later.
   - Line 28 opens the payload as a stream and line 29 makes the call to the method that will remove the macros.
   - Line 30 saves the new file back into SharePoint, complete with the updated file extension to indicate that this is a macro-free file.
   - Line 31 removes the original macro-enabled file from the document library.
   - Lines 32, 33, 37, 38, 43, and 44 set some of our custom properties.
   - Line 46 is the return statement we already had in place.

Listing 5-4. *The Meat of Our Execute Method—Accomplishing Some Work Before We Return a Status*

```
SPFile file = PayloadItem.File;
string sFileExtension = Path.GetExtension(file.Name);
this.ParentList = PayloadItem.ParentList;
if (
(sFileExtension.ToLower() == ".docm")
|| (sFileExtension.ToLower() == ".xlsm")
|| (sFileExtension.ToLower() == ".pptm")
)
{
      string sNewFileExtension = string.Empty;
      switch (sFileExtension.ToLower())
      {
          case ".docm":
              sNewFileExtension = ".docx";
              break;
          case ".xlsm":
              sNewFileExtension = ".xlsx";
              break;
          case ".pptm":
              sNewFileExtension = ".pptx";
              break;
          default:
              break;
      }
      try
     {
              this.OriginalDocumentName = file.Name;
              Stream strmFile = file.OpenBinaryStream();
              RemoveMacros(strmFile, sFileExtension);
              PayloadItem.ParentList.RootFolder.Files.Add( ➥
                  PayloadItem.Url.Replace(sFileExtension, ➥
                  sNewFileExtension), strmFile, PayloadItem.Properties, ➥
                  true);
              PayloadItem.Delete();
              this.FinalDocumentName = ➥
                   Path.GetFileName(file.Name).Replace(➥
                   sFileExtension, sNewFileExtension);
              this.IsMacroFree = true;
      }
      catch (Exception ex)
      {
             this.FinalDocumentName = Path.GetFileName(file.Name);
             this.IsMacroFree = false;
      }
}
```

```
41    else
42    {
43        this.FinalDocumentName = Path.GetFileName(file.Name);
44        this.IsMacroFree = true;
45    }
46    return ActivityExecutionStatus.Closed;
```

You'll notice that in various places throughout Listing 5-4 we reference an object called `PayloadItem`. This is a custom property we'll add to our activity in just a few minutes. For now, just know that it stores the `SPListItem` on which the current instance of the workflow is running.

The last major piece of code we need to add to our activity is responsible for actually stripping the macros out of the file and converting the file to an Office 2007 macro-free document type. This is the `RemoveMacros` call made in line 29 of Listing 5-4. Listing 5-5 handles this chore.

Note The code for the `RemoveMacros` method was adapted from a Visual Studio 2005 Code Snippet for the Open XML file formats provided by Microsoft. I would love to claim credit for it, because it's some pretty nifty stuff. However, anybody who knows me will tell you that I'm not that good a programmer... so thank you to the nameless Microsoft employee who put this little gem together. If you'd like to get your sweaty little hands on the code snippets (and I highly recommend that you do), I'll post a link to it on my web site: `www.kcdholdings.com`.

Line numbers in Listing 5-5 are for reference only, but here's a quick rundown of the interesting bits of the action:

- Lines 5 through 8 set up constants. Relationships in the Office 2007 file formats are identified via a URI. These constants store those URI strings.
- The switch statement in lines 11 through 27 sets a URI indicating the macro-free content type URI for each particular type of file—Word, Excel, or PowerPoint.
- Line 28 checks whether we have a valid content type. If we don't, we skip to the end. If we do, we continue on.
- Line 30 opens our package file from the `FileStream` object passed in as a parameter.
- Lines 35 through 40 retrieve the root package part—we'll use this as our launching point to retrieve the other parts that interest us.
- Lines 42 through 47 locate and delete a part with a relationship type matching the `vbaRelationship` URI we specified back in line 6, relative to the root part.
- Lines 48 through 57 do some XML manipulation to remove the node that contains the VBA relationship information.
- Lines 58 through 64 delete and re-create the document part. This is the only way to reset the package to be of a macro-free content type.
- Line 65 closes the package, which writes all of our modifications back to the `FileStream`.

Listing 5-5. *The RemoveMacros Method*

```
        private void RemoveMacros(Stream fs, string sFileExtension)
        {
            // Adapted from code in the Open XML File Formats Code Snippets
            // provided by Microsoft
            const string relationshipType = @"http://schemas.openxmlformats.org➥
                /officeDocument/2006/relationships/officeDocument";
            const string vbaRelationshipType = @"http://schemas.microsoft.com/➥
                office/2006/relationships/vbaProject";
            const string relationshipNamespace = @"http://schemas.openxmlformats. ➥
                org/package/2006/relationships";
            const string vbaFreeRelsContentType = @"application/vnd. ➥
                openxmlformats-package.relationships+xml";
            string vbaFreeContentType = string.Empty;
            Uri relsUri = null;
            switch (sFileExtension.ToLower())
            {
                case ".docm":
                    vbaFreeContentType = @"application/vnd.openxmlformats-➥
                        officedocument.wordprocessingml.document.main+xml";
                    relsUri = new Uri("/word/_rels/document.xml.rels", ➥
                        UriKind.Relative);
                    break;
                case ".xlsm":
                    vbaFreeContentType = @"application/vnd.openxmlformats-➥
                        officedocument.spreadsheetml.sheet.main+xml";
                    relsUri = new Uri("/xl/_rels/workbook.xml.rels", ➥
                        UriKind.Relative);
                    break;
                case ".pptm":
                    vbaFreeContentType = @"application/vnd.openxmlformats-➥
                        officedocument.presentationml.presentation.main+xml";
                    relsUri = new Uri("/ppt/_rels/presentation.xml.rels", ➥
                        UriKind.Relative);
                    break;
                default:
                    break;
            }
            if ((vbaFreeContentType != string.Empty) && (relsUri != null))
            {
                using (Package onePackage = Package.Open(fs, FileMode.Open, ➥
                    FileAccess.ReadWrite))
                {
                    PackagePart startPart = null;
                    Uri startPartUri = null;
```

```
                foreach (System.IO.Packaging.PackageRelationship relationship➥
                      in onePackage.GetRelationshipsByType(relationshipType))
                {
                    startPartUri = PackUriHelper.ResolvePartUri(new Uri("/",➥
                          UriKind.Relative), relationship.TargetUri);
                    startPart = onePackage.GetPart(startPartUri);
                    break;
                }
                PackagePart relsPart = onePackage.GetPart(relsUri);
                foreach (System.IO.Packaging.PackageRelationship relationship➥
                    in startPart.GetRelationshipsByType(vbaRelationshipType))
                {
                    Uri vbaUri = PackUriHelper.ResolvePartUri(startPartUri, ➥
                        relationship.TargetUri);
                    onePackage.DeletePart(vbaUri);
                    break;
                }
                NameTable nt = new NameTable();
                XmlNamespaceManager nsManager = new XmlNamespaceManager(nt);
                nsManager.AddNamespace("r", relationshipNamespace);
                XmlDocument xDocRels = new XmlDocument(nt);
                xDocRels.Load(relsPart.GetStream());
                XmlNode vbaNode = xDocRels.SelectSingleNode(➥
                      @"//r:Relationship[@Target='vbaProject.bin']", ➥
                      nsManager);
                if (vbaNode != null)
                {
                    vbaNode.ParentNode.RemoveChild(vbaNode);
                }
                XmlDocument xdoc = new XmlDocument(nt);
                xdoc.Load(startPart.GetStream());
                onePackage.DeletePart(startPart.Uri);
                relsPart = onePackage.CreatePart(relsUri, ➥
                      vbaFreeRelsContentType);
                startPart = onePackage.CreatePart(startPartUri, ➥
                      vbaFreeContentType);
                xDocRels.Save(relsPart.GetStream(FileMode.Create, ➥
                      FileAccess.Write));
                xdoc.Save(startPart.GetStream(FileMode.Create, ➥
                      FileAccess.Write));
                onePackage.Close();
            }
        }
    }
```

So, we've nearly completed our activity. The hard-core code is done; we have just a few more things to take care of. First we need to set up the `PayloadItem` property that we referenced in our code earlier. We'll take care of that next.

Adding Custom Properties

Custom properties for an activity are functionality equivalent to custom properties on other .NET components. There are two ways to implement these properties, though—as regular component properties or as dependency properties. We're going to take a look at both approaches as we progress through our examples. I will assume that you are familiar with regular properties using member variables, and so won't cover them in any great detail here. For more information on dependency properties, see the sidebar "Dependency Properties Are Your Friends."

DEPENDENCY PROPERTIES ARE YOUR FRIENDS

Among other things, dependency properties in our Office workflows give us the ability to tie our activity properties to values that will not exist until runtime. Typically, this is going to be something from the `WorkflowProperties` collection, but there is nothing that says it has to be. In our example, we're tying our `PayloadItem` dependency property to whatever `SPListItem` the workflow is running on. When the workflow executes, that value will be available to us, but it is not available at design time. We can't even code for it in our activity because the bridge from the activity to the workflow won't exist until runtime.

At design time, the property is rendered as shown here. We can specify what value we want, and can operate on the object as an `SPListItem`.

⊟ PayloadItem
Name
Path

This isn't to say that you should always use dependency properties. If the property you are working on is not dependent on the specific workflow instance—for example, you just need to collect a simple string from the Designer—you can write regular component-type properties with a member variable backing it up.

Dependency properties are great for when you need them, but otherwise, they just introduce overhead and complexity. So, if you need them—great, use them. If not, keep things simple and use regular properties.

We'll start with dependency properties. In their ongoing effort to be helpful, Microsoft has provided us with a very easy way to add new dependency properties to our workflow activities through the Code Snippet functionality introduced in Visual Studio 2005. Within the Workflow category is a snippet for inserting a dependency property. Use that snippet to insert a skeleton into our class file. Make the few modifications necessary to convert the snippet to the contents of Listing 5-6 and our custom property is complete.

Listing 5-6. *The Final Source for Our Custom Property Definition*

```
public static DependencyProperty PayloadItemProperty =➥
    DependencyProperty.Register("PayloadItem", typeof(➥
    Microsoft.SharePoint.SPListItem),➥
    typeof(KCD.SharePoint.Activities.MacroStripperActivity));
```

```
        [DesignerSerializationVisibilityAttribute(➥
    DesignerSerializationVisibility.Visible)]
        [BrowsableAttribute(true)]
        [DescriptionAttribute("List Item the Workflow is operating upon")]
        [CategoryAttribute("Configuration")]
        public SPListItem PayloadItem
        {
            get
            {
                return
((SPListItem)(base.GetValue(KCD.SharePoint.Activities.MacroStripperActivity.➥
                    PayloadItemProperty)));
            }
            set
            {
                            base.SetValue(KCD.MacroStripper.➥
                    PayloadItemProperty, (SPListItem)value);
                     (SPListItem)value);

            }

        }
```

Each of the attributes decorating our property in Listing 5-6 means something different to Visual Studio and the Workflow Designer. They are described briefly in Table 5-3.

Table 5-3. *Design-Time Property Attributes*

Attribute	Description
`DesignerSerializationVisibilityAttribute`	Controls how the property will be serialized. Possible values for this attribute are: `Visible`: Specifies that the property should be serialized. Use this value for simple properties. `Hidden`: Specifies that the property should not be serialized. `Content`: Specifies that contents of the object should be serialized. Use this value for complex properties and collections.
`ValidationVisibilityAttribute`	Controls validation of the values supplied for the property by the workflow builder. Possible values for this attribute are: `Optional`: The property can be null. `Required`: The workflow builder must supply a value. `Hidden`: No validation will occur.
`BrowsableAttribute`	Controls whether or not the property is displayed in the Properties window. Possible values are `true` or `false`.

Table 5-3. *Design-Time Property Attributes*

Attribute	Description
`DescriptionAttribute`	A brief description of the property to help the workflow builder understand what the property is used for. This is displayed in the Properties window of Visual Studio.
`CategoryAttribute`	Indicates the category in which the property appears within the Properties window of Visual Studio.

That takes care of an example of using a dependency property, but as I said, you don't always need a dependency property. Sometimes a regular old simple property will do the trick quite nicely. Listings 5-7 through 5-10 show the standard properties that we need for our solution.

Listing 5-7. *Nothing Special Here—Just a Regular Old Property*

```
private string _finalDocumentName;
      [DesignerSerializationVisibilityAttribute(DesignerSerializationVisibility.➥
          Visible)]
      [BrowsableAttribute(false)]
      [DescriptionAttribute("Name of macro-free document in Document Library")]
      [CategoryAttribute("Configuration")]
      public string FinalDocumentName
      {
          get { return _finalDocumentName; }
          set { _finalDocumentName = value; }
      }
```

You'll notice in Listing 5-7 that this property is not going to show up in the Properties window because its `BrowsableAttribute` is set to `false`. This property is going to be accessed in our Workflow code in Chapter 6 to retrieve the name of the macro-free document.

Next up (Listing 5-8) is another property that is only used in code. This time it is the opposite of the previous property—it stores the original name of the document before we started tearing it apart and looking to put it back together again.

Listing 5-8. *A Property to Store the Original Name of Our Payload's Document*

```
private string _originalDocumentName;
[DesignerSerializationVisibilityAttribute(DesignerSerializationVisibility.Visible)]
[BrowsableAttribute(false)]
[DescriptionAttribute("Original name of document in Document Library")]
[CategoryAttribute("Configuration")]
```

```
public string OriginalDocumentName
{
    get { return _originalDocumentName; }
    set { _originalDocumentName = value; }
}
```

One more property is shown in Listing 5-9. This time around, we're storing a reference to the SPList that our workflow is running within. As before, this is going to be used later in Chapter 6.

Listing 5-9. *Setting Up Our ParentList Property*

```
private SPList _parentList;
[DesignerSerializationVisibilityAttribute(DesignerSerializationVisibility.Visible)]
[BrowsableAttribute(false)]
[DescriptionAttribute("SPList item containing document")]
[CategoryAttribute("Configuration")]
public SPList ParentList
{
    get { return _parentList; }
    set { _parentList = value; }
}
```

Last but not least, we need to set up a property we can check from the workflow to see whether or not we successfully removed the macros from the file. Listing 5-10 shows this code.

Listing 5-10. *The IsMacroFree Property*

```
private bool _isMacroFree = false;
[DesignerSerializationVisibilityAttribute(DesignerSerializationVisibility.Visible)]
[BrowsableAttribute(false)]
[DescriptionAttribute("Indicates whether resulting document is free of macros")]
[CategoryAttribute("Configuration")]
public bool IsMacroFree
{
    get { return _isMacroFree; }
    set { _isMacroFree = value; }
}
```

Wrapping It All Up

Technically, our activity is complete. We don't *have* to do anything more to it. If we stop here, though, there are a few problems:

- Our activity is ugly (and its mother dresses it funny). Right now if a developer were to add our activity to a workflow, it would look like Figure 5-1. While OK, it is a little dull. We need to add some flash and pizzazz.
- In a similar vein, the icon representing our activity in the Visual Studio Toolbox is the generic gear—not very appealing.

- There is nothing in our activity that verifies that the user has supplied a valid value for the `PayloadItem` property.

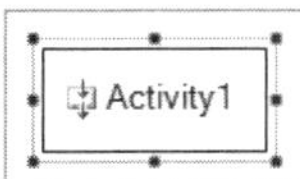

Figure 5-1. *The default look of an activity is dull, dull, boring.*

So, we have a little work still ahead of us after all. Let's start with the Activity Designer.

Activity Designer Class

The Activity Designer class is responsible for controlling the behavior and appearance of our activity in the Visual Studio environment. There are a few somewhat esoteric things that the Activity Designer can do, but the main things it is responsible for are

- Rendering our activity when it is dropped onto the Workflow Designer canvas
- Controlling the actions available on the context menu for our activity (in activity-lingo, these are known as *verbs*, and we'll cover how to add new ones in Chapter 9)

For now, all we're going to do is add a little eye candy to our activity—we'll make it look a bit nicer than the default. Before we get to the code to make this happen, let's take a look at what we're aiming for. Figure 5-2 shows the end result of our Activity Designer class—a little more appealing than the default presentation, no?

Figure 5-2. *The end result of our Activity Designer class is a more visually appealing activity.*

So, how do we get to Figure 5-2 from Figure 5-1? It actually involves *two* classes and a few overridden methods, but all in all it's pretty easy. To begin with, we need to declare our Activity Designer class. Listing 5-11 shows this piece. Looking at this code, you'll see that this class is also decorated with an attribute—`ActivityDesignerTheme`. We'll get to that in just a few minutes.

Listing 5-11. *Declaring an Activity Designer Class for Our Activity*

```
[ActivityDesignerTheme(typeof(MacroStripperDesignerTheme))]
public class MacroStripperDesigner : ActivityDesigner
{
```

The visual appearance of our activity is controlled by three rectangles:

- The rectangle bounding the entire activity
- The rectangle controlling the size and placement of the text space
- The rectangle controlling the size and placement of the image space

Listing 5-12 shows the code to specify the size of our activity. For this first rectangle (bounding the entire activity), this is all we can specify. You'll notice that I have specified a size for our activity that is wider than the default size for the Microsoft activities. This is to resolve a minor annoyance I have with the default activities—the name of the activity wraps across multiple lines, making it annoying to read. There is plenty of horizontal space on the Designer—why not make use of it? If you're a purist, the default dimensions are 91 pixels by 43 pixels. Just change the arguments of your Size object and you're back to conformity... boring.

Listing 5-12. *Specifying the Size of our Activity As It Is Drawn on the Workflow Designer Canvas*

```
protected override Size OnLayoutSize(ActivityDesignerLayoutEventArgs e)
{
     base.OnLayoutSize(e);
     return new Size(200, 45);
}
```

■ **Note** Technically, we can control the entire presentation of our activity by overriding the OnPaint event and handling all of the drawing ourselves. While I understand the appeal to this and appreciate the technical challenge, I'm not sure I see the value in taking things to this level. If you disagree, there are some neat samples floating around of highly customized activity presentations—including at least one that shows an animated GIF for your activity. It's pure eye candy, but neat in small doses.

The next two rectangles are controlled by overriding a few properties from our base class. The first is a property called ImageRectangle and controls the size and placement of the image for the activity (clever, huh?). The code for this is shown in Listing 5-13. The second is called—wait for it—TextRectangle. The code is in Listing 5-14. In both cases, the code calculates the size and placement of a Rectangle object based on the size of the activity rectangle (this.Bounds) and some simple math.

Listing 5-13. *Setting Up the Placement of Our Activity's Image*

```
protected override Rectangle ImageRectangle
{
     get
     {
         Rectangle rectActivity = this.Bounds;
         Size size = new Size(20, 20);
         Rectangle rectImage = new Rectangle();
         rectImage.X = rectActivity.Left + 5;
         rectImage.Y = rectActivity.Top + ((rectActivity.Height - size.Height) / 2);
         rectImage.Width = size.Width;
         rectImage.Height = size.Height;
         return rectImage;
     }
}
```

Listing 5-14. *Setting Up the Placement of Our Activity's Text*

```
protected override Rectangle TextRectangle
{
     get
     {
          Rectangle rectActivity = this.Bounds;
          Size size = new Size(170, 40);
          Rectangle rectText = new Rectangle();
          rectText.X = this.ImageRectangle.Right + 5;
          rectText.Y = rectActivity.Top + 2;
          rectText.Size = size;
          return rectText;
     }
}
```

The last piece for this class is to load the image that gets displayed with our activity. The code is shown in Listing 5-15. If you skip this step, the default image will be loaded. Looking at Listing 5-15, you'll see that we're loading the image from a resource. In order for this to work, you'll need to add an image resource to your project.

Listing 5-15. *Loading the Image for Our Activity*

```
protected override void Initialize(Activity activity)
{
     base.Initialize(activity);
     Bitmap img = KCD.SharePoint.Activities.Properties.Resources.➥
          MacroStripperImage;
     this.Image = img;
}
```

That's it for the Activity Designer class. With that done, we can go back to our MacroStripperActivity class declaration and decorate it with the following attribute: `[Designer(typeof(MacroStripperDesigner))]`. This causes our Activity to make use of the new Designer we just created.

ActivityDesignerTheme

The next piece to take care of is the `ActivityDesignerTheme` class referenced in the attributes decorating our Activity Designer as shown in Listing 5-11. The Activity Designer class controlled the structure of our activity; `ActivityDesignerTheme` controls the colors, the look, and various other visual elements. All of the code we are using is shown in Listing 5-16. This code is pretty straightforward. We set a few colors and set the background.

Listing 5-16. *The ActivityDesignerTheme Class, Which Controls the Color and Styling of Our Activity*

```
public class MacroStripperDesignerTheme : ActivityDesignerTheme
{
```

```
    public MacroStripperDesignerTheme(WorkflowTheme theme)➥
          : base(theme)
    {
        BackColorStart = Color.White;
        BackColorEnd = Color.LightSlateGray;
        BackgroundStyle = System.Drawing.Drawing2D.LinearGradientMode.Horizontal;
        ForeColor = Color.Black;
    }
}
```

We're done with the modifications to our activity's appearance inside the Visual Studio Designer canvas. Jump back to Figure 5-2 if you forget what we were aiming for. It wasn't a lot of code, which is good, and it makes things look a little nicer. If you or your company plan on making a number of activities—and certainly if that is part of the business you're in—it would probably be a good idea to settle on a single Activity Designer class used for all of your activities. It will help lend some cohesion and allow workflow builders to differentiate between your custom activities and those that come out-of-the-box.

■ **Note** If you load your activity's class file in the visual designer, it will still look like Figure 5-1. This view does not reflect our customizations. One other thing, while I'm at it—the `ActivityDesigner` and `ActivityDesignerTheme` classes are only refreshed when you shut down Visual Studio. So if you make changes to this class and rebuild your project, you won't see the changes until you restart Visual Studio.

ToolboxItem Class

The next class we're going to tackle not only handles a visual element of our activity—the icon that shows up in the Visual Studio Toolbox—but also does some work when our activity is dropped on the canvas. For this first look at ToolBoxItem, we're not going to do anything when the activity is dropped on the canvas—we'll be taking a look at that when we build a composite activity later in the chapter. Typically you would use this functionality to control the adding and removing of child activities on a composite activity, so for now, we're simply going to change the icon shown in the Toolbox.

■ **Note** This isn't to say that you can't use the ToolboxItem class to control the events when a simple activity is dropped onto the canvas. You can. It's just more useful for composite activities.

In order to show the icon we want to in the toolbox, we need to take care of a couple of things. While we're at it, we're going to change the contents of the tooltip that pops up when we mouse over our activity in the Toolbox. None of this is going to make or break your activity, but it can be some nice icing to throw on top to really wrap things up.

Listing 5-17 shows the code for our class. It's all pretty self-explanatory. There are two overridden constructors—the first is empty, but necessary nonetheless; the second contains our custom code. The first line deserializes the class. The next three lines configure the text to be displayed on the tooltip. The last line sets the icon shown in the Toolbox to the picture we want to display.

Listing 5-17. *The ActivityToolboxItem Class, Used to Customize Our Activity in the Visual Studio Toolbox*

```
[Serializable]
    internal class MacroStripperToolboxItem : ActivityToolboxItem
    {
        public MacroStripperToolboxItem(Type type): base(type)
        {
        }

        private MacroStripperToolboxItem(SerializationInfo info, ➥
                StreamingContext context)
        {
            this.Deserialize(info, context);
            this.Description = "Remove Macros from Office 2007 Documents";
            this.Company = "KCD Holdings, Inc.";
            this.DisplayName = "Macro Stripper";
            this.Bitmap = new Bitmap(KCD.SharePoint.Activities.Properties.➥
                Resources.MacroStripper);
        }
    }
```

The last piece of code we need to add is an attribute on our activity class to tell it to use the ToolboxItem class. Add the following to the attributes already decorating our activity class: `[ToolboxItem(typeof(MacroStripperToolboxItem))]`. That's it—our activity will now use the custom `ToolboxItem`.

We're just about done. The last thing we need to do is add the image we want to use for the icon as a resource. The image needs to be 16 ×16 and 256 colors. Copy it into your application directory and then use the Properties window for our project to add the existing file as a resource. Verify that the file properties for the item are configured as an embedded resource and you're all set.

So there you are, a custom `ToolboxItem` class for our activity. Figure 5-3 shows the end result of our efforts. Again, pure eye candy at this point, but a nice touch nonetheless. When we revisit the `ToolboxItem` class for the composite activity, we'll see a few more tricks it can do. For now, let's move on to our validator.

Figure 5-3. *Our custom activity and its tooltip, as shown in the Toolbox*

Validator Class

The intention of the validator class is to obviously check—at design and again at compilation—that the various properties of our activity have been set. The goal we're aiming for is to have our activity act the same as the out-of-the-box activities—complete with the error notification in the visual designer in the form of the exclamation point in the red circle on the activity itself and in the Properties window, as well as the smart tag link to the offending property as appropriate.

Sounds like a pretty tall order. It might be time to call in Aunt Matilda. The good news is that it's actually dirt simple—fewer than 20 lines of code—and over half are open or close braces.

If you remember back a few pages to our Activity Definition class, you'll recall that we have five properties defined, but only one that is editable by the workflow builder through the Properties window—`PayloadItem`. It is of type `SPListItem` and stores the `SPListItem` that the current instance of the workflow is acting upon. We use it in our activity to access the ListItem and grab the document we need to strip macros from.

We won't be able to do much if that property isn't set, so we really want to make sure that it is. Also thinking back to the Activity Definition, you'll recall that we set this as a dependency property. This does complicate things just a little, but as you'll see, not too badly.

To begin with, we need to add another class. This one will derive from `ActivityValidator` and contain a single overridden method. Listing 5-18 shows the full source for this one. Again, line numbers are only for reference. Here's a quick rundown of the interesting bits:

- Line 5 creates a `ValidationErrorCollection` object and populates it by calling the `Validate` method of our base type. This ensures that if there are other validation errors caught by the base functionality, we will still report them.

- Line 6 casts the `obj` parameter as an instance of our activity.

- Line 7 checks that we need to continue our validation. The first check ensures that our validator is indeed being used for our activity. The second check makes sure that we're running in the Visual Studio Designer (or another designer) and not as part of the compilation of our validator class itself. If we don't have a parent, then we're not part of a workflow.

- Line 9 is the bit that is different because we used a dependency property. The call to `IsBindingSet` checks to see whether our property is bound to a property of the workflow. While technically our property still does not have a value at design time, this binding will ensure that we have one at runtime and so we'll let it slide for now.

- If we get to line 11, we know that we're not bound, so we need to check our property value. If it's null, we add a new `ValidationError` to our `ValidationErrorCollection` in line 13.

- Line 13 looks pretty innocuous, but it is really the heart of our validation. The parameter we pass in to the `GetNotSetValidationError` method is the name of our property. Behind the scenes, this is what generates our smart tag notification and wires it up to the correct property in the Properties window. Good stuff.

- Finally, line 17 returns our `ValidationErrorCollection` object, which contains our errors as well as errors added from the base class.

Listing 5-18. *The Validator Class, Which Ensures That Our PayloadItem Property Has a Value*

```
public class MacroStripperActivityValidator : ActivityValidator
{
   public override ValidationErrorCollection Validate(ValidationManager
      manager, object obj)
   {
      ValidationErrorCollection activityErrors = base.Validate(manager,
         obj);
      MacroStripperActivity msa = obj as MacroStripperActivity;
      if ((null != msa) && (null != msa.Parent))
      {
         if (!msa.IsBindingSet(MacroStripperActivity.PayloadItemProperty))
         {
            if (msa.GetValue(MacroStripperActivity.PayloadItemProperty)
               == null)
            {
               activityErrors.Add(ValidationError.
                  GetNotSetValidationError("PayloadItem"));
            }
         }
      }
      return activityErrors;
   }
}
```

Note All of the supporting classes we've added—designer, theme, toolbox item, and now validator—can be either added to the same source file as our Designer or moved out to separate source files. It's really a matter of preference. It makes no difference to the functionality.

As before, we need to associate our custom validator with our activity. Once again, this is done with an attribute. Add this code to the growing list of attributes decorating our activity: `[ActivityValidator(typeof(MacroStripperActivityValidator))]`.

The end result of this class is that our validation now looks and acts just like the built-in validation. Figure 5-4 shows the end result.

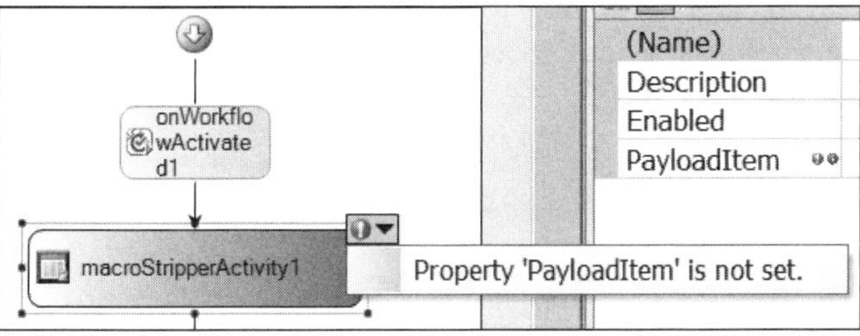

Figure 5-4. *Our validation is now fully integrated—just like the out-of-the-box activities.*

Finishing and Compiling

If you're impatient like me, you've been doing interim compilations as you completed each class. That's fine. But now it's time to compile the whole activity for real.

Keep your fingers crossed.

Congratulations! You have just built your first WF activity.

Deploying Our Activity

So perhaps those congratulations seem a bit empty. After all, we don't really have anything to show for our work yet. Our activity has compiled but all we have is a DLL—not much to write home about. We can't run the activity directly and see it work. This is one drawback to any component development effort and it certainly applies to activities.

Fortunately, deploying activities is easy; they're just components, after all. There are the two standard options, neither of which should be foreign to you if you've done .NET development before:

- *Deploy to the global assembly cache (GAC)*: Requires the standard steps—strong naming, GACUtil, etc.
- *Deploy to the file system*: Requires a simple file system copy

For the purposes of this book, either option is fine. In either case, you then just need to add the assembly to the Toolbox manually. This is no different than adding any other component. As I've been told I have an unerring ability to state the obvious; however, I'll walk you through managing activities in the Toolbox in Chapter 6.

So now we have our custom activity built and deployed, but we still need a workflow to test it with. We'll cover that in the next chapter. Right now it's time to cover the other half of the activity-writing world—composite activities.

Building a Custom Composite Activity

We just spent 20 or so pages building a simple activity. Now we're going to turn our attention to building a custom composite activity. Don't worry; it won't take another 20 pages. I'll move through this material a little faster—covering mostly just the deltas.

As we covered back in the introduction to this chapter, composite activities are constructs for allowing workflow builders to control the flow of their workflow by dictating the path taken through the process and which activities execute under which circumstances, as well as the execution of actions before, during, or after the activities added by the workflow builder are executed. Either usage is a perfectly valid one for composite activities.

The composite activity we are going to build is going to be of the latter variety—it will execute some actions prior to executing any activities added by the workflow builder.

Scenario: Logging Workflow Processing

As KCD makes its way through workflow-enabling its processes, the developers find themselves with a common scenario that comes into play repeatedly. One of these is a requirement for logging. Quite often they need to add logging to their workflows to write information out to the history log for the workflow. Occasionally, this information is needed during development but not necessary during production.

The process of adding and configuring a bunch of LogToHistoryList activities is tedious. On the opposite end of the spectrum, taking the time to remove or disable them all before deploying to production is equally tedious.

There has to be a better way...

Fortunately, there is. Creating a custom composite activity that includes the logging component is pretty simple. Taking things one step further, adding a condition that controls the circumstances under which the logging happens is even easier.

After creating this component, workflow builders will be able to add it to their workflows, add their components to it, and set a global variable to control whether or not the logging happens.

Let's get started.

Setting Up the Environment

The beginning of our process for a composite activity is no different than that for a simple activity.

1. Create a project based on the Workflow Activity Library project template. For this example, I'm naming my project **KCD.Sharepoint.Activities.Composite**.

2. Close the Designer window that opens by default.

3. Rename the `Activity1.cs` file to **LoggerActivity.cs**.

4. Add references to the following assemblies:

   - `Microsoft.Sharepoint`
   - `Microsoft.Sharepoint.WorkflowActions`

5. Open the `LoggerActivity.cs` file in Code view.

6. Add the following to the top of the file with the rest of the `using` statements: `using Microsoft.SharePoint.WorkflowActions;`.

Part of the functionality of a composite activity is to control the execution of its children (wow, taken out of context, that sentence ends in a very dark, disturbing way). What this means is that not only does our activity need to initiate the execution of each child activity, it also needs to listen for the event fired when the child is finished executing so it can inform the runtime that the child activity is closed. In order to listen for this event, we need to implement an interface: `IActivityEventListener`. Right now, our class inherits from `SequenceActivity`, which is fine. We just need to add the interface information to the end of it. Add the following to the end of the class line, immediately after SequenceActivity:

```
, IActivityEventListener < ActivityExecutionStatusChangedEventArgs >
```

Yes, the comma is required.

The next piece of code we need to add is for two dependency properties. We covered dependency properties in the simple activity earlier so I won't rehash it here. Flip back to the "Adding Custom Properties" section if you need a refresher, but the Code Snippet really makes this a pretty simple operation. The first dependency property is going to be called Condition and is of type ActivityCondition. This property will be used to determine whether we should write anything to the log. Because this property is of type ActivityCondition, it will be displayed in the Visual Studio Properties window just like Condition properties for other activities—which we'll look at further in Chapters 6 and 8. As mentioned in the scenario, we are going to be tying this property to a global variable so that workflow builders can control the logging for their entire workflow from a single place.

The next dependency property we need to add is a Boolean flag used to indicate whether our activity is executing. As we'll see, this will tie into the process of catching the event fired when our child activities finish processing. We'll call it Running and as mentioned, it is of type bool.

We'll see both of these properties in action in just a moment. Next, though, we need to revisit our old friend the Execute method. Remember, it is this method that is called by the workflow host to start our activity processing.

Coding the Activity

Listing 5-19 shows the full contents of our Execute method. As before, line numbers are included for reference only. Here's a rundown of what happens in the method:

- Lines 3 and 4 set some values so that we can keep track of the process of our activity. Running is the property we created earlier. ActivityStarted is a local variable used to flag that our activity has started a child activity running. We'll use it at the end to determine what value to return.

- Line 5 checks the Condition property we set up by calling its Evaluate method. If the condition set by the workflow builder indicates we should do some logging, we'll continue on with lines 6 through 16. Otherwise, we jump right to line 18 and begin executing our child activities.

- Lines 7–16 loop through our child activities looking for the logging activity, which we actually add in the ToolboxItem class in just a few minutes. In the ToolboxItem class we will set a value in the UserData property so we could identify our activity here.

- Line 18 begins a loop through the child activities of our composite activity that have their Enabled property set to true. This loop ends on line 27.

- Line 23 is where we set things up to be able to catch the event fired off when our child activity finishes executing. We make use of the generic RegisterForStatusChange method and pass in a parameter that specifies what event it is that we are looking for—Activity.ClosedEvent.

- Line 24 actually executes our child activity within the context passed in for our activity.
- Line 25 sets our `ActivityStarted` variable so that we know that we have launched at least one child activity.
- Because they are contained within the loop started on line 18, lines 23–25 execute once for each enabled child activity.
- Line 28 sets up our return value based on whether or not we started up any child activities. If we did, we return a value indicating that our activity is still running. We'll take care of closing out our activity when we handle the close events for our children. If we did not fire up any child activities, we just pass back a value indicating that our activity is closed and done processing.

Listing 5-19. *The Execute Method for Our Composite Activity*

```
1   protected override ActivityExecutionStatus Execute(➥
        ActivityExecutionContext executionContext)
2   {
3       this.Running = true;
4       bool ActivityStarted = false;
5       If (this.Condition.Evaluate(this, executionContext))
6       {
7           for (int i = 0; i < this.Activities.Count; i++)
8           {
9               if ((string)this.Activities[i].UserData["logger"] == "logger")
10              {
11                  LogToHistoryListActivity logger = (➥
                      LogToHistoryListActivity)this.Activities[i];
12                  logger.HistoryDescription = string.Format(@"Begin ➥
13                      Activity Execution:{0} with {1} enabled Children", ➥
                      this.QualifiedName, ➥
                      this.EnabledActivities.Count.ToString());
14                  break;
15              }
16          }
17      }
18       for (int childNum = 0; childNum < this.EnabledActivities.Count; ➥
           childNum++)
19       {
20           Activity child = this.EnabledActivities[childNum] as Activity;
21           if (null != child)
22           {
23               child.RegisterForStatusChange(Activity.ClosedEvent, this);
24               executionContext.ExecuteActivity(child);
25               ActivityStarted = true;
26           }
27       }
```

```
        return ActivityStarted? ActivityExecutionStatus.Executing : ➥
          ActivityExecutionStatus.Closed;
    }
```

Next up is our event to process our child activities as they close. Listing 5-20 shows the code for this, and here is a rundown of the highlights:

- Line 6 causes our activity to stop listening to events for the particular child that we're running for now. Since we have already received the `Closed` event for this child, there is no need to keep listening.
- Line 12 is the real meat of this method. It is contained within another loop through all enabled child activities so it will process for all child activities. It is responsible for checking the execution status of all of the child activities of our activity. If one of those children has a status of anything other than Initialized or Closed, then we can't close yet. If, however, all of the child activities are in one of those two states, then it is safe to close our activity.
- Line 16 handles the process of notifying our workflow host that we are done processing. It will only execute if the check in line 15 indicates that we are done; all of our child activities are done processing.

Listing 5-20. *Listening for Our Child Activities to Finish*

```
1    void IActivityEventListener<ActivityExecutionStatusChangedEventArgs>.➥
                OnEvent(object sender, ActivityExecutionStatusChangedEventArgs e)
2    {
3        ActivityExecutionContext context = sender as ➥
   ActivityExecutionContext;
4        if (e.ExecutionStatus == ActivityExecutionStatus.Closed)
5        {
6            e.Activity.UnregisterForStatusChange(Activity.ClosedEvent, this);
7            LoggerActivity lgr = context.Activity as LoggerActivity;
8            bool finished = true;
9            for (int childNum = 0; childNum < lgr.EnabledActivities.Count; ➥
               childNum++)
10            {
11                Activity child = lgr.EnabledActivities[childNum];
12                if ((child.ExecutionStatus != ActivityExecutionStatus. ➥
                  Initialized) && (child.ExecutionStatus != ➥
                  ActivityExecutionStatus.Closed))
13                    finished = false;
14            }
15            if (finished)
16                context.CloseActivity();
17        }
18    }
```

The last code for our Activity Definition class is to handle the cancellation of our activity—for any number of reasons. We'll cover cancellation in Chapter 9, but for now, just know that if our composite activity is canceled, we need to handle canceling all of our child activities. Listing 5-21 shows this code. The code for this method is pretty straightforward. As with the previous two listings, we loop through all of our enabled child activities (lines 4 through 14). Line 7 checks to see whether our current child activity is currently executing. If it is, line 9 cancels it and line 10 sets a local variable that indicates we have just canceled a child activity. Lines 12 through 14 repeat a similar pattern, this time for child activities in a Faulting state. Finally in line 15 we determine our return value. If all of our child activities were closed before we got to them, we can tell our host that we are finished. If we had to signal a child activity to close, we return a value of `Canceling`.

Listing 5-21. *Handling the Potentiality of Canceling Our Children When We Are Canceled*

```
1     protected override ActivityExecutionStatus Cancel(ActivityExecutionContext➥
               executionContext)
2     {
3         bool cancelled = true;
4         for (int childNum = 0; childNum < this.EnabledActivities.Count; ➥
             childNum++)
5         {
6             Activity child = this.EnabledActivities[childNum];
7             if (child.ExecutionStatus == ActivityExecutionStatus.Executing)
8             {
9                 executionContext.CancelActivity(child);
10                 cancelled = false;
11             }
12             else if ((child.ExecutionStatus == ➥
              ActivityExecutionStatus.Canceling) || (child.ExecutionStatus ➥
              == ActivityExecutionStatus.Faulting))
13                 cancelled = false;
14         }
15         return cancelled ? ActivityExecutionStatus.Canceling : ➥
      ActivityExecutionStatus.Closed;
16     }
```

That does it for the Activity Definition class.

Just as with our simple activity earlier, a composite activity is made up of multiple classes. We covered all the standard ones back in the simple activity. We're going to touch on some of them again here, but only as deep as we need to in order to build our composite activity. If you're interested in looking at these in further detail, we took care of that earlier in the chapter.

The first "other" class we're going to look at is the `ActivityToolboxItem` class. The class file is not listed in the Solution Explorer in Visual Studio so we're going to have to add it fresh. Add a new class file named `LoggerActivityToolboxItem.cs`.

The first thing we need to add is some `using` statements, and then set up our class and a few constructors. Listing 5-22 shows the code for this. There's nothing overly special about any of this except for the serialization elements, but even that is pretty standard .NET stuff.

Listing 5-22. *Setting Up Our Class with Two Available Constructors*

```
using System;
using System.ComponentModel;
using System.ComponentModel.Design;
using System.Runtime.Serialization;
using System.Workflow.ComponentModel;
using System.Workflow.ComponentModel.Design;
using Microsoft.SharePoint.WorkflowActions;

namespace KCD.Sharepoint.Activities.Composite
{
    [Serializable]
    internal class LoggerActivityToolboxItem : ActivityToolboxItem
    {
        public LoggerActivityToolboxItem(Type type): base(type)
        {
        }
        private LoggerActivityToolboxItem(SerializationInfo info, ➥
         StreamingContext context)
        {
            this.Deserialize(info, context);
        }
```

The only other code we need to add to this class is an override of the `CreateComponentsCore` method, shown in Listing 5-23. This method is called by Visual Studio when you add an activity to the Designer. It gives us the opportunity to do some processing before our activity is added to a workflow. In our case, we are going to use that to add the LogToHistoryList activity as a child of our activity. We will also add some information to the `UserData` property so that we can identify it later. We saw the other half of this back on line 9 of Listing 5-19 earlier. At the end, we simply return our activity and Visual Studio goes on its merry way.

Listing 5-23. *The CreateComponentsCore Method*

```
protected override IComponent[] CreateComponentsCore(IDesignerHost host)
{
    System.Workflow.ComponentModel.CompositeActivity activity = ➥
        new LoggerActivity();
    LogToHistoryListActivity logger = new LogToHistoryListActivity();
    logger.UserData["logger"] = "logger";
    activity.Activities.Add(logger);
    return new IComponent[] { activity };
}
```

The next and last class we need to add to our activity is the Activity Designer class. Unlike the simple activity where we made significant modifications to the look of our activity via the designer class, this time around, we're not going to change the look at all. Instead, we're going to make use of some additional functionality exposed via our base class (`SequentialActivityDesigner`) to control how our activity manages its child activities as well as the process of new activities being added.

To take care of this, we need to add three methods. First, add another class file to your solution and replace the default contents with the contents of Listing 5-24.

Listing 5-24. *Setting Up Our Class*

```
using System;
using System.Collections.Generic;
using System.Collections.ObjectModel;
using System.Workflow.ComponentModel;
using System.Workflow.ComponentModel.Design;

namespace KCD.Activities
{

    public class LoggerActivityDesigner : SequentialActivityDesigner
    {
```

Next up, we need to override the first of our methods. This one allows you to control what happens when a workflow builder attempts to drop an activity into ours. In our scenario, we want to make sure that our LogToHistoryList activity is and remains the first child activity. Listing 5-25 shows the code for this, which is surprisingly simple. It is not evident from the code, but the net effect is to not allow users to drop an activity in front of our LogToHistoryList activity. In the Designer, this translates to not showing the workflow builder the small green plus sign indicator that marks valid drop locations for the space in front of our activity—a pretty slick outcome for only one line of code.

Listing 5-25. *Keeping Our LogToHistoryList Activity As the First Child*

```
public override bool CanInsertActivities(HitTestInfo insertLocation, ➥
            ReadOnlyCollection<Activity> activitiesToInsert)
{
    return insertLocation.MapToIndex() != 0;
}
```

This takes care of part of the functionality required to keep our LogToHistoryList activity first. There are two other situations we need to take care of—moving activities that have already been added to our activity, and deleting the LogToHistoryList activity. Listing 5-26 is similar to Listing 5-25 and has the same effect—it prevents users from dropping (in this case as part of a move operation) an activity in front of our LogToHistoryList activity. Listing 5-27 is a bit different but still pretty simple. It merely checks whether the activity (or one of the activities, it there are multiple) being deleted is our LogToHistoryList activity. If so, it simply disallows the operation.

Listing 5-26. *Controlling Activity Moves*

```
public override bool CanMoveActivities(HitTestInfo moveLocation, ➥
            ReadOnlyCollection<Activity> activitiesToMove)
{
     return moveLocation.MapToIndex() != 0;
}
```

■ Note Listing 5-27 hints at some pretty powerful capabilities that are available to us—the ability to restrict the activities our composite activity can contain based on any number of properties or details. For more capabilities and scenarios available to you, see the sidebar "Box? What Box?"

Listing 5-27. *The Final Piece to Keeping Our LogToHistoryList Activity As the First Child*

```
public override bool CanRemoveActivities(ReadOnlyCollection<Activity> ➥
            activitiesToRemove)
{
     foreach (Activity a in activitiesToRemove)
     {
         if ((string)a.UserData["logger"] == "logger")
         {
             return false;
         }
     }
     return true;
}
```

With all of our supporting classes created, the last step is to decorate our activity class with the attributes that cause it to use the new capabilities. Add the following attributes just above the class declaration for the LoggerActivity class:

```
[Designer(typeof(LoggerActivityDesigner))] ➥
             and[Toolboxitem(typeof(LoggerActivityToolboxitem))]
courier
```

Compiling and Finishing

That's it. All of our code is written and everything's ready. Go ahead and compile.

It's about as exciting as last time, isn't it? We have nothing but a DLL to show for our efforts (though it is a very nice-looking DLL).

We covered deployment earlier in this chapter—go ahead and flip back if you need a refresher, but the options are the old standards—file system or GAC; the choice is up to you.

We'll make use of this composite activity in Chapter 6 so I'll leave it until then to walk you through using it.

■Note We didn't cover it here, but a composite activity supports all of the same capabilities for custom presentation, themes, toolbox icons, validation, etc. In Chapter 6 we're going to make use of a custom composite activity to replicate a `foreach` loop that does make use of all of these elements.

BOX? WHAT BOX?

The examples we walked through in this chapter were pretty concrete. They covered some good material, but let's face it, unless you're building a MacroStripper activity or a simple LoggerActivity, some of it isn't of much use. One of the goals I have for this book is not just to walk you through a specific scenario, but to help you understand how that very specific example can be abstracted to a more generic understanding of the applicability of the concepts covered. So, without further ado, here are some of my thoughts:

- The capabilities of custom validator, designer, and toolbox item classes are pretty powerful. Our custom composite activity here was pretty lightweight in this regard, but there's no reason you can't get very granular with this. You can get down to the level of controlling exact placement of specific activities within your composite activity.
- The Information Worker or Portals and Collaboration spaces are rife with opportunities for custom activities. Some ideas I had:
    - *Document generation*: Creating aggregated documents built from multiple documents or other contents is intriguing.
    - *Document manipulation*: Similar to what we did with the MacroStripper, but you can manipulate any aspect of your Office documents, spreadsheets, or presentations.
    - *Collaborative workspace creation and management*: Why not automate the process of creating and retiring WSS collaborative sites? Collect information in a form (covered in Chapter 7) and have custom sites built and configured without requiring end users to jump through a bunch of hoops. You can also log pertinent information as part of the process.
    - *Automated publishing*: Sure, if your environment is pure WSS/MOSS this is likely unnecessary, but many situations require interoperability with disparate systems. Requirements for activities to move documents and other content in and out of other systems are going to be abundant in the not-too-distant future. Many vendors will begin offering these activities on their own eventually, but that may take longer than you or your clients can wait.

That's what I've got for now, but it's 4 in the morning and the neurons aren't firing fully. With a little thought, I'm sure you can come up with many other situations that call for custom activities.

Remember, WF in general, and Office workflows in particular, are quite powerful. Don't let your thinking be constrained by any artificial limitations. Thinking outside the box is a good thing.

Summary

Here's the abridged version of this chapter:

- Activities are the building blocks of a workflow.
- Activities are specialized .NET components.
- Simple activities do one task.
- Composite activities control workflow execution and activity processing and can add functionality either before or after the activities process.
- Composite activities are containers for other activities.
- WF ships with a set of activities out-of-the-box.
- SharePoint adds more activities to cover SharePoint- and Office-specific tasks.
- Only four of the default WF activities are officially supported (for now).
- Custom properties can either be added as regular component properties or dependency properties.
- Building a custom activity is primarily a matter of providing an `Execute` method and notifying WF when we are done.
- A complete activity can be made up of up to seven distinct classes, though only one class is required.
- Deploying a custom activity is a matter of either installing into the GAC or copying the DLL to a `\bin` folder.
- We have the same facilities open to us to build activities as Microsoft does. There is nothing special about their activities that we couldn't reproduce with the tools available to us mere mortals.

CHAPTER 6

Building a Workflow with Visual Studio 2005

In Chapter 4 we built a workflow using the SharePoint Designer. It gave us a nice, wizard-based approach to creating our custom workflow. That tool will suffice for many situations, including

- Building basic workflows from the provided actions and conditions
- Quickly creating and deploying workflows on a single list or library
- Allowing power users to create their own workflows

But what if your needs are more complicated? What if you need to have more control over your workflow processing, or deploy that workflow to more than one site? For these and many other scenarios, you're going to need a full developer platform. Rather than creating a whole new tool, Microsoft has opted instead to simply extend Visual Studio with the Visual Studio 2005 Extensions for Windows Workflow Foundation. As developers, this makes our lives much easier—we're already familiar with the core tool—Visual Studio—and the programming paradigm. We just need to pick up a few nuances of the extensions.

Getting Started

If you're following along at home, we already installed the extensions and the MOSS or WSS SDK, which contains our project templates, in Chapter 2, so we don't need to rehash that here.

New Project Types

Visual Studio itself should not be new to anyone reading this book, and we already saw some of the project templates, so I'm only going to cover the new items here. The first thing to notice is the addition of yet another category of projects to the New Project dialog box. We now have a SharePoint category under both Visual C# and VB .NET. This category contains two templates:

- *SharePoint Server Sequential Workflow Library*: Used for standard serial and parallel flow workflows
- *SharePoint Server State Machine Workflow Library*: Used for state machine workflows

We'll be making use of both of these templates in the course of this chapter. We'll get started with a simple sequential workflow and then build a state machine workflow later in the chapter to wrap things up.

■ **Note** These names only apply if you have the MOSS SDK installed. If you only have the WSS SDK, the names are simply *SharePoint Sequential Workflow Library* and *SharePoint State Machine Workflow Library*, respectively. I know that is a huge gulf to bridge, but let's see how we do overcoming it. It also means that if you have both SDKs installed, you'll have all four templates—how are we *ever* going to come to peace with that?

Each type of workflow is built in a similar, visual fashion; in either case, you lay out the structure of your workflow—the activities that will perform the work—in a graphical environment known as the Workflow Designer. As this tool is integrated with Visual Studio 2005, the experience should be very familiar to anyone who has worked with Visual Studio. Figure 6-1 shows a view of the Workflow Designer canvas for sequential workflows as well as the Toolbox filled with some of the default activities. Figure 6-2 shows the Workflow Designer canvas for a state machine workflow. It looks different, but functionally is quite similar.

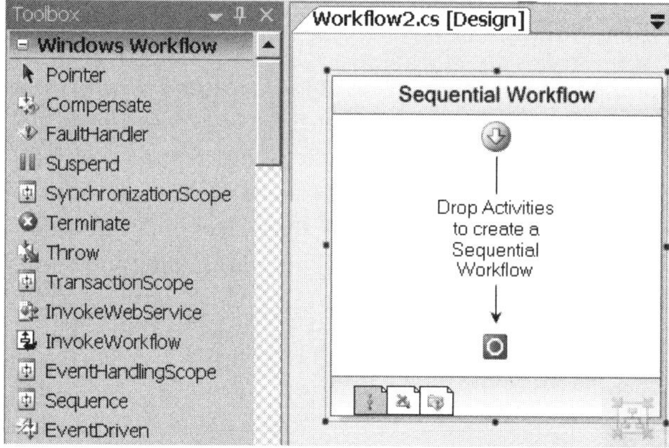

Figure 6-1. *The Workflow Designer in Visual Studio for a sequential workflow*

The Workflow Designer is a powerful extension to Visual Studio 2005. It brings the simplicity of drag-and-drop construction without sacrificing the power of full access to the code. Looking at the Designer in Figure 6-1, you can pretty quickly see how the rest of the process for a sequential workflow is going to go. At the top of the Designer is a small icon with a downward-facing arrow. This signifies the beginning of our workflow. Opposite this at the bottom is a circle icon signaling the end of our workflow. Anything we need to do will happen between those points. The arrow connecting those two icons indicates the flow of our business process. Building a state machine workflow is not as immediately apparent, but the concepts and process are quite similar.

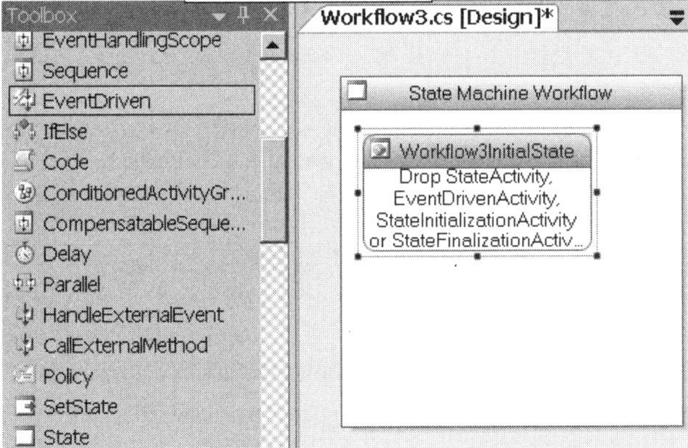

Figure 6-2. *The Workflow Designer in Visual Studio for a state machine workflow*

At a high level, the process for either type of workflow is as follows:

1. Drag activities from the Toolbox and drop them on the design canvas. Remember from Chapter 5 that activities are just .NET components. This is no different than dropping them on a Windows or a web form.
2. Set the properties of the activities via the Visual Studio Properties window.
3. Write code as necessary in your code-behind file to perform the specific tasks of your workflow.

That's it. As with anything else, the devil is in the details, but at a high level, that's what it takes to build either a sequential or a state machine workflow. We'll get into those pesky little details throughout the rest of this chapter.

Building a Sequential Workflow

Our first custom workflow is going to utilize the activity we built in Chapter 5. If you'll recall, that activity removes macros from Office 2007 documents.

Scenario: Removing Macros

As discussed previously, KCD is concerned with preventing macro viruses from entering their network via documents posted by partners and clients on their various externally facing sites. The MacroStripper activity developed previously will do the work of removing the macros; now they just need to implement a workflow to make use of it.

To make this work, you design a workflow that can be used across multiple document libraries to cover all documents posted by outside sources. The full, high-level process for this workflow is as follows:

1. Log the beginning of the workflow.
2. Attempt to remove macros from the document

3. If no macros are present in the document, or all macros were successfully removed, log the end of the workflow and end the workflow.

4. If the macros could *not* be successfully removed:

   - Send an email to each registered owner of the site the document was loaded into, informing them of the problem.

   - Send an email to the author of the document, indicating that there was a problem.

5. Log the end of the workflow, including the results of the macro removal.

The workflow will be developed and deployed to all site collections that are externally accessible and then associated with each appropriate document library.

■ **Note** Anyone familiar with the BizTalk Orchestration Designer is going to breeze through this example. The Workflow Designer for sequential workflows is nearly identical to the Orchestration Designer, so the concepts, interface, and design are all already familiar to you.

Now that we know what we're building, let's get started. The first thing we need to do is create a new project. Open the New Project dialog box and select whichever flavor of Sequential Workflow Library you have the template for. For this example, I've named the solution **DocCleaner**. Once the project is created, it will open in Visual Studio. So far, there's really nothing different from any other Visual Studio project. Before we start working in the files, let's take a look at the pieces that make up our project. Take a look at the Solution Explorer; the Project template has added the following files for us:

- `feature.xml` (located in `DeploymentFiles\FeatureFiles`)—Initially a mostly blank file. It will be used to package our workflow as a feature and deploy it to SharePoint. We'll look at this file later in this chapter when we talk about deploying our workflow.

- `workflow.xml` (located in `DeploymentFiles\FeatureFiles`)—Another mostly blank file for the time being. This is the final piece we need for deployment. We'll also cover this one later.

- `manifest.xml` (located in `DeploymentFiles\ProductionDeployment`)—Used for packaging our workflow into a solution package. We'll cover production deployment preparation later in this chapter.

- `wsp_Structure.ddf` (located in `DeploymentFiles\ProductionDeployment`)—Also used for production deployment and covered later.

- `PostBuildActions.bat` (located in `DeploymentFiles`)—A batch file used for deployment. We'll look at this one later, too.

- `workflow1.cs`—Finally, here's the file we need to actually construct our workflow. We'll start with this file.

The Properties and References items are standard Visual Studio 2005 stuff. There are also a couple of references to the SharePoint assemblies added for us.

Before opening it, right-click on the `Workflow1.cs` file and rename it to **DocCleanerWF.cs**. Click Yes if Visual Studio prompts you to update references to our renamed file.

Working in the Designer

Now it's time to begin our workflow. Open the `DocCleanerWF.cs` file by double-clicking on it. The Workflow Designer, shown in Figure 6-3, will open. Man, is that exciting.

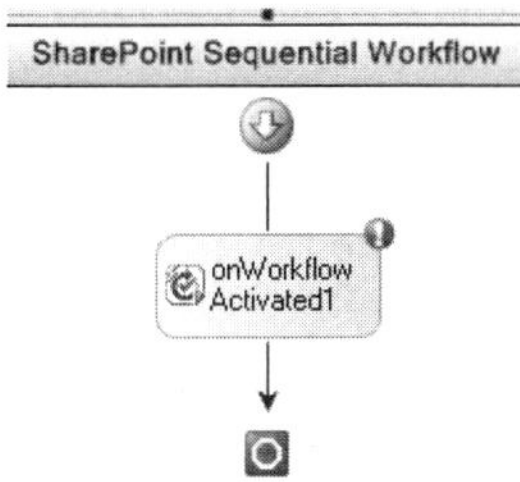

Figure 6-3. *The Visual Studio Workflow Designer gets things started for us by adding one activity.*

The workflow template has already placed one activity on the Designer canvas for us. This activity is an instance of the onWorkflowActivated activity. The template has placed this activity because it is required that this activity be the first one in every SharePoint workflow since it is our gateway back to SharePoint.

■ **Caution** Every SharePoint workflow *must* begin with an onWorkflowActivated activity.

Typically, there is certain information that you will need in order to be able to do the work of your workflow. In the architecture of a WF workflow, the majority of this information will come from the workflow host. In the case of our SharePoint workflows, remember, our host is SharePoint. The information we will typically need is things such as

- The `SPListItem` that the workflow is running upon
- The `SPList`, `SPWeb`, and `SPSite` that contain the `SPListItem`
- The user that initiated the workflow
- Information from the association and initiation forms (we'll cover forms in Chapter 7)

Access to this information is through an instance of an `SPWorkflowActivationProperties` object, which is created for us by the onWorkflowActivated activity and named `workflowProperties`. Details on some of the more useful members of this object in relation to a SharePoint workflow are provided in Table 6-1. You'll see an example of working with these properties in our code later in this chapter. One other thing that the onWorkflowActivated activity does for us is set up our correlation tokens. We'll cover these later in the chapter.

Note While this book is not about building a custom workflow host, the onWorkflowActivated activity hints at an important point to keep in mind if you do need to build your own host. WF allows a workflow host to pass any information to its workflows that it needs to. This is a powerful capability.

Table 6-1. *Useful Information Available Through the WorkflowProperties Object*

Property	Type	Description
`AssociationData`, `InitiationData`	`string`	Stores data from an incoming association or initiation form that started the workflow. This string can be in any format, although, for Office workflow forms, it would be XML corresponding to the XML schema for the form.
`HistoryList`	`SPList`	The reference to the SharePoint list designated to store entries related to the processing of our workflow.
`HistoryListId`	`GUID`	The identifier of the SharePoint list designated as the history list for the particular instance of this workflow.
`HistoryListUrl`	`string`	The URL of the SharePoint list designated as the history list for the particular instance of this workflow.
`Item`	`SPListItem`	The SharePoint list item that the current instance of our workflow is working on.
`ItemId`	`integer`	The identifier of the SharePoint list item within the parent list that triggered the workflow instance.
`ItemUrl`	`string`	The URL of the SharePoint list item that triggered the workflow instance.
`List`	`SPList`	The reference to the SharePoint list our workflow is associated with.
`ListId`	`GUID`	The identifier of the SharePoint list that owns the item that triggered the workflow instance.
`ListUrl`	`string`	The URL of the SharePoint list that owns the item that triggered the workflow instance.
`Originator`	`string`	The name of the SharePoint user that triggered the workflow instance.
`OriginatorEmail`	`string`	The email of the SharePoint user that triggered the workflow instance.
`OriginatorUser`	`SPUser`	The `SPUser` object representing the person who initiated the instance of our workflow.
`Site`	`SPSite`	Stores a reference to the `SPSite` object that the current instance of our workflow is running within.

Table 6-1. *Useful Information Available Through the WorkflowProperties Object*

Property	Type	Description
`SiteId`	`GUID`	The identifier of the SharePoint site that owns the item that triggered the workflow instance.
`SiteUrl`	`string`	The URL of the SharePoint site that owns the item that triggered the workflow instance.
`TaskList`	`SPList`	A reference to the SharePoint list designated to store workflow tasks for the current instance of our workflow.
`TaskListId`	`GUID`	The identifier of the SharePoint list designated as the task list for the particular instance of this workflow.
`TemplateName`	`string`	The name of the workflow template that the current instance of our workflow is based on.
`Web`	`SPWeb`	Stores a reference to the `SPWeb` object our workflow instance is running within.
`WebId`	`GUID`	The identifier of the `SPWeb` that owns the item that triggered the workflow instance.
`Workflow`	`SPWorkflow`	Stores a reference to the current instance of our workflow.
`WorkflowId`	`GUID`	The identifier of the current instance of our workflow.

■ **Note** Having separate object and ID (for example `Web` and `WebID`) properties at first seems a little extraneous—after all, the ID is available as `object.ID`. The reasoning behind this is related to performance. The object properties instantiate an instance of the object and load it into memory—a potentially expensive operation. If all you need to do is access the ID, grab it from the ID property, as this does not incur the same performance hit. The ID property is stored as a simple GUID—with much less performance impact.

The first step in building our workflow is to add the activities we will need. By default, Visual Studio will show the default WF activities in the Toolbox. If it does not show the SharePoint activities for your installation, you'll need to add them manually. These activities are stored in the `\Program Files\Common Files\Microsoft Shared\Web Server Extensions\12\ISAPI\Microsoft.SharePoint.WorkflowActions.dll` assembly. See the sidebar "Managing Activities in the Toolbox" for information on how to add the activities to your Toolbox.

I generally like to add all of my activities to the Designer canvas and set the `(Name)` property so that each has a unique name, and then go back and set the rest of properties at the end. This allows me to keep my focus on getting my process correct as I build the model and then go back and fill in the details.

MANAGING ACTIVITIES IN THE TOOLBOX

There are two ways to add your custom activities to the Toolbox in Visual Studio. Starting with the easiest:

- If your custom activity project is in the same solution as your workflow project, the activity will automatically be added to the Toolbox under a heading taken from the activity project name, as shown here:

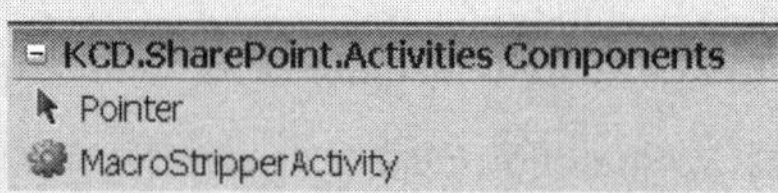

- One potential drawback to this approach is that your custom activity is only available in the Toolbox for the current project. This may or may not meet your needs. Another quirk about this approach is that while the activity will be the most recently compiled version from your project, it will not show any custom Toolbox item elements, such as icons. You will always get the default gear icon, as shown in the accompanying graphic.
- In other scenarios, you will need to manually add the activity to the Toolbox. This is *almost* no different compared with adding other components to the Visual Studio Toolbox:
    - Right-click on the Toolbox.
    - Select Choose Items from the context menu.
    - In the Choose Toolbox Items dialog box, click on the Activities tab (this is the one different thing).
    - Click the Browse button and navigate to the location of your activity's assembly.
    - Click on the name of your activity DLL and click OK.
    - Click OK in the Choose Toolbox Items dialog box.
- Your activity is now available in the Toolbox, underneath the heading that was active when you started, as shown here:

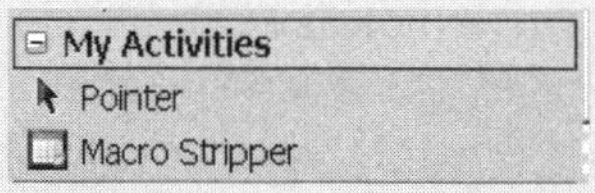

You'll notice in this graphic that our custom class for the Toolbox item that we added in the last chapter is used to deliver the icon and tooltip for the activity.

If you're borderline OCD, as I am, you can organize your activities by adding multiple tabs to the Toolbox. This is standard Visual Studio functionality.

Finally, looking at the Choose Toolbox Items dialog box, you can see how to remove items from the Toolbox. Deselecting the checkbox to the left of the activity in the list and clicking OK will remove it from the Toolbox, which you can also do by right-clicking on a specific activity and selecting Delete from the context menu.

Adding Activities

Adding activities is simply a matter of dragging them from the Toolbox and dropping them onto the Designer canvas where we need them. The Designer even helps us out by lighting up each valid location to drop an activity with a small green plus sign icon:

■ Caution If you drag an activity out of the Toolbox you'll see it is possible to add an activity above the onWorkflowActivated activity even though, as I mentioned earlier, the onWorkflowActivated activity needs to be the first activity in our workflow. This is because the Designer does not know to stop us. Having the onWorkflowActivated activity come first is a SharePoint restriction. The Designer will let us build and compile a workflow with another activity first, but if we deploy it and try to run it, SharePoint will yell at us—the exact message is "Correlation value has not been initialized on declaration *<correlation_token_name>* for activity *<name_of_activity>*" or something similar, depending on which activity you have first.

To get started with our example, we need the following activities, added in this order, starting right below the onWorkflowActivated activity:

- *LogToHistoryListActivity*—Used to write an entry to the history list for our workflow at the beginning of processing. Set the `(Name)` property to **hlogBegin**.
- *MacroStripper*—The custom activity we wrote in Chapter 5. Set the `ID` property to **macroStripper**.
- *IfElse*—Branches our workflow conditionally depending on whether the posted document is now macro-free. Leave the `ID` property at the default.
- *ForEach*—A custom activity available from Microsoft on the .NET Framework 3.0 site (`wf.netfx3.com`). I'll post a link directly to it on my web site: `www.kcdholdings.com`. Add it to the first branch of the IfElse activity. Leave the `ID` property at the default.
- Two *SendEMail* activities, which are part of the SharePoint activity set—Add one inside the ForEach and one just after it. Set the `ID` properties to **emlError** for the first and **emlAuthor** for the second.
- Another *LogToHistoryListActivity*—Used to write an entry to the history log at the end of our workflow to indicate the end of our processing. Add it after the IfElse, at the very end of the workflow. Set the `ID` property to **hlogEnd**.

Figure 6-4 shows how these activities need to be laid out in the Designer. Simply drag each from the Toolbox and drop it in the proper place. Note that when you drop the IfElse activity, it is going to have two branches by default. For this example, we are not going to do anything in the else branch, so you can either leave it in place but empty, or right-click on it and delete it. I went with the latter simply because it makes things look cleaner. If you ever need it back again, you can always add another branch via the context menu.

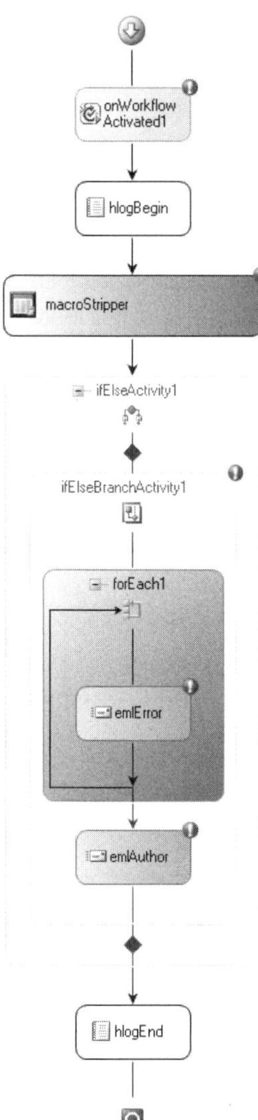

Figure 6-4. *The Workflow Designer*

Another interesting thing to note is the LogToHistoryList activity. As covered in Chapter 3, the history list for our workflow is set up by an administrator when they associate our workflow with a document library. What this means to us is that we have no idea of the name, URL, or any other details of the history list. So how do we write information to a list we know almost nothing about? We don't. That's why this activity exists. We tell this activity the information we'd like to record, and the SharePoint workflow host does some magic behind the scenes to write this information to the proper history list. If you ask me, it's a rather slick solution to a somewhat thorny problem.

With each of the activities in place, you can get a good picture of how the workflow will run, as shown in Figure 6-4. This is why I like to drop all of my activities first. It lets me look at my workflow as a whole and make sure I get all of the pieces laid out before I start customizing them. This is obviously a very simple workflow; nonetheless, it helps to have the activities all set in the proper order before you go setting properties and writing code.

■ **Note** If you look at Figure 6-4, you'll see an unfamiliar activity—the ForEach activity. This does not ship out of the box, and is not part of the SharePoint activities. Back in Chapter 5, I mentioned one additional source of activities—the WF and SharePoint developer communities. ForEach is a perfect example of the former. It was posted to the Microsoft workflow community site as a sample activity for use in WF workflows. Because our Office workflows are nothing more than specialized WF workflows, we can make use of it. You can get your hands on this little treasure at `wf.netfx3.com`.

You'll notice in Figure 6-4 that some of our activities each have an error indicator—the small red circle with the exclamation point inside. This is design-time validation. The author of these activities is telling us that we need to take some action in order to use these activities. We touched on this in Chapter 5 when we were creating our custom activity and writing our custom validators. Here it is in action.

You can probably guess what each activity needs, but to see for sure, move your mouse over the error indicator and click on the drop-down arrow that appears. This smart tag tells us exactly what we need to do in order for our instance of the activity to pass the validation test, as indicated in Figure 6-5.

Figure 6-5. *Smart tags warn us of validation errors before we compile.*

■ **Tip** For missing property value errors such as this one, if you click on the error message itself, it will take you directly to the appropriate place in the Properties window where you need to take action.

With our activities in place, we can go in and start setting properties—not only to fix validation errors, but also to just get the workflow doing what we need. Table 6-2 shows the properties that need to be set for each activity. As you're changing the properties for each activity, take a look around at the other properties. You'll begin to get a good sense of what is possible.

Table 6-2. *Setting Properties on Our Workflow Activities*

Activity	Property	New Value	Description
onWorkflowActivated1	CorrelationToken	workflowToken	For information on correlation tokens, see the sidebar "Correlation Tokens?" later in this chapter.
onWorkflowActivated1	CorrelationToken\OwnerActivityName	DocCleanerWF	For information on correlation tokens, see the sidebar "Correlation Tokens?" later in this chapter.
onWorkflowActivated1	workflowProperties\Name	DocCleanerWF	
onWorkflowActivated1	workflowProperties\Path	workflowProperties	The name of the variable that represents our SPWorkflowActivation ➥ Properties object. This object is created automatically and the name cannot be edited here.
hlogBegin	EventID	WorkflowStarted	
hlogBegin	MethodInvoking	setBeginLog	After you enter the method name here, Visual Studio will jump you over to Code view with a method signature created for you. The code for this is in Listing 6-3.
macroStripper	PayloadItem	workflowProperties.Item	This dependency property cannot be edited directly. Click on either the ellipsis in the value field or the small blue information icon to load the Binding dialog box. Navigate down to workflowProperties.Item, as shown in Figure 6-6.
ifElseBranchActivity1	Condition	Declarative Rule Condition	We go into much more detail on rules and conditions in Chapter 8.
ifElseBranchActivity1	ConditionName	*<leave blank>*	I'll walk you through setting this in just a minute.
ifElseBranchActivity1	ConditionExpression	*<leave blank>*	I'll also walk you through setting this in just a minute.

Table 6-2. *Setting Properties on Our Workflow Activities (Continued)*

Activity	Property	New Value	Description
forEach1	Items	workflowProperties.Item.ParentList.ParentWeb.AssociatedOwnerGroup.Users	Like the payloadItem property earlier, you can again use the Binding dialog box to set this property (but you'll have to access it via the little blue icon). For our scenario, we're going to use the Owners collection for our SharePoint site. The forEach property will iterate through its child activities once for every member of this collection.
emlError	CorrelationToken	workflowToken	You can just select this from the drop-down. For information on correlation tokens, see the sidebar "Correlation Tokens?" later in this chapter.
emlError	From	*<a valid email address in your environment>*	
emlError	MethodInvoking	sendErrorEmail	After you enter the method name here, Visual Studio will jump you over to Code view with a method signature created for you. The code for this is in Listing 6-1.
emlError	Subject	Error Removing Macros	
emlAuthor	CorrelationToken	workflowToken	You can just select this from the drop-down. For information on correlation tokens, see the sidebar "Correlation Tokens?" later in this chapter.
emlAuthor	From	*<a valid email address in your environment>*	
emlAuthor	MethodInvoking	sendAuthorEmail	After you enter the method name here, Visual Studio will jump you over to Code view with a method signature created for you. The code for this is in Listing 6-2.
emlAuthor	Subject	Document at KCD Holdings Client Portal	

Table 6-2. *Setting Properties on Our Workflow Activities (Continued)*

Activity	Property	New Value	Description
hlogEnd	`EventId`	`workflowCompleted`	
hlogEnd	`MethodInvoking`	`setEndLog`	After you enter the method name here, Visual Studio will jump you over to Code view with a method signature created for you. The code for this is in Listing 6-4.

Note When you have finished setting all of the property values indicated in Table 6-1, there will still be an error indicator on the onWorkflowActivated activity. To get rid of this, you will need to edit the Designer file (`DocCleaner.designer.cs`). Find the line that reads `activitybind.Name = "Workflow1"` and change it to read `activitybind.Name="DocCleanerWF"`. For some reason this isn't updated when we rename our workflow code file.

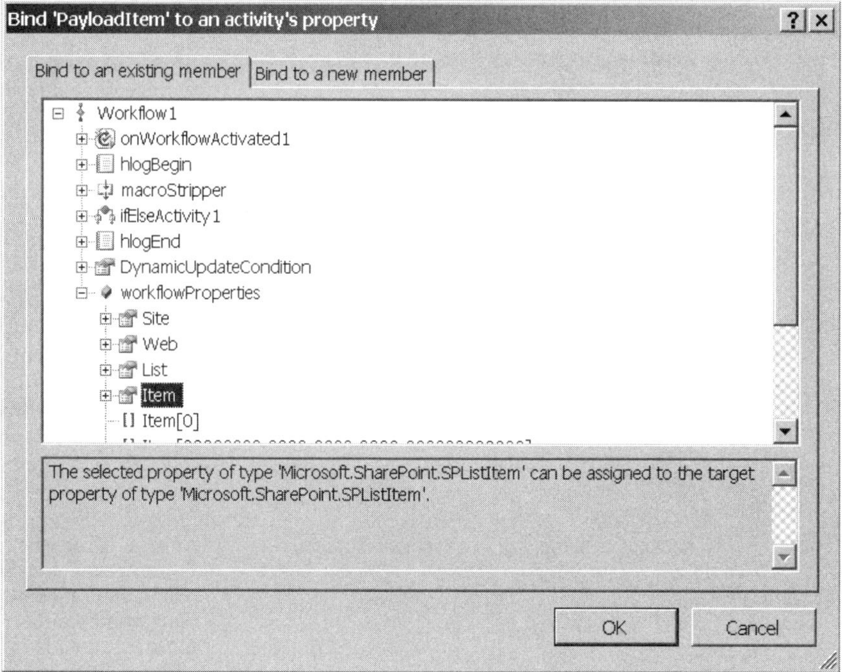

Figure 6-6. *This dialog box allows you to connect properties to elements of your workflow.*

■ Caution Interestingly, the validator for the SendEmail activity does not make us set any of the typical information associated with sending an email—To, From, Subject, Body, etc. Presumably this is because this information is, or can be, set in code. However, be aware that you will not receive any warnings about this in the Designer or when you build your workflow. At runtime, your activity will throw an error when it tries to execute the SendEmail activity if this information is not set. You can either set the properties directly or set them via the `Headers` property.

Table 6-2 takes care of setting most of our properties. We'll get to the code for the couple of activities that need it in a moment. First, if you click back into the Designer view, you'll see that we still have a validation error in one of our activities—the IfElseBranch. If you click on the error indicator on the Designer, you'll see the smart tag pop up that tells you that the `Condition` property is not set. In order to tackle this one, we need to take a brief foray into activity conditions. We go much further into this topic in Chapter 8; we'll just touch upon it here.

For now, think of conditions as a mechanism for determining the circumstances under which an activity executes. It can get more complex than that, but that's a pretty close first pass. By way of example, the simplest condition is on a basic IfElseBranch activity—such as we have in our scenario. The logic of the activity is pretty straightforward—if a certain condition is true, execute the activities in the branch; otherwise, move on to the second branch and evaluate its condition. While this logic can certainly get more complicated, all activity conditions essentially break down to this simple state, and the heart of this logic is the condition that is evaluated.

The condition that is evaluated must result in either a true or a false. Each activity that contains this logic will take different actions based on the return value from the condition evaluation, but the expression itself always results in a Boolean evaluation. Conditions can be applied as either of the following:

- *A Code Condition*, which means that you write code that results in a Boolean value to indicate whether or not the condition evaluates to true or false, thereby controlling how the activity processes.
- *A Declarative Rule Condition*, which means that you define the logic that controls how the activity processes utilizing the built-in Condition Editor. Technically, you're still writing code in the Condition Editor, but the code itself is simpler since it consists of basic comparisons between fields, variables, and values.

Selecting between these two options is done in the Properties window for your activity, as shown in Figure 6-7.

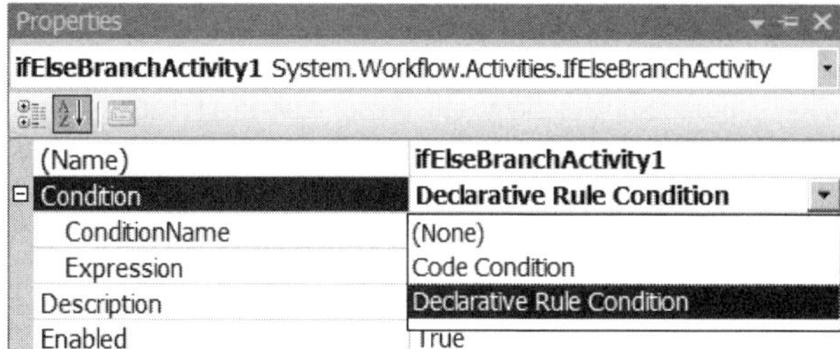

Figure 6-7. *You select which type of condition to use in the Properties window.*

For our IfElseBranch activity, we're going to make use of a Declarative Rule Condition, so go ahead and select it in the drop-down in the Properties window. After you make that selection, expand the `Condition` property and you'll see that we now have two subproperties to set—`ConditionName` and `Expression`. Clicking in the `ConditionName` field will show a small ellipsis button. Click this button to launch the Condition Editor, shown in Figure 6-8.

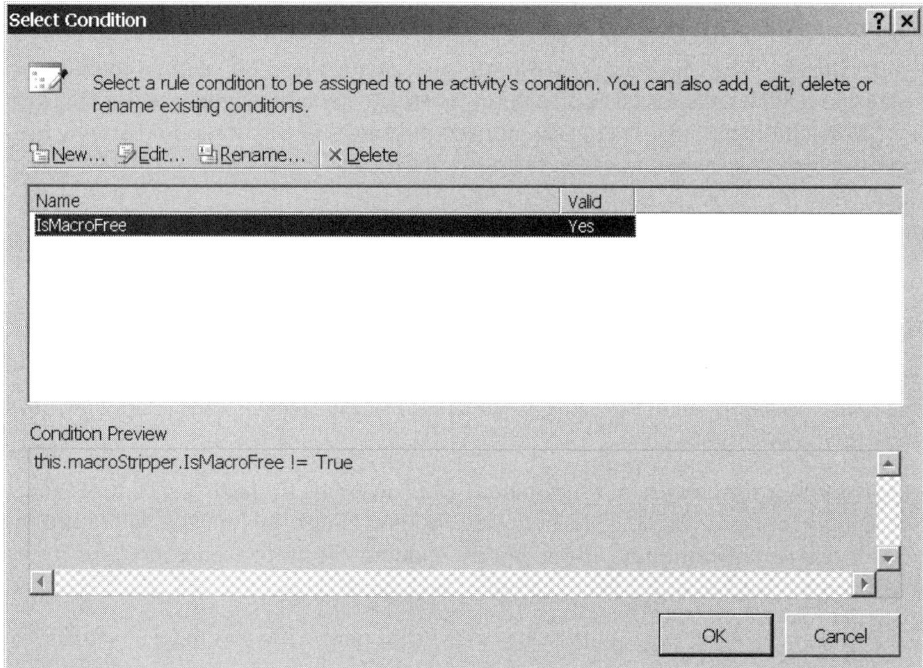

Figure 6-8. *The Condition Editor allows you to specify conditions.*

Again, we'll look at this tool further in Chapter 8, so for now, just click the New button, type a condition of `this.macroStripper.IsMacroFree != True`, and we'll move on. Save your condition and return to the Designer. You'll notice that none of our activities now show a validation error. If we were impatient, we could build our solution and not receive any errors. But we're not impatient, are we?

CORRELATION TOKENS?

So just what exactly *is* a correlation token and what does it do for us? Good question. It's actually a lot easier than it may sound. A correlation token is essentially a means of uniquely identifying each instance of a workflow, modification, or task.

To understand this, you need to understand a little bit about how workflows are processed. When SharePoint needs to initiate a workflow, it does not spawn a unique set of objects. Instead, if one instance of the workflow is already running when the second initiates, the second will reuse the objects from the first. This provides us with a huge performance boost, but means that we need to be able to keep the instances straight. Correlation Token properties ensure that the single activity object is operating on the correct payload instance and accessing the correct details about the workflow.

All we need to do is set the proper correlation token property and then we can go on our merry way—blissfully unaware of all of the sticky bits happening behind the scenes.

By far, the single hardest thing about correlation token is keeping them straight. There are three different places where correlation tokens come into play:

- Workflows
- Tasks
- Modifications

and the tricky part is making sure that you assign the correct correlation token in each scenario. This gets even more difficult when you have multiple tasks and multiple modifications in a workflow. Each distinct task or modification gets its own distinct correlation token.

Eilene Hao, one of the Microsoft Program Managers for Office Workflows, produced an excellent guide to correlation tokens on the SharePoint team blog (`http://blogs.msdn.com/sharepoint/archive/2006/11/23/developing-workflows-in-vs-part-3-five-steps-for-developing-your-workflow.aspx`). Check out the full posting, but I've reproduced her table in Table 6-3 (thanks, Eilene!) as it provides a lot of good detail—more than you think after a simple first pass.

Table 6-3. *Keeping Correlation Tokens Straight*

Workflow Token	Task Token	Modification Token
OnWorkflowActivated	CreateTask	EnableWorkflowModification
OnWorkflowItemChanged	CreateTaskWith➥ContentType	OnWorkflowModified
OnWorkflowItemDeleted	UpdateTask	
SetState	DeleteTask	
SendEmail	CompleteTask	
UpdateAllTasks	RollbackTask	
	OnTaskChanged	
	OnTaskDeleted	
	OnTaskCreated	

The table shows us where each SharePoint activity falls with regard to correlation tokens. If you're using an OnWorkflowItemDeleted activity, you use the workflow token. If you're using the UpdateTask activity, use the task token. So far, it makes perfect sense. The one activity that is a bit counterintuitive, though, is the UpdateAllTasks activity. It gets the workflow token, not the task token, which might be what you would expect. If you think a little further about it, though, it makes sense. This activity does not work on a single task, so there is not a single task token to assign to it. Instead, it gets the workflow token and is then tied to all tasks in the workflow.

The best example, and again, one that I stole from Eilene, is as follows: *if you have in a sequence the activities CreateTask, OnTaskChanged (to wait for the user to edit his task), then CompleteTask, you want these three activities to map to the same task in SharePoint; you do this by specifying the same correlation token in all three (from the same blog entry cited earlier).*

■ **Note** The plumbing of WF and SharePoint as a workflow host and correlation is beyond the scope of this book. For our purposes, we just need to know how to set the correlation token property. If you'd like to read more about correlation, take a look at `http://wf.netfx3.com`.

Writing All That Code

The last thing we need to do to wrap up our workflow is add the code to our methods. We'll take care of that now. As you'll recall, Visual Studio automatically created method signatures for us as we set some of our properties, so all we need to do now is go into our code file and add the code.

The first method we're going to tackle is `sendErrorEMail`. Click in the method body and add the code in Listing 6-1. There's not really anything special to this code; we just set the `To` and `Body` properties for our email. Remember, though, that this activity sits inside the ForEach activity so it is going to execute once for each member of the `Owners` group from the site that owns the document library with which our workflow is associated. We access the `CurrentItem` property of the ForEach activity to set the `To` field properly.

Listing 6-1. *Configuring the sendErrorEMail Activity*

```
this.emlError.To = ((SPUser)this.forEach1.CurrentItem).Email;
this.emlError.Body = string.Format(@"The following document was
                posted to {0} - {1}.  The automatic process was unable to
                successfully remove the macro parts from the document package.
                This document will be unavailable to end users until it is
                manually processed.{2}",
                this.macroStripper.ParentList.ParentWeb.Title,
                this.macroStripper.ParentList.Title,
                this.macroStripper.FinalDocumentName);
```

Next up is the code to configure the To and Body properties of the sendAuthorEmail activity. This code, shown in Listing 6-2, is quite similar to the previous code, except that we set the To property to the email address of the person who posted the document. We access this piece of information from the workflowProperties object.

Listing 6-2. *Configuring the sendAuthorEmail property*

```
this.emlAuthor.To = this.workflowProperties.OriginatorEmail;
    this.emlAuthor.Body = string.Format(@"The document ({0}) you
    recently posted to the KCD Holdings Client portal has encountered
    a problem.  KCD policy prohibits the posting of documents with
    embedded macros.  We were unable to automatically remove the
    macros from your document.  Therefore it has been quarantined
    until it can be processed manually.",
    this.macroStripper.OriginalDocumentName);
```

The next two code listings are going to handle setting the text that gets written to our history list—one at the beginning of processing and one at the end. Listing 6-3 shows the code for our setBeginLog method. Listing 6-4 handles setEndLog.

Listing 6-3. *Logging the Beginning of Our Workflow*

```
this.hlogBegin.HistoryDescription = string.Format(@"
    Processing: {0}.  Attempting to remove macros",
    this.workflowProperties.Item.Name);
```

Listing 6-4. *More Logging...*

```
string sHistoryOutcome = @"Processing complete: ";
if (macroStripper.IsMacroFree)
{
    sHistoryOutcome += "Macros successfully removed";
}
else
{
    sHistoryOutcome += "Macros NOT successfully removed";
}
this.hlogEnd.HistoryDescription = sHistoryOutcome;
```

There you have it—all of the code for our workflow in 30 lines; not too shabby. While this example is pretty basic, it nonetheless makes an important point: our workflow itself does not contain any real business logic. All of the real *work* of our workflow is done using activities. All that the code in our workflow itself does is tie those activities together and handle some runtime configuration and logging. We've centralized our business logic into objects and simply reused that logic where we needed to.

Compiling and Wrapping Up

Before we can compile, we need to configure our assembly to be strongly named because it is going to be deployed to the GAC. I'll assume that you know how to do this.

So there you have it—your first Office 2007 workflow. Go ahead and compile. If neither of us made any typos, everything should compile OK and you can give yourself a pat on the back.

Congratulations on a job well done.

OK, so this is only marginally better than the feeling after compiling our activity in the previous chapter. We still have nothing to test and play with—just a boring old DLL file. Where's the fun in that?

We need to complete one more step before we have something to actually show for all of our work. We need to deploy and associate our workflow. We'll cover all that next.

Read on, MacDuff...

Deploying Our Workflow

Be glad you're tackling deployment in the final release of the product. In the beta cycle, deployment was a nightmare of interrelated moving parts that practically set you up for failure the first few times you tried it.

OK, so maybe it wasn't *that* bad, but it is a lot easier now. We're going to start with a deployment for development and testing, and then circle back and go through a deployment for production. They are different. For development, there are two files we need to work with:

- `feature.xml`
- `workflow.xml`

■ **Note** Deploying our workflow to SharePoint is going to make use of the SharePoint *Features* functionality. While you can get through this section without a deep understanding of Features, it would help if you had some knowledge. When we get to the section on production deployment, we'll raise the bar a little further and talk about SharePoint *Solutions*.

Taking these one at a time, we'll start with `feature.xml`.

Open the `feature.xml` file that the project template has created for your solution (under `DeploymentFiles\FeatureFiles` in the Solution Explorer). Initially, there's really nothing of much value in this file, other than some instructions on inserting a Code Snippet. Make sure that your cursor is positioned at the end of the file and then follow the instructions provided to insert the `feature.xml` Code Snippet. You will end up with a file that looks like Figure 6-9.

■ **Tip** If the workflow Code Snippets aren't showing up, click on Tools ➤ Code Snippets Manager, select XML from the Language drop-down, and add `C:\Program Files\Microsoft Visual Studio 8\Xml\1033\Snippets\SharePoint Server Workflow` to your snippets collection.

```
feature.xml*
<?xml version="1.0" encoding="utf-8"?>
<!-- _lcid="1033" _version="12.0.3111" _dal="1" -->
<!-- _LocalBinding -->

<!-- Insert Feature.xml Code Snippet here.  To do this:
1) Right click on this page and select "Insert Snippet" (or press Ctrl+K, then X)
2) Select Snippets->SharePoint Workflow->Feature.xml Code -->
<Feature  Id="GUID"
          Title="Default Title"
          Description="This feature is a workflow that ..."
          Version="12.0.0.0"
          Scope="Site"
          ReceiverAssembly="Microsoft.Office.Workflow.Feature, Version=12.0.0.0, Culture
          ReceiverClass="Microsoft.Office.Workflow.Feature.WorkflowFeatureReceiver"
          xmlns="http://schemas.microsoft.com/sharepoint/">
  <ElementManifests>
    <ElementManifest Location="workflow.xml" />
    <ElementFile Location="MyForm.xsn"/>
  </ElementManifests>
  <Properties>
    <Property Key="GloballyAvailable" Value="true" />

    <!-- Value for RegisterForms key indicates the path to the forms relative to feature
    <!-- if you don't have forms, use *.xsn -->
    <Property Key="RegisterForms" Value="*.xsn" />
  </Properties>
</Feature>
```

Figure 6-9. *Our feature.xml file after inserting the Code Snippet*

Figure 6-9 loses a little bit of its usefulness when it gets printed in bland and white, but take a look on your screen. The parts highlighted in green are the ones we're interested in. These are the pieces we need to customize for our particular workflow. Table 6-4 provides details on the changes we need to make to each of these entries in our `feature.xml` file.

Table 6-4. *Customizing feature.xml After Inserting the Code Snippet*

Entry	New Value	Description
`Id`	Create a new Registry-format GUID (but be sure to delete the opening and closing braces after inserting it).	This entry uniquely identifies your new Feature.
`Title`	`DocCleaner`	This value will show up in the list of Features deployed to your site.
`Description`	This Feature encapsulates the custom workflow to remove macros from Office documents.	The description will show up underneath the title in the list of Features.

Table 6-4. *Customizing feature.xml After Inserting the Code Snippet*

Entry	New Value	Description
`ElementManifest\Location`	`workflow.xml`	Leave this entry set to its default. Since our `workflow.xml` file is located in the same directory as our `feature.xml` we don't need to specify the full path to it. If for some reason, this were not the case, you would need to specify the full path and filename for your workflow definition file.
`ElementFile`		You can delete this whole tag, leaving just one `ElementManifest` tag nested within the `ElementManifests` tag.

The other elements of the file can remain as is. Save and close `feature.xml`; we're done with it.

■ **Note** When our workflow is deployed, `feature.xml` will be copied to the server underneath the `FEATURES` folder. When you specify a path, for example for the `ElementManifest` attribute, make sure that your path is relative to the server folder hierarchy.

Open up `workflow.xml` from the Solution Explorer. Repeat the same process to insert the `workflow.xml` Code Snippet. Your screen should look like Figure 6-10. Table 6-5 details the changes to make.

```
workflow.xml*
<?xml version="1.0" encoding="utf-8" ?>
<!-- _lcid="1033" _version="12.0.3015" _dal="1"   -->
<!-- _LocalBinding   -->

<!-- Insert Workflow.xml Code Snippet here.  To do this:
1) Right click on this page and select "Insert Snippet" (or press Ctrl+K, then X)
2) Select Snippets->SharePoint Workflow->Workflow Template->Workflow.xml Code -->
<Elements xmlns="http://schemas.microsoft.com/sharepoint/">
  <Workflow
       Name="My Workflow"
       Description="This workflow ..."
       Id="GUID"
       CodeBesideClass="ProjectName.Workflow1"
       CodeBesideAssembly="ProjectName, Version=3.0.0.0, Culture=neutral, PublicKeyToken=publicKeyToken"
       TaskListContentTypeId="0x01080100C9C9515DE4E24001905074F980F93160"
   AssociationUrl="_layouts/CstWrkflIP.aspx"
       InstantiationUrl="_layouts/IniWrkflIP.aspx"
       ModificationUrl="_layouts/ModWrkflIP.aspx">
    <Categories/>
    <!-- Tags to specify InfoPath forms for the workflow; delete tags for forms that you do not have -->
    <MetaData>
      <Association_FormURN>associationFormURN</Association_FormURN>
      <Instantiation_FormURN>instantiationFormURN</Instantiation_FormURN>
      <Task0_FormURN>taskFormURN</Task0_FormURN>

      <Modification_GUID_FormURN>modificationURN</Modification_GUID_FormURN>
      <Modification_GUID_Name>Name of Modification</Modification_GUID_Name>

      <StatusPageUrl>_layouts/WrkStat.aspx</StatusPageUrl>
    </MetaData>
  </Workflow>
</Elements>
```

Figure 6-10. *Our workflow.xml file after inserting the Code Snippet*

Table 6-5. *Customizing workflow.xml After Inserting the Code Snippet*

Entry	New Value	Description
`Name`	`DocCleaner`	The name of our workflow as it will appear to administrators when they associate it to a list.
`Description`	This workflow removes macros from Office 2007 files	The description will appear to administrators when they select our workflow during the association process.
`Id`	Create a new Registry-format GUID (again, be sure to delete the opening and closing braces after inserting it)	This entry uniquely identifies your new workflow.
`CodeBesideClass`	`DocCleaner.DocCleanerWF`	The name of your project and the name of your workflow class, separated by a period.
`CodeBesideAssembly`	(The fully qualified strong name of your assembly)	For help retrieving the proper value for this entry, see the sidebar "What's in a (Strong) Name?"

Table 6-5. *Customizing workflow.xml After Inserting the Code Snippet (Continued)*

Entry	New Value	Description
TaskListContentTypeId AssociationUrl InstantiationUrl ModificationURL Association_FormURN Instantiation_FormURN Task0_FormURN Modification_GUID_FormURN Modification_GUID_Name		We're not using any forms for this workflow—we cover forms in Chapter 7. You can go ahead and delete all of these entries. Just be careful that you don't inadvertently delete the StatusUrl attribute and the closing angle bracket from the workflow tag when you delete the rest of the attributes (yes, that is experience talking...)

Leave everything else at its defaults. When you're all finished, your workflow.xml file ought to look similar to Figure 6-11. That takes care of workflow.xml.

```
workflow.xml
<?xml version="1.0" encoding="utf-8" ?>
<!-- _lcid="1033" _version="12.0.3015" _dal="1"   -->
<!-- _LocalBinding   -->

<!-- Insert Workflow.xml Code Snippet here.  To do this:
1) Right click on this page and select "Insert Snippet" (or press Ctrl+K, then X)
2) Select Snippets->SharePoint Workflow->Workflow.xml Code -->
<Elements xmlns="http://schemas.microsoft.com/sharepoint/">
    <Workflow
         Name="DocCleaner"
         Description="This workflow removes macros from Office 2007 files"
         Id="020347B2-A53B-417a-8092-004F09890ABC"
         CodeBesideClass="DocCleaner.DocCleanerWF"
         CodeBesideAssembly="DocCleaner, Version=1.0.0.0, Culture=neutral, PublicKeyToken=20dfe4897269146c"
         StatusUrl="_layouts/WrkStat.aspx">
        <Categories/>
        <!-- Tags to specify InfoPath forms for the workflow; delete tags for forms that you do not have -->
        <MetaData>
            <AssociateOnActivation>false</AssociateOnActivation>
        </MetaData>
    </Workflow>
</Elements>
```

Figure 6-11. *Our completed workflow.xml file*

WHAT'S IN A (STRONG) NAME?

To retrieve the correct name for your assembly, you've got two choices (well, really you've got more, but only two that make much sense). First, you could add the DLL to the global assembly cache (GAC) (c:\windows\assembly) and check the value from there. You will need to strong-name your assembly before adding it to the GAC. This option requires you to piece together the various pieces of data into the full string that you need:

```
(Assembly Name), (Version), (Culture), (PublicKeyToken)
```

where:

- `Assembly Name` is the filename of your assembly, minus the extension.
- `Version` is the full major/minor/build/revision version of your assembly.
- `Culture` is the culture supported by your assembly (typically `neutral`).
- `PublicKeyToken` is the public key portion of the key pair used to sign the assembly.

The first four columns in the default view of the GAC give you all of this information—you just need to retype it properly or go into the properties for the assembly, copy out each element, and paste it into the right place. If you're lazy and/or a bad typist, like me, retyping those values—especially the public key token—is asking for trouble. Copying and pasting is equally fraught with the potential for mistakes. There has to be a better way.

Fortunately, there is—Lutz Roeder's .NET Reflector, a little utility that is quite likely more important than the discovery of fire. If you're not already familiar with it, Google "roeder reflector" and it should be your top hit. Download the ZIP file and extract the EXE—there's nothing to install. Run the EXE, drag your assembly and drop it on the top portion of the screen, select it from the list, and retrieve the full strong name string we need from the bottom portion of the screen. You can copy the `Name` string right from Reflector and paste it into your `workflow.xml` file. The following screenshot shows this bad boy in action:

Now we're at the point where Microsoft really cleaned up the deployment process coming out of the beta. Previously, there was a file named `install.bat` that did the actual deployment. Hold your comments about doing deployment with a batch file because it really makes perfect sense, and, guess what... we're still using one; it's just better hidden from us, *and* we don't need to edit it manually the way we did during the beta. The reason that the batch file (how '80s!) makes perfect sense is because of the tasks it is completing. At a very high level, the major steps it performs for us are as follows:

1. Copy the required files to a directory on the server.
2. Adds your assemblies to the GAC.
3. Verify the InfoPath forms. Again, we're not using forms, but there is no harm in this line executing.
4. Install and activate the Feature, making it available on the site for which you specified a URL.
5. Reset IIS so that your changes are recognized by the server.

As you can see, when you look at what is happening, a batch file is the best way to go. Fortunately, as I said, things are a lot easier now. We no longer need to edit the file manually and it is integrated right into the build process within Visual Studio for us by the MOSS SDK project templates.

Configuration of the deployment is handled right from within Visual Studio. Inside your project properties is a tab called Build Events. Click it and you'll see an entry for the postbuild event that looks like Listing 6-5. The last parameter on that command line is the one we're interested in. It starts out as `NODEPLOY`. This tells the batch file to build our project but not to do any of the deployment steps. This allows us to do interim builds to see how things are progressing and whether we've broken anything, without wasting time deploying to the server before we're ready.

Listing 6-5. *The Postbuild Command*

```
call "$(ProjectDir)\DeploymentFiles\PostBuildActions.bat"➥
 "$(ConfigurationName)" "$(ProjectDir)" "$(ProjectName)" ➥
"$(TargetDir)" "$(TargetName)" NODEPLOY
```

Once you have completed your development and are ready to deploy, simply change the `NODEPLOY` parameter to `DEPLOY`. Now, as part of the build process, the batch file will perform the steps to deploy our workflow to the server.

■ **Tip** There is one additional option available to control the processing of our build and deployment cycle. If you have made changes *only* to the code files—either through the Designer or by actually writing code—all you need to do is update the assembly in the GAC. There is no need to redeploy the whole Feature to SharePoint. In this case, append a `QUICK` parameter at the end of the postbuild command line (after `DEPLOY`). Now upon a successful build, the GAC will be updated and IIS reset so that your new assembly is used. Just remember to take this parameter off if you make changes to forms or any of the XML files or they will not be updated.

Getting back to our example, we're now ready to actually deploy our project to our development server. Go into properties and change `NODEPLOY` to `DEPLOY` and you're ready to go (that was easy). Save your solution before continuing and then build your project. You'll notice that the output from the batch deployer is shown in the output window within Visual Studio. You may see some error messages, for example when GACUtil tries to remove your assembly (the `-uf` line in `postbuildactions.bat`). The first time you deploy, there is nothing to remove. There are other similar situations like this, especially the first time you run the deployment. If you see other errors, however, you'll need to do some troubleshooting. It is likely that the problem will be in a misconfigured `feature.xml` or `workflow.xml`, or perhaps you forgot to sign the assembly.

If there are no unexpected error messages, you're done. Your workflow Feature is successfully installed. Now we can test it out.

THE ENABLED PROPERTY

As we hopped around in this chapter and examined the various activity properties, you may have noticed one property we haven't talked about that is common to all activities—even the custom activity we built in Chapter 5. I'm talking about the `Enabled` property. We didn't specifically add it to our MacroStripper activity so how did it get there and what does it do?

The `Enabled` property is added by the base activity class that ultimately all activities derive from. As far as usage, it does exactly what you think it would do: it indicates whether the activity is marked as *commented out.* When we're writing code, commenting out a particular block of code is a common activity. Perhaps it's code we're still working with, or old code that we're not quite ready to get rid of yet. It could be code we're refactoring or reworking for performance reasons; developers comment out code for any number of reasons.

The `Enabled` property of an activity gives you the same capability in a workflow. If you have activities on the Designer canvas that you need to leave in place but don't want to have as part of your compiled workflow, simply set their `Enabled` property to `false`. The activity and all of its property settings, code, and so forth will remain in place. It just won't be compiled into your workflow DLL.

Disabled activities are indicated in the Designer with a semitransparent coloring over the activity.

Testing Our Workflow

We're getting closer to something we can actually feel good about. We've built an activity, built a workflow around it, and deployed that workflow to our server. Now let's see how it works.

In order to test our workflow, we need to go through the following steps:

1. Associate the workflow with a document library.
2. Create an instance of the workflow on a specific document.
3. Sit back and marvel at the sheer wonder of our accomplishment.

Tip You may not need to worry about the next step. I'm using a prerelease version of the `PostBuildActions.bat` file to write this part of the chapter. Some people at Microsoft are telling me that this step should not be necessary. It has been all through the beta, when it also shouldn't have been, so I'm leaving the step in just in case. Try it the first time you deploy an activity and see if you need it.

The first time we deploy our workflow to the server, there is one additional step we need to take care of—activating the Feature on our site collection. To take care of this, from the Site Actions drop-down menu, select Site Settings. If need be, navigate to the settings for the top-level site. Underneath the heading Site Collection Administration, click the link for *site collection features*. On the next screen, locate the entry for our DocCleaner workflow and click its Activate button. Now we can continue with a more typical test. Step 1 is pretty straightforward. From the Settings page for your document library, click the Workflow Settings link. Next you'll see the Add a Workflow screen. Figure 6-12 shows the completed version of this form for our workflow. There are only two pieces of information we need to change:

- Select DocCleaner as the workflow template.
- Enter **DocCleaner1** as the unique name for our instance.

All of the other settings can be left at their defaults for our example. Click OK to associate your workflow with the document library. If you're interested in the various other settings on this page, the descriptive text to the left provides some pretty good detail. You could also refer back to Table 3-1 in the "Solving the Problem: The Workflow Administrator's Role" section of Chapter 3.

After the workflow is successfully associated with the document library, you will be taken to the Change Workflow Settings screen for your document library. So far, so good; now it's time to load up a document and kick off our workflow.

Step 2 actually tells SharePoint that we want to run our workflow on a specific document. First, make sure that there is an Office 2007 document utilizing the new file formats in the document library you associated with in step 1. For this first run, make sure it is a document that contains macros. Later on, if you'd like, you can run it through for a nonmacro document. Run your mouse over the name of the document and select Workflows from the context menu, as shown in Figure 6-13.

Tip When you create your macro-enabled document, make sure the macro is actually in the document, and not the template it is based on (typically `Normal.???m`). If the macro is in the template instead of the document, our activity will (rightly so) not remove it. Yep, that's experience talking...

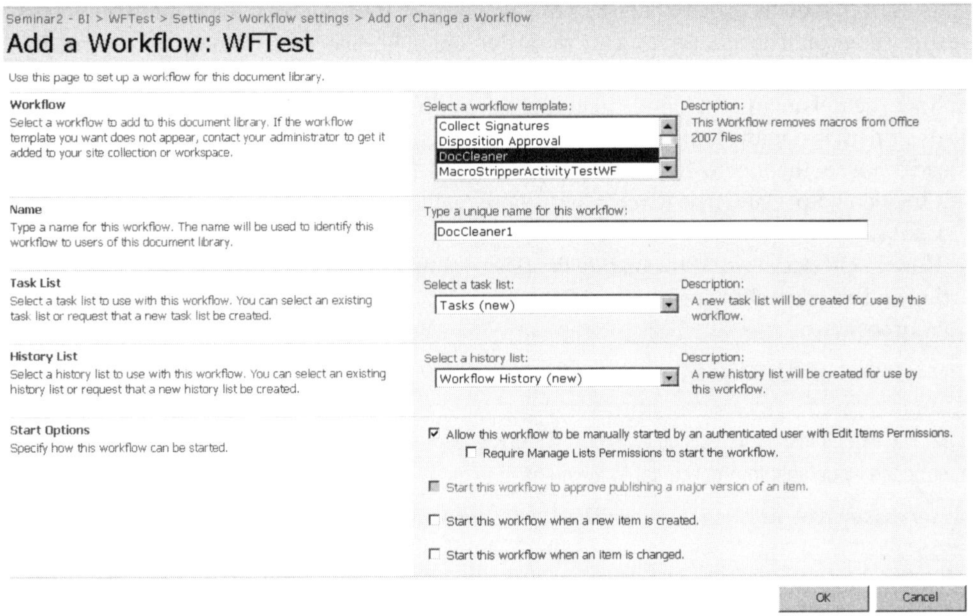

Figure 6-12. *The completed Add a Workflow form for our workflow*

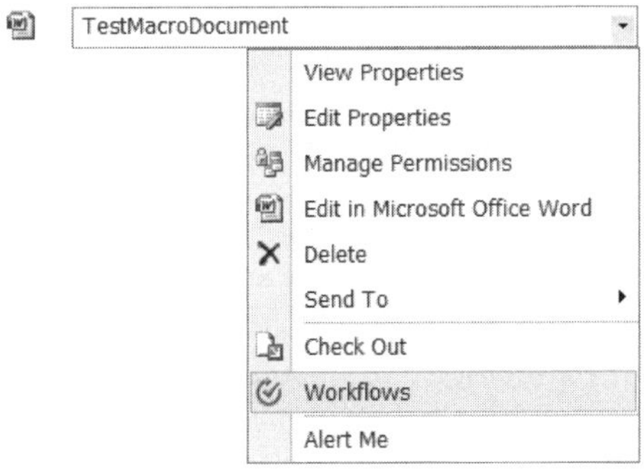

Figure 6-13. *Launching a workflow on a particular document*

The next screen that comes up, shown in Figure 6-14, shows the available workflows for this document library. Click the name of our workflow (DocCleaner1) and get ready for step 3.

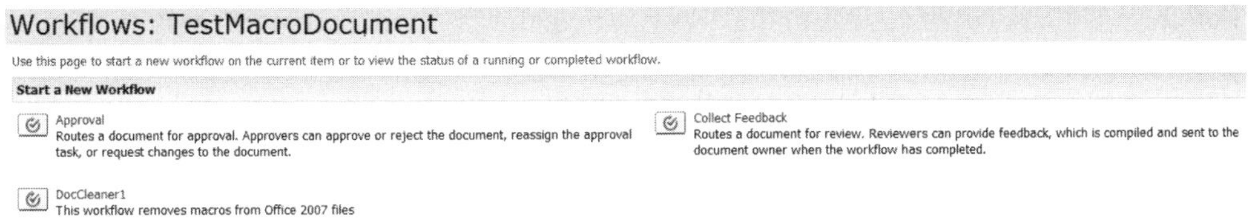

Figure 6-14. *The available workflows in our document library*

The last part of the process, step 3, is the fun part—we take a look at the fruits of our labors. The first thing you'll notice, right on the main document library screen that we are returned to, is that our document is gone. Yes, there is a document there, but if you run your mouse over it, you'll see the full document name, including the extension, in the status bar of the browser. The document is not any longer a macro-enabled document (DOCM, XLSM, or PPTM) but instead is now of the macro-free variety (DOCX, XLSX, PPTX). Go ahead and click on the document to open it up. Check the macros list—there really is nothing there anymore.

Cool.

Now go check the workflow history list. There should be an entry showing our workflow starting and an entry showing our workflow finishing.

Way cool...

■ **Tip** The default history list, called Workflow History, does not show up on the Quick Launch or the All Site Content page by default. In order to get to it, you need to navigate to it manually. The address will be

`http://<base_site_url>/Lists/Workflow%20History/AllItems.aspx`

Wrap Up

So there you have it: a complete sequential workflow from start to finish. Again, the example we walked through was pretty simple, but the process you would follow for an infinitely more complex workflow would be the same. We looked at pretty much all the options for configuring a workflow that we have available to us.

■ **Note** For the record, the options we didn't cover were all pretty basic and self-explanatory. I'm going to go out on a limb and assume that you're all intelligent enough to figure out what, for example, an option labeled *Start Workflow When a New Item Is Created* does. That's the type of stuff I skipped over. If you have questions, feel free to ping me at my web site: `www.kcdholdings.com`.

That wraps up our foray into sequential workflows. Next up: state machines...

Building a State Machine Workflow

At a high level, building a state machine is fundamentally identical to building a sequential workflow. The devil is, of course, in the details, where they are completely different. In this section, we'll explore those differences by looking at another problem encountered at KCD Holdings and see how a simple state machine workflow comes to the rescue.

First, though, let's start at the high level and see where the two models are the same. In both types of workflow, we do the following:

- Add activities from the Toolbox
- Set properties on activities in the Properties window
- Write code in event handlers and other standard Visual Studio constructs
- Configure our deployment with two XML files
- Deploy our workflow as a feature
- Test our workflow through the browser

If you think that list looks like most of what we've covered in the last 20-something pages, you're absolutely right. The majority of the *mechanics* of building a state machine are identical to the process we covered for a sequential workflow, or nearly enough so as to not matter. There are a few differences in the Designer that impact how we add and configure our activities, but they are not that significant.

The only thing that is significantly different is the model or paradigm we follow for our workflow process and the impact that has on how our workflow is built. Let's go through a quick refresher on state machines so we all start from the same place.

Essentially, a state machine is based on the concept of conditions ("states") and transitions. A condition is a set of circumstances that indicate the current status or situation of the process being modeled. Events occur and cause a transition from one condition to another. Unlike sequential workflows, there is no defined path through the workflow. Instead, the path taken by the workflow is determined by the events that occur as the workflow is processing. A state machine can only be "in" one condition at a time.

State machines are good at modeling both complex processes as well as simpler process. They excel at modeling nondeterministic processes—that is, processes that do not have a prescribed path that is known at design time. Finally, due to their nature and the inherent event-driven paradigm, state machines are naturally suited to modeling processes that progress based on the occurrence of a trappable event from a collection of events known and planned for at design time.

■ **Note** If you'd like a refresher on state machines, complete with pictures, please flip back to Chapter 1. Otherwise, we're done with the dictionary definition and so we will be moving on.

So, that's a good dictionary definition. Let's start to look at state machines in the real world.

Exploring State Machines and the State Machine Designer

You saw a screenshot of the Designer for state machines back in Figure 6-2, but you likely didn't pay much attention to it. We'll need to correct that here. Go ahead and create a new project in Visual Studio using the SharePoint State Machine Workflow Library template. Don't worry about what you call it or anything like that; we'll be throwing this project away before we walk through our sample state machine. We're just going to use it to explore for a bit. Figure 6-15 shows our workflow when we open our `Workflow1.cs` file in the Designer for the first time. The project template for the state machine workflow has kindly added one state activity to our

Designer to get us started. We're going to take a minute and explore the Designer environment for state machines because it is somewhat different from what we've seen before. We'll make use of the one state activity that was added for us to poke around.

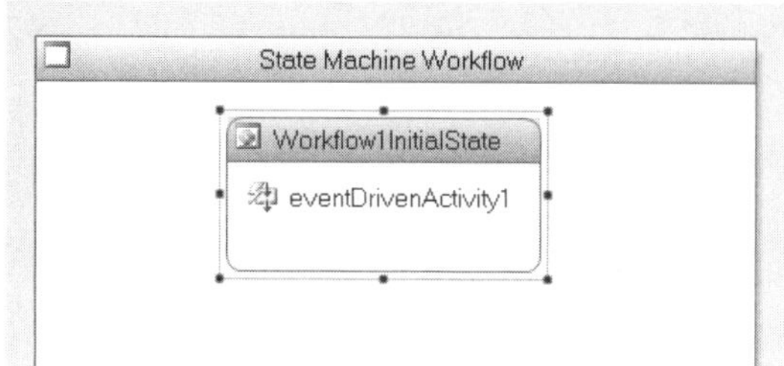

Figure 6-15. *The initial Designer for our state machine workflow*

You'll notice that the Designer for state machines is entirely freeform. You can place activities anywhere you need to and drag them around at will. Remember, there is no set path through a state machine workflow so the structured Designer of the sequential workflow would not work here.

The one activity on the Designer is a state activity. By default, it is named Workflow1InitialState because it is just that—the first state in our workflow. If you think back to the beginning of our sequential workflow, you'll remember that I said it had to start with an onWorkflowActivated activity in order to function in the SharePoint environment. So the questions you're likely asking are "Why are things different for a state machine? Why doesn't it need to begin with an onWorkflowActivated?" Those are both very astute questions and you're very observant for having brought them up. The answer is that things aren't different and the state machine does start with an onWorkflowActivated. You just can't see it yet.

To get to the bottom of this mystery, we need to explore a fundamental element of the state machine Designer. Looking at Figure 6-15, it looks like it contains just the one state activity, which then includes the nested eventDrivenActivity. Looks can be deceiving. It turns out that the state activity is a special type of composite activity with a quite unique Designer of its very own.

Double-click on the eventDrivenActivity1 in the Designer and the magic will be revealed—a view inside the eventDrivenActivity showing its children, as shown in Figure 6-16.

Now you can see the onWorkflowActivated activity. I told you it was here.

Looking at Figure 6-16, the eventDrivenActivity should look familiar—it looks an awful lot like some of the sequential activities we've seen already. In fact, it looks like we could add more activities underneath the onWorkflowActivated activity and have them executed in sequence; and, in fact, that is exactly the case. When we're walking through the construction of our state machine workflow, we'll add more activities to the EventDrivenActivity to have them do the work we need.

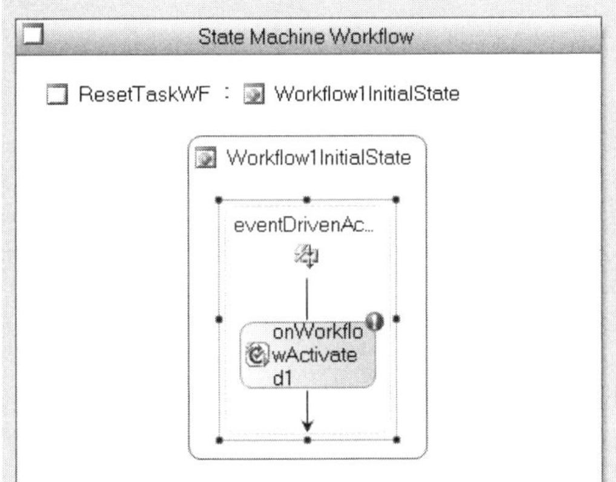

Figure 6-16. *Opening the secret door reveals more of the inner workings of our state machine.*

We're going to leave this piece alone for now and come back to it when we're building our workflow. We have a few more Christmases Past to visit before we can settle in, so let's get going, Ebenezer. At the top of Figure 6-16 you'll see two links—one for the name of our workflow and the other for the name of the activity we're currently examining. Each of those links will take us back to the high-level view of our workflow—the former to the beginning of the workflow and the latter to a view of the current activity. For our small-potatoes workflow, they both operate the same. Go ahead and click either one to go back.

The next thing we're going to take a look at is adding new activities to our workflow. There's not anything different here, so just drag any activity out of the Toolbox and drop it any old place on the Designer. Go ahead, just pick an activity and add it.

Now, unless you're cleverer than I am (which admittedly, isn't all that impossible) you probably weren't successful. As you might expect, it turns out that the only activities you can add directly to the workflow itself is a state activity or an EventDriven activity. It's not too much of a stretch, considering that this is a state machine; it is made to handle states and transitions, which is essentially what these two activities represent. We'll go into more detail on these two activities in just a bit.

So now we'll add a state activity to the Designer. Grab it and drag it out; drop it anywhere you like. Remember, this is a freeform canvas. I've expanded the height of the activity slightly so you can read all of the text, but Figure 6-17 shows our state activity after dropping it on the canvas. It tells us which activities we can drop on it:

- State activity
- EventDriven activity
- StateInitialization activity
- StateFinalization activity

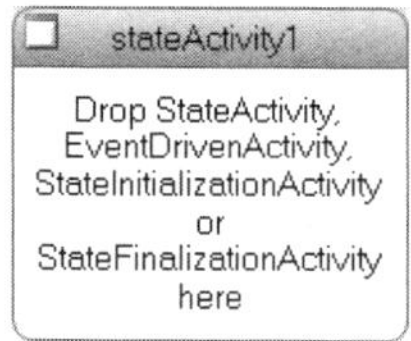

Figure 6-17. *The state activity gives us a clue as to the children it can contain.*

Let's take a look at these one at a time.

StateInitialization Activity

The StateInitialization activity will fire as our state machine transitions into our state. We can use it to execute other activities as soon as the transition happens. If you double-click on the StateInitialization activity on the canvas, you will also be taken to a lower-level view, similar to what we saw before. In this view, you can add additional activities as children of the StateInitialization activity to be executed sequentially.

A state activity can contain zero or one StateInitiation activities. If it exists, it will always be executed, although nothing prevents you from adding conditional activities (IfElse, While, etc.) activities as children of the StateInitialization to control processing at a more granular level. If you try to add more than one StateInitialization activity, the Designer will not let you.

Unlike the next activity we'll look at, this activity can be added to your workflow and not contain any children. In this case, it just won't do anything.

EventDriven Activity

The next activity we can work with at this level is the EventDriven activity. You add it to the state activity in the same way, and you can double-click on it to see its children. When you do so for the first time, you'll see a little bit of the specifics of this activity. The error message that shows up tells us that not only can the EventDriven activity contain other activities as children, but in fact it *must* contain at least one child activity. So unlike the other activities we're looking at here, if you add an EventDriven activity, you have to add at least one child activity to it.

If you add just about any activity to the EventDriven activity, you'll see a bit more of the specifics of this activity. Go ahead and add an activity, say a Code activity, to the EventDriven activity. You can add it but you'll see that the error indicator is still there. Click on the smart tag and you'll see a new error message: "The first 'EventDrivenActivity' child should implement 'System.Workflow.Activities.IEventActivity', such as 'HandleExternalEventActivity' or 'DelayActivity'." The wording is perhaps a little misleading—the use of *should* implies that you can get away with not implementing the interface when in fact it is a requirement. It really ought to read *must.*

Anyway, back to our walkthrough. Wording issues aside, what the error message tells us is that the first child activity inside our EventActivity must implement the stated interface. Without going too far into the inner working of the interface, this requirement is in place because the EventDriven activity needs to be able to subscribe to specific events so that it can respond to them.

Nine activities fit this bill. From the default WF activity set, we have

- HandleExternalEvent
- Delay

And from the SharePoint activities, we have

- OnTaskChanged
- OnTaskCreated
- OnTaskDeleted
- OnWorkflowActivated
- OnWorkflowItemChanged
- OnWorkflowItemCreated
- OnWorkflowItemDeleted

In reality, all of these SharePoint activities are just customized versions of the HandleExternalEvent activity, preconfigured for specific events from within the SharePoint host.

All of this brings us to the final piece of information that you need to know about the EventDriven activity—it does just what the name says. It executes its child activities as a response to a specified event. Each EventDriven activity can subscribe to exactly one event—no more, no less. If you attempt to add more than one of the nine activities from the previous lists, you will get an error in the Designer telling you that this is a no-no. This is the defining element of this activity. It allows your workflow to control the processing of its child activities. It allows you to say essentially, "Just because something has transitioned me to a certain state doesn't mean that I am going to do anything about it yet. I'm going to wait until my subscribed event happens before I proceed."

This is important in our Office workflows. See the sidebar "Designing Office State Machines" for more information.

■ **Note** We'll see this in a few minutes when we finally get around to building our sample workflow, but you can support multiple events in a given state by adding multiple EventDriven activities to the state and subscribing each to different events.

DESIGNING OFFICE STATE MACHINES

I'm going to speak in some generalities here for a minute to try to help you understand how state machines are *typically* designed in an Office, Information Worker scenario. Notice the emphasis on *typically* and cut me a little slack. Yes, I know there are many, many situations that can differ from this model, but we're looking at things from a high level right now.

Typically (there's that word again), the various components of a state machine are used as follows:

- In the single StateInitialization activity you can have for a given state, you do whatever processing you need to and then create tasks and assign them to users. You would also typically include some logging here.
- Next in the chain would be one or more EventDriven activities—one for each potential event that you are interested in responding to. OnTaskChanged is usually going to be one of those events you're interested in. Each EventDriven activity is going to include a SetState activity to effect a transition to a new state. Exactly what state that is depends on many factors, including what event was handled.
- Finally in the single StateFinalization activity each state can have, you will do some processing to close things out for this state. This may include things such as
  - Logging
  - Closing out tasks as appropriate

Again, remember that we're talking in generalities here, but that list is a pretty good approximation of how most Office state machines will be built. This is, in fact, the design we implement in our example.

There is nothing in SharePoint or WF that locks you into this. Numerous other scenarios are possible, but they will all be some variation of this. Perhaps you won't use a StateInitialization activity and you'll create tasks directly in your EventDriven activity. That's fine. Perhaps you won't have a StateFinalization activity and your process will jump immediately to the next state. That's fine, too. Perhaps the only "event" your EventDriven activity will handle is the signaling of a Delay activity so in a sense it always processes. That, too, is OK.

The only thing you can't do is not have an EventDriven activity in your state. This is because it is the EventDriven activity that must contain the SetState activity that is what causes your process to transition to the next state. The only exception to this rule is your "completed" state, which cannot contain any other activities as it signifies the end of your workflow.

StateFinalization Activity

The StateFinalization activity does just what you would expect: it gives you the opportunity to execute some activities just before the workflow transitions out of a state. It is the antithesis of the StateInitialization activity we just looked at. Other than its place in the processing order, it is exactly the same as the StateInitialization activity.

State Activity

The last activity that can be added directly to a state is another state activity. You may wonder what the ability to nest states gets you; the answer is that it gets you a pretty decent form of event inheritance. EventHandler activities can be defined at the parent state level, and the child states can have those events available as potential targets for a transition. This functionality is not something we're going to look at as part of our simple example here, but take a look at the sidebar "Recursive Composition—Nesting States" for some further exploration of this topic.

STATE MACHINE VS. SEQUENTIAL—A WORKFLOW SMACKDOWN

Beyond the obvious world of states such as Waiting for Approval and Approved, transitions such as OnDocumentPublished and onDocumentApproved and other states and transitions of their ilk, the applicability of states and transitions is a bit more difficult than in other scenarios where the states and approvals can easily number in the dozens or even hundreds. I have to admit that I had a long struggle to come to grips with the benefit that state machines bring to the information worker world. I've got a pretty good picture now, but I know that there are still elements that I'm not at peace with yet. The one thing I am certain of, though, is that I'm convinced of the value of state machines—so much so, that most of the workflows I'm building for clients these days are state machines. I tend to put up a pretty good fight when someone tries to implement a process as a sequential workflow when I know that a state machine would be a much better approach.

OK, all of that aside, how did I come by this preference for state machines and how can you achieve the same Zen-like level of workflow nirvana? Read on.

Typical processing in an Office workflow scenario would go as follows:

1. Create content and post for review.

2. Reviewers review and offer feedback.

3. Integrate feedback and submit document for approval.

4a. Approver reviews and approves. Go to 5a.

4b. Approver reviews and rejects. Go to 5b.

5a. Content is published to a wider audience.

5b. Content is returned to author.

6. Process ends.

Naturally there will be significant variations from scenario to scenario when you get down to specific details, but remember, we're talking in generalities here so this is a pretty good description of processing.

So why is a state machine better than a sequential workflow? The answer lies in four parts:

1. The wildcard is that review and approval can occur on multiple levels whereby one level can trump another level's response, causing the process to short-circuit or branch arbitrarily. This is what showcases the power of a state machine. It represents an occurrence that is global to the entire process—meaning that it can happen at just about any point. Building this into a sequential workflow almost always results in an ugly mess of loops and conditional evaluations. It is much cleaner in a state machine, especially with judicious use of nested states—which we look at in the sidebar "Recursive Composition—Nesting States."

2. The realization that each of the items we've listed is really a combination of states and events already. Posted, Feedback Offered, Approved, Rejected, Published—these are all states that content can exist in. The trigger to move between these states is always an event—Author posts content, Reviewer offers feedback, Approver rejects, etc.

3. While our list pretty much covers the majority of information worker workflows, it is by no means all encompassing. As soon as you toss in things such as translations, automated processing, external lookups, and so forth, things get a little murkier. You're beginning to move out of the realm of human workflow and skirting the edges of machine workflow. State machines work very well in situations such as these. In these situations, the external processes are services that can respond to and signal events that our state machine can interact with. We're moving our workflows into the realm of a service architecture with the inherent benefits of loose coupling, isolation, and so forth.

4. Human interaction is rarely definable in a neat little package of a primarily straight-line processing that a sequential workflow prescribes. Toss into the mix the fact that over time processes change and things get even trickier. Even if you were able to shoehorn your process into a nice, neat sequential workflow in the beginning, over time changes and exceptions will make it unwieldy. A state machine is much less susceptible to these types of problems.

OK, that's it, time to get down off my high horse. That's my take on things; I'm sure your view of the world will be different and more than one of you will be wondering who whacked me with the *stupid* stick. My final advice would be to use what makes the most sense in your situation. While I prefer a state machine, I also realize that it does not fit the bill in every situation, and in some situations just plain will not work at all. So, look at the needs and restrictions of each situation and head down the road that makes the most sense. Don't just blindly head down one road or another.

There are a few last things to look at in the Designer before we get to building our state machine. First of all, in your sample project, notice that the state that was added automatically for us by the template is named Workflow1InitialState. This touches on a concept that says that each state machine must have one state designated as the *Initial* state. This is where our workflow begins its processing. At the opposite end, there can be, but doesn't have to be, a state designated as the *Completed* state. It will not be unusual to have a state machine that does not ever really end. It continues moving from state to state in response to various triggers. It may live in a given state for years, but it technically never ends, so we don't have *have* to have a Completed state. With that said, I typically add a Completed state to my state machines because I can usually think of some situation that would bring about the end of the workflow.

There are two ways to designate these special states:

1. Right-click on an activity and select either Set as Initial State or Set as Completed State.

2. Click on the Designer canvas itself and look at the Properties window for the workflow as a whole. You'll see an `InitialStateName` property and a `CompletedStateName` property.

To stop a state from being designated as one of these special roles, you need to either remove it from the property name in option 2 or else assign another activity to that state via the context menu. Finally, you can tell visually in the Designer which activities are fulfilling the Initial and Completed roles because the icon in the header of the activity changes, as shown in Figure 6-18.

Figure 6-18. *The various icons for state machine activities indicate the role they play.*

It's a little hard to see in Figure 6-18, but the icon for the Initial state is a small green circle with a white arrow inside—the same icon used to signify the beginning of our sequential workflow. The icon for the Completed state is the red square with the white circle that signified the end of our sequential workflow.

Lastly, realize that our workflow itself is a state activity. In the Designer, that means that the entire canvas is a great big state activity with all the rights, privileges, and responsibilities thereof. The importance of this will dawn on you after you read the sidebar on recursive composition.

RECURSIVE COMPOSITION—NESTING STATES

As mentioned earlier, it is possible to nest one state activity within another. The benefit of this is that an EventDriven activity defined on the parent state activity is available on any of its child states. For our Office workflows, this means that if you were to define an EventDriven activity on a parent level to handle an onWorkflowItemChanged event, that event can be handled from any state within the parent.

The real benefit of this, and part of what makes state machines so powerful, is subscribing to events at the workflow level—global events that can occur at any point during the process. By defining them at the workflow level (remember, the top-level workflow is nothing more than a great big state activity), they can be captured and handled regardless of which state the workflow is in currently. Events like items being deleted are a perfect example of the benefit this offers. Instead of having to define a handler for this as part of every state, it can be defined once at the workflow level.

Working in the Designer

Our foray into state machines and the Designer for them is done; now we can go ahead and build our first state machine workflow. Let's take a look at the scenario we're going to tackle.

Scenario: Preventing Outdated Tasks

One problem KCD has encountered as they increase their use of workflow is outdated task assignments. For example, Sue in Marketing creates a document detailing plans for a marketing campaign for a new product and posts it to the Marketing department's collaboration section on the intranet. After posting the document, Sue manually kicks off the Marketing Campaign workflow. Sue does not need to assign users to tasks because, as part of the workflow, a task is assigned to the current members of the campaign review committee—a virtual team that rotates its members quarterly and is made up of employees from all over the world. Sue does not know who the current members of the review committee are, although she could find out if she needed to. The workflow encapsulates the logic to look up the current team members and assign tasks appropriately.

Shortly after posting the document, Sue receives an email from the product manager informing her that the product has encountered a production problem and is going to be delayed for six weeks. Sue knows that this changes the marketing campaign schedule that is part of the document, and also means that the deadlines on the tasks assigned to review the document are now no longer valid. Sue modifies the document and reposts it to the portal. She also updates the metadata for the document—one piece of which is the due date used by the workflow process to assign task deadlines.

The problem is that the tasks that were created by the workflow are still assigned to the users. As mentioned, Sue does not know who was assigned a task when the workflow started. She could look it up and send them an email notifying them that the schedule has changed and that they can hold off on completing their task, but that would take hours and she's busy. She decides just to let them figure it out. After all, what's the harm? So they complete their tasks a bit early—at least the document is correct so they'll see the right data.

You can see where this is going...

Meanwhile, in London, Robert, part of the current campaign review committee, sees the task assigned to him. He is busy trying to get things wrapped up before he goes away on vacation for two weeks, but the deadline for this task falls right smack in the middle of his time off. He puts aside other work and begins reading the document immediately, adding his comments as he goes. Two hours later, he gets to the end of the document where the marketing schedule is. At first he thinks it is a mistake, but he checks again and sure enough, the schedule is six weeks off what the task assignment told him. There's two hours of time he won't get back. He stops working on the document and tries to get back to the other, more pressing items on his to-do list so he can go away on vacation and think seriously about finding a new job...

So perhaps this scenario is a bit stilted, but the ability to react to changing conditions in our environment is going to be key for our workflows. While I'm sure it would be possible to implement this as a sequential workflow, it would likely involve a morass of While and Parallel activities. As you'll see, in a state machine, this type of scenario is easy.

■ **Note** To keep matters simple, we're only going to walk through the elements of this scenario that are specific to state machines—namely building out the event-driven process so we can respond to changes on the document and its metadata. The other portions of the process—creating and updating tasks, retrieving information from SharePoint lists and other data sources, and so forth are all pretty standard SharePoint development fodder. We'll put placeholders in so you can see where things will be happening, but I really just want to keep the focus on the state machine elements.

To get started we need to create a new project of the SharePoint State Machine Workflow Library type. If you created a playground project to explore things in the previous section, you can close it and don't worry about saving the changes. For my example, I'm going to name the new project **ResetTaskOnChange**. We'll go through the same beginning steps for this project as we did for the sequential one earlier. If you need details, flip back to the beginning of this chapter, but here are the steps in summary:

1. Create the project.

2. Rename `workflow1.cs` to **ResetTask.cs**.

3. Examine the files in the solution. Notice that they are the same as the sequential workflow.

4. Open the `ResetTask.cs` file in the Designer.

We explored the Designer already in the previous sections, so we can just go directly to the tasks to build our workflow.

Configuring the Top Level

As we've already seen, you add activities to a state machine the same as any other workflow. Go ahead and add two more state activities to the canvas. With the Initial state added by the template for us, that makes a total of three states. Add a StateInitialization activity, two Event-Driven activities, and a StateFinalization activity to one of the state activities. Notice that the activities always reorder themselves to Initialization–EventDriven–Finalization regardless of the order you drop them.

All of the activities for this level are in place, so let's go ahead and set some properties; at this level, that only means giving our states and other activities meaningful names. Table 6-6 shows what we're going to change the names to.

Table 6-6. *Renaming States and Activities*

Old Name	New Name
workflow1InitialState	InitialState
stateActivity1	TaskCreatedState
stateActivity2	CompletedState
stateInitializationActivity1	InitTaskCreatedState
eventDrivenActivity1	onWorkflowActivated
eventDrivenActivity2	onTaskChanged
eventDrivenActivity3	onWorkflowItemChanged
stateFinalizationActivity	FinalizeTaskCreatedState

■ Note While not a requirement, a good practice to adopt is to name your EventDriven activities for the event they handle—typically *on<Event_Name_Here>* as we did here. Similarly, states are typically named *state<Descriptive_Name>* or *<Descriptive_Name>State*. We used the latter for our example.

When we rename our states the designation as the Initial and Completed states gets lost, so we need to redo the designation. Right-click on CompletedState and select Set As Completed State from the context menu. Right-click on InitialState and select Set As Initial State.

The last thing we need to do is build our transitions. There are two ways to do this—we'll cover them both. The first is a visual approach and the second is, well, not a visual approach. Personally I find the former to be easier most of the time, but you can make up your own mind. Also, if you are going to decide at runtime which state your process will transition to, you have to use the second approach.

For the first approach, we are going to build a transition from the onWorkflowActivated EventDriven activity to the TaskCreatedState activity. This means that when our workflow is initiated, it will transition to the TaskCreatedState. We're not setting any conditions on it, so this transition will happen every time our workflow runs. To set this up, use the following steps:

1. Click on the onWorkflowActivated activity to select it.
2. Run your mouse over the small blue dot in the middle of the right vertical border of the activity until your cursor changes to a crosshair-like effect. The change is kind of subtle but you'll see what I mean.
3. Click and drag down to the top center of the TaskCreatedState activity. A Visio-like connector will follow your mouse and attach itself permanently to the two activities once you release your mouse.

That's it for the first method. If you double-click on the onWorkflowActivated activity, you'll see that a SetState child activity has been added and configured to transition to the TaskCreatedState.

For the next transition, we are going to react to our workflow task being changed. However, we'll only transition to the Completed state if the task was actually marked as complete. Otherwise, we'll just stay right where we are. We'll need to do some runtime decision making for this one.

To build this transition, follow these steps:

1. Double-click on the onTaskChanged activity to go to the view of its children.
2. Add an IfElse activity to the onTaskChanged activity.
3. Add a SetState activity to the first ifElseBranch activity. One note of caution—there are two SetState activities in the Toolbox: one for state machines and one for SharePoint. We want the former. It is in the Windows Workflow tab on the Toolbox.
4. Set the `TargetStateName` property of the SetState activity to `CompletedState` by selecting it from the drop-down list.

Don't worry about the validation errors for now; we'll come back to take care of them in just a minute. Click on the ResetTask link to return to the top-level view.

■ **Note** There is no transition kicked off by the onTaskChanged activity. As you'll see in a moment, the only function of that activity is to update the due date for tasks based on information supplied with the payload item.

When you're done to this point, this top level of your workflow is complete and should look like Figure 6-19. The Designer lets you drop activities anywhere so your screen won't look exactly like mine, but as all the pieces are there, the layout doesn't matter.

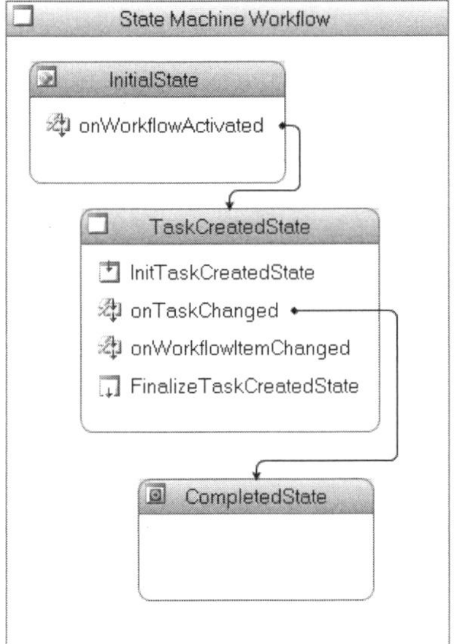

Figure 6-19. *A look at the finished top level of our state machine*

Configuring the Child Level

The next pieces that we need to configure are all one level down from where we've spent the majority of our time so far. This will take care of all of the child activities.

First up will be the onWorkflowActivated activity in the InitialState activity. Double-click on it to see its children. All we need to do is fix up the `CorrelationToken` property (and possibly the `WorkflowProperties\Name` property—it depends on how you did your renaming). `CorrelationToken` should be set to `workflowToken` and the name for both the `CorrelationToken` and the `WorkflowProperties` properties should be `ResetTask`. We're done with this first task, so go ahead and click on the ResetTask link in the Designer to take us back to the top level.

Next we will take care of the child activities for the InitTaskCreatedState activity, so go ahead and double-click on it. Drag a CreateTask activity from the Toolbox and add it to the InitTaskCreatedState activity. Set the properties as shown in Table 6-7. Any properties not listed in the table can be left at their defaults.

Table 6-7. *Configuring Properties for the CreateTask Activity*

Property	New Value	Notes
`CorrelationToken`	`taskToken`	
`CorrelationToken\OwnerActivityName`	`taskCreatedState`	
`MethodInvoking`	`InitCreateTask`	The code for this method is shown in Listing 6-6.
`TaskID`	`taskID`	Click on the ellipsis in the value field to bring up the Binding dialog box and create a new field (not a property) named `taskID`. The various subproperties of `TaskId` will be filled in appropriately.
`TaskProperties`	`taskProperties`	Again use the Binding dialog box to create a new field named `taskProperties`.

Moving on, we can tackle the onTaskChanged EventDriven activity next. Again, double-click on it to bring up the child view. There are a few error indicators on this screen, so we'll take care of them. First of all, at the top of the activity is an error that tells us we need to add an activity above our IfElse that implements the `IEventActivity` interface. Drag an onTaskChanged activity from the SharePoint section of the Toolbox and drop it above the IfElse. The first error goes away.

We now need to configure the onTaskChanged activity; the details are in Table 6-8.

Table 6-8. *Configuring Properties for the onTaskChanged Activity*

Property	New Value	Notes
`CorrelationToken`	`taskToken`	Select the value from the drop-down list.
`TaskId`	`taskID`	Use the Binding dialog box to bind to the existing `taskID` field that we created earlier.
`AfterProperties`	`afterProps`	Use the Binding dialog box to create a new field named `afterProps`. This field will get a hash table of property values in place *after* the task is edited.

The last issue we need to fix on this screen is to set the `Condition` for the IfElseBranch activity. Configure the `Condition` property as a Declarative Rule Condition. Use the Condition Editor dialog box to create a new condition named **TaskCompleted** with a value of `this.onTaskChanged1.AfterProperties.PercentComplete == 1`.

We don't need the `else` portion of our IfElseBranch, so you can go ahead and delete it. That's all we need to do on this screen; simply click the ResetTask link at the top of the canvas to return to the top level.

The next EventDriven activity we need to configure is the onWorkflowItemChanged activity. Double-click on it to go to the child view. We need to add three activities here:

1. One that implements the `IEventActivity` interface
2. One Code activity
3. One UpdateTask activity

Add the activities in the order shown here. This time around we'll use the onWorkflow-ItemChanged activity for the IEventActivity activity. Add it to the top of the canvas and then you'll need to set its `CorrelationToken` property to `workflowToken`. Next add a Code activity to the onWorkflowItemChanged activity. Change its `ExecuteCode` property to `updateDueDates`. We'll add the code for this in a bit. Finally, add the UpdateTask activity below the Code activity. Set its `CorrelationToken` property to `taskToken`. Use the Binding dialog box to bind its `TaskId` property to the existing `taskID` field we created as part of the CreateTask activity. Also use the Binding dialog box to connect its `TaskProperties` property with the existing `taskProperties` field we created. We're done with this EventDriven activity. You can close out of it and return to the top level.

The last child activity we need to configure is going to be on the FinalizeTaskCreatedState activity. From its child view, we need to drag in a CompleteTask activity. Set its `CorrelationToken` to `taskToken` from the drop-down list, and bind its `TaskId` property to our existing `taskID` field. Close out of the child view and return to the top-level view.

We're almost there. The last thing we need to do in our workflow itself is to add some code. Open `ResetTask.cs` in Code view. You'll see a couple of variables and two empty methods. Add the code in Listing 6-6 to the `InitCreateTask` method. This code is pretty simple. It creates a new GUID in order to uniquely identify our new task and then sets some properties of the task itself.

■ Note As I mentioned previously, I'm cutting out certain portions of this scenario to keep the focus on the state machine aspects. The `GetCurrentReviewers` method is a perfect example of that. In the full-blown solution, this retrieves information from a SharePoint list that stores the names of the current members of the Marketing Campaign Review Committee. For this sample, I just have it returning a single value, which is hard-coded. The entire contents of the `GetCurrentReviewers` method is `return @"mossrtm\marketingreviewer";`. You'll need to replace that with a valid account in your environment.

Listing 6-6. *The InitCreateTask Method*

```
this.taskID = Guid.NewGuid();
this.updateDueDates(null, null);
this.taskProperties.AssignedTo = GetCurrentReviewers();
this.taskProperties.Title = "Marketing Campaign Review";
```

Add the code in Listing 6-7 to the `updateDueDates` method. This code is responsible for calculating the due dates for the task created by this workflow based on some metadata values supplied with the payload item. Naturally in a production system, we would perform an actual calculation as opposed to using a random number generator. As I've said, though, I want to keep the focus on state machines and not get bogged down making you type irrelevant code.

Listing 6-7. *Generating random task due dates*

```
Random rand = new Random();
this.taskProperties.DueDate = DateTime.Now.AddDays(➥
                rand.Next(5, 15));
```

Deploying and Testing

Fortunately, deploying a state machine is no different than deploying a sequential workflow. Edit your two XML files (`workflow.xml` and `feature.xml`) and change your postbuild command line (`DEPLOY` instead of `NODEPLOY`). I covered specific instructions for this earlier in this chapter, so I won't rehash it all here. Just remember to configure your project for strong naming before compiling and that your Feature name is now ResetTaskOnChange.

After the build and postbuild process is complete, you need to create a new workflow association with a list in SharePoint and then actually kick off an instance of the workflow on a list item or document. Again, the steps for this were covered earlier in this chapter.

Once the workflow has processed, you should have a task assigned to the name you specified in the `GetCurrentReviewers` method. There are three things we want to try out in order to verify that our state machine is actually doing what it is supposed to do:

1. Change a piece of metadata (such as the title) or upload a new copy of the document, overwriting the existing document. Either one of these will trigger the `onWorkflowItemChanged` event and we should see a new due date (coming from the random number generator) for our task when we refresh the view of the task details. Our workflow should not change to a Completed state.

2. Modify the task, but don't mark it Complete or set its % Complete column to 100%. The `onTaskChanged` event should fire within our workflow, but it shouldn't change anything until we it is marked as Complete (or technically until its % Complete is 100%).

3. Change the task again, this time marking it as 100% complete. Check the workflow status again. It should be marked as Completed.

There you have it: a complete, functioning state machine workflow. Nice work. You rock. Go ask your boss for a raise.

Deploying to Production

So far, we've been doing our deployment in a nonproduction environment. We've been using the provided `PostBuildActions.bat` file to do all of the work for us. That's been all fine and dandy for a development environment, but now we're ready to deploy to production. What do we need to do now?

(I love being the bearer of good news...)

The short answer is *hardly anything*. The long answer is *OK, there are three steps.*

1. Switch Visual Studio to a Release build and compile as normal.
2. Grab the WSS Solution package file (.wsp) from the \bin\Release\Package folder of your solution and copy it to your production server.
3. Run the following commands, replacing paths and filenames as appropriate:
   - <path>\stsadm.exe -o addsovution -filename <path>\filename>.wsp
   - <path>\stsadm.exe -o deploysolution -name <path>\filename>.wsp -local -allowGacDeployment -force
   - <path>\stsadm.exe -o installfeature -filename <path>\feature.xml -force
   - <path>\stsadm.exe -o activatefeature -filename < path>\feature.xml -force -url http://localhost/ -force

When we switch Visual Studio to a Release build, the PostBuildActions.bat file automatically creates our WSS Solution deployment files for us. All we need to do is deploy them just the same way we deploy any other WSS solution.

See, you didn't even need your Easy Button for that.

Summary

We covered a lot of ground in this chapter, introducing a whole new landscape of functionality now available in Visual Studio. Here is a summary of the major points:

- The SharePoint SDKs (MOSS and WSS) add new project types to Visual Studio for our workflow projects. The names vary slightly depending on which SDKs you have installed
- In many ways, workflow projects are no different from any other project in Visual Studio. All of our code is still written in our class file, we have objects to create and manage, and all object properties are set in the Properties window.
- The visual workflow Designer is very similar to the BizTalk Orchestration Designer for those of you who have worked in that environment before.
- An instance of the onWorkflowActivated activity must be first in every SharePoint workflow.
- The onWorkflowActivated activity is our gateway back to our workflow host by way of the workflowProperties object it provides.
- Activities are managed in the Toolbox just like any other component in Visual Studio.
- Design-time validators warn us visually of errors configuring our activities.
- The WSSHistory activity provides functionality similar to the Windows Event Log for our workflow instances.
- The Enabled property allows you to comment out activities, removing them from your compiled workflow but keeping them in the Designer.

One major (and I do mean *major*) item we did not cover in this chapter is debugging. I figured that your code never fails and so you wouldn't need to worry about debugging—actually, I saved that for Chapter 9. The short answer is that our workflows are extremely debuggable. The long answer is in Chapter 9.

Speaking of Chapter 9 (nice segue, huh?), I'll add a plug for it here. We took a pretty happy path through our first workflows here. This was intentional because most of the time things should work pretty smoothly. There are some sticky bits that will rear their ugly heads periodically and Chapter 9 will help you deal with them. See if your question is answered or your problem is solved; if not, ping me at my web site (`www.kcdholdings.com`) and I'll see what I can do to help out.

CHAPTER 7

Workflow Forms

Welcome to Chapter 7. In this chapter we're going to explore (obviously) Workflow forms. We've discussed forms in various places throughout the book so far, and we've seen examples of many different types of Workflow forms—in both a browser and directly integrated into the Office client applications. In the previous chapter, we created a workflow, but it was one that did not use any forms. In this chapter, we're going to look at introducing forms built in InfoPath 2007 and ASP.NET to our Workflow arsenal. Microsoft has provided us with rich, nearly limitless capabilities to extend our forms experience. By the time we're done with this chapter, we'll have covered everything you need to know (and some things you probably don't) about Workflow forms in the 2007 Office System.

Types of Forms

The first thing we need to understand is specifically what forms we're talking about. There are two ways to classify the Workflow forms we deal with:

- *By technology*: ASP.NET or InfoPath
- *By function*: Association and initiation forms, modification forms, and task forms

The two technologies are just a delivery mechanism. Functionally, they are equivalent, and each of the functional types of forms can be rendered via either technology. The three functional classifications each serve a different purpose in the workflow lifecycle. We'll briefly cover each of these classifications.

Introducing InfoPath

InfoPath forms are designed and built in the InfoPath Office client application. InfoPath was introduced in Office 2003 but undergoes some serious upgrades in Office 2007. The major enhancement in Office 2007 is the addition of the Forms Server. This newcomer is responsible for taking a form designed in InfoPath and rendering it as standards-compliant HTML accessible from any modern browser. In addition, one nifty new feature introduced by MOSS 2007 is the ability to wrap these rendered forms directly in the Office 2007 client applications—looking for all the world like native Office dialog boxes. Cool.

Although the benefits of this technology are many for nearly any scenario, the case that interests us now is how this impacts our workflows. We've already seen several examples of InfoPath forms being rendered through the Forms Server. In Chapter 3, when we discussed the out-of-the-box experience, we saw some of these forms integrated into the Office client applications. To refresh your memory without forcing you to flip back to Chapter 3, lose your place in this chapter, and toss the book away in frustration, I'll include another screenshot here, shown in Figure 7-1. To show both sides of this coin, Figure 7-2 shows the same InfoPath form rendered into the browser. Again, the backend form is the same and was only built once—in InfoPath; we're just rendering it via a different technology.

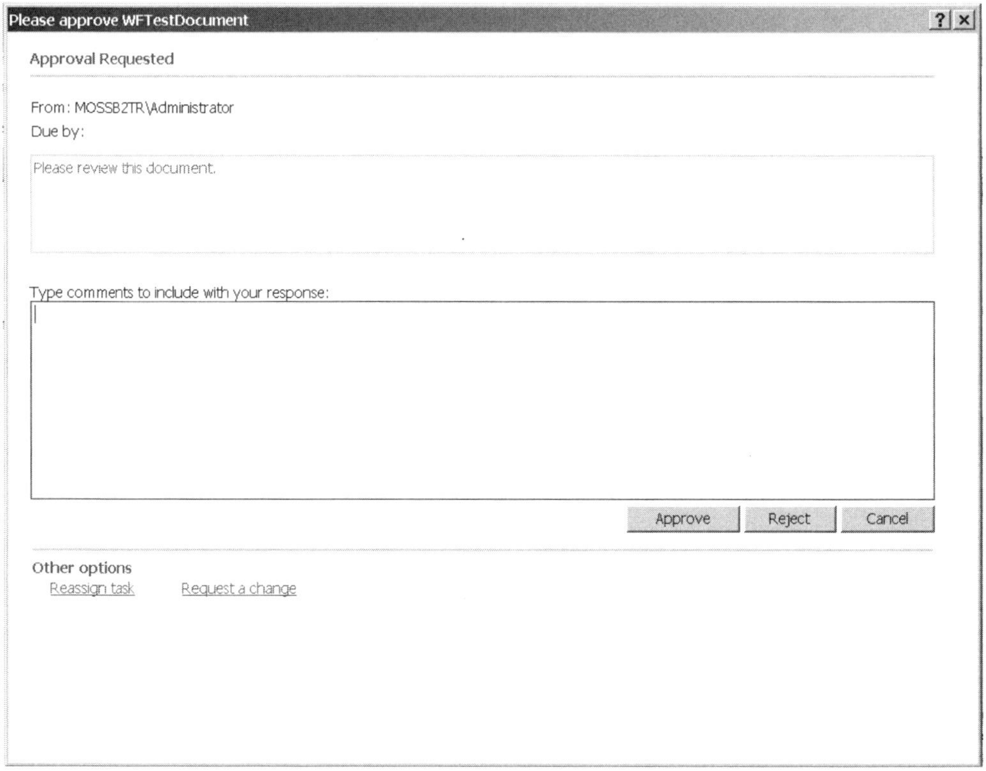

Figure 7-1. *The Forms Server renders InfoPath forms as standards-compliant HTML—shown here rendered directly in the Office client applications.*

The primary benefits we derive from this technology include

- The ability to utilize the rich design-time experience of InfoPath to develop our forms.
- The ability to develop the forms once and utilize them in multiple situations—namely both a browser and the Office client applications. We don't need to develop duplicate forms to handle each different client application.

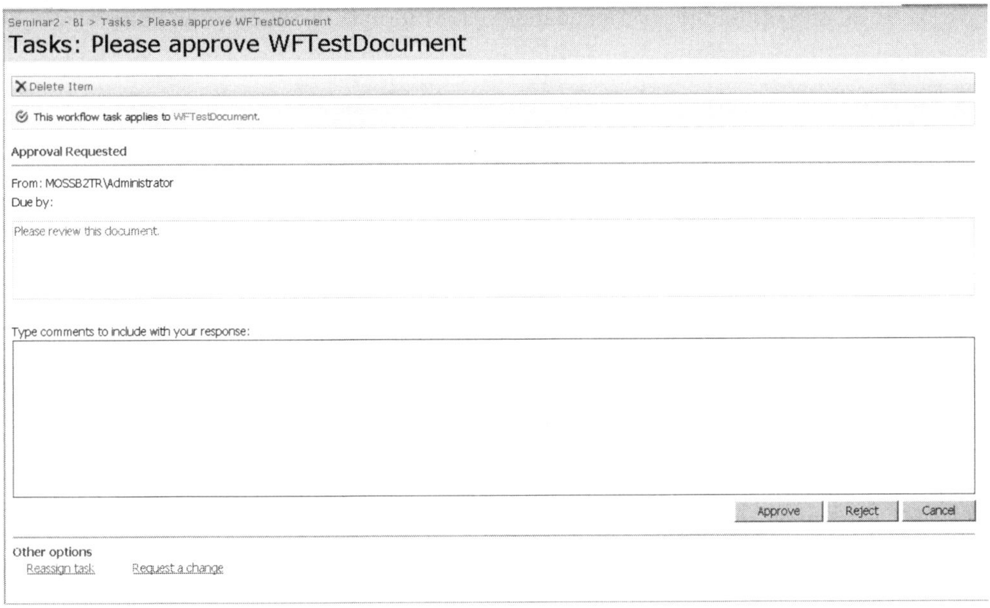

Figure 7-2. *InfoPath forms rendered as HTML can, of course, also be viewed in a browser. Here is the same form as in Figure 7-1, displayed in a browser.*

■ **Note** One thing to keep in mind about these browser and Office client renditions of InfoPath-based forms is that they do require the Forms Server technology be installed in your environment. Without the Forms Server, InfoPath forms are only consumable from within the InfoPath client—not nearly as useful. MOSS ships with a derivative of the full-blown Forms Server known as simply Forms Services. This allows for the browser-based forms and the forms to be integrated into the browser but does require MOSS. WSS alone won't cut it. Even WSS and a full Forms Server implementation won't get you the Office client integration—that is strictly MOSS territory.

ASP.NET

ASP.NET forms are nothing new and aren't anything to write home about. Their use in Office Workflow is pretty typical as a primarily web-based application. There are some special requirements to keep in mind as you develop these forms, but we'll delve into building these forms a little later in this chapter. For now, just keep in mind that all of your ASP.NET skills will be useful here and that without some flavor of the Forms Server in your environment, this is the only option available to you for Workflow forms.

Figure 7-3 shows a sample of a standard ASP.NET form in use during a workflow.

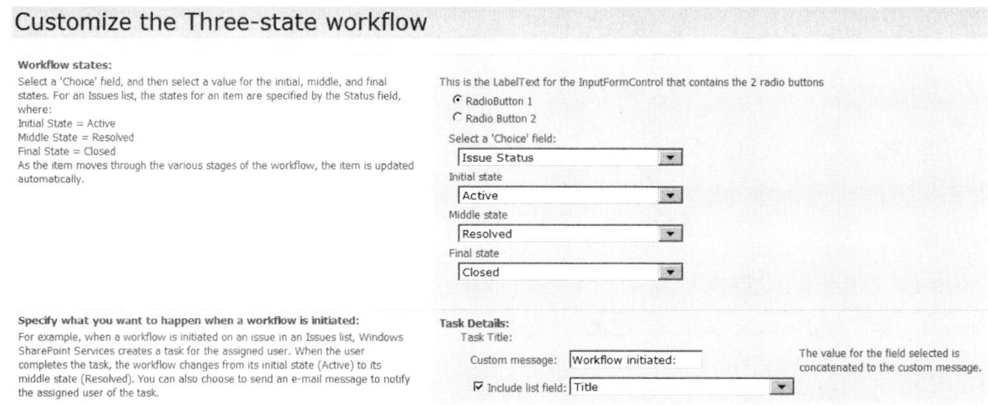

Figure 7-3. *Eminently useful in many situations, regular old ASP.NET web forms find yet another home in workflows where the new Forms Server is not available.*

Association and Initiation Forms

Association and initiation forms, while serving distinct purposes within the workflow lifecycle, are typically lumped together because they both are utilized before a workflow is begun. These forms are the first grouping in our functional breakdown of Workflow forms.

Association forms are used by administrators when they make a workflow available on a particular list, document library, or content type. Figure 7-4 shows an example of an association form. The function of these forms is to allow the administrator to specify parameters to customize a workflow—including listing the names of participants who will be assigned tasks. Initiation forms are similar to association forms, except that they are utilized when an instance of the workflow is kicked off for a particular document or list item. Quite often, data collected from the association form is used to set default values for fields on the initiation form. The initiation form can either allow editing of these default values or won't allow editing. Figure 7-5 shows a sample of an initiation form.

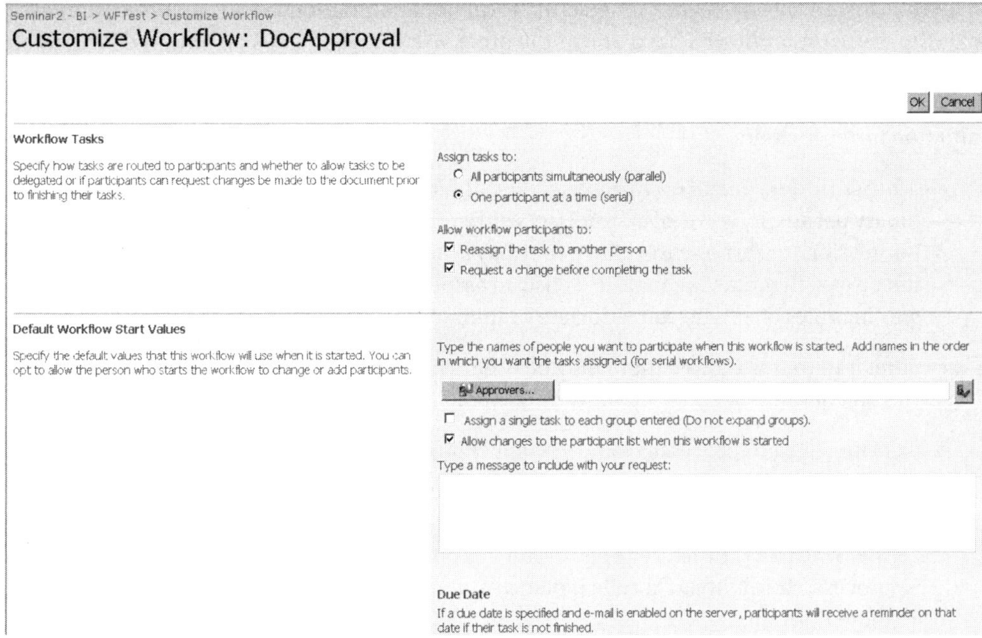
Seminar2 - BI > WFTest > Customize Workflow
Customize Workflow: DocApproval
OK Cancel
Workflow Tasks
Specify how tasks are routed to participants and whether to allow tasks to be delegated or if participants can request changes be made to the document prior to finishing their tasks.
Assign tasks to:
All participants simultaneously (parallel)
One participant at a time (serial)
Allow workflow participants to:
Reassign the task to another person
Request a change before completing the task
Default Workflow Start Values
Specify the default values that this workflow will use when it is started. You can opt to allow the person who starts the workflow to change or add participants.
Type the names of people you want to participate when this workflow is started. Add names in the order in which you want the tasks assigned (for serial workflows).
Approvers...
Assign a single task to each group entered (Do not expand groups).
Allow changes to the participant list when this workflow is started
Type a message to include with your request:
Due Date
If a due date is specified and e-mail is enabled on the server, participants will receive a reminder on that date if their task is not finished.

Figure 7-4. *A workflow association form is used to specify default values when attaching a workflow to a document library or list.*

Seminar2 - BI > WFTest > WFTestDocument > Workflows > Start Workflow

Start "DocApproval": WFTestDocument

Request Approval

To request approval for this document, type the names of the people who need to approve it on the **Approvers** line. Each person will be assigned a task to approve your document. You will receive an e-mail when the request is sent and once everyone has finished their tasks.

Add approver names in the order you want the tasks assigned:

Approvers... MOSSB2TR\Administrator

Assign a single task to each group entered (Do not expand groups).

Type a message to include with your request:

Please Review This Document

Due Date

If a due date is specified and e-mail is enabled on the server, approvers will receive a reminder on that date if their task is not finished.

Give each person the following amount of time to finish their task:

Day(s)

Notify Others

To notify other people about this workflow starting without assigning tasks, type names on the CC line.

CC...

Start Cancel

Figure 7-5. *Initiation forms are used by workflow initiators to specify parameters for their particular instance of a workflow.*

While technically neither an association form nor an initiation form is required, the vast majority of the time, you will need one or the other. We'll cover details on how to do this later in this chapter. Besides the obvious function of allowing users to specify participants for their workflow instances, a few other situations that could be handled via custom association or initiation forms include

- *More granular control over processes*: The ability to associate or initiate a workflow is a binary permission on a given list. Users either have the right to do it or don't. If they have permission to start one workflow, they have the right to start every workflow. This may not be exactly what you need. In a custom association or initiation form, you could apply specific rules over who can associate or initiate a particular workflow.
- Similar to that situation, there may be other criteria for limiting which workflows can run on content:
  - *Dates*: Certain processes may only apply during certain times throughout the year.
  - *Content of the payload itself*: Employee reviews may require one process for "Meets Expectations" or "Exceeds Expectations" reviews, but a totally separate process for "Below Expectations" reviews. While this could be handled within a single workflow process, the ability to handle it before a workflow is actually started just provides more flexibility.
- *Logging*: In some environments, it may be necessary to record or audit the processes that were attached to a particular document library. No workflows have actually begun yet, and so logging to a workflow history list is not appropriate. This would be more along the lines of process-control auditing.

Modification Forms

Modification forms, as the name cleverly implies, are those forms that allow users to make changes to a workflow once it is in progress. We saw this in Chapter 3 when we discussed the ability to reassign tasks or request changes to a task. Figure 7-6 shows one of these screens again for reference.

Workflow modifications are a powerful capability that is only touched on lightly in the sample workflows that ship with MOSS. The capability is really quite open-ended. It gives you the capability to make changes to a running workflow while it is in progress for any reason identified by your business process, or more likely a one-off exception to your business process. Perhaps it is a change in the process flow based on some new information. Perhaps it is a change based on a new threshold level for approvals.

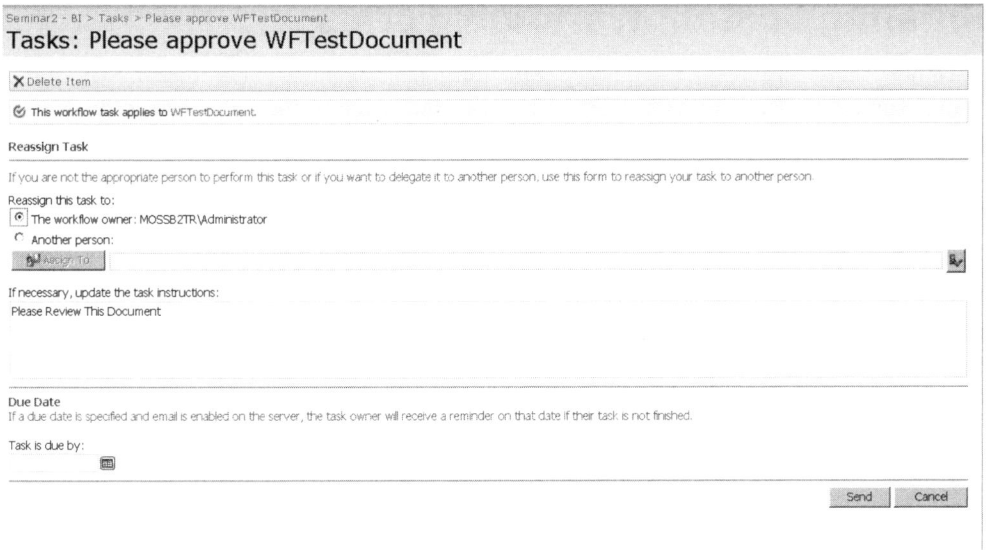

Seminar2 - BI > Tasks > Please approve WFTestDocument

Tasks: Please approve WFTestDocument

Delete Item

This workflow task applies to WFTestDocument.

Reassign Task

If you are not the appropriate person to perform this task or if you want to delegate it to another person, use this form to reassign your task to another person.

Reassign this task to:

The workflow owner: MOSSB2TR\Administrator

Another person:

Assign To

If necessary, update the task instructions:

Please Review This Document

Due Date

If a due date is specified and email is enabled on the server, the task owner will receive a reminder on that date if their task is not finished.

Task is due by:

Send Cancel

Figure 7-6. *Modification forms, like this Reassign Task form, allow users to make changes to in-progress workflows.*

Imagine this scenario: you are reviewing a document for a new wonder drug your company is working on. The day before the document landed on your To-Do list, the FDA levied a hefty fine against another pharmaceutical company for some infraction related to their internal documentation. Now here you are with a similar document sitting on your desktop. Before you add your comments and pass the document along, you'd really like to run it past someone in the legal department to get their input in light of the new landscape. When the document workflow was constructed, there was no facility for a legal review at this point in the process—that comes later. If, however, the workflow supports modifications during its processing, you can route the document over to someone in legal and have them review it before you do. Crisis averted thanks to workflow modification.

Task Forms

While similar to the previous two types of forms in the functionality provided, task forms are a unique beast. Due to the underlying architecture of SharePoint, a task form for a workflow is not simply a form associated with the workflow. Instead, it needs to work with other constructs within SharePoint—task lists. For basic functionality, and in most cases, we can largely ignore this and simply use the default form that ships with SharePoint.

Creating Custom Workflow Forms

Now that you have a good understanding of the role played by forms in our workflows, it's time to dig in and build some forms. We're going to walk through two different scenarios in this chapter—perhaps this is where the scenario model I've presented up to this point begins to fall apart a little. The scenarios covered here start to feel a bit forced or contrived. Forgive me for that, but I think it's important to walk through both ASP.NET and InfoPath forms to see how to implement each. We'll start with the InfoPath forms and wrap up the chapter with ASP.NET forms.

In each case, we'll be building a brand-new workflow in Visual Studio to meet the needs of our scenarios. Since we already covered the steps for building the workflow project and adding activities, I'm not going to cover them in great detail here. I'll just list the information you need to set up and let you work through the process on your own. If you need help with anything, refer back to Chapter 6 for a refresher.

Scenario 7-1: Using InfoPath Forms

As mentioned previously, using InfoPath forms is an extremely attractive option *if* you have some version of MOSS installed in your environment. You could also have WSS and Forms Server installed, although in this case you would not get the integration between the forms and the Office client applications—but it's still a step up from ASP.NET.

For this scenario, we're going to assume that we have MOSS installed. We'll start by creating our Visual Studio project, adding and configuring our activities, and preparing for deployment. Before we deploy, however, we'll build and configure our forms and configure our workflow to use these new forms. After that, we'll continue packaging our workflow into a Feature, deploying it and testing it.

Scenario: Global Marketing Campaigns

In the KCD Holdings Global Marketing department, a common occurrence is naturally the creation of new marketing campaigns. Often, however, these campaigns are not new. Instead, they have begun as local campaigns that were successful and are now going to be adapted and introduced globally. The local marketing director in the region that originated the campaign needs to review global campaigns that originated in their region. They do not actually approve the campaign, but they are given the opportunity to offer suggestions to fine-tune the campaign based on their experience as the originating region.

A task is assigned to a marketing traffic coordinator, however. This person is responsible for coordinating all of the resources necessary for a successful campaign. The task assigned to the traffic coordinator is for them to review the marketing plan document and approve of schedules and so forth.

To facilitate this process, each workflow is constructed to notify the appropriate regional marketing director via email and assign a task to the traffic coordinator. The initiation form will present the workflow originator with an interface that will allow them to specify the email address for the appropriate regional marketing director and the traffic coordinator.

■ Note This workflow is intentionally simplistic. Among other things, in a real production application, we would get the name of the marketing director and look up their email address. To keep things simple and to keep the focus on the forms, we'll just collect their email address on the form for now.

We've already covered building workflows and adding activities in Chapter 6. The focus here is on the forms so I didn't want to get us distracted. Naturally, your workflows can be as complex or as simple as you need them to be. The information collected in your forms can be as much or as little as you require. However, regardless of complexity, the basic principles covered here will apply in every case.

To begin with, we need to create our workflow project in Visual Studio. Select a Sequential Workflow project and name it **MarketingCampaign**. After the project is created, rename the default `Workflow1.cs` to `MarketingCampaign.cs`.

Adding and Configuring Activities

Open this file in the Designer and follow these steps:

1. Add a SendEmail activity to the canvas directly below the default OnWorkflowActivated1 activity.
2. Drag and drop a CreateTask activity directly below the SendEmail.
3. Add a While activity after the CreateTask activity.
4. Add a Sequence activity inside the While activity.
5. Add an onTaskChanged activity inside the Sequence activity.
6. Add an UpdateTask activity inside the Sequence, after the onTaskChanged.
7. Add a CompleteTask activity at the end, after the While activity.

When you are done, your Designer canvas should look like Figure 7-7. Don't worry about the property errors indicated by the exclamation points. We'll take care of them next.

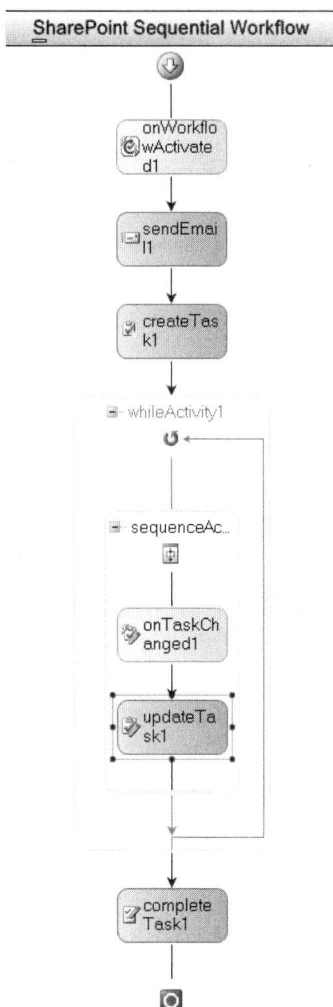

Figure 7-7. *The Designer canvas with our activities dropped into place*

Tables 7-1 through 7-7 provide details on customizing the properties of each of our activities. Set the properties of each activity as indicated. If a particular property is not listed, just accept the default value.

Table 7-1. *Property Settings for the OnWorkflowActivated1 Activity*

Property	Setting	Notes
`CorrelationToken\OwnerActivityName`	`MarketingCampaign`	Select the value from the drop-down list.
`Invoked`	`onWorkflowActivated`	Visual Studio will automatically create a method framework with the proper signature for us.
`WorkflowProperties\Name`	`MarketingCampaign`	

■ **Tip** After making the changes in Table 7-1 there will still be an error indicator shown. You need to manually change an item in the `MarketingCampaign.designer.cs` file. Open the file, find the line that looks something like `activitybind2.Name = "Workflow1";`, and change the value to `MarketingCampaign`. For some reason, this isn't caught during the refactoring when we rename our class file.

Table 7-2. *Property Settings for the SendEmail1 Activity*

Property	Setting	Notes
`CorrelationToken`	`workflowToken`	If you select from the property drop-down list, the `OwnerActivityName` subproperty will be automatically set.
`CorrelationToken\OwnerActivityName`	`MarketingCampaign`	
`From`	`admin@kcdholdings.com`	Set to a valid email address in your development system.
`MethodInvoking`	`onSendEmail`	We'll set the `To` and `Body` properties for our email programmatically in this method at runtime.
`Subject`	`Marketing Campaign Submission`	

Table 7-3. *Property Settings for the CreateTask1 Activity*

Property	Setting	Notes
`CorrelationToken`	`taskToken`	You'll need to type this value in.
`CorrelationToken\OwnerActivityName`	`MarketingCampaign`	
`MethodInvoking`	`onCreateTask`	
`TaskId`	`Activity = MarketingCampaign, Path = taskID`	Click the ellipsis in the `TaskId` property field, select the Bind To New Member tab, and enter **taskID** as the new member name. Select the Create Field radio button and click OK. A new variable of type `Guid` will be created and automatically associated for us.
`TaskProperties`	`Activity = MarketingCampaign, Path = taskProperties`	As before, if you click the ellipsis and use the Bind To New Member tab, the proper variables will be created for you.

Table 7-4. *Property Settings for the While Activity*

Property	Setting	Notes
`Condition`	`Code Condition`	
`Condition`	`taskComplete`	This subproperty is the name of the method that the While activity uses to determine whether it is finished processing. We'll add the code to this in a bit.

Table 7-5. *Property Settings for the onTaskChanged Activity*

Property	Setting	Notes
`AfterProperties`	`afterProperties`	Use the Bind dialog box to create a new member field with the proper name and data type.
`BeforeProperties`	`beforeProperties`	Use the Bind dialog box to create a new member field with the proper name and data type.
`CorrelationToken`	`taskToken`	If this isn't available in the drop-down list, you'll need to type it in by hand.
`CorrelationToken\OwnerActivityName`	`MarketingCampaign`	
`Invoked`	`onTaskChanged`	This method will be called when the activity is executed.
`TaskId`		Use the Bind dialog box to bind to the existing `taskID` property.

Table 7-6. *Property Settings for the UpdateTask Activity*

Property	Setting	Notes
`CorrelationToken`	`taskToken`	
`CorrelationToken\ OwnerActivityName`	`MarketingCampaign`	
`TaskId`		Use the Bind dialog box to bind to the existing `taskID` variable.
`TaskProperties`		Use the Bind dialog box to bind to the existing `taskProperties` variable.

Table 7-7. *Property Settings for the CompleteTask1 Activity*

Property	Setting	Notes
`CorrelationToken`	`taskToken`	Select from the drop-down list.
`TaskId`		Use the Bind dialog box to bind to the existing `taskID` property.

Note As I said before, this chapter is on forms. If you need a refresher on correlation tokens, activities, etc., please flip back to Chapter 6. It's all covered in far more detail there. I blew through it all pretty quickly here so we could keep our focus on the forms.

All of our activities are now configured. They don't actually *do* anything, but they are all configured. If you take a look at the code-behind file, you will see the six variable declarations and the five methods that Visual Studio has created for us. Although it's not a requirement, I'm semi-OCD so I like to move all of my variable declarations to the top of the class file (right under the constructor) and keep the methods at the end of the class file in the same order as the activities they belong to.

Note If you're coming back through this section for the ASP.NET forms, this is the point at which you want to stop, check the flux capacitor, and jump ahead to the ASP.NET forms again. If this is your first time through this chapter, you have no idea what I'm talking about here. Just ignore this little note for now. It will all become clear in about 20 pages.

Building Our Forms in InfoPath

We're going to leave Visual Studio for a minute before getting into any of the coding aspects of our workflow and go through the process of building our forms. You could continue and write your code and do the forms later. I prefer to do it this way for two reasons:

- Some pieces of the coding part of the project (like schema definitions and field names) are dependent on the forms. Building the form first lets you drop everything in place as you write your code.
- The rich design environment of Visual Studio is a great place to fine-tune your requirements and prototype the user interface for end users before writing much, if any, code. If the users change a requirement after you've written code (I can hear your startled gasps—that *never* happens!), it's a lot harder to change. If all you've done is drop some activities onto the canvas and put together some forms in InfoPath, changes are a lot easier to absorb. In addition, these two aspects deliver some nice eye candy to show to end users to help explain the process.

So, let's dig into InfoPath. We'll build the initiation form first and then the task form.

■ **Note** For our scenario, there is no data that we need to collect when a workflow is associated with a particular list so we will not be using an association form. The process of working with an association form would be nearly identical to what we'll cover here for an initiation form.

Building the Initiation Form

Open InfoPath 2007 and select the option to design a new, blank form. The InfoPath design view opens and presents you with a blank form and the Design Tasks tool pane. Click the Controls option and drag two textboxes onto your form. Double-click on the first textbox to bring up its Properties window. On the Data tab, change the Binding Field name to **marketingdirectoremail**. At the bottom of the Data tab, in the Validation and Rules section, select the Cannot Be Blank checkbox. Click OK to close the window. Repeat the process for the second textbox, but change the Binding Field name to **trafficcoordinator**.

■ **Caution** Be careful with your field names—XML is case sensitive. All of the field names you enter in InfoPath here end up as XML elements. A misplaced capital letter can really throw things into a tizzy.

Drag a Button control out onto the form and, in its Properties window, change its Label to **Submit**. In order to wire it up to actually submit our form, we need to add some rules:

1. At the bottom of the General tab, click the Rules button.
2. Name the rule something clever, like **Submit**.
3. Click the Add Action button.
4. Select Submit Using a Data Connection from the drop-down menu.
5. Click the Add button.

6. In the Data Connection wizard, accept the default of Create a New Connection to Submit Data by clicking Next.
7. Select To the Hosting Environment… for your destination, then click Next.
8. Click Finish to close the wizard.
9. Click OK to close the Add Action dialog box.

Once our form is submitted back to the server, there is one last thing we need to do—close the form. We handle that with another rule. Follow steps similar to those earlier (starting with step 3) to add a Close the Form action. You must uncheck the If Changes Have Not Been Saved checkbox before clicking OK. Click OK a few more times to exit the dialog boxes.

Add some descriptive labels directly onto the form to indicate what data goes into each field. When you are done, your form should look like Figure 7-8.

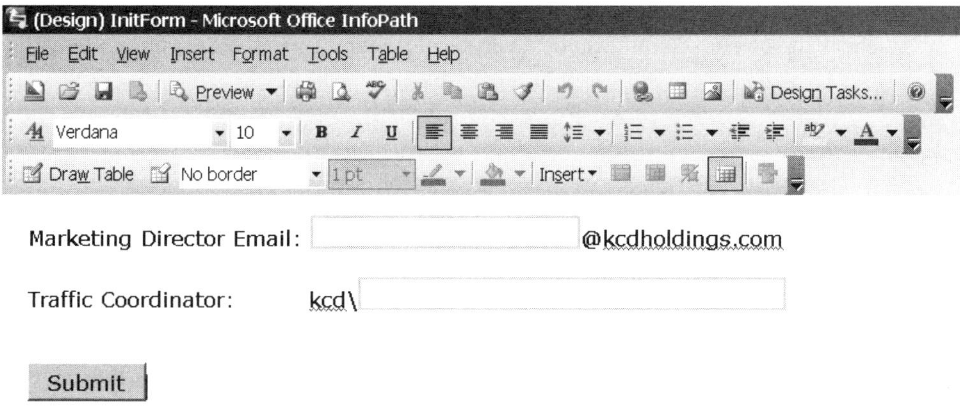

Figure 7-8. *Our basic initiation form all laid out on InfoPath*

This form is pretty straightforward. It presents an interface to collect two pieces of information. The fields are named such that when we access them from our code, they'll make sense. The last thing we'll need to do to make our coding easier is customize our data source a bit. For those of you not familiar with InfoPath, it automatically builds an XML schema (which is called your data source) behind the scenes. When users complete a form, the data is saved in an XML file that matches that schema. In our case, as we'll see in a moment, that XML file is submitted to the server and accessed by our workflow. To make our coding a little bit more straightforward and logical, we're going to rename the top-level element of this schema to something that makes a little more sense. In addition to forming the structure of our XML data, this top-level name also becomes the name of the object we use to access the XML data. To rename this element, in the Controls tool pane, click the Design Tasks link at the top to return to the Design Tasks tool pane. This time, select the Data Source menu option to view the data source for our form. Right-click on the myFields entry at the top of the tool pane and select Properties from the context menu. In the Field or Group Properties dialog box, change Property Name to **InitForm**. You'll see this name reappear shortly in this section and then again when we're writing our code. Click OK to close the dialog box.

The last thing we need to do before publishing our form is to check that it will be able to be rendered into a browser by the Forms Server. We do this with the Design Checker:

1. In the tool pane, again click on the Design Tasks link.
2. From the Tasks menu, select Design Checker.
3. In the Form Options dialog box, in the Browser Compatibility section, select the Design a Form That Can Be Opened in a Browser or InfoPath option and click OK.
4. There should be no errors or warnings.

The last step is to set the security on our form so that it can operate in our environment:

1. Inside InfoPath, click Tools ➤ Form Options.
2. Select the Security and Trust category.
3. Uncheck the box next to Automatically Determine Security Level (Recommended).
4. Select the Domain radio button.
5. Click OK.

That's it; our first InfoPath form is done. All we need to do is save and publish it. First, save the form to your hard drive. To save yourself some hassle, do not save the files to the same directory as your Visual Studio solution or to a subdirectory of that solution folder—I'll explain why in just a moment.

We can now publish our form:

1. Click File ➤ Publish.
2. In the Publishing wizard, select the option to publish To a Network Location and click Next. You might think that you want to publish to a SharePoint server. Ultimately, you're correct—that will be our destination—but for now we're just publishing to a network location. We'll move the forms to the SharePoint server as part of deploying our workflow.
3. Click the Browse button and navigate to your `\DeploymentFiles\FeatureFiles` folder. Make sure that the Form Template Name is set to InitForm and click Next. I mentioned just a bit ago about not saving to your solution folder—this step is why. By publishing our form to our FeatureFiles folder, it simplifies deployment, as we'll see shortly. If we had saved the files here, we would have had a conflict.

4. In the next step of the wizard, it is very important that you clear the alternate access textbox—it must be totally blank or your forms won't be rendered properly by SharePoint. With the field blank, click Next.
5. If you get a warning message about users not being able to access the form from this location, ignore it by clicking OK. Our users will be accessing the form from SharePoint. If you don't get this message box, you didn't set your security to Domain. Shame on you.
6. In the next step of the wizard, click Publish.
7. The final step of the wizard should tell us that our form was successfully published. Keep both checkboxes unselected and click Close.

Our initiation form is now published and ready to go. Before we close it, however, we're going to take one more step to generate some files we'll need while writing our code:

1. Click File ➤ Save As Source Files.
2. Select our solution folder in the dialog box that pops up.
3. Click OK.

That's it. If you look in your solution folder, you should see five new files:

- `manifest.xsf`
- `myschema.xsd`
- `sampledata.xml`
- `template.xml`
- `view1.xsl`

From all of these, we really only need the `myschema.xsd` file, but the others are nice to have. Regardless of your form name, data source name, InfoPath filename, etc., the saved schema file is always called `myschema.xsd`. We'll make use of the XSD file in a few minutes. So that we don't get it confused with the schema from our task form—which we're building next—close your form in InfoPath and then rename `myschema.xsd` to `InitFormSchema.xsd`.

Initiation form built and published—check. It's time to build the task form.

Building the Task Form

The task form is not going to be very different from the initiation form. You can repeat most of the same process from earlier. I'll walk you through it again but in less detail this time. If you have questions, refer to the previous pages.

Create a new form in InfoPath and add controls and label text so that it looks like Figure 7-9.

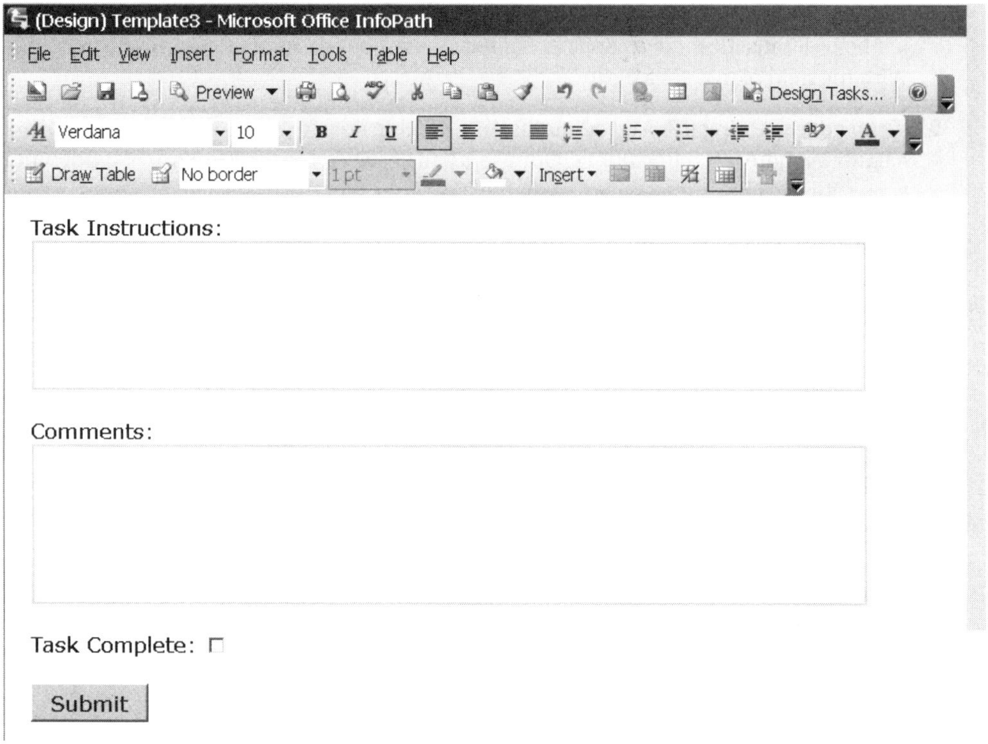

Figure 7-9. *The Design view of our Task Edit form in InfoPath*

The Task Instructions and Comments fields are set up similar to the two textboxes we set up on the initiation form. The only differences are that these two are set to be multiline fields and the Instructions field is set up to be read-only. The Task Instructions textbox should have a field name of `taskinstructions`, the Comments textbox should have a field name of `taskcomments`, and the Task Complete checkbox should have a field name of `taskcompleted`. Set up the Submit button the same as we did on the initiation form earlier. Make sure that the rules for the button are set up the same, too.

There is one unique step for the task form that is not required for any other type of form. When SharePoint is configured to display a task form, it needs a mechanism to pass values from the current task to the form in order to be displayed. This is necessary because of the split nature of tasks between SharePoint and Workflow. While the association and initiation forms are only used by the workflow, this is not true with task forms. Task forms exist as part of SharePoint and can be modified directly within SharePoint—adding a column, for example, through SharePoint for one particular task list; worse still would be the deletion of an existing column. If that task form was passed into a workflow, the workflow would not know how to handle the extra, or missing, column. This could cause all kinds of problems. Instead, Microsoft opted to just pass in the task data as XML. The workflow can parse and deal with any data now because it is not tied to a fixed schema.

Note While task forms can be shared across tasks, there is nothing that requires this. You can have unique task forms for each task in your workflow. You just need to specify the correct information for each task in your deployment files.

The mechanism for receiving this information is an XML file named `ItemMetadata.xml`, which provides the schema for our received data. If any of you worked with workflows during the beta cycle, you know that this file was *required*. Without it, SharePoint would crash whenever you tried to load task forms. In the final release, this problem was fixed. The file is no longer required, though it makes for a pretty boring task form without it, so in all likelihood, you will be using it.

Caution The filename `ItemMetadata.xml` is case sensitive. You must match the case as shown here or you will still get an error, even if the file is otherwise configured and bound correctly.

To configure this correctly, you must create the `ItemMetadata.xml` file and then bind that file to your form as a secondary data source by following these steps:

1. In your solution folder, create a text file named `ItemMetadata.xml`—remember about the case-sensitive filename!
2. Add the following line to the top of the file: `<z:row xmlns:z="#RowsetSchema" />`.

If there are no data elements that you need in your task form, you are finished with this file—you can save and close it. If there are some fields that you need to have available to your form, add them to the file. To do this, for each field that you need available, add the field name as an attribute to the `z:row` tag and set it equal to an empty string. There is one important point to remember for this—you must prefix each field name with `ows_`. For our scenario, we need the `taskinstructions` and `taskcomments` fields available, so we will add an attribute of `ows_taskinstructions` and an attribute of `ows_taskcomments`. Our finished `ItemMetadata.xml` will look like this: `<z:row xmlns:z="#RowsetSchema" ows_taskinstructions="" ows_taskcomments="" />`. After adding an attribute for each field (in our case, just the two) you can save and close the file.

If we're using the `ItemMetadata.xml` file, we need to add the schema to our task form as a secondary data source:

1. From the InfoPath Data Source task pane, click Manage Data Connections.
2. Click Add.
3. Configure the options to create a new connection to receive data.
4. Click Next.

5. Click the option to receive data from an XML document.
6. Browse to your `ItemMetadata.xml` file and select it.
7. Click the Resource Files button.
8. Click Add.
9. Browse to your `ItemMetadata.xml` file and select it.
10. Click OK and then Next.
11. Make sure the option is selected to automatically retrieve data.
12. Click Finish.

Once the data source is created, if you need to retrieve any of the task data for your form, you can bind the specific fields to the new data source. In our case, we need to retrieve the `taskinstructions` and `taskcomments` fields, so we'll bind those to our new data source:

1. Double-click on the `taskinstructions` textbox to bring up the Properties window.
2. Click the function button to the right of the Value textbox.
3. Click the Insert Field or Group button.
4. Select the ItemMetadata (Secondary) data source from the drop-down list.
5. Choose the `ows_taskinstructions` field.
6. Click OK a few times to exit all of the dialog boxes.

Repeat the steps for the `taskcomments` field.

That's all we need to do as a special step for our task form. We can now go back to finishing the task form just as we did earlier with the association form. Repeat the same process from before:

1. Make the form browser-compatible (in the Design Checker).
2. Rename the top-level element of your data source (to **TaskForm**).
3. Change the security setting on the form.
4. Save the form to a folder other than your solution folder.
5. Publish the form to your FeatureFiles folder. Be sure to name the form **TaskForm** and to clear out completely the alternate access textbox.
6. Save the source files for this form and rename the XSD file to **TaskFormSchema.xsd**. When prompted about overwriting files, you can click OK. The only file we really need is the XSD, and that one won't be overwritten because we renamed it in our first go-around.

Both of our forms are now complete. We can close InfoPath and return to Visual Studio to write our code, compile, and deploy.

Writing the Code in Visual Studio

We've created two forms for use in our scenario. The code we write now needs to handle our workflow's interaction with each. Let's get started with the initiation form.

Initiation Forms

Looking at our initiation form, there are a few pieces of information that we collect:

- The name of the senior traffic coordinator
- The email address of the regional marketing director

To work with these pieces of information, we need to assign them to local variables within our workflow class. Declare the private variables shown in Listing 7-1 at the top of your class file.

Listing 7-1. *Private Variable Declarations*

```
private string sTrafficCoordinator = default(String);
private string sMarketingDirectorEMail = default(String);
```

Now that we have a place to store the values, we need to get the values and store them. Then we can use them where and how we need to. To understand the two approaches we could take to retrieve this data from the forms, we need to know how it is made available to us. The `SPWorkflowActivationProperties` class exposes two members that are of interest to us here—`InitiationData` and `AssociationData`.

When our workflow is associated with a particular list by an administrator, the `AssociationData` property gets populated with an XML string that contains the values supplied on the association form. When an instance of our workflow is initiated by a user on a particular list item, the `InitiationData` property gets populated with an XML string that contains the values supplied on the initiation form. A sample schema for these two properties is shown in Listing 7-2. Looking at this schema reveals that our individual properties are stored as XML elements.

Listing 7-2. *A Sample XSD Schema for an Association or Initiation Form*

```
<?xml version="1.0" encoding="UTF-8" standalone="no"?>
<xsd:schema targetNamespace="http://schemas.microsoft.com/office/➥
infopath/2003/myXSD/2006-06-15T12:34:02" ➥
xmlns:my="http://schemas.microsoft.com/office/infopath/2003/ ➥
myXSD/2006-06-15T12:34:02" xmlns:xsd="http://www.w3.org/2001/XMLSchema">
     <xsd:element name="InitForm">
          <xsd:complexType>
               <xsd:sequence>
                    <xsd:element ref="my:trafficcoordinator" minOccurs="0"/>
                    <xsd:element ref="my:marketingdirectoremail" minOccurs="0"/>
               </xsd:sequence>
          <xsd:anyAttribute processContents="lax" namespace="http://www.w3.org/XML/➥
1998/namespace"/>
          </xsd:complexType>
```

```
    </xsd:element>
    <xsd:element name=" trafficcoordinator " type="xsd:string"/>
    <xsd:element name=" marketingdirectoremail" type="xsd:string"/>
</xsd:schema>
```

Listing 7-3 shows a sample of the data from the InitiationData property from our current scenario. This example is quite simple, which makes it easy to see how the data is stored and could be retrieved. Even more complex property structures can be just easily retrieved with some simple XPath expressions.

Listing 7-3. *Sample Data from SPWorkflowActivationProperties.InitiationData*

```
<my:InitForm xml:lang=\"en-US\" xmlns:my=\"http://schemas.microsoft.com/office/➥
infopath/2003/myXSD/2006-06-15T12:34:02\">
    <my: trafficcoordinator >
        kcd\\Administrator
    </my: trafficcoordinator >
    <my: marketingdirectoremail >
        User1@kcd.com
    </my: marketingdirectoremail >
</my:InitForm>
```

Now that you we see how the data entered into our initiation form is available to us, let's discuss the two options for retrieving it and working with it in our workflow:

- Query the InitiationData or AssociationData property, retrieve the XML, and manually parse it to retrieve the information we need.
- Use the .NET Framework command-line tool, xsd.exe, to generate a class based on our particular schema and use XML serialization to create an object based on that class. The values from our forms will then be available as properties of that object.

For this example, we'll use the second approach. In general, this is a far simpler and more robust solution than manually writing a bunch of code that has to be maintained. I strongly recommend that you use this approach.

■ **Note** As mentioned previously, we're not making use of an association form in this scenario. If you need to, the only significant difference would be that you would work with the AssociationData property instead of the InitiationData property. I suppose that was a pretty obvious difference but I figured I'd mention it anyway. If I were being paid by the word, I'd have just picked up an extra 37 cents—look out retirement, here I come!

We have two XSD files that we need to process to build classes from—one for each of our forms. The process for each is identical:

1. Open a Visual Studio 2005 command prompt (there should be an icon for this under Start ➤ All Programs ➤ Visual Studio 2005 ➤ Visual Studio Tools).
2. In the Command window, navigate to your solution folder.
3. Run the following command: `xsd initformschema.xsd /c`.

The XSD utility will whir and pop for a few seconds and then be complete. After a momentary victory dance around your chair, it's time to repeat the process for the other schema file (`taskformschema.xsd`) and then continue.

Back in Visual Studio, add your newly created class files to your project (the new class files are going to be listed under their corresponding XSD files). If you open them to take a look, you'll see that they are made up essentially of just properties—one for each data point we collect on our form. With those in place, we can use them in our code.

Open the `MarketingCampaign.cs` file in Visual Studio. While we were configuring the properties for our activities, an `onWorkflowActivated` property was automatically generated for us when we set the `Invoked` property of the onWorkflowActivated1 activity. Find this method now in the code-behind file and add the code from Listing 7-4 the body of the method.

Listing 7-4. *Using XML Serialization to Retrieve Our Form Values*

```
XmlSerializer serializer = new XmlSerializer(typeof(InitForm));
XmlTextReader rdrInitForm = new XmlTextReader(new System.IO.StringReader➥
(workflowProperties.InitiationData));
InitForm frmInit = (InitForm)serializer.Deserialize(rdrInitForm);

sTrafficCoordinator = @"kcd\" + frmInit.trafficcoordinator;
sMarketingDirectorEMail = frmInit.marketingdirectoremail;
```

At a high level, this code uses the XML contents of the `InitiationData` property to create an instance of the `InitForm` object. The deserialization process maps the values from the XML elements `trafficcoordinator` and `marketingdirectoremail` to properties of the `InitForm` object. Those values are then available to us from there. As mentioned earlier, this process could be handled with manual parsing of the XML but this strategy is much simpler. Unless you need some unique handling, I strongly recommend this approach.

Now that we have the values from our initiation form, we can use them to deliver the functionality we need: sending an email and assigning a task. First we'll cover the email.

Like the `onWorkflowActivated` method, Visual Studio also creates an `onSendEmail` method for us as we set the properties of the SendEmail activity. If you recall from Table 7-2, we set all of the standard email properties except `To` and `Body`. The `onSendEmail` method is called when the activity begins executing but before it attempts to send the email, so it is the perfect place to finish setting these values.

From the initiation form, we have the email address of the person we need to send an email to—the regional marketing director—in the `sMarketingDirectorEMail` variable. As I said before, in a real application we would have collected the name of the marketing director and performed a lookup to retrieve their email address, but for this walkthrough we're keeping non-workflow-related tasks as simple as possible. Setting the `To` property of our SendEmail activity is a simple matter of assigning the value of `sMarketingDirectorEMail` to it, like this:

`sendEmail1.To = sMarketingDirectorEMail + "@kcdholdings.com"`. Naturally you'll need to change the domain name to one that works in your environment.

Easy enough. The other piece of information we need to set for our email is the `Body`. We want to include some information about the particular marketing campaign and a link back to the document in the message to the marketing director. We'll retrieve this information from the `WorkflowProperties` object. Add the code in Listing 7-5 to the `onSendEmail` method.

Listing 7-5. *Setting the Email Body*

```
string sItemTitle = workflowProperties.Item["Name"].ToString();
string sItemURL = workflowProperties.ItemUrl;
sendEmail1.Body = string.Format("New Marketing Campaign: {0}.  URL:{1}", ➥
sItemTitle, sItemURL);
```

That's it for the SendEmail activity. Now we need to add the code to customize our task. Again, Visual Studio has created an empty method for us; go ahead and find the `onCreateTask` method in your code-behind file. Like the `onSendEmail` method, this method is called by the activity before the task is actually created. We need to set up certain parameters for the task before it is created. Add the code in Listing 7-6 to your method.

Listing 7-6. *Creating Our Task in C#*

```
taskID = Guid.NewGuid();
taskProperties.Title = "New Marketing Campaign";
taskProperties.AssignedTo = sTrafficCoordinator;

string sItemTitle = workflowProperties.Item["Name"].ToString();
string sItemURL = workflowProperties.ItemUrl;
string sOriginator = workflowProperties.Originator;

taskProperties.Description = string.Format("New Marketing Campaign: {0}.  URL:{1}", ➥
sItemTitle, sItemURL);
taskProperties.ExtendedProperties["taskinstructions"] = string.Format("Please review ➥
this proposed marketing campaign and let {0} know if there are any scheduling➥
 issues.Thanks!", sOriginator);
```

■ **Caution** Field names in the InfoPath forms and the `ExtendedProperties` object are case-sensitive. If they don't match, you'll have problems.

Looking at either of these code listings, they're pretty straightforward, except perhaps for the last line where we're working with something called `ExtendedProperties`. The `ExtendedProperties` property of the `SPWorkflowTaskProperties` object is a hash table that allows you to store any number and combination of key-value pairs of extra information. In this example, we want to store the instructions for this particular task. These will get passed to the task form we created in InfoPath. The ExtendedProperties mechanism shows some of the flexibility and power available to our workflows.

The last functionality we need to add with code is to check whether or not the traffic coordinator has indicated that their task is complete. There are two elements to this. First, the While activity references a taskComplete method; this method is checked to determine whether the While activity should continue processing. Add this code to the empty taskComplete method: e.Result = !taskCompleted;. Add a variable declaration at the top of your class file with the other variable declarations to create a Boolean variable named taskCompleted. In your code-behind file, you should also have an empty method for onTaskChanged. This method gets called when the associated task is modified by an end user (i.e., when the traffic coordinator submits the task form). In this method, we'll check whether the user has indicated that the task is complete; if so, our While activity can stop looping and the workflow can continue on with the next activity. If not, the While activity will reenter the loop and wait for the task to be changed again. We'll also grab any comments that were submitted and make sure that they get stored in the task so that they can be retrieved again to be displayed. The code that handles this is in Listing 7-7. Go ahead and add it to your empty onTaskChanged method.

■ **Caution** Any of the taskProperties properties that we access are merely snapshots in time. They are not linked to the actual task in any way, so if the task changes, we will not see that change. Similarly, changing these property values will not change the task itself.

Listing 7-7. *Checking Whether the Task Is Complete and Capturing Comments*

```
taskCompleted= bool.Parse(afterProperties.ExtendedProperties➥
["taskcompleted"].ToString());
taskProperties.ExtendedProperties["taskcomments"] = ➥
afterProperties.ExtendedProperties["taskcomments"].ToString();
```

■ **Tip** Notice in Listing 7-7 that we are referencing an object variable called afterProperties. When we were configuring our activities, we created this object (and one called beforeProperties) as part of our onTaskChanged activity. These objects give us access to the original values of our task properties before the user submits the task form (in beforeProperties) as well as the new values submitted on the form (in afterProperties). If we needed to, we could access these properties as part of the onTaskChanged method and do something—disallow changes, log changes, and so forth. In this scenario, we just need to make sure that the comments are saved, but you get an idea of what some of the possibilities are.

All of our code is finished now. We can compile our project and move on to deployment. Ultimately, our assembly is going to be deployed to the GAC, so you're going to have to strong-name it. Configure your key file in the Project properties window (on the Signing tab), save your solution, and then go ahead and build. Take care of whatever rituals you need to before building (personally, I'm fond of the "shake-the-rubber-chicken-over-the monitor-while-chanting" ritual, but you just take whatever approach you're accustomed to in order to appease the compiler gods). If you've lived a righteous life (and if you typed all of the code in correctly), the project will compile. If not, well, you're on your own—go back and review the code in this section and the configuration of your activities. The rest of us are moving on to…

(Cue trumpets...)

Deploying Our Custom Workflow

As we saw in Chapter 6, deployment of our custom workflows is not as straightforward as we would like. We covered most of this in Chapter 6, but I'm going to rehash it here because there are a few new elements (the information to deploy our forms, for example) and the steps and details are so interrelated that just giving you the deltas and forcing you to flip back to Chapter 6 for the rest is a recipe for disaster. Forgive me for the duplication and padding out the book, but in this instance, I think it's worth it. Let's get started.

Be glad you're tackling deployment in the final release of the product. In the beta cycle, deployment was a nightmare of interrelated moving parts that practically set you up for failure the first few times you tried it.

OK, so maybe it wasn't *that* bad, but it is a lot easier now. We're going to cover just the development deployment here. Deploying for production was covered back in Chapter 6 and the steps are nearly identical; I'm sure you'll be able to figure out the slight differences.

For development, there are two files we need to work with:

- `feature.xml`
- `workflow.xml`

■ **Note** Deploying our workflow to SharePoint is going to make use of the SharePoint Features functionality. While you can get through this section without a deep understanding of Features, it would help if you had some knowledge.

Taking these one at a time, we'll start with `feature.xml`.

Open the `feature.xml` file that the project template has created for your solution (under `DeploymentFiles\FeatureFiles` in Solution Explorer). Initially, there's nothing of much value in this file, other than some instructions for inserting a Code Snippet. Make sure that your cursor is positioned at the end of the file and then follow the instructions provided to insert the `feature.xml` Code Snippet. You will end up with a file that looks like Figure 7-10.

■ **Tip** If the workflow Code Snippets aren't showing up, click on Tools ➤ Code Snippets Manager, select XML from the Language drop-down, and add `C:\Program Files\Microsoft Visual Studio 8\Xml\1033\Snippets\ SharePoint Server Workflow` to your snippets collection.

```
Install.bat  workflow.xml  feature.xml*
<?xml version="1.0" encoding="utf-8"?>
<!-- _lcid="1033" _version="12.0.3111" _dal="1" -->
<!-- _LocalBinding -->

<!-- Insert Feature.xml Code Snippet here.  To do this:
1) Right click on this page and select "Insert Snippet" (or press Ctrl+K, then X)
2) Select Snippets->SharePoint Workflow->Feature.xml Code -->
<Feature  Id="GUID"
          Title="Default Title"
          Description="This feature is a workflow that ..."
          Version="12.0.0.0"
          Scope="Site"
          ReceiverAssembly="Microsoft.Office.Workflow.Feature, Version=12.0.0.0,
          ReceiverClass="Microsoft.Office.Workflow.Feature.WorkflowFeatureReceive
          xmlns="http://schemas.microsoft.com/sharepoint/">
  <ElementManifests>
    <ElementManifest Location="workflow.xml" />
    <ElementFile Location="MyForm.xsn"/>
  </ElementManifests>
  <Properties>
    <Property Key="GloballyAvailable" Value="true" />

    <!-- Value for RegisterForms key indicates the path to the forms relative to
    <!-- if you don't have forms, use *.xsn -->
    <Property Key="RegisterForms" Value="*.xsn" />
  </Properties>
</Feature>
```

Figure 7-10. *Our feature.xml file after inserting the Code Snippet*

Figure 7-10 loses a little bit of its usefulness when it gets printed in black and white, but take a look at your screen. The parts highlighted in green are the ones we're interested in. These are the pieces we need to customize for our particular workflow. Table 7-8 provides details on the changes we need to make to each of these entries in our `feature.xml` file.

Table 7-8. *Customizing feature.xml After Inserting the Code Snippet*

Entry	New Value	Description
Id	Create a new Registry-format GUID (but be sure to delete the opening and closing braces after inserting it).	This entry uniquely identifies your new Feature.
Title	MarketingCampaign	This value will show up in the list of Features deployed to your site.
Description	This Feature encapsulates the custom workflow to process a new marketing campaign.	The description will show up under the title in the list of Features.
Element Manifest Location	`workflow.xml`	Leave this entry set to its default. Since our `workflow.xml` file is located in the same directory as our `feature.xml`, we don't need to specify the full path to it. If for some reason this were not the case, you would need to specify the full path and filename for your workflow definition file.
`<ElementFile Location="MyForm.xsn"/>`	*<deleted>*	Delete this entry; we won't need it.

The other elements of the file can remain as is. Save and close feature.xml; we're done with it.

■ **Note** When our workflow is deployed, `feature.xml` will be copied to the server underneath the `FEATURES` folder. When you specify a path, for example for the `ElementManifest` attribute, make sure that your path is relative to the *server* folder hierarchy.

Open `workflow.xml` from the Solution Explorer. Repeat the same process to insert the `workflow.xml` Code Snippet. Your screen should look like Figure 7-11. Table 7-9 details the changes to make.

workflow.xml*

```
<?xml version="1.0" encoding="utf-8" ?>
<!-- _lcid="1033" _version="12.0.3015" _dal="1"   -->
<!-- _LocalBinding   -->

<!-- Insert Workflow.xml Code Snippet here.  To do this:
1) Right click on this page and select "Insert Snippet" (or press Ctrl+K, then X)
2) Select Snippets->SharePoint Workflow->Workflow.xml Code -->


<Elements xmlns="http://schemas.microsoft.com/sharepoint/">
    <Workflow
         Name="My Workflow"
         Description="This workflow ..."
         Id="GUID"
         CodeBesideClass="ProjectName.Workflow1"
         CodeBesideAssembly="ProjectName, Version=1.0.0.0, Culture=neutral, PublicKeyToken=publicKeyToken"
         TaskListContentTypeId="0x01080100C9C9515DE4E24001905074F980F93160"
         AssociationUrl="_layouts/CstWrkflIP.aspx"
         InstantiationUrl="_layouts/IniWrkflIP.aspx"
         ModificationUrl="_layouts/ModWrkflIP.aspx"
         StatusUrl="_layouts/WrkStat.aspx">

        <Categories/>
        <!-- Tags to specify InfoPath forms for the workflow; delete tags for forms that you do not have -->
        <MetaData>
            <Association_FormURN>associationFormURN</Association_FormURN>
            <Instantiation_FormURN>instantiationFormURN</Instantiation_FormURN>
            <Task0_FormURN>taskFormURN</Task0_FormURN>

            <Modification_GUID_FormURN>modificationURN</Modification_GUID_FormURN>
            <Modification_GUID_Name>Name of Modification</Modification_GUID_Name>

            <AssociateOnActivation>false</AssociateOnActivation>
        </MetaData>
    </Workflow>
</Elements>
```

Figure 7-11. *Our workflow.xml file after inserting the Code Snippet*

Table 7-9. *Customizing workflow.xml After Inserting the Code Snippet*

Entry	New Value	Description
Name	MarketingCampaign.	The name of our workflow as it will appear to administrators when they associate it to a list.
Description	This workflow enforces the business process for new marketing campaigns.	The description will show up to administrators when they select our workflow during the association process.
Id	Create a new Registry-format GUID (again, be sure to delete the opening and closing braces after inserting it).	This entry uniquely identifies your new workflow.
CodeBesideClass	MarketingCampaign. MarketingCampaign.	The name of your project and the name of your workflow class, separated by a period.
CodeBesideAssembly	The fully qualified strong name of your assembly.	For help retrieving the proper value for this entry, see the sidebar "What's in a (Strong) Name?" in Chapter 6.
TaskListContentTypeId	0x01080100C9C9515DE4E2400 ➥ 1905074F980F93160.	We did not create a custom content type for our task so we can just accept the default value.

Table 7-9. *Customizing workflow.xml After Inserting the Code Snippet*

Entry	New Value	Description
AssociationUrl	`_layouts/CstWrkflIP.aspx.`	Accept the default value. For information related to this entry, see the sidebar "So Just How Are Our Forms Rendered Anyway?" later in this chapter.
InstantiationUrl	`_layouts/IniWrkflIP.aspx.`	Accept the default value. For information related to this entry, see the sidebar "So Just How Are Our Forms Rendered Anyway?" later in this chapter.
ModificationUrl	`_layouts/ModWrkflIP.aspx.`	Accept the default value. For information related to this entry, see the sidebar "So Just How Are Our Forms Rendered Anyway?"
Association_FormURN		For this scenario, we do not have an association form. You can delete this entire entry—opening tag, value, and closing tag.
<Instantiation_FormURN>	The unique URN for your initiation form.	See the sidebar "Ode on an InfoPath URN" later in this chapter for information on retrieving the proper values.
Task0_FormURN	The unique URN for your task form.	See the sidebar "Ode on an InfoPath URN" for information on retrieving the proper values.
Modification_GUID_ FormURN		For this scenario, we do not have a modification form. You can delete this entire entry—opening tag, value, and closing tag.
Modification_GUID_Name		For this scenario, we do not have a modification form. You can delete this entire entry—opening tag, value, and closing tag.

Leave everything else at its defaults. That takes care of `workflow.xml`.

■ **Note** One thing to notice in Table 7-9—the InstantiationUrl and Instantiation_FormURN entries really are *Instantiation*, even though everywhere else, this form is called the *initiation* form. Someone at Microsoft got their words mixed up…

SO JUST HOW ARE OUR FORMS RENDERED ANYWAY?

In our `workflow.xml` file we accepted the default values for the `AssociationUrl`, `InstantiationUrl`, and `ModificationUrl` entries. That's great, but what exactly do these entries do and what are those ASPX pages that are referenced in the values? The answer is so simple it just might surprise you—someone back at Camp Redmond gets a gold star on the refrigerator for devising a scheme that is the perfect mix of simplicity and power.

I'll use the initiation form as an example, but the association and modification forms operate in a similar way. What happens is this:

When a new instance of a workflow is started on a list item, SharePoint checks the `InstantiationUrl` entry in the `workflow.xml` file for that workflow template. SharePoint now knows which ASPX page to load and its job is essentially done. The ASPX page loads and finishes the process of loading our form, independent of SharePoint. In the case of InfoPath forms, the ASPX page that loads is one provided by Microsoft as part of the product. That ASPX page contains a special web part that handles the rest of the form interaction. It reads the `Instantiation_FormURN` from the `workflow.xml` file to identify the specific form that it needs to load and present to the user. Mission accomplished.

Now we're at the point where Microsoft really cleaned up the deployment process coming out of the beta. Previously, there was a file named `install.bat` that did the actual deployment. Hold your comments about doing deployment with a batch file because it really makes perfect sense, and, guess what—we're still using one; it's just better hidden from us, *and* we don't need to edit it manually the way we did during the beta. The reason that the batch file (how '80s!) makes perfect sense is because of the tasks it is completing. At a very high level, the major steps are

1. Copy the required files to a directory on the server.
2. Add your assemblies to the GAC.
3. Verify the InfoPath forms.
4. Install and activate the Feature, making it available on the site for which you specified a URL.
5. Reset IIS so that your changes are recognized by the server.

As you can see, when you look at what is happening, a batch file is the best way to go. Fortunately, as I said, things are a lot easier now (at least while we're using InfoPath forms). We no longer need to edit the file manually and it is integrated right into the build process within Visual Studio for us by the MOSS SDK project templates.

ODE ON AN INFOPATH URN

Sigh. Bad pun—my apologies to John Keats.

Anyway, as you likely know, URN is an acronym for Universal Resource Name. According to RFC 2141 from the Internet Engineering Task Force (IETF), URNs are "intended to serve as persistent, location-independent, resource identifiers" (`http://www.ietf.org/rfc/rfc2141.txt`). Great, that and five bucks will buy me a coffee. What does that really mean and why should we care?

We care because InfoPath uses URNs to uniquely identify our forms. Technically, URNs are not guaranteed to be unique. It is possible for two InfoPath forms to have the same URN, but you'd almost need to force it to happen. So, for our purposes, consider URNs to be unique. The important part of the URN, harkening back to the IETF definition, is that they are *location-independent*. Unlike URLs, which are very location-dependent, the URNs for our forms are going to be the same whether they come from our local hard drive or whether they are delivered from the SharePoint server. This is important because the location of our forms is almost guaranteed to change. We develop them and set the configuration for them locally and then the deployment process copies them to the SharePoint server.

I won't go into the makeup of the InfoPath URN here. InfoPath generates them for us—we never need to worry about that—so it's not that important to know what the various pieces mean. If you're interested, there's a pretty good blog entry from the InfoPath team located at `http://blogs.msdn.com/infopath/archive/2004/05/20/136165.aspx` that explains the makeup of the InfoPath URN.

Intellectually, all of that is quite stimulating and someday it will win you a trivia contest. But honestly, who cares? All I want to know is "How do I get the URN for my form so I can put it into my `workflow.xml` file, finish this workflow, and go home?" Easy. Open your form from your solution folder (the published version of the form) in Design mode. Click File ➤ Properties and copy the URN from the `ID` field. Paste it into the appropriate place in your `workflow.xml` file and you're good to go.

Configuration of the deployment is handled right from within Visual Studio. Inside your project properties is a Build Events tab. Click it and you'll see an entry for the postbuild event that looks like Listing 7-8. The last parameter on that command line is the one we're interested in. It starts out as `NODEPLOY`. This tells the batch file to build our project but not to do any of the deployment steps. This allows us to do interim builds to see how things are progressing and whether we've broken anything, without wasting time deploying to the server before we're ready.

Listing 7-8. *The Postbuild Command*

```
call "$(ProjectDir)\DeploymentFiles\PostBuildActions.bat"➥
 "$(ConfigurationName)" "$(ProjectDir)" "$(ProjectName)" ➥
"$(TargetDir)" "$(TargetName)" NODEPLOY
```

Once you have completed your development and are ready to deploy, simply change the `NODEPLOY` parameter to `DEPLOY`. Now, as part of the build process, the batch file will perform the steps to deploy our workflow to the server.

Tip There is one additional option available to control the processing of our build and deployment cycle. If you have made changes only to the code files—either through the Designer or by actually writing code—all you need to do is update the assembly in the GAC. There is no need to redeploy the whole Feature to SharePoint. In this case, append a `QUICK` parameter to the end of the postbuild command line (after `DEPLOY`). Now upon a successful build, the GAC will be updated and IIS reset so that your new assembly is used. Just remember to take this parameter off if you make changes to forms or any of the XML files, or they will not be updated.

Getting back to our example, we're now ready to deploy our project to our development server. Open the properties and change `NODEPLOY` to `DEPLOY` and you're ready to go (that was easy). Save your solution before continuing and then build your project. You'll notice that the output from the batch deployer is shown in the output window in Visual Studio. You may see some error messages, for example when GACUtil tries to remove your assembly (the `-uf` line in `postbuildactions.bat`). The first time you deploy, there is nothing to remove. There are other similar situations like this, especially the first time you run the deployment. If you see other errors, however, you'll need to do some troubleshooting. It is likely that the problem will be in a misconfigured `feature.xml` or `workflow.xml`, or you forgot to sign the assembly.

If there are no unexpected error messages, you're done. Your workflow feature is successfully installed. Now we can test it out.

Testing Our InfoPath Forms Workflow

Before we can test our workflow, we need to associate it with a document library. We've previously walked through these steps, but at a high level, they are as follows:

1. From the settings page for the document library, go into Workflow Settings.
2. Add a new workflow based on the Marketing Campaign Workflow template, giving it a unique name.

Because we didn't create an association form, you won't see a form pop up here. After the workflow is associated, we need to kick off an instance of it on a document:

1. From a document in the same document library, select Workflows from its drop-down menu.
2. Click the name that you gave the workflow in step 2 earlier.
3. Our initiation form will now pop up, as shown in Figure 7-12. Fill in valid values for your environment and click Submit.

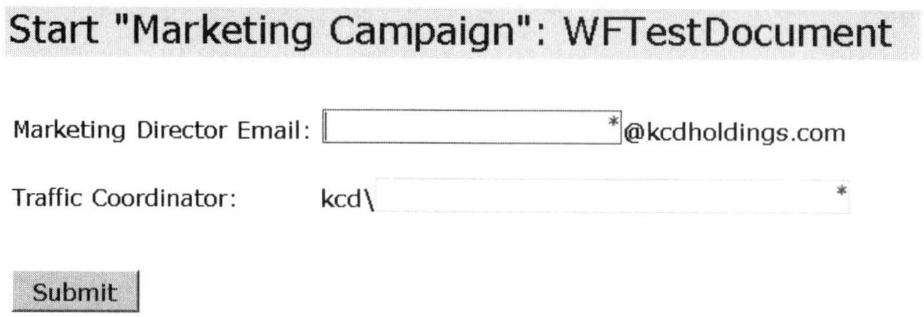

Start "Marketing Campaign": WFTestDocument

Marketing Director Email: * @kcdholdings.com

Traffic Coordinator: kcd\ *

Submit

Figure 7-12. *Our custom initiation form in action*

4. Once the form is submitted, our workflow will create and assign a task to the person you specified as the traffic coordinator and will send an email to the account you specified for the marketing director. The task, using our custom task form, is shown in Figure 7-13. Notice the instructions that we put in programmatically are shown in the read-only Task Instructions field.

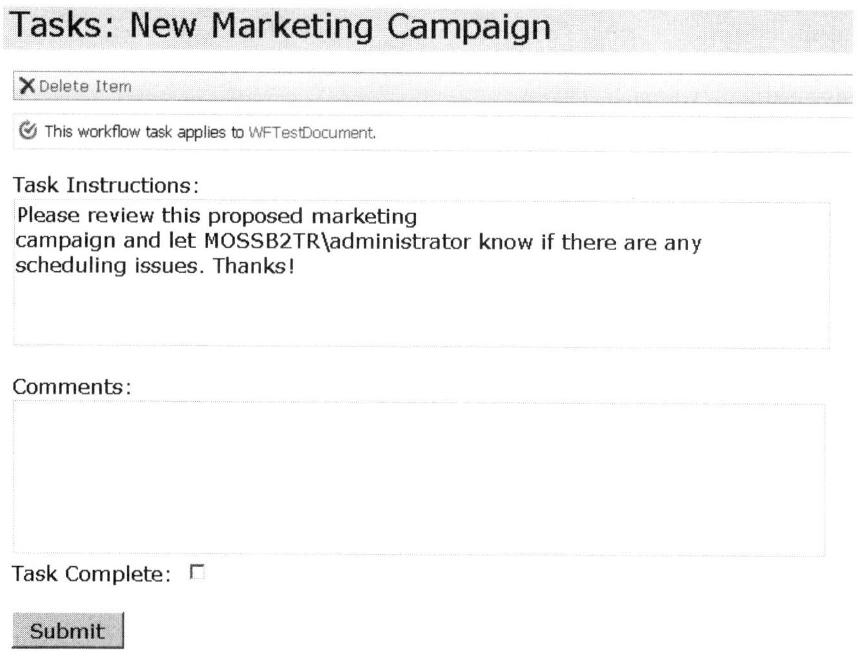

Tasks: New Marketing Campaign

Delete Item

This workflow task applies to WFTestDocument.

Task Instructions:

Please review this proposed marketing
campaign and let MOSSB2TR\administrator know if there are any
scheduling issues. Thanks!

Comments:

Task Complete:

Submit

Figure 7-13. *Our second custom form—this time for task information*

5. Open the task form and add some comments, but do not mark the task as complete. Save the form. The comments will be recorded, but the workflow will not be flagged as complete.

6. Click on the document to open it in Word. If you are logged in as the user to whom the Task is assigned, you will see the Task information in the Business Bar. In this case, you can click the Edit This Task button in Word to see our custom form rendered within the Word client, as shown in Figure 7-14. Notice that it contains the comment we entered in step 5.

New Marketing Campaign

Task Instructions:

Please review this proposed marketing
campaign and let MOSSB2TR\administrator know if there are any
scheduling issues. Thanks!

Comments:

this is a comment entered from a browser

Task Complete: ☐

Submit

Figure 7-14. *Our custom InfoPath form rendered through the Office client. Sweet.*

7. Mark the task as Complete within Word and click Submit.
8. Close Word and refresh your browser. The workflow is now marked as Complete.

■ **Note** The form we built was totally unstyled. If we know we're going to be rendering into the Office client applications, we can spend a little time styling things to look more integrated.

So there you have it: a brand-new workflow, complete with custom forms. Not too bad; give yourself a pat on the back and then let's move on to ASP.NET forms. As you'll see, these are a little harder.

Scenario 7-2: Using ASP.NET Forms

Functionally, using ASP.NET forms for your workflow is no different from using InfoPath forms. You still have association, initiation, task, and modification forms. Users still interact with your forms the same way (well, actually, there is one difference: having the forms display inside the Office 2007 client applications is not an option with anything except InfoPath forms and MOSS).

The one thing that is significantly different—and I'm not kidding when I say *significantly* different—is the work necessary to build the ASP.NET forms. Building the ASP.NET forms is a lot more work. Fortunately, Microsoft has given us some good starting points and some good building blocks to build our forms from MOSS and WSS SDSs. This set of sample code, white papers, and documentation provides a wealth of information to any SharePoint developer.

■**Note** Because I'm a nice guy, I've done a lot of the legwork for you by tearing the sample projects apart and distilling them down to a set of template files and a few code snippets. I'll be referring to these files as we step through this process. Altogether, they constitute several hundred lines of code—most of which we won't need to change. So, instead of making you type all of that out, I've packaged them together and posted them on my web site (`www.kcdholdings.com`). You'll want to download the template files before going much further. While I would love to claim credit for all of this code, I can't. I added about 5 percent on top of what came out of Microsoft's SDKs.

Let's get started. For simplicity's sake, we're going to implement the same scenario with ASP.NET forms as we did for InfoPath forms. Here's a refresher on the scenario.

Scenario: Global Marketing Campaigns

In the KCD Holdings Global Marketing department, a common occurrence is naturally the creation of new marketing campaigns. Often, however, these campaigns are not new. Instead, they have begun as local campaigns that were successful and are now going to be adapted and introduced globally. The local marketing director in the region that originated the campaign needs to review global campaigns that originated in their region. They do not actually approve the campaign, but they are given the opportunity to offer suggestions to fine-tune the campaign based on their experience as the originating region.

A task is assigned to a marketing traffic coordinator, however. This person is responsible for coordinating all of the resources necessary for a successful campaign. The task assigned to the traffic coordinator is for them to review the marketing plan document and approve of schedules, etc.

To facilitate this process, each workflow is constructed to notify the appropriate regional marketing director via email and assign a task to the traffic coordinator. The initiation form will present the workflow originator with an interface that will allow them to specify the email address for the appropriate regional marketing director and the traffic coordinator.

Unlike with the InfoPath forms where there was little real difference between the association and initiation forms (and so we only covered the initiation forms), when using ASP.NET forms the process for association and initiation, while similar, is different enough to warrant covering them both here. It is important to note, however, that you could use the same form for both initiation and association—your form and code-behind will just need to contain an amalgamation of the details covered here for each individual form as necessary for your particular situation. For our scenario, the association form will allow the administrator to provide some initial values as defaults that can be changed in the initiation form.

The first thing we're going to do is to set up our solution. Set up a new SharePoint Sequential Workflow project in Visual Studio called **MarketingCampaignASP**. To make things easier, if you have both MOSS and WSS, make sure that you use the WSS template; it will be the one that says "SharePoint Sequential Workflow". Before we begin working with the actual project itself, there are a few housekeeping items to take care of first:

- In the project's Properties window, configure the project to be signed with a strong name.
- Copy the contents of the `ASPXWorkflow` folder from the templates you downloaded from my web site into the root of your solution. Rename each file by removing `_template` from the filename.
- Rename the default `Workflow1.cs` file to **MarketingCampaignASPWF.cs** in the Solution Explorer.
- Open `MarketingCampaignASPWF.cs` in the Designer. Set the `CorrelationToken\OwnerActivityName` and `WorkflowProperties\Name` for the onWorkflowActivated activity to **MarketingCampaignASPWF**.
- Open `MarketingCampaignASPWF.designer.cs` and rename the one reference to `Workflow1` to **MarketingCampaignASPWF**.
- Build the solution. Yes, I know it doesn't *do* anything yet. This will allow us to grab the fully qualified strong name for our assembly when we need it in just a bit. See how clever we can be?
- Set the six template files we pasted in earlier to be included in the project. You'll likely need to click the Show All Items button at the top of the Solution Explorer in order to see them.

■ **Caution** When you're doing this for real, you'll want to give your ASPX files unique names. They're going to be copied to the `_layouts/` folder so there's the possibility of contention with other forms that you create based off these templates. Make sure you also set the correct names in your workflow definition files.

Now we can start working on our project. As I mentioned before, we're going to implement the same scenario as we did for the InfoPath forms. The first thing we need to do is to add and configure all of our activities. Rather than repeat all of those instructions here, I'll refer you to the section "Adding and Configuring Activities" earlier in this chapter. Go through those steps again and then jump back here to begin working with our forms.

■ **Caution** When you're repeating the steps to add and configure the activities, remember that our workflow name is now **MarketingCampaignASPWF**. Any place that the earlier instructions tell you to enter *MarketingCampaign*, you'll want to enter ***MarketingCampaignASPWF*** instead.

Shoo, now, on with you...
[*Exeunt Omnes...* cue intermission music]

Welcome back, I hope you had a nice trip. Was the earlier part of the chapter any better the second time around? Anyway, now that our activities are all set up, we can continue on with our forms. We'll start with the association form.

ASP.NET Association Forms

When using ASP.NET forms for workflow association, the process the forms implement is always going to follow the same basic steps:

- When the form is first loaded, display the appropriate interface to collect the information that your workflow needs.
- If you are editing an existing association, read content from the stored association data and display it for editing.
- When the form is submitted, call the appropriate method, depending on whether this is a new workflow association or you're editing an existing association (which you can tell by examining the `GuidAssoc` parameter) to process the association:
  - `AssociateWorkflowTemplate` for new associations
  - `UpdateWorkflowTemplate` for editing associations
- If necessary, create the task and history lists for the workflow.
- Set the properties of the `SPWorkflowAssociation` object from the values collected on your form.

We're not going to explore all of these steps in excruciating detail. The code is right in the files and it is pretty straightforward. If you're interested in digging into the functionality in this file a little further, the heart of things is the `BtnOK_Click` event. Take a peek there; the actual *association* happens on about lines 242 and 248—once for lists and once for content types. Everything else is mostly just setting the stage for that event.

■ **Note** There is likely going to be a bug in the RTM version of the sample from the SDK that prevents the sample from working correctly on content types. I don't know if Microsoft will get it fixed in time to be part of the RTM release. I have a copy of an untested potential fix, which I'll test and integrate into my templates before I post them for you. Just keep this in mind if you're working directly with the SDK samples.

The file we're going to start working with is `AssocForm.aspx`; go ahead and open it in Code view. Take 30 seconds and scroll through the contents of the template. It's all pretty standard ASP.NET—nothing to be worried about.

There are three places within this template where we need to add some code. I've conveniently labeled them *Step 1* through *Step 3* so we can stay on track. Step 1 is located near the top of the file. Delete the placeholder text, `Step 1: Assembly Strong Name`, from the `Name` attribute and paste in its place the fully qualified strong name for your assembly. This is why we compiled before doing anything else—the strong name is available to us. If you need help determining the strong name, see the sidebar "What's in a (Strong) Name?" in Chapter 6.

Step 2 is in the line immediately after Step 1, inside the `Inherits` attribute. Again, delete the placeholder text—`Step 2: Namespace.Classname`. In its place, type **MarketingCampaignASP.AssocForm**. We'll be changing the namespace for all of our files as we go through. The class name is for the association form code-behind file, which we'll be editing soon.

Step 3 is about halfway down the file. Here we're going to be adding interface controls so that we can collect information from our users. If you recall from the InfoPath forms, we need to collect two pieces of information in order to run our workflow:

- The name of the traffic coordinator so we can assign a task to them
- The email address of the regional marketing director

so we'll need a text box for each of them. Add the code from Listing 7-9 immediately after the `<asp:Content ID="Content6" ContentPlaceHolderID="PlaceHolderMain" runat="server">` tag. Again, all we're doing here is adding interface controls—nothing special.

■ **Note** If you've used SharePoint much, you'll have noticed that in many places, it presents a pretty slick interface for designating users. It's called the Contact Picker or the People Editor (depending on how it is implemented). We'll take a look at using it in Chapter 9.

Listing 7-9. *Building Our Interface*

```
Traffic Coordinator: kcd\<input type="text" name="TrafficCoordinator" ➥
id="TrafficCoordinator" runat="server" />
<br /><br />
Marketing Director Email: <input type="text" name="MarketingDirector" ➥
id="MarketingDirector" runat="server" />@kcdholdings.com
<br /><br />
```

That's all we need to do with this file, and there's really not much else exciting going on here. You can save and close it. Next up is `AssocForm.cs`, so go ahead and open it.

Once again, I've indicated the steps necessary to customize this file; you'll notice there's only one step. Simply update the namespace to `MarketingCampaignASP` and save and close the file.

That takes care of the changes specific to our association form. There is some generic or reused processing that we need to customize a bit, but we'll get to that soon. First, we'll walk through some similar steps to configure the initiation form.

ASP.NET Initiation Forms

The next form we're going to tackle is the initiation form. While this is similar to the association form in many ways, most notably in the user interface, it performs some different tasks behind the scenes, as you'll see.

When using ASP.NET forms for workflow initiation, the process the forms implement is always going to follow the same basic steps:

- When the form is first loaded, display the interface to collect the information that your workflow needs.
- As appropriate, prepopulate fields on the form with information from the association form.
- When the form is submitted, store the supplied information and start the workflow.

First, we're going to look at the ASPX form itself, so open `InitForm.aspx` and feast your eyes on its coding splendor. You'll notice that it is almost identical to the `AssocForm.aspx` file we looked at earlier. Guess what? The changes we make to this file are nearly identical, too. There is only one exception—the class name in Step 2 is going to be `InitForm` instead of `AssocForm` as it was the first time around.

If you need a refresher, jump back to the section on customizing the association ASPX form; otherwise just plow on through the three steps identified in this template file. When you're done, save and close this one.

■ **Note** If there is information you need to collect only on workflow association (which would typically be done by some type of administrator), you can accomplish this by simply not adding that field to the UI for the initiation form. You'll need to make sure that you can still carry around the information—typically in `ViewState`—there's an example in the comments of the template file.

The next file we need to take a look at is the `InitForm.cs` file. Once again, I've added placeholders where you'll need to make edits.

Step 1: Update the namespace.

Step 2a: Add an entry for each piece of data that you collect only on the association form to store it in `ViewState`.

Step 2b: Add an entry for the same fields from 2a that retrieves the value from `ViewState` and populates the appropriate property.

For the scenario we're walking through, we don't need to worry about Steps 2a and 2b, so just change the namespace in Step 1 to **MarketingCampaignASP** and then save and close the file.

Supporting Files

There are two template files that we haven't touched upon yet: `WFDataPages.cs` and `FormData.cs`. These files play a supporting role in the process—as a common base class for both forms to inherit from (`WFDataPages`) and as a serializable class to store and retrieve our data (`FormData`). We'll look at `FormData` first.

The `FormData.cs` file serves the same function as the class we generated with the XSD utility for the InfoPath forms. It needs to contain at least one public property for each field we make use of on our forms. Open `Formdata.cs` and you'll see a skeleton with an example embedded in the comments. Step 1 again involves updating the namespace. For Step 2, we need to add the code in Listing 7-10 as our property getters and setters.

Listing 7-10. *Properties for Our FormData Class*

```
private string trafficCoordinator = default(string);
public string TrafficCoordinator
{
     get { return this.trafficCoordinator; }
     set { this.trafficCoordinator = value; }
}

private string marketingDirector = default(string);
public string MarketingDirector
{
     get { return this.marketingDirector; }
     set { this.marketingDirector = value; }
}
```

After adding the code from Listing 7-10 you can save and close the `Formdata.cs` file. There are some other elements in there for working with the Contact Selector control, but we'll leave those alone for now; we'll revisit them in Chapter 9.

Open `WFDataPages.cs`. Again, you'll see that I have added placeholders. Step 1 is to update the namespace to `MarketingCampaignASP` as we've done before. In Step 2 we create objects for the various form controls that get displayed to the user on both the association and initiation forms. As I said before, each of the forms inherit from this class, so we can define these objects once centrally and use them in each child form. Because the forms can have different fields, we need to make sure that each is created here so they're accessible for Steps 2a and 2b in the initiation form code-behind (which we covered earlier). For our scenario, add the code from Listing 7-11 after the placeholder text for Step 2.

Listing 7-11. *Creating Objects for Our UI Elements*

```
protected HtmlInputText TrafficCoordinator = new HtmlInputText();
protected HtmlInputText MarketingDirector = new HtmlInputText();
```

Step 3 is within the `PopulatePageFromXml` method, which is responsible for re-creating a `FormData` object from a serialized representation of the data submitted via our forms. All we're doing here is grabbing the data from the `FormData` object and populating the properties for the control that represents our form field. When the form loads, the appropriate values will be displayed. Add the code from Listing 7-12 just under the placeholder for Step 3.

Listing 7-12. *Retrieving Values from FormData*

```
TrafficCoordinator.Value = formdata.TrafficCoordinator;
MarketingDirector.Value = formdata.MarketingDirector;
```

The last customization we need to make is Step 4. It does exactly the opposite of Step 3—it takes the values that were submitted via the form and stores them in `FormData` so that they can be serialized and stored. As before, we potentially have different fields for the two forms and the need to handle them differently, so we're split into 4a and 4b. For our scenario, our code will be exactly the same, so add the code from Listing 7-13 for both 4a and 4b.

Listing 7-13. *Storing Values into FormData*

```
data.TrafficCoordinator = TrafficCoordinator.Value;
data.MarketingDirector = MarketingDirector.Value;
```

That brings us to the end of our templates. Save and close `WFDataPages.cs`. The last code we need to add for this project is to enable our activities to do their work.

Adding Code to Our Activities

We covered all of this ground when we did the InfoPath-based solution but it's scattered throughout the section up there. To keep things nice and simple, I'll just give you the code again. To begin with, open the `MarketingCampaignASPWF.cs` file in Code view and add the variable declarations from Listing 7-14 to the top of the class file.

Listing 7-14. *Global Variables for Our Workflow Class*

```
private string sTrafficCoordinator = default(String);
private string sMarketingDirectorEMail = default(String);
private bool taskCompleted = false;
```

Add the code from Listing 7-15 to the empty `onSendEmail` method. Update the first line to work in your environment.

Listing 7-15. *Code for onSendEmail*

```
sendEmail1.To = sMarketingDirectorEMail + "@kcdholdings.com";
string sItemTitle = workflowProperties.Item["Name"].ToString();
string sItemURL = workflowProperties.ItemUrl;
sendEmail1.Body = string.Format("New Marketing Campaign: {0}.  URL:{1}",sItemTitle,
sItemURL);
```

We're nearly done with this part. Add the code from Listing 7-16 to the `onCreateTask` method.

Listing 7-16. *Code for onCreateTask*

```
taskID = Guid.NewGuid();
taskProperties.Title = "New Marketing Campaign";
taskProperties.AssignedTo = sTrafficCoordinator;
string sItemTitle = workflowProperties.Item["Name"].ToString();
string sItemURL = workflowProperties.ItemUrl;
string sOriginator = workflowProperties.Originator;
taskProperties.Description = string.Format("New Marketing Campaign: {0}.  URL:{1}"➥
,sItemTitle, sItemURL);
taskProperties.ExtendedProperties["taskinstructions"] = string.Format("Please ➥
review this proposed marketing campaign and let {0} know if there are any ➥
scheduling issues.  Thanks!", sOriginator);
```

The `taskComplete` method is short and sweet: add `e.Result = !taskCompleted;` to the empty method.

Last but not least is the `onTaskChanged` method. Add the code from Listing 7-17 and we're done.

Listing 7-17. *Code for onTaskChanged*

```
if (afterProperties.ExtendedProperties.ContainsValue("Completed"))
            {
                taskCompleted = true;
            }
```

If you're impatient, you can go ahead and compile. There wasn't a boatload of new code we added, so things should be OK. If not, either go back and check that you typed everything correctly, or else bag the whole thing and become a Tibetan monk. The choice is yours—I'm all about empowering my readers.

Next up: deployment.

Deploying Our ASPX Forms-Based Workflow

Remember that nice, easy deployment scenario we had for the InfoPath forms? The one where we just set a few options on the command line for our build actions? Yeah, hold onto that fond memory. We're not so lucky this time around. For a WSS-only scenario, we'll be making use of the project templates from the WSS SDK, which do not include the `PostBuildActions.bat` file. Instead, it has its weaker, less friendly sibling `Install.bat`.

Welcome to our nightmare, Alice.

OK, so maybe things aren't all *that* bad. Perhaps I should have done ASPX forms first in this chapter so you wouldn't be pining for the better world of InfoPath forms quite so much. Oh well, water under the bridge now...

To get started, we need to update our deployment files. The first one—`feature.xml`—is similar to the InfoPath version of the file. Insert the WSS version of the snippet and replace the elements. If you need a refresher, flip back to the InfoPath deployment section. Just remember that our solution is now MarketingCampaignASP.

The second file to be edited, `workflow.xml`, is slightly different this go around. The first few elements you edit are the same as before. Beginning with the `TaskListContentTypeId`, though, things get different. Delete the `TaskListContentTypeId` attribute. The `AssociationUrl` and `InitiationUrl` elements need to be set to the appropriate path and filename for our forms. For this scenario, that means `_layouts/AssocForm.aspx` and `_layouts/InitForm.aspx`, respectively. Remember that if you change the names of these files in the file system to make sure they're unique when they get copied to the `_layouts` folder, you need to update these references too. You can go ahead and delete the ModificationUrl attribute as well as the Modification_GUID_Name element a little further down as we're not doing modifications this time around.

That's it for `workflow.xml`; save it and close it.

■ **Caution** If you're doing this development on a machine with MOSS installed (as I am; I know that's going to jump up and bite me at some point here), you'll have a slightly different experience than the WSS-only developers. Everything will work OK for you because MOSS sits on top of WSS, but if you try to deploy your solution to a WSS-only environment, you will have problems. You need to make sure that you remove all MOSS-only elements from your deployment files, as well as from the rest of your project. This includes any InfoPath references, and references to any assembly that begins `Microsoft.Office.SharePoint` or `Microsoft.Office.Workflow` and a few other bits and pieces. Just be careful. You could avoid a lot of this by making sure that you use the proper WSS template to begin with.

The problem with the last piece of our deployment is that it feels like it doesn't belong. It's disconnected from the rest of the work we've been doing. It's not hard; in fact, it's pretty easy. It just doesn't fit in with the rest. Oh well, we just have to suck it up.

Open up the `install.bat` file. At the top of the file are some comments with instructions, which I've duplicated in Listing 7-18 for reference. I'm not going to regurgitate the process here in painful detail as these instructions are pretty good. Instead, I'll just offer some general information and some clarifying points to help you out.

Listing 7-18. *Instructions from install.bat*

```
:: Before running this file, sign the assembly in Project properties
::
:: To customize this file, find and replace
:: a) "MyFeature" with your own feature names
:: b) "feature.xml" with the name of your feature.xml file
:: c) "workflow.xml" with the name of your workflow.xml file
:: d) "http://localhost" with the name of the site you wish to publish to
```

From the instructions in Listing 7-18, you only need to worry about Step `a` for our scenario. We left our `workflow.xml` and `feature.xml` files named with their defaults so we don't need to change them here, which is what Steps `b` and `c` are handling. Technically you could rename these files to anything you want, but if you do, there are a number of places you would need to reflect that change. Personally, I can't think of a compelling reason why you would want to change the filenames. If you need to, though, remember that it is possible.

The first thing to notice about the `install.bat` file is that it is pretty well commented. Each major task being performed by the batch file is preceded by an `echo` statement that tells you what is about to happen. At a very high level, the major steps are

1. Copy the required files to a directory on the server. Notice in this section that the `xcopy` command for the ASPX files will pull from your solution folder (where `install.bat` is located) and all subfolders. In our scenario, we need to customize the name of our Feature—MarketingCampaignASP—in place of MyFeature.

2. Add your assemblies to the GAC. Make sure that you change MyFeature to MarketingCampaignASP on both lines in this section.

3. Installs and activates the Feature, making it available on the site you specify a URL for. Specify the URL to your SharePoint server here or leave it at `http://localhost`, as appropriate. The first set of commands are commented out by default and only need to be uncommented if you rerun `install.bat`. They uninstall and deactivate your Feature from the specified server. The first time you run `install.bat` there is nothing to uninstall/deactivate. It won't hurt to uncomment them for every run, but it is unnecessary.

4. Resets IIS so that your changes are recognized by the server.

■ **Tip** There is one additional change I like to add to the `install.bat` file and that is a `pause` statement at the end, after the `iisreset`. It's not necessary but it can be helpful to go back and review the contents of the command window after the batch file has run. The first time I went through this I had forgotten to strongly name my assembly so it failed when `install.bat` tried to add it to the GAC. If I did not have the contents of the command window to go back through and review, I likely would have spent *hours* troubleshooting why my installation didn't work.

That's it. Make those changes, save your file, and you're ready to deploy. Save your solution before continuing. Open an Explorer window, navigate to your solution folder, and double click on `install.bat`. You may see some error messages, for example when GACUtil tries to remove your assembly (the `-uf` line). The first time you run `install.bat`, there is nothing to uninstall. There are other similar situations like this, especially the first time you run the installer. If you see other errors, however (like my unsigned assembly), you'll need to do some troubleshooting.

If there are no unexpected error messages, you're done. Your Workflow Feature is successfully installed. The moment of truth is at hand. Open a document library, select Document Library Settings from the Settings menu, and then click Workflow Settings from the Permissions and Management section. On the next screen, click the Add a Workflow link.

Finally, we're at the screen we need. Select MarketingCampaignASP from the list of available workflow templates at the top and give it a unique name. Leave all of the other options set at their defaults and simply click the Next button.

Voilà! Our ASPX association form is shown on screen in all of its workflow-form glory—see Figure 7-15. Fill in a valid name and email address for your environment and click OK.

Figure 7-15. *Our ASPX association form*

Go back to your document library and kick off a workflow based on this new association. You'll see our ASPX initiation form, as shown in Figure 7-16, complete with prefilled content that was entered on our association form.

Customize Marketing Campaigns :

Use this page to customize this instance of Marketing Campaigns.

Traffic Coordinator: kcd\ administrator

Marketing Director Email: admin @kcdholdings.com

OK

Figure 7-16. *Our ASPX initiation form*

That's it. Functionally, everything else about our ASPX forms is the same as InfoPath forms. As I said at the beginning, the real difference is the implementation mechanism. To my mind, ASPX forms are a lot more work, but if they're all you have available, at least know that you're not missing out on any important functionality.

■ **Note** Looking at Figures 7-15 and 7-16 it is easy to see that these forms do not look very nice. They look like they were designed by… well, by a developer. You're right; they were. In Chapter 9 I cover some material on making your ASPX forms look nicer and more like they fit in with the rest of SharePoint. This is one area that ASPX form developers have the upper hand over InfoPath form developers.

ABSTRACT THINKING

The basic functionality we covered here can be taken and expanded on for many other situations. We took a fairly straight and narrow path through the functionality, but there's no reason you can't branch out to cover other needs. At a high level, here's what we covered:

- Creating a form that collects information from a user and passes that information in to our workflow, where it is accessible via code. At that point we can do whatever we need to with it—including launching other processes, sending emails, calling web services, programmatically altering documents, etc.
- Setting values on our workflow form programmatically and having them be read-only on the form. These values can be retrieved from anywhere.
- Moving data in a full round-trip—from form to workflow and back to form again. This process can start anywhere (form or workflow) and keep that same round-trip capability.
- Creating, updating, and completing tasks.
- Sending email.

So even though what we saw here was pretty concrete, keep in mind that the capabilities open to you are pretty broad. Take what we covered here and look to apply it to many different situations—the opportunity is there.

Summary

There was a lot of material in this chapter. Here's a quick synopsis:

- Forms allow you to collect any information you need from your workflow participants.
- With some flavor of the Forms Server in your environment, you can build your forms in InfoPath 2007 and have them rendered into a browser.
- With MOSS 2007 installed, you can also have your forms rendered directly into the Office clients that support the new UI.
- With only WSS you are limited to strictly ASPX forms. They're more work, but your solution won't lack any important functionality.
- There are various types of forms to support various functions:
  - Association forms for when an administrator is creating an association between a workflow and a SharePoint list or document library.
  - Initiation forms for when a user is kicking off an instance of a workflow on a particular list item or document.
  - Task forms to customize the look and functionality of tasks assigned to users as part of your workflow.
  - Modification forms to support the functionality of making changes to a workflow in mid-processing.
- A lot of moving parts are involved in getting our forms to work properly as part of our workflow. Follow the steps we've covered here to make sure everything clicks.
- In many situations, association and initiation forms are very similar. The association form allows you to set information that can then be changed in the initiation form. Similarly, the initiation form could be configured to not allow values set in the association form to be changed. It all depends on your business needs.
- There is nothing we need to do differently in order to move our forms down to the Office client applications, so these are all full players in whatever process we need to implement.

PART 4

Turning Things Up a Notch

In the movie *This is Spinal Tap*, there is a great line (OK, there's really more than one, but only one that I'll reference here). The band is talking to the interviewer about their amplifiers and Nigel says something along the lines of "Whereas most amps go to 10, ours go to 11… it's one louder." I'm paraphrasing that pretty heavily, but if you've seen the movie you know the scene I'm talking about. Somewhere in the recesses of poor Nigel's heavily sedated brain, the implication is that this is what makes them louder—it is the extra little bit that they provide for their audience.

Consider this part the "11" setting for this book—it's the little bit extra I provide for you.

We've covered all of the basics and walked through numerous examples of how to operate within and build an Office 2007 Workflow. While you may not be completely comfortable with everything yet, we've at least covered it all. You should know what is possible and know that when you need a refresher on a particular area you can always go back and review the appropriate chapter.

The three chapters in this part, however, take things to a whole new level. No longer are we content with the basics. No longer do we need step-by-step instructions to walk us through each task. The material covered here is more advanced than previous material, and it's possible that you will never need some of it. And that's OK. The information is useful, nonetheless.

Chapter 8, “Workflow Rules,” introduces the WF Rules engine as well as some advanced activities, and proceeds to extend things well past the out-of-the-box capabilities. The solution introduced there to facilitate external management of workflow processing crosses many pieces of functionality and ties them all together into a package that makes your Office workflows eminently more useful and extensible.

Chapter 9, “A Workflow Smorgasbord,” is just that—an eclectic mix of material. While it’s all important, none of it is a big enough topic to get a chapter of its own. Some of this chapter is based on material presented elsewhere, building upon it or filling in details; some of it is entirely standalone.

Chapter 10 is a walkthrough of the Workflow Object Model. It is not an exhaustive dissertation—that would be both boring and foolish. If you want an object reference, you can get it in the Visual Studio Object Browser or the documentation on MSDN. Instead, I look at the major members of the major classes from the Workflow Object Model. I break them down and talk about what the various members are used for and when you will need them. I include code snippets for many of the pieces to help you understand how they can be used.

CHAPTER 8

Workflow Rules

Rules are part of the crunchy goodness in Office workflows. We'll delve more deeply into rules as we progress through this chapter (not that "crunchy goodness" doesn't tell you everything you need to know, but I *do* have a whole chapter to fill here), but think about it this way—without rules as *separately definable entities* the following are true:

- A workflow locks a business process in as a snapshot in time.
- Business logic is tightly intertwined with processing logic.
- Documenting and tracking business logic is made more difficult.

None of these are ideal.

With rules, however, we can extract some of that logic and define it separately. If that part of the logic ever needs to change, we can update the rule and leave the rest of the logic intact. That separation provides for a lot of flexibility and power. You'll see more as we progress through this chapter.

One of the tenets of the Information Worker Revolution is to reduce dependence on IT. If business logic is intertwined with code and processing logic, business departments can never fully take ownership of it—they will always be dependent on IT to modify and deploy that logic when it changes.

An example will help to drive this idea home:

Early in its experience with Office 2007, KCD Holdings targeted the employee review process as a key process to be modeled and introduced using workflows and Office 2007. It was a classic example of document routing, approval, and feedback. Based on their research, they felt that they would be able to introduce this process using largely out-of-the-box activities stitched together with a minimal amount of custom code.

The only sticky bits were related to the various approval levels for pay raises. This year, they had budgeted for a 5 percent raise as the maximum that would be permitted within any department without additional executive approval. The final review step in their process would always look like Figure 8-1. However, knowing their business, they knew that the threshold percentage that would trigger additional approval requirements would change every year.

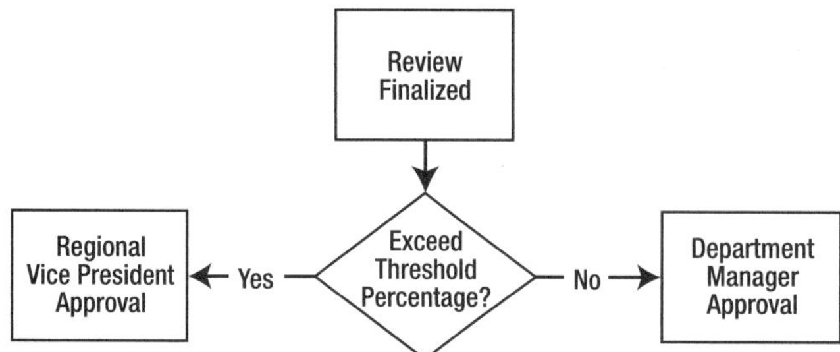

Figure 8-1. *Final approval on the KCD Employee Review workflow would always follow these steps.*

They toyed with a few options as they worked to design the process:

- *Wrapping the threshold percentage in a web service called by the workflow*: Each year, all they needed to do was update that web service. While this was appealing, they knew that it would still require intervention by IT and also that it was not practical as their use of Workflow grew—having one (or more) web services for every business process was not a recipe for an easily maintainable architecture.
- *Storing the threshold value in a simple XML configuration file*: Again, this would fit the bill for this particular scenario, but it was not a desired architecture for significant long-term use by multiple processes. In addition, it only stores a single value—not the logic of the condition itself. If the logic changes slightly from "greater than *x* percent" to "greater than *x* percent or less than *y* percent," then this approach will not work.
- *Hard-coding the threshold value and business logic directly into the workflow code*: Again, this would solve the immediate problem, but it presented many others—dependence on IT, versioning issues, and deployment problems, just to name a few.
- *Implementing the threshold value as an entry on the association or initiation form for the workflow*: This approach came in a close second, but because the employee reviews were stored in multiple document libraries across the portal, they wanted to avoid having to update the threshold value multiple times when it changed. They felt that the chances of one document library not being updated with the new value were too great and would cause too many problems. Like the XML file discussed earlier, this too only stores a simple threshold value.
- *Storing the threshold value as a SharePoint list item and writing code to access it from within the process*: This approach was also appealing for many reasons, including its simplicity. However, like the XML file or forms-based approaches, this too only stores a simple threshold value.
- *Using the Workflow Rules engine* and configuring the threshold value and business logic as an externally accessible rule, which could be read by each workflow instance and maintained separately from the process itself by a business user.

Naturally, as this is a chapter on rules in Workflow, they chose the last option.

Although that example is very simple, it should help to clarify the benefit of a separate rules engine. Expanding on it slightly, any decision in a workflow that uses discrete data points as factors in the decision is a candidate for the Rules engine. This would include, but is certainly not limited to

- Timeframes for reviewing documents
- Policy details for document retention, disposition, etc.
- Approval paths for purchase requisitions, travel requests, etc.

Like many other things, there is more than one way to skin this cat. Many factors will drive how you go about solving your particular problem. As alluded to earlier, a close second to implementing rules is to simply collect the information on an association or initiation form, which we covered in Chapter 7. Honestly, this would certainly be easier to implement than a foray into the Rules engine. However, it does have a few shortcomings when compared to rules:

- *Duplication*: Rule values are duplicated every time the workflow is implemented. If you're only using the workflow in one or a few lists or document libraries, this may not be a big deal.
- *Versioning*: With the form approach, there is no (easy) way to track and control the values that are applied to a specific instance.
- *Control*: Using rules, specifically in the way we are going to cover in this chapter, will allow you to define and manage the rules centrally.
- *Auditing*: In highly regulated environments, it may be necessary to be able to report on or verify the specific rules that were implemented at a certain point in time. The approach we are going to take in this chapter could easily be extended to support full auditing and reporting by treating the rules as records and utilizing the full record-management capabilities of MOSS.

So with that understanding of when and why to use rules, let's begin our investigation.

■ **Note** This chapter is going to be slightly different from previous ones in that there is not a single scenario that we are going to walk through. Rather, in this chapter, we're going to build a custom piece of functionality that will be useful across many scenarios. For this chapter, the functionality we're building out is a custom activity to implement rules defined externally from our workflow as well as a simple Windows Forms application to define and manage those external rules.

Rule Mechanics

Before going much further into rules, and certainly before we can build our own rules-based workflow, we need to cover a bit of the *what* and *how* for rules in Office workflows. In the first place, where exactly can you use rules in an Office workflow? Good question. The answer is that there are two situations in which rules come into play:

- As *conditions* on activities such as
    - IfElseBranch
    - While
    - ConditionedActivityGroup
    - Replicator

  (We covered each of these at a high level in Chapter 3—we'll cover them in more detail here.)
- As a full *ruleset* on the Policy activity. We touched only briefly on the Policy activity in Chapter 3. We'll cover it in more detail (including an explanation of just what the heck a *ruleset* is) in just a bit. Our actual implementation in this chapter is going to replicate much of the functionality of the Policy activity but allow us to define and store our rules outside of the workflow itself.

The difference between these two situations is related to the complexity of the rule being applied and the manner in which it is applied.

■ **Note** This is probably a good time to fill you in on one little caveat... the use of the Policy activity and rulesets is not officially supported by Microsoft for Office workflows. In conversations with some Microsoft people, it appears that this is simply because it is not a scenario that they tested. There is nothing in the product to preclude their use, and as you'll see, everything works and is not that different from any other custom activity. Plus, the value provided is too useful to just pass up.

Let's start with activity conditions. Activity conditions are local to a particular activity. Generally they are used to indicate whether one specific activity executes. For example, the simplest condition is on a basic IfElse activity. The logic of the activity is pretty straightforward—if a certain condition is true, execute the logic in the first branch; otherwise, execute the logic in the second branch. Although this logic can certainly get more complicated, all activity conditions essentially break down to this simple state, and the heart of this logic is the condition that is evaluated.

The condition that is evaluated must result in either a `true` or a `false`. Each activity that contains this logic will take different actions based on the return value from the condition evaluation, but the expression itself always results in a Boolean evaluation. Conditions can be applied as either of the following:

- *Code Condition*: Means that you write code that results in a Boolean value to indicate whether the condition evaluates to `true` or `false`, thereby controlling how the activity processes.
- *Declarative Rule Condition*: Means that you define the logic that controls how the activity processes utilizing the built-in Condition Editor. Technically, you're still writing code in the Condition Editor, but the code itself is simpler as it consists of basic comparisons between fields, variables, and values.

The latter is considered a part of the Rules engine, while the former is strictly custom code. You select between these two options in the Properties window for your activity, as shown in Figure 8-2. If you opt to write custom code, you are not utilizing the Workflow Rules engine—which may be perfectly acceptable in some cases. Although this is a chapter on the Rules engine, we'll take a little time to explore the Code Condition here just so we're presenting a complete picture.

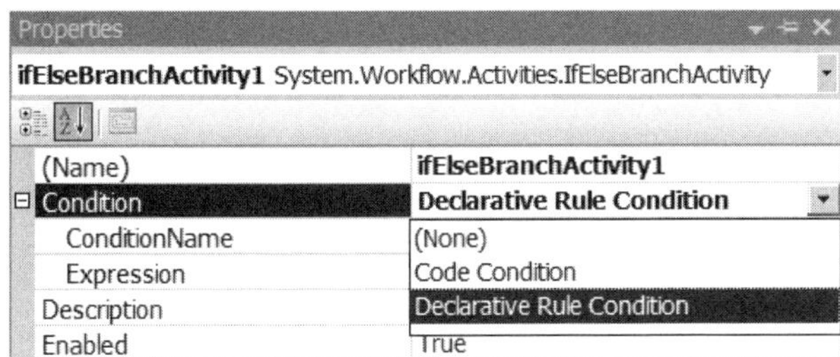

Figure 8-2. *Select which type of condition to use in the Properties window.*

Code Conditions

When you opt to write your condition as code, you specify a method name as the `ConditionName` property and Visual Studio automatically creates a method for you with the proper signature, as shown in Listing 8-1. All you need to do is write your code to arrive at either a `true` or a `false`. You then set the `Results` property of the `ConditionalEventArgs` parameter (the parameter `e` in Listing 8-1) for your method and all is right with the world.

Listing 8-1. *A Shell for Our Condition Method*

```
private void conditionCheck(object sender, ConditionalEventArgs e)
 {
 }
```

Code Conditions can contain any combination of the following:

- Inline code
- Method calls
- Calls to a web service

Your business needs and coding practices determine specifically what will go into the method evaluated for your condition. I recommend as a good habit that you avoid inline code and utilize method calls for code in your assembly and web services for code outside your assembly. It's just easier to maintain and reuse your logic that way. A simple method call example is shown in Listing 8-2. The call to the `checkAuthor` method could just as easily be a call to a web service.

Listing 8-2. *A Simple Condition Evaluation to Control the Flow of Our Process*

```
private void conditionCheck(object sender, ConditionalEventArgs e)
{
    e.Result = checkAuthor(this.workflowProperties.Originator);
}

private bool checkAuthor(string sAuthor)
{
    if (this.workflowProperties.Item["Author"].ToString().ToLower() == sAuthor.➥
ToLower())
    {
        return true;
    }
    else
    {
        return false;
    }
}
```

The code executed inside your method call (or in inline code) can do whatever you need it to, getting as complex as necessary. The benefit of Code Conditions is that they are easy for developers to wrap their minds around. They live in code, so writing a few more lines of code is easy. The problem with this approach is primarily that only coders can understand and maintain these conditions. Business departments can't touch them.

■ **Note** While this may seem like pretty good job security for developers, most good developers I know would not want a job that has evolved into mostly maintaining values in a bunch of rules. After a very few times of changing a 5 to a 6, recompiling and redeploying, most good developers are thinking that they don't want to be secure in this job anymore. The ability to farm these types of things off to business users means that the developers can do things quite a bit more interesting.

If you are dead set on implementing your rules and business logic entirely in code, do yourself a favor and at least strip the rules out into a separate assembly. In your Code Condition, you then just instantiate that object and call the appropriate method. That way, when the rules change, you only need to update that assembly and don't have to touch the rest of your logic. If you play your cards right, you can do a lot with this approach but it's more work than necessary.

Declarative Rule Conditions

As alluded to earlier, Declarative Rule Conditions are part of the Workflow Rules engine. "Great," you say. "What does that mean?" Hang on there, Beppo, we're getting to it. Declarative Rule Conditions are, as the name implies, declared and therefore not compiled. At runtime, they are interpreted and evaluated to determine a course of action.

Interpreted? Wait, doesn't that slow things down? Yes, it does—slightly. However, if you ever actually notice the extra nanoseconds this adds to your processing you can call Microsoft and complain. Otherwise, don't worry about it.

Declarative Rule Conditions on activities offer us a simple way to separate our condition from the rest of our logic. They don't get us all the way to the promised land of fully separate, externally maintainable rules, but they take us a step in the right direction. The step they take is to allow us to create a condition once and utilize it in multiple places *from within the same workflow.*

One other important feature of Declarative Rule Conditions is that they can be dynamically updated at runtime. Wait! Isn't that what we're looking for—the ability to dynamically manipulate our rules at runtime? Yes, it is. I'm glad you're paying attention. It is important to note, however, that due to the nature of SharePoint as a Workflow *host,* our ability to manipulate our conditions at runtime is significantly more limited than in the rest of the WF world. Essentially, what this means is that while a given workflow instance can manipulate its *own* conditions dynamically at runtime, there is no simple way to manipulate the conditions from outside the workflow. Drat. So close and yet so far.

■ **Tip** When I said our ability to manipulate our conditions at runtime is "significantly more limited" back there, you really ought to read that as *while not impossible, it's really difficult and probably not worth the time.* I know some very stubborn developers (myself included) and if I said *impossible* there, they would spend hour after hour hacking together code to make it work just because it's a challenge. Really, folks, read on; there is a better way.

In my opinion, this limits the usefulness of Declarative Rule Conditions for Office workflows as it makes them not very different from well-crafted Code Conditions. Although it is true that you can't (easily) update your code at runtime, if the solution is well architected and well written, you can achieve the same end with the use of method parameters and some global variables. As mentioned earlier, even separating all of your rules out into a separate assembly provides a lot of the same benefits of Declarative Rule Conditions.

We will cover more details on Declarative Rule Conditions, however, for a few reasons:

- They still provide some value for our Office workflows. The tool exists and in some cases it will be the best tool for the job, so we should make sure it is available in our arsenal.
- In many ways, Declarative Rule Conditions are simpler to implement, maintain, and work with than Code Conditions. (The developer in me just let out a gasp of disbelief...)
- When we do reach the promised land of externally maintainable rules, there will still be the need for either Code or Declarative Rule Conditions, so they don't go away. We'll see a return of Declarative Rule Conditions in the example at the end of the chapter.

Declarative Rule Conditions on our activities make use of the Condition Manager, shown in Figure 8-3. The Condition Manager provides access to the Condition Editor, a simple wizard that allows us to manage the conditions available to us in the current workflow. So, for example, if another activity elsewhere in our workflow needed to make the same evaluation as Condition1 shown in Figure 8-3, it could simply reuse the condition—we would not need to re-create it. This provides some of the value of Declarative Rule Conditions, but is no different than utilizing a Code Condition and pointing at the same method call.

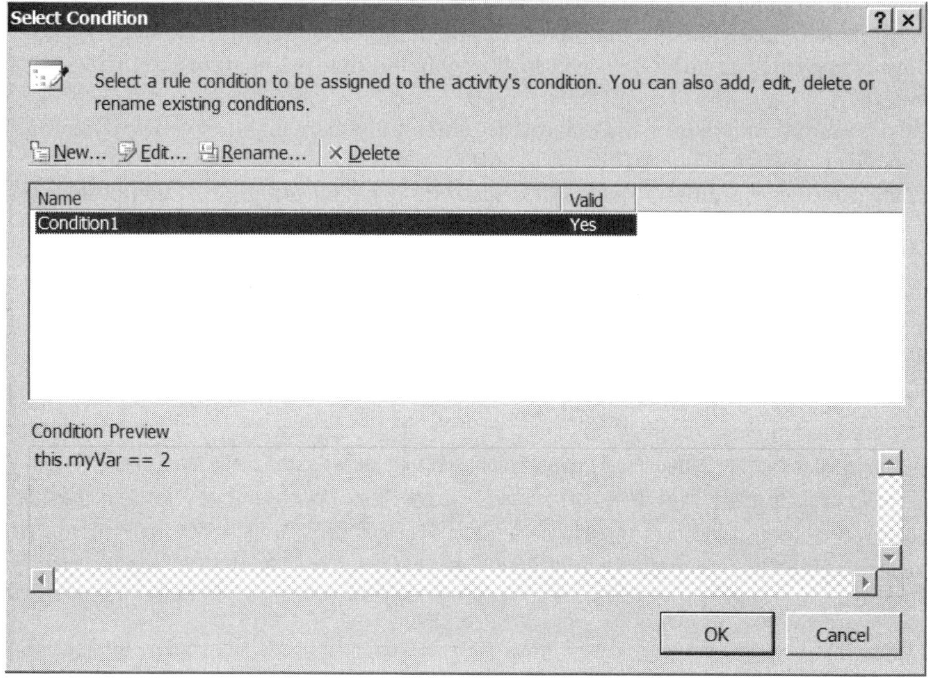

Figure 8-3. *The Condition Manager showing a very simple Declarative Rule Condition*

The Condition Editor is really the heart of setting up Declarative Rule Conditions. Let's take a look at how it works and what it lets us do. First of all, to access the Condition Editor, you need to specify *Declarative Rule Condition* as the type of condition for your activity. Next, click the ellipsis in the `ConditionName` property to open the Condition Manager. The buttons across the top of the Condition Editor (New, Edit, Rename, Delete) are pretty self-explanatory, so I won't go into detail on each one. Just remember that they are the options available to you when working with Declarative Rule Conditions. Notice that clicking on a condition will show you a preview of the contents of that condition in the lower half of the Condition Editor window. This avoids having to open each condition to find the one you need. Remember, conditions defined anywhere in your workflow will be available to all of the activities in your workflow. Conceivably, then, in a complex workflow this dialog box could get quite busy.

Clicking on either the New or the Edit button will bring up the Condition Editor dialog box, shown in Figure 8-4. The only difference is obviously that in the former case you are creating a new rule so the dialog box is blank, whereas in the latter you are changing an existing rule so the contents of that condition will be shown, as in Figure 8-4.

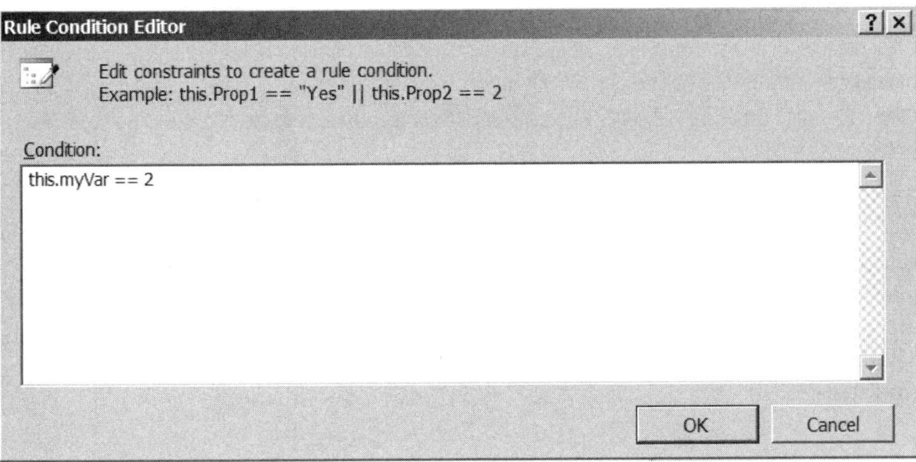

Figure 8-4. *Editing an existing condition in the Condition Editor*

Creating a condition is a simple matter—just type it in. Whatever you type needs to evaluate to a Boolean condition, and while this is the "if" statement, you don't actually type in "if…". To assist you, the Condition Editor supplies capabilities similar to IntelliSense. This means that if you type **this** or **some_object_name** followed by a period, an IntelliSense-like window will pop up showing you the available members for that object, as shown in Figure 8-5. You also get a little indicator—the exclamation point in the red circle on the right side of Figure 8-5—when your condition is not valid.

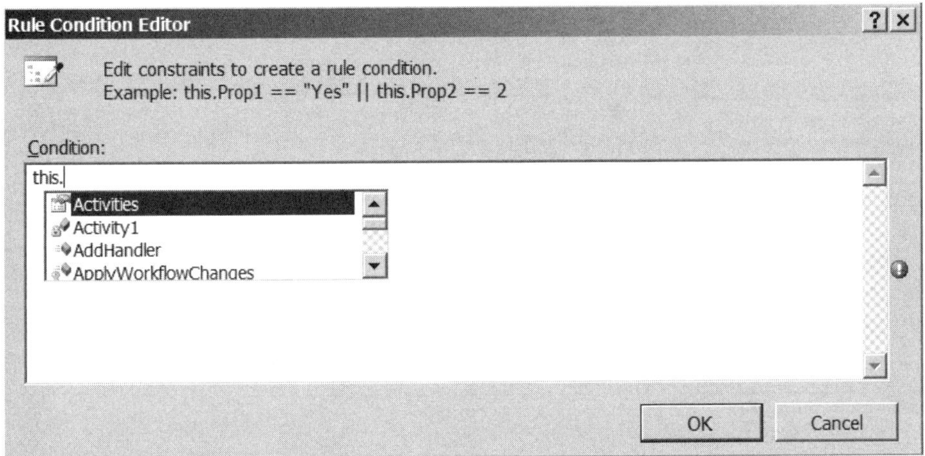

Figure 8-5. *The Condition Editor supplies an IntelliSense-like feature for creating our conditions.*

■ **Note** For objects, only *static* members are available for use within conditions. For the object `this`, which represents the current workflow, all properties, variables, and methods are available—just as if we were writing inline code. Keep this in mind if you are creating objects for use inside your conditions—to be accessible, members must be static.

So writing our condition is a simple matter of setting up our comparisons to arrive at a Boolean result. But what can those comparisons look like? Each side of the comparison will be a property, variable, method, or other member of either the current workflow or a referenced object (static members only). In between will be an operator. The available operators are shown in Table 8-1.

Table 8-1. *Available Operators for Our Rules*

<table>
<tr><th>Symbol</th><th>Operation</th></tr>
<tr><td>== or =</td><td>Equality</td></tr>
<tr><td><</td><td>Less than</td></tr>
<tr><td>></td><td>Greater than</td></tr>
<tr><td><=</td><td>Less than or equal to</td></tr>
<tr><td>>=</td><td>Greater than or equal to</td></tr>
<tr><td>+</td><td>Addition</td></tr>
<tr><td>-</td><td>Subtraction</td></tr>
<tr><td>*</td><td>Multiplication</td></tr>
<tr><td>/</td><td>Division</td></tr>
<tr><td>MOD</td><td>Modulus (division remainder)</td></tr>
<tr><td>AND or &&</td><td>Boolean AND</td></tr>
<tr><td>OR or ||</td><td>Boolean OR</td></tr>
<tr><td>NOT or !</td><td>Negation</td></tr>
<tr><td>|</td><td>Bitwise OR</td></tr>
<tr><td>&</td><td>Bitwise AND</td></tr>
</table>

So, each of the following is an example of a valid condition:

- `this.Enabled != True`
- `myObject.myStaticMethod(this.workflowProperties.AssociationData ➥ ["Some_Property"]) != String.Empty`
- `this.workflowProperties.Item.Attachments.Count >= 0 && this.➥ workflowProperties.Item.Attachments.Count < 5`
- `this.some_variable + this.another_variable >= 3`

Pretty straightforward stuff. The last thing we need to cover with regard to Declarative Rule Conditions is how they are stored and applied. We've already said that these conditions are not compiled, so what happens with them? Where do they go? What are they all about, Alfie? If you take a look in the Solution Explorer inside Visual Studio after creating a condition, you will see a new file has been added to your project. It will be the name of your workflow class file with a `.rules` extension—for example, `MyRulesWorkflow1.rules`. If you open the file in Visual Studio, you will see a whole lot of very verbose XML. I say it's verbose because, for example, for the simple condition `this.workflowProperties.Item.Attachments.Count > 0`, the resulting XML is 36 lines long.

Ouch.

I'm not going to show you an example here because we're not going to do anything with it and it would just fill the page with a lot of unattractive XML. The XML itself is pretty straightforward. If you take a few minutes to analyze it, you'll come to grips with the logic behind it all. It makes heavy use of `CodeDom`, so a familiarity with that would be helpful.

Oh, OK, stop whining, I'll show you an example of a `.rules` file. But don't blame me if you get a hernia carrying this book around. Figure 8-6 shows the `.rules` file for a Declarative Rule Condition of `this.workflowProperties.Item.Attachments.Count > 0`. As you can see in Figure 8-6, it is quite lengthy. In my ongoing effort to be a good, helpful author, I added some indicators for the important parts:

A: The name of our condition in case we need to use it over again or refer to it in documentation

B: The operator that sits between the left and right portions of our condition

C-F: The left side of our condition, shown from the inside out

G: The right side of our expression—in this case, simply the value we're comparing against

That's it, a simple `.rules` file. As I said, verbose, but not difficult to understand. If you happen to be a code-masochist, you could write a utility to generate the properly formed XML. As I mentioned before, we are somewhat limited with what we could do with the conditions. In a pure WF project, you can dynamically load and modify these `.rules` files at runtime based on your needs. In that case, the schema and details of the `.rules` file would be far more important.

For our Office workflows, however, we need to take a slightly different approach, which we're sneaking up on. I can sense the anticipation building…

```
<RuleDefinitions xmlns="http://schemas.microsoft.com/winfx/2006/xaml/workflow">
  <RuleDefinitions.Conditions>
    <RuleExpressionCondition Name="Condition1"> A
      <RuleExpressionCondition.Expression>
        <ns0:CodeBinaryOperatorExpression Operator="GreaterThan" B
            xmlns:ns0="clr-namespace:System.CodeDom;Assembly=System, Version=2.0.0.0,
            Culture=neutral, PublicKeyToken=b77a5c561934e089">
          <ns0:CodeBinaryOperatorExpression.Left>
            <ns0:CodePropertyReferenceExpression PropertyName="Count"> C
              <ns0:CodePropertyReferenceExpression.TargetObject>
                <ns0:CodePropertyReferenceExpression PropertyName="Attachments"> D
                  <ns0:CodePropertyReferenceExpression.TargetObject>
                    <ns0:CodePropertyReferenceExpression PropertyName="Item"> E
                      <ns0:CodePropertyReferenceExpression.TargetObject>
                        <ns0:CodeFieldReferenceExpression FieldName="workflowProperties"> F
                          <ns0:CodeFieldReferenceExpression.TargetObject>
                            <ns0:CodeThisReferenceExpression />
                          </ns0:CodeFieldReferenceExpression.TargetObject>
                        </ns0:CodeFieldReferenceExpression>
                      </ns0:CodePropertyReferenceExpression.TargetObject>
                    </ns0:CodePropertyReferenceExpression>
                  </ns0:CodePropertyReferenceExpression.TargetObject>
                </ns0:CodePropertyReferenceExpression>
              </ns0:CodePropertyReferenceExpression.TargetObject>
            </ns0:CodePropertyReferenceExpression>
          </ns0:CodeBinaryOperatorExpression.Left>
          <ns0:CodeBinaryOperatorExpression.Right>
            <ns0:CodePrimitiveExpression>
              <ns0:CodePrimitiveExpression.Value>
                <ns1:Int32 xmlns:ns1="clr-namespace:System;Assembly=mscorlib, Version=2.0.0.0,
                  Culture=neutral, PublicKeyToken=b77a5c561934e089">0</ns1:Int32>
              </ns0:CodePrimitiveExpression.Value>                     G
            </ns0:CodePrimitiveExpression>
          </ns0:CodeBinaryOperatorExpression.Right>
        </ns0:CodeBinaryOperatorExpression>
      </RuleExpressionCondition.Expression>
    </RuleExpressionCondition>
  </RuleDefinitions.Conditions>
</RuleDefinitions>
```

Figure 8-6. *The .rules file for a simple single expression condition. Brevity is not its strong suit.*

Policy Activity

Our goal is to be able to control our workflow from an external source without having to recompile and redeploy, and we haven't quite gotten there yet. The constructs we've been looking at will be a part of the solution, but before we can add the external control, we'll need to introduce the final player I mentioned a little while ago—the Policy activity.

The Policy activity takes the simple conditions we have explored so far in this chapter and tacks a `then` and an `else` on the end. The function of the conditions—either Code or Declarative—is to be the `if` part of an `if-then-else` statement. The policy, with its rulesets (which we'll explore shortly), is the full `if-then-else`, plus a bit more.

The Policy activity is one of the default activities that ship with WF. Its primary function, at a high level, is simply to manage the creation and execution of rules within a ruleset. I know I've tossed the word *ruleset* around a few times and I haven't defined it yet, so let's take care of that now.

■ Definition A *ruleset* is a collection of business rule definitions that together serve to describe the full logic of a solution.

The rule definitions that make up the ruleset consist of

- `if-then-else` expressions:
  - One or more conditions
  - Zero or more actions taken if the condition(s) evaluate to `true`
  - Zero or more actions taken if the condition(s) evaluate to `false`
- Metadata to control execution:
  - Name
  - Priority
  - Active flag
  - Reevaluation conditions

In addition, the ruleset itself has an attribute that lets you specify the specific chaining behavior for the ruleset as a whole. (Chaining behavior? Forget it—we're on a roll…)

So, there you have it. Ready to move on? I thought not. That definition may have created more questions than it answered—like just what is chaining behavior. OK, let's take a deeper look at rulesets.

Rulesets

First and foremost, rulesets are just that—*sets* of *rules*... a collection of business logic that are interrelated and so are treated as a unit. A rule, as already mentioned, is an `if-then-else` statement. That part of understanding rulesets is pretty straightforward. What you're likely having a harder time understanding is some of the metadata elements from the previous list. Let's break them down a little bit.

Starting with the easy ones.

- *Name*: Simply a label to use to refer to the rule.
- *Priority*: Again, simple; indicates the order in which the rules within a ruleset should execute. Higher priority trumps lower priority and executes first. By default, all rules have a priority of 0. To indicate that a particular rule should execute last without changing the priority of all other rules, you can specify a negative priority number.
- *Active*: Also dirt simple; a simple Boolean flag that indicates whether the individual rule should be processed at all. This allows you to temporarily remove rules from execution processing without deleting them.

That takes care of all but two pieces of metadata—one on the individual rules and one on the whole ruleset. These last two are more complicated and related to the same functionality. First up: reevaluation conditions. This is a simple binary choice—Always or Never. Rules can be reevaluated based on the chaining settings (which we'll cover in a moment), and this property allows you to override the reevaluation caused by chaining for each individual rule. This will make more sense in a moment, but basically it comes down to always reevaluate a specific rule when necessary or never, ever, reevaluate. Evaluations are a result of chaining, so let's get to that.

Chaining

First a warning: if you try to jump in with both feet and tackle chaining and all of its implications head on, your head is likely to explode. On one level, chaining can be very, very complicated and trying to come to grips with all of the potential ramifications can be a daunting task. On the other hand, chaining itself is quite a simple concept. If you start with simple examples and get a good understanding of how chaining works and what it offers to your workflows, you can safely venture into deeper waters without needing to wrap your head in duct tape and put plastic up on the walls.

So, the basics. At a very basic level, chaining is nothing more than a mechanism for identifying, managing, and responding to dependencies between rules. There, that's not too difficult. Let's take a look at an example. If I have the three rules shown in Listing 8-3, the dependencies are fairly obvious.

Listing 8-3. *A Basic Ruleset to Help Us Understand Chaining*

```
Rule 1 (Priority: 2) - If y=3 then b=9
Rule 2 (Priority: 3) - If x=1 then a=2
Rule 3 (Priority: 1) - If z=4 then x=1
```

The single dependency between these rules is fairly obvious: Rule 2 is dependent on Rule 3 because the condition in Rule 2 is based on the value of x, which is set in the action of Rule 3.

If we start with values of

```
x=5

y=7

z=4

b=6

a=3
```

we can walk through the execution process fairly easily:

1. Rules are processed in descending order of their priority so Rule 2 executes first with x at its initial value of 5. The condition (`if x=1`) evaluates to `false` so the action for the rule never executes.

2. Next in descending priority order is Rule 1 with a priority of 2. Rule 2 executes with y at its initial value of 7. The condition (`if y=3`) evaluates to `false` so the action for the rule never executes. So far, so good—nothing has happened.

3. Rule 3 will execute last because it has the lowest priority. When Rule 3 executes, z still has its original value of 4 because it has not been changed by any of the preceding rules. The condition for Rule 3 (`if z=4`) evaluates to `true` so the action executes, setting x to 1.

4. Without chaining, processing would stop right here. However, because of chaining, dependencies are taken into account and Rule 2 will be reevaluated because it has a dependency on Rule 3.

5. Rule 2 is reevaluated, this time with a value of 1 for `x`. In this case, the condition (`if x=1`) evaluates to `true` and so the action sets `a` to a new value of 2.

6. No other dependencies exist within our ruleset and so processing stops here.

Our process ends with the following values:

```
x=1

y=7

z=4

b=6

a=2
```

Whew. That was a pretty simple example—no `else` pieces for our conditions, no multiple dependencies, simple priorities, etc.—and I can feel my head straining against the duct tape.

Chaining is unbelievably powerful but it's also very easy to get in over your head. Fortunately, Microsoft has made things simple for us mere mortals for most of the situations we're likely to find ourselves in. Out of the box, chaining such as we just went through would all be handled for us automagically. We wouldn't have to worry about it unless we needed our process to operate differently. Then we need the duct tape. If you're a glutton for punishment and want to test out your newfound understanding of chaining, take a look at the sidebar "Cleanup in Aisle 4."

CLEANUP IN AISLE 4

So now you're feeling all cocky in your new knowledge of rulesets and chaining and want to try out one that's a bit more complex. Here's a challenge for you—see how you do.

Start with initial values of

- `x=1`
- `y=2`
- `z=3`
- `a=4`
- `b=5`

Now set up your rules as shown here. Walk through the process manually and see what you come up with. Here's a hint for you: pay attention to the Reevaluation settings.

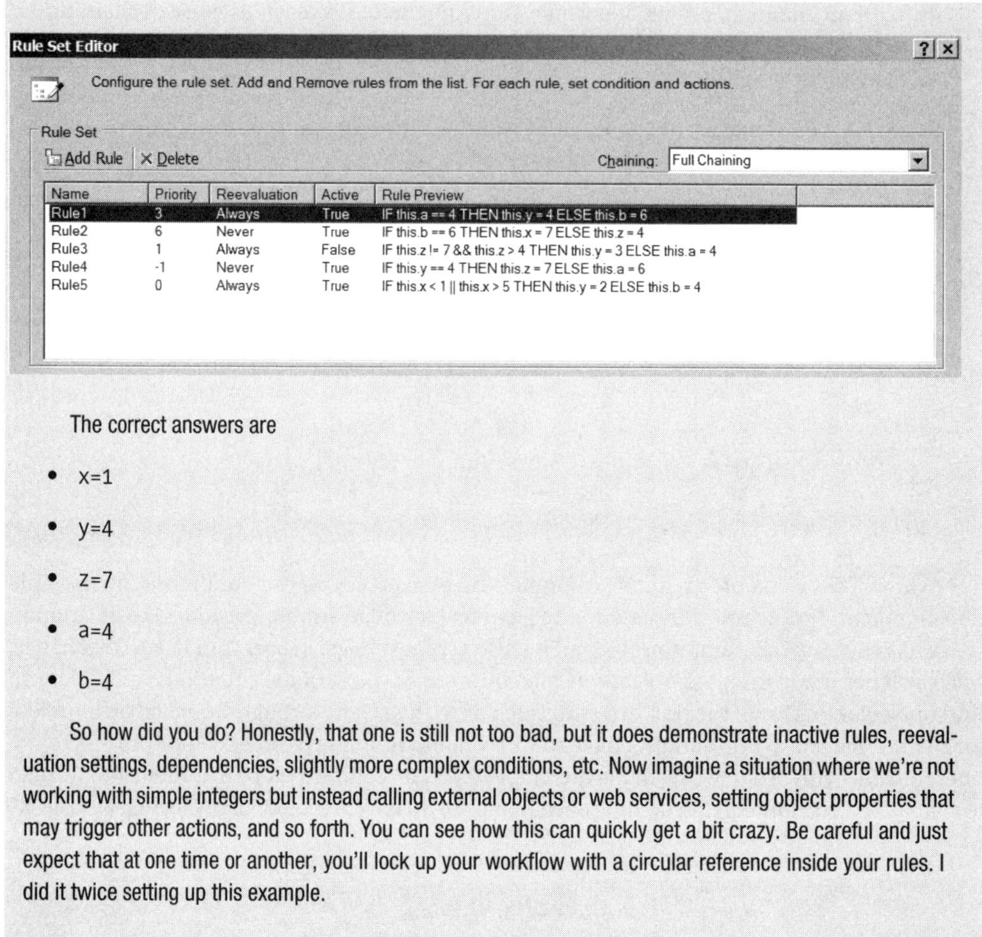

The correct answers are

- x=1
- y=4
- z=7
- a=4
- b=4

So how did you do? Honestly, that one is still not too bad, but it does demonstrate inactive rules, reevaluation settings, dependencies, slightly more complex conditions, etc. Now imagine a situation where we're not working with simple integers but instead calling external objects or web services, setting object properties that may trigger other actions, and so forth. You can see how this can quickly get a bit crazy. Be careful and just expect that at one time or another, you'll lock up your workflow with a circular reference inside your rules. I did it twice setting up this example.

The heart of chaining is the identification of dependencies. There are three ways that dependencies can be identified in our rules:

- *Implicit*: These are what we saw earlier. The Rules engine walked our ruleset before executing any rules and identified situations where a value used in the condition of one rule is modified in the action of another rule. This represents an implicit dependency. There's not much more to implicit dependencies so we won't go any further. Most of the time, this is what you'll use.
- *Attribute-based*: Used when a rule invokes a method. Because of the potential web of dependencies and interrelations once code starts stepping into method calls, this mechanism allows a developer to explicitly identify how methods should be accounted for when determining ruleset dependencies. We'll delve more deeply into this in the next section.

- *Explicit*: This type of dependency control is only useful in situations where a property is updated by a call to a method that for one reason or another (perhaps it is a third-party control) cannot be modified to add attribute-based dependency information. We'll look at this in just a moment.

Attribute-Based Dependencies There are three specific attributes available for developers to decorate their methods with for use with rules:

- `[RuleRead("property_name")]`: The associated method reads the specified property value.
- `[RuleWrite("property_name")]`: The associated method writes to the specified property.
- `[RuleInvoke("method_name")]`: The associated method makes a call to another method. The first method gets decorated with `RuleInvoke` and the name of the second method. The second method gets decorated with `RuleRead` or `RuleWrite` and the name of the property involved.

■ **Tip** Like conditions, methods and properties of objects used in rules must be static.

For example, a method called by a rule that modifies the property `RequisitionValue` would be decorated as shown in Listing 8-4.

Listing 8-4. *Using RuleWrite*

```
[RuleWrite("RequisitionValue")]
private void SetRequisitionTotal(int iReqID, int iDiscountPercent)
{
    // do some processing here...
    RequisitionValue = ...
}
```

An example of using `RuleRead` is shown in Listing 8-5.

Listing 8-5. *Using RuleRead*

```
[RuleRead("RequisitionValue")]
private double GetRequisitionTotal(int iReqID)
{
    // do some processing here...
    return RequisitionValue
}
```

Finally, an example of `RuleInvoke` is shown in Listing 8-6. Note the use of `RuleWrite` as well on the called method.

Listing 8-6. *Last, but Not Least, RuleInvoke*

```
 [RuleInvoke("SetRequisitionTotal")]
private void UpdateRequisitionDetails(int iReqID)
{
     // do some processing to determine discount percentage here...
     SetRequisitionTotal(iReqID, iDiscountPercent);
}

[RuleWrite("RequisitionValue")]
private void SetRequisitionTotal(int iReqID, int iDiscountPercent)
{
     // do some processing here...
}
```

Explicit Dependencies

Explicit dependencies are identified by use of an `Update` statement, which is added directly to a rule in the Rule Set Editor, as shown in Listing 8-7.

Listing 8-7. *Using the Update Statement for Explicit Identification of Dependencies*

```
If a>3 then Some_External_Method(b)
Update(b)
```

As mentioned previously, this only comes into play when you can't modify the invoked method for some reason. Using the `Update` statement to explicitly identify a dependency should be pretty rare. Most of the time, dependencies will be handled implicitly. In cases where we use methods in our rules, attribute-based identification should suffice.

Wrapping Up Rulesets

Now that we have a pretty good understanding of chaining, there are just a few more items to cover to complete our understanding of rulesets:

- As mentioned before, each ruleset has a property that allows us to control chaining for the ruleset as a whole. The following three options are available:
  - *Full chaining*: Chaining is unrestrained and will execute as described earlier.
  - *Sequential*: Essentially chaining is turned off. Rules are executed only once and only in descending priority order.
  - *Explicit*: Turns off attribute-based and implicit and only processes dependencies explicitly identified with `Update` statements. While this might be extreme, this option provides the rule author with the greatest level of granular control over chaining within a given ruleset.
- Utilizing the `Halt` directive in the action part of a rule will cause the ruleset to immediately stop processing and to return control to the next statement in the workflow.

So that's it. Chaining and rulesets are now fully integrated into your vocabulary. You're a ruleset expert. You dream about attribute-based dependencies. Great, let's get back to the Policy activity.

Using the Policy Activity

To recap, the primary purpose of the Policy activity is to oversee the execution of a ruleset. If you drag a Policy activity out onto your workflow and look at its properties, you'll see a property called `RuleSetReference`. Clicking on the ellipsis in this property field will bring up the RuleSet Manager. This screen allows you to choose which ruleset defined in the current workflow you wish to apply with this Policy activity. A sample of this dialog box is shown in Figure 8-7. You'll notice that it looks very similar to the Declarative Condition Manager we saw back in Figure 8-3.

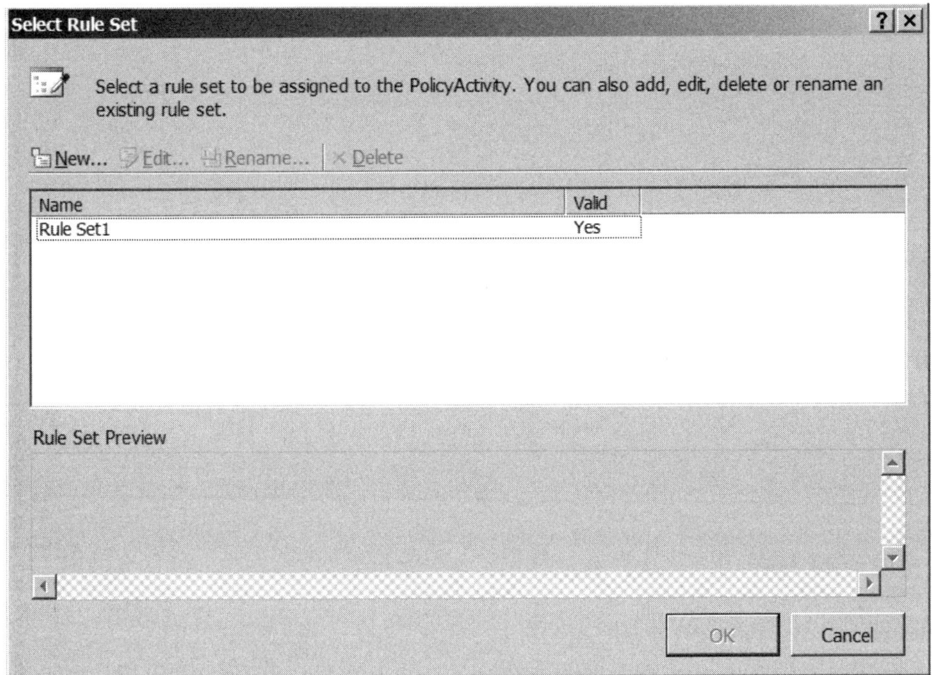

Figure 8-7. *The RuleSet Manager allows you to choose which ruleset to apply via the Policy activity.*

Clicking the New or Edit button opens the Rule Set Editor, which allows you to manage the rules that are part of the ruleset and also the chaining behavior and other metadata about the ruleset. An example of the Rule Set Editor is shown in Figure 8-8. The options available on this screen should be pretty familiar to you from our walkthrough of ruleset functionality. We'll explore the Rule Set Editor in more detail shortly as part of our process of building our externally manageable ruleset activity at the end of this chapter.

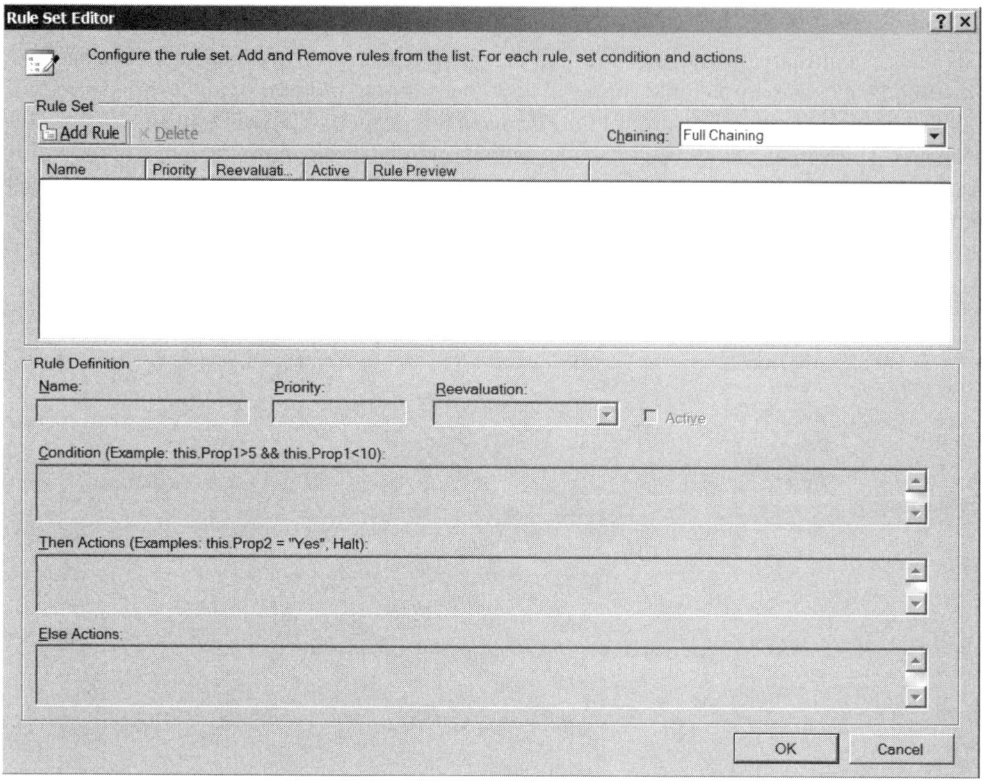

Figure 8-8. *The Rule Set Editor is somewhat more complex than the simple Declarative Condition Editor we saw earlier.*

The more astute among you will have noticed that I slipped in a little knock against the Policy activity a few paragraphs back when I introduced the RuleSet Manager. For those of you that missed it, here it is again: *This screen allows you to choose which ruleset defined in the current workflow you wish to apply with this Policy activity.* The key to my knock against the Policy activity is *defined in the current workflow.* Drat. We *still* can't get at our rulesets from outside of our workflow.

Double-drat.

So, the Policy activity gets us pretty close but not all the way there. To take the final step we need to do some coding—some pretty heavy-duty coding. For what it's worth, even the full WF does not have the capability to support external rule management out of the box, so this isn't just a slight against Office workflows. It is a capability that is conspicuously absent from the current version of all WF-based workflows.

In an apparent nod to the importance of this functionality, and perhaps as a harbinger of things to come in future releases of the WF engine, Microsoft has published a sample on the Windows Workflow Foundation section of the .NET 3.0 Framework site that shows how to store rulesets in SQL Server and dynamically load them into a workflow at runtime.

■ Tip The External Ruleset Demo application is available from `http://wf.netfx3.com/files/folders/rules_samples/entry309.aspx` at the time of this writing. Because it is still in beta, I expect that the sample will be updated for the production release and will likely be available from a different URL. You may need to dig around the WF section to find it.

"Great!" you say. "I'll just take a look at that sample application to make my rulesets externally accessible. I don't need to read any more of this inane drivel."

Not so fast, bucko. Sorry to burst your bubble, but the WF sample referenced earlier won't work for Office workflows. Sorry. You're stuck reading my inane drivel.

In the rest of this chapter, we're going to build a custom activity, a custom document library, a Windows Forms application to rehost the Rule Set Editor, and finally a sample workflow to show it all in action.

SOMETIMES IT'S JUST TOO MUCH

Now that you understand the Policy activity and are embarking on an exploration of our custom ExternalPolicy activity, you may be wondering why the simple Declarative Rule Conditions exist at all. The answer is that sometimes you don't need the `then` and the `else`. Back in the "Rule Mechanics" section of this chapter, you'll recall that I mentioned that the conditions were used on activities such as

- IfElseBranch
- While
- ConditionedActivityGroup
- Replicator

These activities do not need the `then` or the `else`—those are both provided by the activity itself or the activities they contain. Think about it, the IfElseBranch only needs to know whether or not it executes. If it does, the activities added to it will do the necessary work. If it does not, control passes on and nothing within that branch executes. The other activities that use conditions are similar.

Conditions are perfect for this scenario because they only signal how the process should flow. Throwing a policy into this, whether or not it is externally maintainable, would be overkill. Simplicity is a goal we should all shoot for.

Office Workflow External Policy Solution

As I mentioned earlier, the WF sample application will not work in Office workflows, so we need to take a different approach. While we're at it, we might as well take care of a few other issues with the sample application.

- The sample application stores rulesets in SQL Server (actually SQL Express). We have SharePoint at our disposal, so we'll change this to store our rulesets as documents in a custom document library.
- The sample application implements its own versioning functionality. We'll make use of SharePoint versioning.
- The sample application is not very approachable by nontechnical users. It references assemblies, types, and a few other technical details that would make business users blanch. Since one of our goals is to provide a tool to business users that allows them to manage rules without the help of IT, we'll make the rule management tool a little less technically focused.

So, without further ado, let's get started.

Note The full source code for all of the pieces utilized here is available at `www.kcdholdings.com`. If you don't feel like typing in all of the code for this solution, you can simply download it and follow along at home.

To understand what we're about to step into, let's take a look at our goals. We want to

- Duplicate the functionality of the Policy activity, namely the management and execution of rulesets.
- Make our rulesets editable from a process divorced from our workflow.
- Utilize SharePoint for storage, versioning, and security.
- Deliver a rule management application that nontechnical business users can understand and work with.

There are two primary processes to be implemented via our code: rule management and rule execution. We'll start with rule execution via a custom activity.

External Policy Activity

To execute externally defined rules within our workflows, we first need to retrieve them and then we can execute them. To do this and make this process flexible so that it can be used in multiple scenarios, we're going to create a custom activity to implement the following process:

1. Retrieve the serialized ruleset from the SharePoint document library.
2. Deserialize the ruleset into a ruleset object.
3. Execute the ruleset.

Create a new activity Library with a project name of KCD.Workflow.Rules and give the activity class a clever name, such as **ExternalPolicy**. When the solution is created, open up the activity in Code view and add the contents of Listing 8-8 to the top with the other `using` statements. Add references to Microsoft.SharePoint.dll and System.Windows.Forms.dll to your project and we can continue on.

■ **Note** I'm joking about the name for this activity. The name you use here is referenced again in the RuleSet Manager. If you change the name here, you'll need to change it in line 21 of Listing 8-17.

Listing 8-8. *The using Statements for Our Solution*

```
using System.Xml;
using System.Windows.Forms;
using System.Drawing.Design;
using System.Windows.Forms.Design;
using Microsoft.SharePoint;
using System.IO;
```

The next piece we're going to tackle is the custom properties for our activity. To make this activity work, we need three pieces of information:

- The URL of the SharePoint site that stores the ruleset documents
- The name of the document library on that site that stores the ruleset documents
- The name of the ruleset document to apply

Listing 8-9 shows all of the code for the properties we'll use to capture this information. The `SourceSiteURL` property is the same as the properties we set up on our activity in Chapter 5—it just makes sense to use a dependency property. If you need a refresher on dependency properties, jump back to Chapter 5. Other than that, there is nothing special about this property.

Listing 8-9. *Setting Up Our Properties*

```
public static DependencyProperty SourceSiteURLProperty =
    DependencyProperty.Register("SourceSiteURL",
    typeof(string),
    typeof(KCD.Workflow.Rules.ExternalPolicy));

public string SourceSiteURL
{
    get
    {
        return ((string)(base.GetValue(
            KCD.Workflow.Rules.ExternalPolicy.SourceSiteURLProperty)));
    }
```

```
        set
        {
            base.SetValue(
                KCD.Workflow.Rules.ExternalPolicy.SourceSiteURLProperty,
                value);
        }
    }

    public static DependencyProperty DocumentLibraryProperty =
        DependencyProperty.Register("DocumentLibrary",
        typeof(string),
        typeof(KCD.Workflow.Rules.ExternalPolicy));

    [Description("Name of Document Library storing Ruleset information"),
    Editor(typeof(docLibSelector), typeof(UITypeEditor))]
    public string DocumentLibrary
    {
        get
        {
            return ((string)(base.GetValue(
                KCD.Workflow.Rules.ExternalPolicy.DocumentLibraryProperty)));
        }
        set
        {
            base.SetValue(
                KCD.Workflow.Rules.ExternalPolicy.DocumentLibraryProperty,
                value);

        }
    }

    public static DependencyProperty RuleSetNameProperty =
    DependencyProperty.Register("RuleSetName", typeof(string),
        typeof(KCD.Workflow.Rules.ExternalPolicy));

    [Description("Name of RuleSet to Apply"),
    Editor(typeof(RuleSetSelector), typeof(UITypeEditor))]
    public string RuleSetName
    {
        get
        {
            return ((string)(base.GetValue(
                KCD.Workflow.Rules.ExternalPolicy.RuleSetNameProperty)));
        }
```

```
        set
        {
            base.SetValue(
                KCD.Workflow.Rules.ExternalPolicy.RuleSetNameProperty,
                value);
        }
    }
```

The other two properties are a bit different, though, and for the same reason. They both make use of dependency properties, but in each case, we need to control the choices available to the user of our activity. For the document library, we want to make sure that they enter a valid document library name for the site specified by the URL. To do this, we'll present them with a list of document libraries. For the second case, they need to select a ruleset document from that document library. In addition, the ruleset they select needs to be valid for the workflow they are building. Again, we'll present them with a list to choose from. To accomplish this, we will set up custom property editors for each of these two properties.

■ **Note** As we'll see in a bit, our rules are going to be interacting with the members—variables, properties, and methods—of our workflow. Therefore, each ruleset is tightly bound to a particular *type*—the specific workflow assembly. This is somewhat limiting and will result in some problems, but let's face it—there's no good way around it. We just need to live with it.

The property editors are attached to the appropriate property by means of an attribute: `Editor(typeof(docLibSelector), typeof(UITypeEditor))`. The first type (`docLibSelector`) is the name of the class we'll build as our editor. The second type is always `UITypeEditor`. We'll cover these a little more when we actually build the editors.

The next thing we need to take care of is overriding the `Execute` method. Again, we saw this in Chapter 5 so I won't go into a lot of detail about the mechanics of executing activities; I'll just give you the code in Listing 8-10. At a high level, this code uses the properties to retrieve the ruleset document from the SharePoint document library as XML. It deserializes that XML to create a ruleset object and then executes that ruleset.

Listing 8-10. *Code to Retrieve and Execute Our External Ruleset*

```
protected override ActivityExecutionStatus Execute(
            ActivityExecutionContext context)
        {
            string sFullURL = this.SourceSiteURL + @"/" + this.DocumentLibrary
                + @"/" + this.RuleSetName + ".ruleset";
            WorkflowMarkupSerializer serializer = new WorkflowMarkupSerializer();
            XmlUrlResolver resolver = new XmlUrlResolver();
            System.Net.NetworkCredential myCredentials =
                new System.Net.NetworkCredential(
                "Administrator", "password", "Mossb2tr");
```

```
            resolver.Credentials = myCredentials;
            XmlReaderSettings settings = new XmlReaderSettings();
            settings.XmlResolver = resolver;
            XmlReader reader = XmlReader.Create(sFullURL, settings);
            RuleSet ruleSet = (RuleSet)serializer.Deserialize(reader);
            reader.Close();
            Activity targetActivity = Utility.GetRootWorkflow(this.Parent);
            RuleValidation validation = new RuleValidation(
                targetActivity.GetType(), null);
            RuleExecution execution = new RuleExecution(validation,
                targetActivity, context);
            ruleSet.Execute(execution);
            return ActivityExecutionStatus.Closed;
        }
```

The execution of the ruleset in this manner is duplicating the functionality of the default Policy activity. Essentially, it walks through the individual rules contained within the ruleset and evaluates them—keeping the various properties of the rules and the ruleset (reevaluation condition, chaining settings, priority, etc.) in mind as it does so.

■ **Note** Yes, in the middle of Listing 8-10 I have a hard-coded username and password. Trust me, that's only for this sample code. I strongly recommend that you implement your choice of the various impersonation methods floating around. Hard-coding this information directly into your assembly is a bad, bad idea. Even retrieving the information from a configuration file would be a better option. While I'm at it, there are a number of things that I would change in Listing 8-10 in addition to the hard-coded user credentials—the complete lack of error control comes immediately to mind. If you're implementing this in a production environment, you'll want to apply your own rigorous coding standards. For now, let's just keep things simple.

In the middle of Listing 8-10, you'll notice a call to a `GetRootWorkflow` method. The code for this method is provided in Listing 8-11. All it does is call itself iteratively until it reaches the top of the activity hierarchy, which represents our workflow itself. I have this method separated out in a utility class because I use it from various places in development projects.

Listing 8-11. *The GetRootWorkflow Method Used by Our Custom Activity*

```
public static CompositeActivity GetRootWorkflow(CompositeActivity activity)
        {
            if (activity.Parent != null)
            {
                CompositeActivity workflow = GetRootWorkflow(activity.Parent);
                return workflow;
            }
```

```
            else
            {
                return activity;
            }
        }
```

The last piece of this section of the solution is to build the custom property editors for the `DocumentLibrary` and `RuleSetName` properties. I'm only going to cover these pieces at a pretty high level because they're really not related to workflow rules. Listing 8-12 shows the full class for the first editor, used by the `DocumentLibrary` property. It is all SharePoint development 101—grab the document libraries and present them in a list box; nothing special there. The rest of the code is mandated by the custom property editor.

Listing 8-12. *The Custom Property Editor for the DocumentLibrary Property*

```
public class docLibSelector : UITypeEditor
        {
            IWindowsFormsEditorService frmEditor = null;

            public override UITypeEditorEditStyle GetEditStyle(
                ITypeDescriptorContext context)
            {
                return UITypeEditorEditStyle.DropDown;
            }

            public override object EditValue(ITypeDescriptorContext context,
                IServiceProvider provider, object value)
            {
                ExternalPolicy parent = (ExternalPolicy)context.Instance;
                string sSourceSiteURL = parent.SourceSiteURL;
                if (sSourceSiteURL != null)
                {
                    frmEditor = (IWindowsFormsEditorService)
                        provider.GetService(
                        typeof(IWindowsFormsEditorService));
                    ListBox lbDocLibs = new ListBox();
                    SPSite site = new SPSite(sSourceSiteURL);
                    SPWeb web = site.OpenWeb();

                    foreach (SPDocumentLibrary dl in web.GetListsOfType(
                        SPBaseType.DocumentLibrary))
                    {
                        lbDocLibs.Items.Add(dl.Title);
                    }
```

```
                lbDocLibs.SelectedValueChanged +=
                    new EventHandler(lbDocLibs_SelectedValueChanged);
                frmEditor.DropDownControl(lbDocLibs);
                return lbDocLibs.SelectedItem;
            }
            else
            {
                MessageBox.Show(@"You must specify a Source
                Site URL first!");
                return null;
            }

        }

        void lbDocLibs_SelectedValueChanged(object sender, EventArgs e)
        {
            frmEditor.CloseDropDown();
        }
    }
```

The next custom editor is similar to the previous one. It handles the process of presenting the user with a list of valid rulesets to be utilized. A ruleset is considered valid for the current workflow if the name of the workflow containing the activity matches the value of the `WorkflowName` column in the document library. We'll cover setting that value to the proper value when we build the RuleSet Manager application in a bit. As before, the code for all of this is straightforward SharePoint development. We use an `SPQuery` object to filter our result set and loop through the `SPListItemCollection` to populate the list box. Listing 8-13 shows you this code.

Listing 8-13. *The Custom Property Editor for the RuleSetName Property*

```
public class RuleSetSelector: UITypeEditor
    {
        IWindowsFormsEditorService frmEditor = null;

        public override UITypeEditorEditStyle GetEditStyle(
            ITypeDescriptorContext context)
        {
            return UITypeEditorEditStyle.DropDown;
        }

        public override object EditValue(ITypeDescriptorContext context,
            IServiceProvider provider, object value)
        {
            ExternalPolicy parent = (ExternalPolicy)context.Instance;
            string sSourceSiteURL = parent.SourceSiteURL;
            string sDocLibName = parent.DocumentLibrary;
```

```
    if (
        (sSourceSiteURL != null)
        && (sDocLibName != null)
        )
    {
        frmEditor = (IWindowsFormsEditorService)
            provider.GetService(
            typeof(IWindowsFormsEditorService));
        ListBox lbRuleSets = new ListBox();
        SPSite site = new SPSite(sSourceSiteURL);
        SPWeb web = site.OpenWeb();
        SPDocumentLibrary dl = (SPDocumentLibrary)
            web.Lists[sDocLibName];

        CompositeActivity workflow =
            Utility.GetRootWorkflow(parent.Parent);

        SPQuery qry = new SPQuery();
        qry.Query = string.Format(
            @"<Where><Eq><FieldRef Name='WorkflowName' />
            <Value Type='Text'>{0}</Value></Eq></Where>",
            workflow.QualifiedName);
        SPListItemCollection lic = dl.GetItems(qry);
        if (lic.Count > 0)
        {
            foreach (SPListItem li in lic)
            {
                lbRuleSets.Items.Add(
                    Path.GetFileNameWithoutExtension(li.File.Name));
            }
        }
        lbRuleSets.SelectedValueChanged +=
            new EventHandler(lbRuleSets_SelectedValueChanged);
        frmEditor.DropDownControl(lbRuleSets);
        return lbRuleSets.SelectedItem;
    }
    else
    {
        MessageBox.Show(@"You must specify a
        Document Library first!");
        return null;
    }
}
```

```
        void lbRuleSets_SelectedValueChanged(object sender, EventArgs e)
        {
            frmEditor.CloseDropDown();
        }
    }
```

Note I won't walk through building the auxiliary classes for our activity—the Designer, toolbox item, etc. We covered that in Chapter 5 so there's little reason to rehash it here. In my copious spare time, I'll be wrapping up all of the code from the book and posting it on my web site so you can go there to grab it all if you're interested in the final product: `www.kcdholdings.com`.

That's it. Build and deploy the activity as we did in Chapter 5 and we're ready to move onto the RuleSet Manager application.

Rule Management

Ruleset management is the other half of our solution. For this we'll be building a Windows Forms application. Before getting to the code, I'll walk you through the functionality provided by the application so that the source code makes a little more sense.

At a high level, the functionality of this application is as follows:

1. Allow the user to select which workflow template they wish to create a ruleset for. The list of available templates is filtered to only show those that make use of our ExternalPolicy activity.

2. Once the user has selected a template, allow them to either select an existing ruleset to edit or create a new ruleset. The names of existing rulesets are retrieved from a SharePoint document library.

3. Present the Rule Set Editor provided by Microsoft to manage the rules and ruleset properties.

4. Save the ruleset back to our SharePoint document library.

Only two screens make up the user interface for our solution—and one of them is provided by Microsoft—so we need to create only one. Figure 8-9 shows the form we'll be building. The other form is the Rule Set Editor provided by Microsoft and shown back in Figure 8-8.

Note As I mentioned while we were building the ExternalPolicy activity, each ruleset is going to be manipulating member variables of a given workflow template. Therefore, the ruleset is tightly bound to that specific workflow template's Type. We're trying to hide some of the ugliness of types and members from our users, so we'll do all of that work in the background. All we need them to do is select the workflow template for which they wish to build a ruleset.

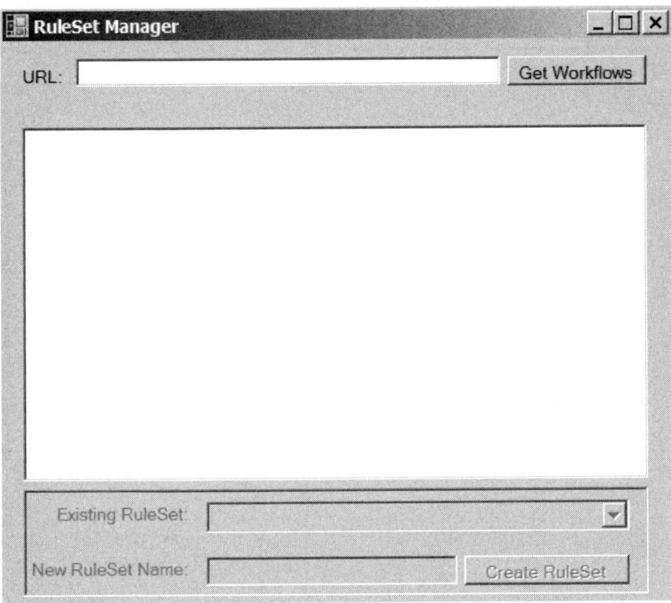

Figure 8-9. *The RuleSet Manager form we'll build for our solution*

Now that we have an idea of what we're building, let's go ahead and get started. To begin, create a new Windows Forms application in Visual Studio 2005 and add controls to the form so that it looks like Figure 8-9. Table 8-2 shows the details for the controls that matter. Most importantly, for the code to operate, you need to set the control names properly.

Table 8-2. *Control Properties for Our Rule Manager Solution*

Control	Property	Value	Description
TextBox	`(Name)`	`txtSiteURL`	Holds the URL for the site (duh) that contains our ruleset documents.
Button	`(Name)`	`btnGetWorkflows`	Initiates the process to retrieve the list of workflow templates from the site specified in `txtSiteURL`.
Button (`btnGetWorkflows`)	`Text`	`Get Workflow Templates`	
ListBox	`(Name)`	`lbWorkflows`	Holds the list of workflow templates, filtered on those that use the ExternalPolicy activity.
Panel	`(Name)`	`pnlRuleSets`	All of the controls below the list box are contained in this panel. It's just easier to work with them as a unit when they're in a container.

Table 8-2. *Control Properties for Our Rule Manager Solution (Continued)*

Control	Property	Value	Description
Panel (`pnlRuleSets`)	`Enabled`	`False`	All of the controls will be enabled once the user selects a workflow from the list box.
ComboBox	`(Name)`	`cmboExistingRulesets`	Stores the list of rulesets already created for the selected workflow. Also enables the creation of a new ruleset (by selecting New).
Label	`(Name)`	`lblRuleSetName`	This label is different from the others because we programmatically control its `Enabled` property during the course of the solution.
Label(`lblRuleSetName`)	`Enabled`	`False`	Starts out as disabled.
TextBox	`(Name)`	`txtRuleSetName`	Holds the name of a new ruleset to be created.
TextBox (`txtRuleSetName`)	`Enabled`	`False`	Starts out as disabled.
Button	`(Name)`	`btnRuleSet`	Initiates the process to show the Rule Set Editor.
Button (`btnRuleSets`)	`Text`	`Create RuleSet`	We'll change this programmatically depending on whether we're editing an existing ruleset or creating a new one.

With all of the visual elements set up, we can now start working with the code (finally!). Listing 8-14 shows the extra namespace references we need to add to the top of our code file. You'll need to add references to your project as appropriate for these namespaces.

Listing 8-14. *Namespace References*

```
using Microsoft.SharePoint;
using Microsoft.SharePoint.Workflow;
using System.IO;
using System.Xml;
using System.Xml.XPath;
using System.Reflection;
using System.Workflow.Activities.Rules.Design;
using System.Workflow.Activities.Rules;
using System.Workflow.ComponentModel.Serialization;
```

The next step is to create a new class for an object we will use throughout the rest of the code to store information about the available workflows. After the default class created for you by Visual Studio, add the code from Listing 8-15. It's just a collection of properties, so I won't step you through each one. We'll see them in action in just a few minutes.

Caution In order to be able to work with the Visual Studio visual form designer, it is important that this class come *after* the form class in your code file. If it doesn't, Visual Studio will bark at you.

Listing 8-15. *Our Utility WorkflowData Class for Storing Information About the Available Workflows*

```
public class WorkflowData
 {
     private string _name;
     public string Name
     {
         get { return _name; }
         set { _name = value; }
     }

     private Guid _id;
     public Guid ID
     {
         get { return _id; }
         set { _id = value; }
     }

     private string _assemblyName;
     public string AssemblyName
     {
         get { return _assemblyName; }
         set { _assemblyName = value; }
     }

     private Type _assemblyType;
     public Type AssemblyType
     {
         get { return _assemblyType; }
         set { _assemblyType = value; }
     }
 }
```

Listing 8-16 shows the last piece of setup code for our solution—it just sets up a few variables for us. I'll leave you to decipher this complex set of code on your own. Add the code to the top of the class and we can move on.

Listing 8-16. *Three of the Most Complex Lines of Code You'll Ever Encounter*

```
List<WorkflowData> WFDataCollection = new List<WorkflowData>();
string sWorkflowName = string.Empty;
string sSiteURL = string.Empty;
```

With all of that out of the way, now we can get on to some *fun* code (did I just say "fun code"? I'm such a geek). Anyway, the code shown in Listing 8-17 handles the click event for the Get Workflows button. Double-click the button in the Designer to have Visual Studio automagically create and associate the method for you and then just add the code—line numbers are for reference only. There are a few interesting things about this method:

- Line 10 sets up an instance of the `WorkflowData` class that we created in Listing 8-15.
- Line 13 begins a loop through all of the workflows that have been installed on the site indicated by the provided URL. The rest of the method is within this loop.
- Lines 15 through 21 check that the workflow is using the ExternalPolicy activity we created earlier. Since the rulesets we create with this application are only useful to our ExternalPolicy activity, there's no sense in showing other workflows.
- Line 15 makes a call to the method `GetAssemblyName`. We'll be creating that method in a few minutes.
- Lines 23 through 27 are the meat of this method—everything else is just qualifying and leading up to these five lines. These lines fill out our `WorkflowData` object and add it to the collection of `WorkflowData` objects we created back in cryptic Listing 8-16. Finally, line 27 simply adds the name of this workflow template to our list box so that it's available for users to select.

Listing 8-17. *Getting the Workflows That Use Our ExternalPolicy Activity*

```
1           Cursor.Current = Cursors.WaitCursor;
2           sSiteURL = txtSiteURL.Text;
3           sSiteURL.Replace(@"\","/");
4           if (!sSiteURL.EndsWith("/"))
5           {
6               sSiteURL += "/";
7           }
8           SPSite site = new SPSite(sSiteURL);
9           SPWeb web = site.OpenWeb();
10          WorkflowData wfd = null;
11          SPWorkflowTemplateCollection wftc = web.WorkflowTemplates;
12          string sAssemblyName = string.Empty;
13          foreach (SPWorkflowTemplate wft in wftc)
14          {
15              sAssemblyName = GetAssemblyName(wft.Id.ToString());
16              if (sAssemblyName != string.Empty)
17              {
18                  Assembly a = Assembly.Load(sAssemblyName);
19                  foreach (AssemblyName mod in a.GetReferencedAssemblies())
20                  {
```

```
                    if (mod.FullName.ToLower().Contains("externalpolicy"))
                    {
                        wfd = new WorkflowData();
                        wfd.Name = wft.Name;
                        wfd.ID = wft.Id;
                        WFDataCollection.Add(wfd);
                        lbWorkflows.Items.Add(wfd.Name);
                    }
                }
            }
        }
        Cursor.Current = Cursors.Default;
```

The next chunk of code is shown in Listing 8-18 and it's a doozy. It is the handler for the `SelectedIndexChanged` event on our list box, so it will fire every time the user selects a new workflow from the list. Again, line numbers are for reference only.

- Line 4 begins the fun by checking whether we have already retrieved the name of the assembly for the selected workflow template. If not, line 6 makes a call to the `GetAssemblyName` method (which we saw in Listing 8-17 and will be adding shortly) and stores the result back in the `WorkflowData` collection. This ensures that each workflow is queried only once to find out its assembly information. After that, we store it in our `WorkflowDataCollection` object.

- Line 8 loads the assembly so that we can begin iterating through its contained types in line 9.

- Lines 11 through 16 set the `AssemblyType` parameter in our `WorkflowData` collection for the appropriate type within the assembly. We're looking for a type that descends from one of the workflow base classes—`SequentialWorkflowActivity` or `StateMachineActivity`. At a minimum, the assembly is going to contain a `settings` type, which is why we filter on the name of the base type.

■ **Note** Yes, there is a certain amount of fragility to this approach. If there are other types within the assembly that descend from one of those base types, it could break things—or at least produce unexpected results. For now, we're going to live with this. If I come up with a better solution, I'll post it to my web site: `www.kcdholdings.com`. If you have any ideas, I'd love to hear them.

- Line 17 begins our interaction with SharePoint. In lines 17 through 20 we connect to SharePoint and the document library that contains our ruleset documents. Yes, in line 19 I have hard-coded the name of the document library. You could easily change the code to read it from any number of other places; this was just a bit simpler for this demo. In the activity, as you recall, we coded functionality to let the developer select the document library. Doing so here would likely just confuse the user, which is never a good idea.

- Lines 20 through 22 query the document library for items where the `WorkflowName` column match the name of the workflow we're working with. Again, remember that rulesets are tightly bound to a workflow template and shouldn't show the user rulesets that are not applicable to the workflow they have selected.
- Finally, lines 23 through 29 loop through and add each ruleset name to the combo box. They're now available for the user to choose from.

Listing 8-18. *Retrieving the Rulesets Applicable to the Selected Workflow*

```
1          Cursor.Current = Cursors.WaitCursor;
2          cmboExistingRulesets.Items.Clear();
3          pnlRuleSets.Enabled = false;
4          if (WFDataCollection[lbWorkflows.SelectedIndex].AssemblyName == ➥
               null)
5          {
6              WFDataCollection[lbWorkflows.SelectedIndex].AssemblyName = ➥
                  GetAssemblyName(WFDataCollection➥
                  [lbWorkflows.SelectedIndex].ID.ToString());
7          }
8          Assembly a = Assembly.Load(WFDataCollection➥
              [lbWorkflows.SelectedIndex].AssemblyName);
9          foreach (Type type in a.GetTypes())
10          {
11                  if ((type.BaseType.Name.ToLower() == ➥
                            "sequentialworkflowactivity") || ➥
                            (type.BaseType.Name.ToLower() == ➥
                            "statemachineworkflowactivity"))
12              {
13                  WFDataCollection[lbWorkflows.SelectedIndex].AssemblyType = ➥
                      type;
14                  break;
15              }
16          }

17          SPSite site = new SPSite(sSiteURL);
18          SPWeb web = site.OpenWeb();
19          SPDocumentLibrary dl = (SPDocumentLibrary)web.Lists["Rules"];
20          SPQuery qry = new SPQuery();
21          qry.Query = string.Format(@"<Where><Eq>➥
              <FieldRef Name='WorkflowName' /><Value Type='Text'>{0}</Value>➥
              </Eq></Where>",➥
              WFDataCollection[lbWorkflows.SelectedIndex].AssemblyType.Name);
22          SPListItemCollection lic = dl.GetItems(qry);
```

```
            if (lic.Count > 0)
            {
                foreach (SPListItem li in lic)
                {
                    cmboExistingRulesets.Items.Add➥
                      (Path.GetFileNameWithoutExtension(li.File.Name));
                }
            }
            cmboExistingRulesets.Items.Insert(0,"<New>");
            cmboExistingRulesets.SelectedIndex = 0;
            pnlRuleSets.Enabled = true;
            Cursor.Current = Cursors.Default;
```

A few times in the last few listings, we've referenced a method named `GetAssemblyName`. Listing 8-19 finally shows the code for this method. This one is a little different from the rest in that it does some XML parsing instead of working with SharePoint or workflows. Again, we'll just step through the highlights:

- Line 4 begins our loop through the `Features` directory on our server. We grab any files named `workflow.xml` that we find and load them into an `XmlDocument` object.
- Line 10 retrieves the GUID ID of the workflow and line 11 checks to see whether it matches against the workflow template selected by the user. If not, this iteration ends and we continue the loop.
- If line 11 does match, then we have found the `workflow.xml` file for the workflow selected by the user. Lines 13 and 14 can do some additional querying to retrieve the internal name of the workflow (the `Name` attribute of the `<Workflow>` XML tag) and the fully qualified assembly name (from the `CodeBesideAssembly` attribute).
- Since we've now found what we need, there is no reason to continue looping, so line 15 short-circuits the loop and drops us into line 18, which simply returns the assembly name.

Listing 8-19. *Getting the Name of the Assembly for the Selected Workflow from Its workflow.xml File*

```
1         private string GetAssemblyName(string WFID)
2        {
3            string sRetVal = string.Empty;
4            foreach (string sFileName in Directory.GetFiles(@"C:\Program Files\➥
                   Common Files\Microsoft Shared\➥
                   web server extensions\12\TEMPLATE\ FEATURES\", ➥
                   "workflow.xml", SearchOption.AllDirectories))

5            {
6                XmlDocument xDoc = new XmlDocument();
7                xDoc.Load(sFileName);
8                XmlNamespaceManager nsMgr = new XmlNamespaceManager
                   (xDoc.NameTable);
```

```
                nsMgr.AddNamespace("def",
                    "http://schemas.microsoft.com/sharepoint/");
                string wfid = xDoc.SelectSingleNode(
                    "/def:Elements/def:Workflow/@Id",nsMgr).InnerText;
                if (wfid.ToLower() == WFID.ToLower())
                {
                    sWorkflowName = xDoc.SelectSingleNode(
                      "/def:Elements/def:Workflow/@Name", nsMgr).InnerText;
                    sRetVal = xDoc.SelectSingleNode(
                      "/def:Elements/def:Workflow/@CodeBesideAssembly",
                      nsMgr).InnerText;
                    break;
                    }
            }
            return sRetVal;
        }
```

■ **Note** The code in Listing 8-19 only works because we are running it on our SharePoint server. For a real production environment, this method will need to be made into a web service and various security aspects taken care of in order to allow businesspeople to run the application from their desktop.

Listing 8-20 shows the code to handle the click event on our `btnRuleSet` object. Like Listing 8-18, its pretty long; fortunately, though, most of it consists of auxiliary-type code that is simply supporting the real work of this method.

- Lines 4 through 12 set things up for creating a new ruleset.
- Lines 13 through 26 handle the editing of an existing ruleset, with line 24 creating the ruleset object by deserializing the XML stored in the document library. We saw this in the ExternalPolicy activity as well.
- Lines 29 and 30 show how easy it is to instantiate and show the Rule Set Editor provided by Microsoft.
- If the user clicks OK in the dialog box (as opposed to Cancel, checked in line 32), we grab the ruleset from the dialog box (line 34).
- If there are any rules (checked in line 35), lines 37 through 48 save the information back to SharePoint, including setting the `WorkflowName` column for the `SPListItem` to the name of the selected workflow template.

Listing 8-20. *Editing the Rulesets and Saving the Information to SharePoint*

```
        RuleSet rs = null;
        if (cmboExistingRulesets.SelectedItem.ToString() == "<New>")
        {
            if (
              (txtRuleSetName.Text == null)
              || (txtRuleSetName.Text == string.Empty)
              )
            {
                MessageBox.Show("Please specify a name for the RuleSet");
            }
            else
            {
                rs = new RuleSet(txtRuleSetName.Text);
            }
        }
        else
        {
            string sFullURL = sSiteURL + "Rules/" + ➥
              cmboExistingRulesets.SelectedItem + ".ruleset";
            WorkflowMarkupSerializer serializer = ➥
              new WorkflowMarkupSerializer();
            XmlUrlResolver resolver = new XmlUrlResolver();
            System.Net.NetworkCredential myCredentials;
            myCredentials = new System.Net.NetworkCredential("Administrator", ➥
              "password", "MossRTM");
            resolver.Credentials = myCredentials;
            XmlReaderSettings settings = new XmlReaderSettings();
            settings.XmlResolver = resolver;
            XmlReader reader = XmlReader.Create(sFullURL, settings);
            rs = (RuleSet)serializer.Deserialize(reader);
            reader.Close();
        }
        if (rs != null)
        {
            RuleSetDialog ruleSetDialog = new RuleSetDialog(➥
              WFDataCollection[lbWorkflows.SelectedIndex].AssemblyType, ➥
              null, rs);
            DialogResult result = ruleSetDialog.ShowDialog();
            WorkflowMarkupSerializer serializer = ➥
              new WorkflowMarkupSerializer();
```

```
32              if (result == DialogResult.OK)
33              {
34                  rs = ruleSetDialog.RuleSet;
35                  if (rs.Rules.Count > 0)
36                  {
37                      MemoryStream ms = new MemoryStream();
38                      string sFilename = rs.Name + ".ruleset";
39                      XmlWriter writer2 = XmlWriter.Create(ms);
40                      serializer.Serialize(writer2, rs);
41                      writer2.Flush();
42                      SPSite site = new SPSite(sSiteURL);
43                      SPWeb web = site.OpenWeb();
44                      SPDocumentLibrary dl = ➥
                          (SPDocumentLibrary)web.Lists["Rules"];
45                      SPFile newfile = dl.RootFolder.Files.Add(➥
                          sFilename, ms.ToArray(), true);
46                      newfile.Item["WorkflowName"] = sWorkflowName;
47                      newfile.Item.Update();
48                      writer2.Close();
49                      MessageBox.Show("RuleSet Saved");
50                      cmboExistingRulesets.Items.Add(rs.Name);
51                      cmboExistingRulesets.SelectedItem = rs.Name;
52                      txtRuleSetName.Text = string.Empty;
53                  }
54              }
55          }
```

■ **Note** Yes, once again, I have a hard-coded username and password (line 19). In your production system you really don't want to do this. Impersonation is your friend; let it help you.

We're almost done. Listing 8-21 shows the code for the `SelectedIndexChanged` event on the combo box. The code is straightforward (unlike that impenetrable Listing 8-16) and only handles some minor housekeeping, so I won't walk you through it.

Listing 8-21. *Closing with Some Housekeeping*

```
if (cmboExistingRulesets.SelectedIndex == 0)
{
    btnRuleSet.Text = "Create RuleSet";
    lblRuleSetName.Enabled = true;
    txtRuleSetName.Enabled = true;
}
else
{
    btnRuleSet.Text = "Edit RuleSet";
    lblRuleSetName.Enabled = false;
    txtRuleSetName.Enabled = false;
}
```

So there you have it—the whole code base for the RuleSet Manager application. Go ahead and build and hope for the best. If neither of us made any typos, it should all compile and run just fine. Of course, if you try to walk through the process, it will fail because there are still a few things to wrap up:

1. We need a document library to store the ruleset documents in. You should call it **Rules** (unless you changed it in the RuleSet Manager code), and it needs a column called **WorkflowName**, which is a required, single-line-of–text-field.
2. We need to build and deploy a workflow that makes use of the ExternalPolicy activity. We'll handle that in the next section.

Putting It All Together—A Sample Workflow

To see everything in action, we just need to build a sample workflow that uses our ExternalPolicy activity. This workflow won't do anything useful—we just want to show off to all of the cynics in the crowd that our solution actually works.

Figure 8-10 shows the final product of the sample workflow in the Workflow Designer. It contains our new activity plus an IfElse activity and two SendEmail activities. We have a variable defined in the code that is used in two places:

- The first IfElseBranch checks the variable as part of its Declarative Rule Condition to see whether it should execute.
- The ExternalPolicy activity sets the value of the variable as part of the execution of the external ruleset.

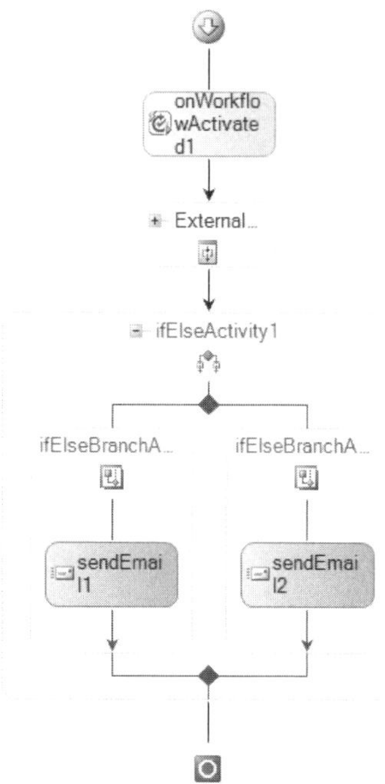

Figure 8-10. *Our sample workflow makes use of the custom activity we wrote to retrieve and execute a ruleset stored outside of our workflow.*

There are only a few lines of custom code for this project. With the first, we set up a variable at the top of the class file: `int myFlagVariable = 0;`. The other code is shown in Listing 8-22 and it simply sets the `Body` property of the SendEmail activities to a value that will tell us which branch of the `if-else` executed.

Listing 8-22. *Setting the Email Body*

```
private void sendEMailA(object sender, EventArgs e)
{
    this.sendEmail1.Body = "Branch 1 executed, so myFlagVariable = 7";
}

private void sendEMailB(object sender, EventArgs e)
{
    this.sendEmail2.Body = "Branch 2 executed, so myFlagVariable <> 7";
}
```

From here, the process will get a little strange due to the nature of the solution. The problem is that we have a bit of the *which came first—the chicken or the egg* syndrome here. As I've mentioned before (are you sick of it yet?) rulesets are tightly bound to the workflows they are based on. In our scenario, we need to specify in the activity the name of the ruleset we'd like to implement. We also need to build that ruleset, which means that we must point it at our assembly. To remedy this, we'll set enough of the properties so that we can compile and deploy and then go back and build our ruleset. Last, we'll reopen the workflow, specify the ruleset we just built, and then redeploy. It's a little bit of jumping back and forth for us as developers, but for the end users it will not be nearly so complicated. The real benefit of all of this is still that when the rules change in the future, we can just edit the ruleset without touching the workflow itself.

■ **Note** If you were wondering, this is why none of the properties of the ExternalPolicy activity were specified as required—we need to compile the workflow before we can set them all.

Table 8-3 specifies values for the properties we need to set in order to be able to compile.

Table 8-3. *Properties for Our External Policy Test Workflow*

Activity	Property	Value
IfElseBranchActivity1	`Condition`	Declarative Rule Condition
IfElseBranchActivity1	`Condition Name`	`Check Flag Variable`
IfElseBranchActivity1	`Expression`	`this.myFlagVariable == 7`
SendEmail1	`CorrelationToken`	`workflowToken`
SendEmail1	`MethodInvoking`	`SendEmailA`
SendEmail1	`Subject`	`External Policy Test`
SendEmail1	`To`	*<a valid email address in your environment>*
SendEmail2	`CorrelationToken`	`workflowToken`
SendEmail2	`MethodInvoking`	`SendEmailB`
SendEmail2	`Subject`	`External Policy Test`
SendEmail2	`To`	*<a valid email address in your environment>*

With the activities configured, configure the project to be signed with a strong name key file and then compile your workflow. After compiling (so you can get the strong name of the assembly), make sure you edit the `workflow.xml`, `feature.xml`, and `install.bat` files, and then go ahead and deploy. If you need a refresher on how to deploy the workflow, jump back to Chapter 6. Chapter 7 also covers workflow deployment, but in Chapter 7 we make use of Workflow forms so things are a little different from what we need here.

■ **Caution** When configuring the `workflow.xml` file, make sure that you set the `Name` attribute to the name of your class. We look for this value when we're determining which rulesets are valid for a given workflow template.

With the workflow deployed, we can fire up the external RuleSet Manager application and configure a new ruleset. Although it's not referenced anywhere, give the new ruleset a meaningful name—I'll be calling mine `myFlagVariable`. Add a rule to the ruleset and set the condition for the rule to `1==1` so that it always executes. Add the following code to the Then actions for the rule:

```
this.myFlagVariable = 9
```

Then click OK to save the ruleset.

Close the RuleSet Manager application and go back to the test workflow project. Set the properties for the ExternalPolicy activity as shown in Table 8-4.

Table 8-4. *Property Values for the ExternalPolicy Activity*

Property	Value
`SourceSiteURL`	*<URL of the SharePoint site that has the Rules document library>*
`Document Library`	`Rules`
`RuleSetName`	`myFlagVariable`

You won't need to make any other changes, so compile and redeploy. Go into a SharePoint document library and add an instance of the test workflow. Kick off the workflow instance on a document, and after whirring and popping for a few seconds, SharePoint will report back that the workflow is complete. If you go in and check your email, you'll see a new message indicating that branch 2 executed. This is just as we expected.

Now, to put things to the test, fire up the external RuleSet Manager application again and change the Then actions for the `myFlagVariable` ruleset to

```
this.myFlagVariable = 7
```

Don't change anything else. Back in SharePoint, rerun the same workflow instance on the same document. The email you receive this time will indicate that branch 1 executed. Again, just as we expected.

Congratulations. You have just successfully altered the processing of a workflow without touching the compiled workflow assembly or changing anything in SharePoint.

Sigh. You might be thinking that this is no big deal. All we did was change which branch of an `if-else` fired and sent out a different email—not a very useful accomplishment. You're right; by itself, this is not going to make anyone's life any easier. Take a minute and think, though. The implications of this are huge. All we were working with here were simple conditions, simple actions, and simple activities, so all we got were simple results. In a more complicated scenario, this is an incredibly powerful capability. To make yourself feel better, take a look at the "Houston, We Have Liftoff" sidebar.

HOUSTON, WE HAVE LIFTOFF

So you're feeling a little let down. All of the work and gyrations in this chapter leads to what feels like a hollow victory. Yep, join the club. When I was writing this chapter, I was constantly fighting with myself over whether it should be included. I've already mentioned that it is not officially supported by Microsoft. The examples I was working through in the book were small potatoes. Should I just drop it and write a chapter about something else? Even a chapter on alpaca farming might be more useful.

In the end, it took a few comments from one of my technical reviewers (thanks, Eilene!) and some more thought on just what functionality this solution provided to convince me that the material really did provide value. Here are some of the thoughts I had as I came to peace with the material:

- While the functionality would not be widely used in Office 2007 workflows, when it was used, it would be a major boon to the situation.
- The examples in the chapter were intentionally kept simple—only one rule per ruleset and even then just working with simple integer values. I did this to keep the focus on the solution, not the scenario. There is nothing that prevents your rulesets from being incredibly complex, including any of the following, just to name a few options:
  - Calling external objects or web services.
  - Setting multiple values as part of a `Then` condition.
  - Including multiple rules per ruleset. As hinted at in the complex ruleset example back in the "Cleanup in Aisle 4" sidebar, the ability to handle extremely complex scenarios is built into the WF framework. We're just tapping into a tiny piece of it.
- We're only creating one ruleset per workflow template in our examples. The solution, however, supports multiple rulesets per workflow template. This means that each instance of a workflow template can have its own ruleset. So, for example, if you create a single Approval workflow template, each department that implements it can have their own ruleset to customize the processing to meet their needs.
- Rulesets are stored as XML files in the SharePoint document library. The full document-management capabilities (also including the record-management capabilities) are available to you for approval, versioning, and so forth. You can also easily move these documents around if you need to support multiple environments. Flexibility is a strong suit of this solution.
- All you've really hard-coded into your workflow is that a decision needs to be made at a certain point and that the workflow will react to that decision. You have not locked in any details of what goes into making that decision.

In addition, the functionality does not need to be limited to true decision-based rules. As seen in our final walkthrough, a condition can be set such that it *always* executes (i.e., `if 1=1`). In this case, the ruleset is not making a decision, but the `Then` condition will still execute. What you have on your hands now is a simple process to allow nontechnical (albeit still trained) business users to maintain their workflows. The core interface is all built—at most you'll need to tweak things a bit to fit into your specific situation.

So, yes, on the surface, this chapter may not seem like much of a big deal. In the end, though, the sky's the limit—Houston, we do indeed have liftoff. Where you go from here is entirely up to you.

Summary

We covered a lot of ground in this chapter. Here's a quick refresher:

- Rules allow your workflow to take alternate execution paths, based on identified conditions.
- Among other things, without rules as *separately definable entities*:
  - A workflow locks a business process in as a snapshot in time.
  - Business logic is tightly intertwined with processing logic.
  - Documenting and tracking business logic is made more difficult.
- Simple conditions, based on values and variables known at the time the workflow is created, can be handled more easily within the confines of the workflow itself. Rules allow you to future-proof your workflows. All you've really hard-coded into your workflow is that a decision needs to be made at a certain point and that the workflow will react to that decision. You have not locked in any details of what goes into making that decision.
- There are two types of simple conditions—Code Conditions and Declarative Rule Conditions.
- Various activities support simple conditions. IfThenElse, While, ConditionedActivityGroup, and so forth all include some basic facility for logical evaluation. None of them provide anywhere near the possibility of the Policy activity.
- A *ruleset* is a collection of business rule definitions that together serve to describe the full logic of a solution.
- Rulesets are incredibly powerful, supporting various reevaluation conditions, priority-based execution ordering, and multiple chaining scenarios.
- Chaining refers to the process of having the execution of one rule cause another rule to be reevaluated.
- Chaining is built on dependencies between rules within a ruleset. When one rule updates a value that is used by the condition of another rule, the second rule is considered to be *dependent* on the first.
- Dependencies can be identified implicitly (the default), based on attributes, or explicitly.
- The ultimate goal of this chapter is to provide functionality that allows for the management of rulesets entirely divorced from the process of building a workflow.

CHAPTER 9

A Workflow Smorgasbord

This chapter contains a collection of topics—all related to Workflow in Office 2007, but not necessarily otherwise related to each other—hence the title of the chapter. As I said in the introduction for this part, all of the material is important, but none of it fit in anywhere else or was sufficient to warrant a chapter unto itself. In the interest of providing as complete a picture as possible about Workflow, I collected it all and present it here for your edification. There's a little smattering of many topics here—hopefully you'll find at least one or two interesting and useful.

Note One of my goals here is to get you thinking outside of the box just a bit. The rest of the book has been pretty straightforward and operated well within the bounds of how most people will use Workflow in Office 2007. This chapter specifically is an attempt to push that envelope a little. I hope you'll find the information here a little thought provoking. You may even find yourself thinking, "That's pretty cool" as you make your way through one or two sections.

So, without further ado...

Dehydration

Not many people know this, and it is not well documented by Microsoft, but managing and executing workflows is hard work and if you leave your SharePoint servers out in the blazing sun like most people do, they can easily become dehydrated. If this happens, your business processes will slow down as the server processes scream out for fluids... um, no. That's not what dehydration means in workflow terms.

In workflow terms *dehydration* means that we persist our workflow (to disk, typically) and remove it from memory. There isn't anything you need to be concerned with for this—SharePoint, as our workflow host, takes care of it for us. I just want to spend a little time talking about dehydration so you understand what it is and why it exists. It will come into play when we talk about workflow processing in a bit, but still not in any way that we need to actually do anything about.

If you recall from Chapter 1, one of the interfaces provided by WF to be implemented in the various workflow hosts is *persistence*. There are various terms for this persistence—unloading and passivation are two others that I've heard—but dehydration seems to be the most common.

Workflows, especially human-centric workflows, are typically long-running processes. Analyzed in computer timeframes, even if a document is approved within two or three minutes, it is still a long time to a processor that can complete millions of instructions per second. From the computer's point of view, it's keeping information in memory for eons while it waits for another ice age to pass before it gets to move on to the next step of the process.

If all we're executing is a few workflows at a time, there would not be such a problem storing the information in memory. But WF is built to scale to handle nearly any load of concurrent workflows. If we had to store all of that information in memory, then we'd have a problem on our hands. The ability to store this information in some sort of persistent storage while we aren't actively working with it comes to our rescue here.

One other problem—and one that presents itself even if we only had one workflow ever running on our system—is that all of the information about that workflow stored in memory will be lost if the server crashes. There will be no way to recover the current status of the workflow without it having been persisted in some way.

Dehydration takes care of this for us, and it does it automatically so that most of the time, we don't need to think about it much. Essentially, dehydration occurs when our workflow is waiting for some event to occur.

There is, as you've probably guessed, a complementary aspect to dehydration known as *rehydration*. This is the process of taking the information about a workflow that has been persisted, loading it back into memory, and assigning a thread to continue processing. Just like dehydration, this is entirely automatic—it is triggered by an event that our workflow is listening for. There is nothing we need to do to make this happen.

The persistent storage medium for SharePoint workflows is tables in the SQL Server database. This means that when SharePoint needs to unload an idle workflow, it serializes the information and stores it in SQL Server. When it needs to rehydrate, it reads the information from the tables and spins the workflow back up.

We'll see when we talk about SharePoint workflow processing that there are reasons we would want to force our workflow to dehydrate and mechanisms to support doing just that.

Reality Check

Up to this point, the book has been pretty "happy-path" and hasn't focused much on things too far off the beaten path. I tried to stay at a level of "this is how things will go when everything is working right" because, honestly, that is how things will be *most* of the time. Unfortunately, as we all know, things don't *always* work right. So, we need to pop off the rose-colored glasses and spend some time looking at some of the sticky bits we'll encounter. There's nothing too scary in this section—just some things you need to be aware of if you're going to make a serious run at this.

Here we go…

Workflow Processing

There is an important point about the processing of our SharePoint workflows that you need to understand. It's not going to be a factor often in your workflows, but when it does come into play, it will do so in a major way—especially as you begin to build more and more complex workflows.

■ **Tip** Quite possibly, this little section is the most important part of the book. If you're doing workflow development, you need to know the information here if you want to avoid a lot of headaches. Unfortunately, this information is not very well publicized by Microsoft. Read it, read it again, photocopy the page and hang it in your cube. When you're about to tear your hair out troubleshooting a workflow, refer back to it. It will probably help.

What I'm talking about is the way the SharePoint batches the workflow operations. When a workflow executes, all of the operations (CreateTask, UpdateTask, etc.) are collected into a single batch. They are not processed as they are encountered. When the workflow reaches a state where it is about to dehydrate (see the previous section), the entire batch is executed as a single SQL transaction.

There are two primary benefits to this, two significant *gotchas* and one thing to simply keep in mind. First the benefits:

- *Performance*: Because the operations are batched, performance is much better than if each individual operation were immediately executed as a standalone SQL transaction.
- *Rollback*: If any of the operations fail, the process of rolling back to the last known good state is greatly simplified.

And now the drawbacks:

- The big exception to this rule is non-SharePoint activities—whether built by us or by Microsoft. Non-SharePoint activities do not participate in this batch process model. If you write custom code inside a Code activity that updates the database, that operation will be committed immediately. It is not included as part of the batch. Similarly, if you write custom code that attempts to access a task created earlier in the workflow, the task may not exist yet. It depends on whether the batch has executed. While on the surface this may not appear to be a big deal, the implications are actually quite far-reaching. We'll cover the potential problems and some potential workarounds in the rest of this section.
- As mentioned in the dehydration section, when the workflow is persisted, objects are serialized and stored—which is great unless the objects aren't serializable. What type of objects might that be a problem for? Well, certainly any custom, nonworkflow objects unless you explicitly mark them as serializable—but also minor things like, say, `SPList`. (`SPList`, a minor item in SharePoint? No, that was sarcasm. Certainly this is a hugely important object in just about any custom SharePoint solution.) Depending on some specific details about the objects in question, at worst, your workflow will fail when it attempts to dehydrate. At best, any nonserializable objects will be invalid after a dehydration/rehydration cycle.
- The last disadvantage is not too much of a big deal, but something to keep in mind nonetheless. Because the batch can be rolled back as a unit, there is no explicit error handling that we need to do there (not that we can't add our own custom error handling—we'll get to that in a bit), but the low-level elements of ensuring that the database is reset to a valid state are taken care of for us. However, this does complicate error handling a bit because we'll need to keep track of which activities we need to handle manually. Certainly, we'll need to handle any custom activities. We'll also need to handle any nonSharePoint activities. We'll cover error handling later in this chapter. This just makes things more interesting.

So, with all of that now out of the way, what do we do? How can we still write the complex workflows we need to in order to get our jobs done while taking these issues into account? Fortunately, it's pretty easy. We just need to know when our workflow is going to dehydrate. If we can identify those points, we can identify where we're going to have batches being committed and therefore where we need to pay a little extra attention.

As mentioned earlier, our workflow will dehydrate when it is in a waiting state. From a practical point of view, this means that our workflow will dehydrate any time it reaches an *Onxxx* activity (for example, OnTaskCreated). Workflows will also dehydrate whenever they reach a Delay activity. So, if we have code that we want to execute, but only, say after a new task is actually created, put it inside the OnTaskCreated activity. The workflow will dehydrate until the task is actually created, then wake up and continue with the code we placed in the OnTaskCreated and we'll be fine. You could also place this code on the other side of a one-second Delay activity and you would be OK, but this is not using things the way they were meant to be used. The *Onxxx* activities exist so that we can be sure that we're on the opposite side of a dehydrate/rehydrate cycle before continuing.

In a similar fashion, our error handling just needs to be aware of where our process is in regard to a dehydrate/rehydrate cycle before continuing, *and* know what activities we need to handle manually.

The last issue we need to be aware of as we progress is reinstantiating objects as necessary after a dehydrate/rehydrate cycle. This can get a little trickier in complex scenarios, but shouldn't be too bad if you plan your workflow before coding it. Just remember that, while they're built in a fashion similar to any other program, they do not execute that way. Check your objects before you use them and you'll be OK.

All in all, this section seems a little scary, but it really isn't. We just need to think things through more before we start hacking code and we have to test a little better throughout and on the back end. Come to think of it, that's all stuff most people need to get better at anyway.

■ **Tip** One final word of advice on this topic: if you are implementing "standard" human-workflow constructs—tasks, notifications, documents, list items, etc.—*use the SharePoint activities whenever possible.* The more you can get into the standard workflow processing batches, the better off you are going to be. There should rarely, if ever, be a reason to duplicate this functionality in custom code.

Debugging

Once again, reality needs to intrude ever so slightly on our foray into workflow. We are not all coding gods. Not every single line of code we write is perfect and pristine as soon as we type it. Not every method does exactly what we (think we) told it to do the first time.

Sorry to burst your bubble, but this means that we need to debug our code.

Debugging Workflows

Fortunately, debugging our workflows is not any different from debugging any other .NET code we write, except for one added capability. We still set breakpoints, we still use watch windows, and we still step through code and use the various other debugging tools in Visual Studio.

After building and deploying (at least to the GAC if not a full-feature deployment), simply attach to the W3WP process (the one with a type of `Workflow`). In the browser, go ahead and start an instance of your workflow on an item. When the runtime gets to your breakpoint, it will jump you back over to Visual Studio, just as you would expect. Debugging at this point is no different than any other .NET debugging you've ever done.

The one additional thing you can do with debugging workflows is set a breakpoint in the Designer by right-clicking on an activity. Honestly, I don't see much value in this. If I'm debugging, I want to look right at the code—not just know that it has hit a certain activity. I suppose there would be some value in stepping through your workflow execution process at the activity level if you have multiple potential paths through your workflow and you simply need to confirm the path that is being taken. Other than that, I don't see Designer-set breakpoints being of much use—but that's just my opinion.

Debugging Activities

Hark back to Chapter 5 when we were building our first activity. Remember how I said it was really nothing more than a .NET custom control? Guess what? Debugging activities is exactly the same as debugging any other custom control. Set your breakpoint, run the workflow that contains your activity, and the runtime will pause when it gets to your breakpoint.

Debugging in the SharePoint Designer

This is going to be the shortest section in the book. You *can't* debug your workflows in the SharePoint Designer.

Next, please!

Debugging Tips

There are just a few more pieces to keep in mind when you're debugging:

- When your workflow fails at some point, you will get an ultra-useful message of either *Failed on Start* or *Error Occurred.* Not that either of those doesn't give gobs of helpful information right out of the gate, but they do mean different things:
  - *Failed on Start* typically means that something prevented SharePoint (as the workflow host) from launching your workflow. Perhaps it can't find the workflow DLL—check that things deployed properly and that the version of your assembly matches the information in the strong name in the `workflow.xml` file. Debugging your workflow here likely won't reveal anything.
  - *Error Occurred* typically means that your workflow was launched but encountered an error. In this case, you'll want to debug your workflow as it will likely turn something up.
- In either case, you can occasionally get useful information from the workflow's cancellation and error report available from the Workflow Status page.

- Check the Event log—occasionally useful tidbits show up in there.
- Check the log files located at `\Program Files\Common Files\Microsoft Shared\Web Server Extensions\12\Logs`. Again, depending on the nature of the problem, you can often get useful information from here. If you do go this route, start from the end of the file and work up. There will be a ton of information that is irrelevant to our workflow, which you'll need to ignore, but if there is something logged about your workflow, it will likely be very useful. I can tell you that this piece has saved me hours of head-scratching trying to figure out what was going wrong.

So that's it. Keep the information about workflow processing in mind and understand your debugging options, and the rest of the time you can remain in the happy, lotus-land of workflow development.

Going Mobile

In today's business world, it is not unusual to have various members of your team working remotely—which could mean in another office but still connected to your corporate network, but more and more often, it means that they are in an airport, sitting in traffic as they drive from client site to client site, or even sitting on the sidelines watching their kid's soccer or lacrosse game. In the first case—when they're in a remote office—there's really nothing we need to do to make our workflows accessible to them. They're likely using their laptop and they're on the network. Assuming that connectivity to the remote office is at an acceptable speed, it's no different than if they were sitting down the hall. They can be full participants in our workflows.

What about some of the other scenarios? What about when they are in an airport and the only connectivity they have is via their smartphone? What do we need to do to allow them to participate in our workflows?

Nothing.

Yep, that's right. Through the magic of MOSS and WSS, users on mobile devices can participate in our workflows without us having to lift a finger and without forcing them to interact with the SharePoint site's regular pages across their cellular connection. Cool.

There are a few things to keep in mind, however:

- The Office 2007 applications are not available for mobile devices yet (and I can't find anyone talking about when they will be) so the functionality of the SharePoint integration is limited. In many ways, the experience will be similar to users of previous Office versions. What this means is that things such as the Business Bar and Workflow forms being integrated directly into the client will not be available. Also, if documents are only available in the new file formats, they will not be able to be opened from a mobile device.
- Due to the nature of SharePoint Mobile views (discussed in a moment), mobile users can participate in existing workflows but cannot initiate new workflows. In this case, you would want to look into the various auto-start options for workflows.
- Data connection speeds will also be considerably reduced—even the best cellular networks are not on the same level as high-speed LANs. This is just another thing to keep in mind.

Accessing SharePoint and specifically our workflow functionality from a mobile device will make heavy use of two pieces of the Office System: SharePoint Mobile views and Outlook synchronization with SharePoint. We'll take a quick look at each of these before walking through the experience of a mobile user within a workflow scenario.

SharePoint Mobile Views

SharePoint Mobile views is perhaps one of the best-kept secrets in MOSS and WSS v3. In a nutshell, Mobile views are a window into your SharePoint content for a mobile device. Every site, list, and document library in SharePoint 2007 is capable of supporting Mobile views right out of the box. For our workflows, this means that our workflow-enabled document libraries, our task lists, and our history lists will all be available from a properly equipped mobile device.

As mentioned earlier, the functionality available out of the box *is* a little limited. Users will only be able to interact with existing workflows—they will not be able to create new workflow instances or perform much of the administration functionality we've discussed. Nonetheless, this is a powerful capability to have available to us with no effort on our part.

Accessing these Mobile views is easy; simply append `/_layouts/mobile` to the end of your site URL and SharePoint takes care of the rest. So, for example, if your site had a URL of `http://portal.kcdholdings.com`, the Mobile view would be accessible at `http://portal.kcdholdings.com/_layouts/mobile`. If you have a SharePoint site available to you and a mobile device that you can access the site with, go ahead and try it out. You'll see something akin to Figure 9-1. You can see that what is generated for us is only a textual representation of our site, but on a mobile device with limited screen real estate and limited bandwidth, that's really all we want.

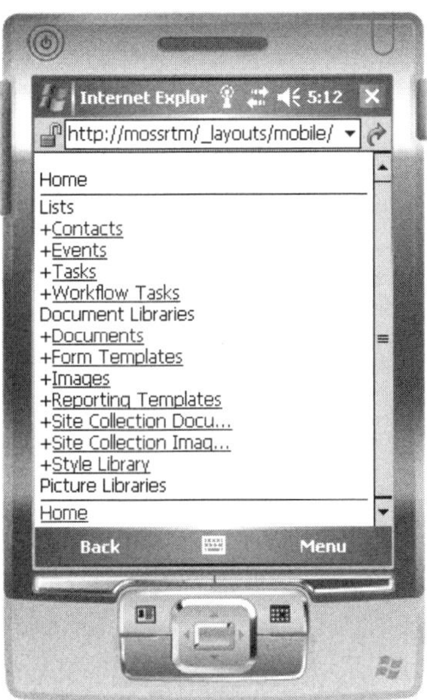

Figure 9-1. *SharePoint content on a mobile device. Cool, way cool.*

Part of what you'll see in this view is the gold at the end of our workflow rainbow—access to both the document libraries themselves but also the Workflow task list. We'll walk through the whole experience for our mobile workflow participants in just a few minutes.

SEE WHAT ALL THE BUZZ IS ABOUT WITHOUT BUYING A NEW PDA

If you don't have a device available that can access the Internet, you can still see what all of the buzz is about by one of two methods:

- If you have access to Visual Studio 2005, you can utilize the emulator tools built into that tool. You may still want to download a new ROM image from the URL listed next.
- If you do not have VS 2005, you can use Microsoft's Mobile Device Emulator. You'll need to download both the emulator itself along with the ROM images for the machine type you want to emulate. You can get both of these from here: `www.microsoft.com/downloads/details.aspx?FamilyId=C62D54A5-183A-4A1E-A7E2-CC500ED1F19A&displaylang=en`. I'll also post links to them on my web site: `www.kcdholdings.com`.

If you're going the first route, you can either use one of the images that comes with Visual Studio or download a new image from the "Emulator Images for Visual Studio 2005" section of this page: `http://msdn.microsoft.com/mobility/downloads/Emulator/default.aspx`. The installation is pretty vanilla and shouldn't give you any fits.

If you are going with door #2, you first need to download the ZIP file for the emulator itself. Open the ZIP file and run the `vs_emulator.exe` file, which will install the emulator. After that installation finishes, download and install the ROM image you need. Personally I use the Windows Mobile 5 image available at the site because, well, because I run Windows Mobile 5 on my device and it was just easier. You can use any of the "Emulator Images for Microsoft Device Emulator 1.0" available here: `http://msdn.microsoft.com/mobility/downloads/Emulator/default.aspx`. Again, the installation is pretty vanilla.

Whichever emulator tool and ROM image you're using, there are one or two things to configure before you can load a SharePoint Mobile view:

- If you do not have the Virtual Machine Network Driver for Microsoft Device Emulator installed on the machine you are trying to install the emulator on, you'll need to download and install it from here: `www.microsoft.com/downloads/details.aspx?familyid=DC8332D6-565F-4A57-BE8C-1D4718D3AF65&displaylang=en`.
- Before you can use either of the emulators, you'll need to configure networking so that it can access your server. To do this, follow these steps:
  - In the emulator program itself (i.e., not in the mobile device image), click File ➤ Configure and then select the Network tab.
  - Select the checkbox next to Enable NE2000 PCMCIA Network Adapter and Bind To and click OK.
  - Inside the emulated mobile device, click Start ➤ Settings and select the Connections tab. (This step will be slightly different depending on which version of Windows Mobile you are running.)
  - Open Network Cards and click on the NE2000 Compatible Ethernet Driver to modify its settings.

- Configure the IP Address, Subnet mask Default Gateway, and Name Server settings to valid values for your network and click OK.
- Click OK in the warning that pops up about the new settings being applied.
- Click OK a few more times to return to the Today screen.
- Once again in the emulator program itself, click File ➤ Configure and then select the Network tab.
- Ensure that the checkbox next to Enable NE2000 PCMCIA Network Adapter and Bind To is still selected and click OK. Repeating these steps here simulates removing and reinserting the PCMCIA network card in the device, which forces the new settings to take effect. If this doesn't work, reset the Guest (i.e., emulated) operating system.

That's it. The emulator is now ready to browse your SharePoint site and wow you with the automatic Mobile views. Fire up IE Mobile and connect to your SharePoint site. Just remember to append `/_layouts/mobile/` to the site URL or you'll end up browsing the full SharePoint site. While this isn't too bad running an emulator on your machine that is likely sitting on a high-speed network, it can be mind-numbingly slow on a standalone mobile device across a cellular network.

If you want to close the emulator and be able to fire it up again to browse the Mobile views, make sure that you save state before closing the emulator. Otherwise, you'll have to repeat all of the steps in this sidebar to reconfigure the network cards.

There may be a few extra steps to configure inside your emulator—it all depends on how your machine and network is set up. This, however, gets you most of the way there. You'll need to take it the rest of the way.

Outlook Synchronization With SharePoint

We've already talked about the integration between SharePoint 2007 and Outlook 2007. The integration with a mobile device is simply an extension of that. Workflow tasks and emails that are delivered to Outlook will be delivered to the mobile device the next time the user synchronizes their mobile device with Exchange. Our workflow information just comes along for the ride. Links inside emails or tasks will open inside IE Mobile and take the user to the appropriate page on the SharePoint server. One drawback is that unless we specifically craft a mobile URL, the links will take the mobile user to the full-fidelity site page. It's not the worst thing in the world, but it can be a little painful on a mobile device. (See the accompanying tip for some information on making this a little better.)

We'll see this integration in the next section as we walk through the mobile experience.

■ **Tip** The experience for our mobile users interacting with tasks assigned to them is going to be better if we use a custom workflow for the simple reason that we can control things a bit better and set values (for links, descriptions, etc.) that will work better from their mobile devices. The out-of-the-box workflows will still work, and even a custom workflow built with the SharePoint Designer can function—but really, if you want to truly support a sizable mobile workforce, you'll need to create custom workflows in Visual Studio and craft links specifically for them.

To allow this synchronization to happen, you need to go through just a few steps in both SharePoint and Outlook. I covered them in detail in Chapter 3, complete with pictures, so I'll just hit the steps here:

1. From the list that you want to synchronize into Outlook (in our case, the task list), click the Actions menu and then select Connect to Outlook.
2. If it is not already open, Outlook will open on your desktop.
3. A dialog box will pop up asking you to confirm that you want to connect the list to Outlook. Go ahead and click Yes.
4. Outlook will whir and pop for a few seconds and then your list will be synchronized.

From now on, every change made to the list item, *either in Outlook or in SharePoint,* will be synchronized across to the other. As we'll see in just a minute, this can be easily extended to our mobile devices.

■ **Note** Only Outlook content that synchronizes with your mobile device will be available, so not every SharePoint list that you connect to Outlook will be available on your mobile device.

The Mobile Experience

As mentioned earlier, mobile users can only be participants in workflows; they cannot manually kick off a workflow. To help you understand what mobile users can and cannot do, we'll walk through the participant experience for a mobile user, including a few screenshots.

First, if a user is browsing a SharePoint Mobile view from a mobile device, they will initially see a view similar to the one shown earlier in Figure 9-1. It is simply a textual listing of the lists available on the site. From there, if they click to browse the task list, they will see a Mobile view of the items in that list—including any workflow tasks assigned to them. An example of this is shown in Figure 9-2.

The experience in this view is perhaps not the best—if there are a number of tasks in the view, the user will have to do a lot of scrolling. Nonetheless, for something we get out of the box, this is going to go a long way. As you can see in Figure 9-2, users have the choice of opening the document (in Word Mobile—remember, there are none of the Office 2007 client integration elements available in Word Mobile), displaying the task, or editing the task. If they choose to edit the task, they will see a screen similar to Figure 9-3. Again, not the best interface, but on a mobile device the UI is less important than the raw information.

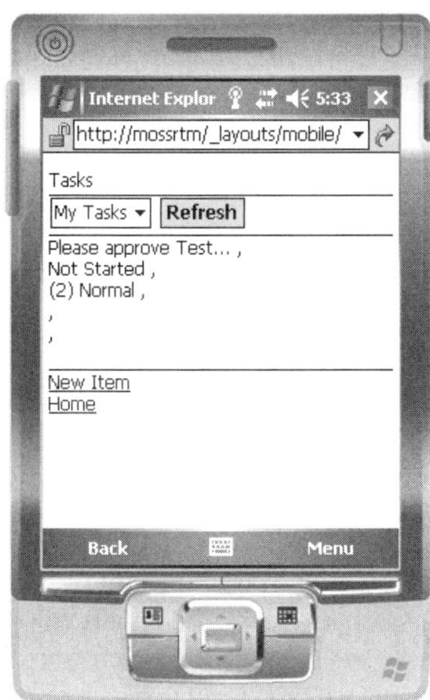

Figure 9-2. *Our workflow tasks viewed through a mobile device*

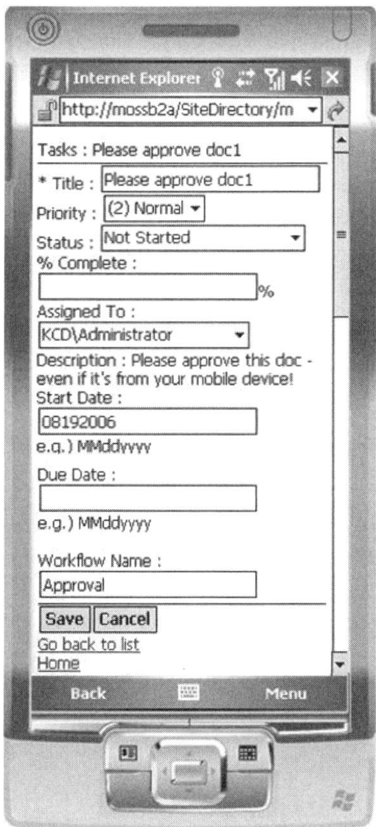

Figure 9-3. *Our workflow task shown on a mobile device*

Note Before you ask, no, that isn't the real size of my mobile device screen in Figure 9-3. I Photoshopped two images together to show you the whole screen in one shot. You can thank me later…

With these two views of the task, I can perform my work from wherever I am when I am assigned the task. If I need to review a document, I can download it into Word Mobile, read it, and then provide feedback or approval/rejection—all from my mobile device.

The experience reviewed above is a pull scenario—the user needs to be browsing the Mobile views in order to see the task assigned to them. I don't know about you, but the form factor on my mobile device is still just a little too limiting for me to casually browse the company intranet on a whim. I need a reason to go there. This is where the push aspect of the mobile experience comes into play. This experience, too, is easy.

If properly configured, as covered earlier, SharePoint will synchronize our task list to our mobile device. Assuming that our mobile device is already synchronizing tasks and emails with our Exchange server, there's nothing else we need to do. Our workflow tasks and emails will show up on our device just the same as any other email or task. And because the synchronization is two-way, if we update the task on our device, the next time we synchronize the Outlook task will be updated and then the SharePoint task will be updated by Outlook. Pretty nifty.

Note I'm not showing you any screenshots here because if you have a mobile device, you already know what tasks and emails look like on your device. If you don't have a mobile device capable of supporting email and tasks, um… can I ask why not?

Note Seriously, though, if you don't have a mobile device that supports email and tasks, showing you an example of an email and a task won't provide much value. Skip back to the sidebar "See What All The Buzz Is About Without Buying a New PDA" and you'll be able to see for yourself.

That's it. Our workflows are now fully mobile.

SUPPORTING A MOBILE WORKFORCE

One additional thing to think about when planning for your road warriors is allowing them to work from their laptops. There are a few options for this:

- Users can choose one of the various tethering options, which would allow them to use their mobile device as a modem and connect to it from their laptop. It's a bit slow, but they can then browse the intranet as if they were on the network and so will not need to muck about with Mobile views and the inherent limitations.

- If tethering is not an option, users can achieve the same end manually—have them use the Mobile views to see tasks and download documents. Once the documents are on their mobile devices, they can move them to their laptops via one of three mechanisms:
  - Using a USB cable and ActiveSync.
  - Using a Bluetooth Personal Area Network.
  - Using the modern version of the old *sneaker net*—save the file to the removable memory card in their phone, pop the card into their laptop, and open it from their laptop. Do the reverse when they need to load the documents back to the portal. Various adapters are available if the two devices don't support a common card format.

One added benefit of any of these options is the fact that users will be able to work with Office 2007 format documents with any of these options. They won't, however, unless they're tethered, see any of the Office 2007 constructs such as the Business Bar and Workflow forms.

Fault Handling

The functionality provided by fault handling in our workflows is no different from what you expect in typical .NET applications: you try something and then catch any errors and handle them. The implementation, however, is turned 90 degrees from what you would expect. Starting from the top, fault, or error, handling in our workflows is going to have the same capabilities as any other .NET application:

- Faults can be caught within a local scope, or globally for the entire workflow.
- Unhandled exceptions will cause the workflow to immediately halt execution and shut down.
- Handled exceptions can be processed and allow your workflow to either continue processing or shut down gracefully, with as much logging or notifications as you need.

We'll cover the details on these as we go through the rest of this section. First, let's review some of the mechanics of how you configure fault handling in workflows.

The primary construct for handling errors is the FaultHandler activity. We'll walk through using this activity in just a bit, but at a high level, each FaultHandler activity is associated with one particular type of exception and contains other activities that dictate how the particular error is handled.

Like any other error handling, the goal of fault handling in WF is to trap errors as they occur, respond according to our business rules, and ideally allow the workflow to continue processing. If continuation is not possible, we need to clean things up and return our documents or other content to a stable, manageable state.

At a global level, exception handling can be applied to the entire workflow. To do this you are going to make use of the three little tabs (shown in Figure 9-4) at the bottom of the Workflow Designer pane in Visual Studio that we haven't paid much attention to as yet. Specifically, we're going to focus on the rightmost tab.

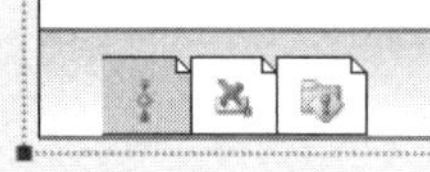

Figure 9-4. *The tabs at the bottom of the Workflow Designer in Visual Studio provide access to the fault handling functionality.*

Clicking on that tab will reveal the Workflow Exceptions design canvas, shown in Figure 9-5. Even the most cursory glance will reveal that the Exceptions design canvas looks nearly identical to the Workflow Designer we've worked with so far. That is not an accident. Configuring our exception handling is just configuring another part of the workflow. Looking at Figure 9-5 a little more closely, you'll see it consists of a single composite activity of type `faultHandlersActivity`. This composite, like all of the others we've seen so far (Sequence, Parallel, While, IfElse, etc.) is made to serve as a container for other activities. This one is a little special, though, because it is made to store only one type of activity: the FaultHandler activity mentioned earlier. If you try to add any other type of activity to it, the Designer will not let you.

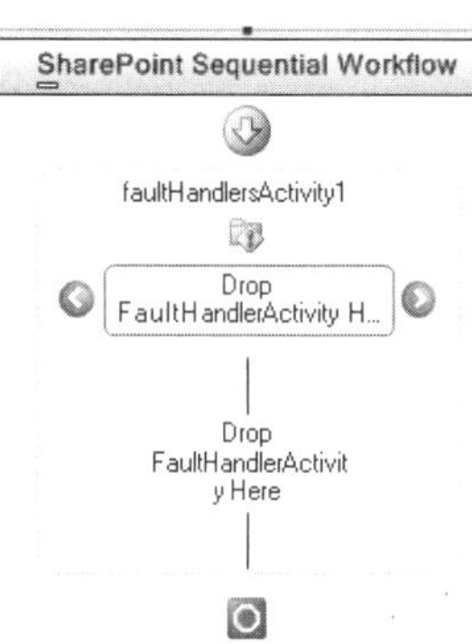

Figure 9-5. *The Workflow Exceptions design canvas looks remarkably like the regular Workflow Designer canvas we've already worked with.*

One other thing that is different about this composite activity is the manner in which it displays its children. Because each of the children is another composite activity, the tree display could get very ugly, very fast. To help alleviate this, Microsoft has coded the faultHandlersActivity to display its children in a unique way—essentially each FaultHandler gets its own design canvas. Each FaultHandler child dropped onto the faultHandlersActivity parent will be displayed in the small ribbon-like construct at the top of the activity. The two blue arrow icons allow you to scroll back and forth between the FaultHandler activities that have been added. The main body of the activity below this will display the child activities from the currently selected FaultHandler.

That's a little confusing. Let's walk through an example to help clarify things:

1. Open or create any workflow.

2. From the designer canvas, click the right-hand tab located at the bottom of the screen. This will open the Workflow Exceptions design canvas.

3. From the Toolbox, drag two FaultHandler activities and drop them onto the faultHandlersActivity on the canvas

4. Click on the first FaultHandler activity—indicated by this icon on the left side: 

5. Drag a Code activity and drop it into the body of the faultHandlerActivity1 activity—where the small green plus sign has appeared.

6. Click on the second FaultHandler activity—indicated by same icon shown in step 4, this time on the right side.

   Notice that the Code activity has disappeared. This is because we are now working with a different FaultHandler activity.

7. Drag an IfElse activity from the ToolBox and drop it into the body of the faultHandlerActivity2—again where the small green plus sign has appeared. Add another Code activity to the left-hand branch.

8. Click back on the first FaultHandler—you'll see that the Code activity is still in place.

If you click back and forth between the two FaultHandler activities, you'll see that everything is still intact—you just have two totally distinct environments in which to handle errors. This, of course, begs the question of why you need separate environments. The answer is that you need multiple environments in order to explicitly handle different types of errors. It is the equivalent of the code shown in Listing 9-1.

Listing 9-1. *The Code Equivalent for Our Workflow Fault Handling Constructs*

```
try
{
    //do something
}
catch (System.NullReferenceException exNull)
{
    //handle a null reference exception
}
catch (System.ArithmeticException exArith)
{
    //handle an arithmetic exception
}
catch (System.Exception ex)
{
    //catch-all to handle any other error
}
```

Each FaultHandler activity represents one of the catch blocks in Listing 9-1.

Configuring Fault Handlers

There are two ways to configure fault handling for our workflows—declarative or imperative. The imperative type of fault handling requires setting one set of properties, creating variables, and writing some code to handle the error however we need to. We'll show this option in a minute. Declarative handling is slightly different. When we handle our workflows declaratively, we work exclusively in the Designer—adding activities to the canvas and setting properties to handle our exception. We don't write any code. We'll cover this next.

Declarative Fault Handling

Declarative fault handling is all about adding activities to the canvas and configuring them to handle the exception according to your business rules. One of the primary distinctions of this approach is that it is somewhat generic in nature; the only real information you know about the fault is its type—and that only because, as we saw earlier, each FaultHandler is configured to handle a particular type of error.

So, how do we work with this style of fault handling? As you would expect, it's really pretty straightforward if you're comfortable with the Workflow Designer.

1. From the Exceptions tab in the Workflow Designer, drag a FaultHandler activity out onto the canvas.

2. Make sure that the FaultHandler activity is selected and open the Properties window.

3. Inside the Properties window click on the ellipsis for the Fault Type property. This will bring up a dialog box, shown in Figure 9-6. This dialog box allows you to specify which type of error this particular FaultHandler activity will take care of.

4. Once you've specified the type of error to be handled by this FaultHandler activity, you can add whatever activities you need to in order to handle the error.

5. If you need to handle more than one exception type, drag another FaultHandler activity out and configure it in the same way.

OK, I have to jump in here and editorialize a bit. I don't understand the usefulness of declarative fault handling (except for one circumstance, which I'll get to in just a minute). Here's the problem I see—if I'm catching and handling an error, I want to be pretty specific about the way I handle it. Also, in most cases, the error being thrown is likely unique to the workflow that is running. Because of these two points, I need my handler to be specific, which means that I'm likely adding a Code activity and writing some code. Once I've crossed that line, I'm into the realm of imperative fault handling.

The only exception I see to this is if all you are doing is simple logging. In that case, write a custom, generic logging activity that will write the information to whatever logging medium you require, add it to the Designer for your fault handler, and you're good to go. No coding required, but you still get some useful information and didn't have to write any code specific to this handler.

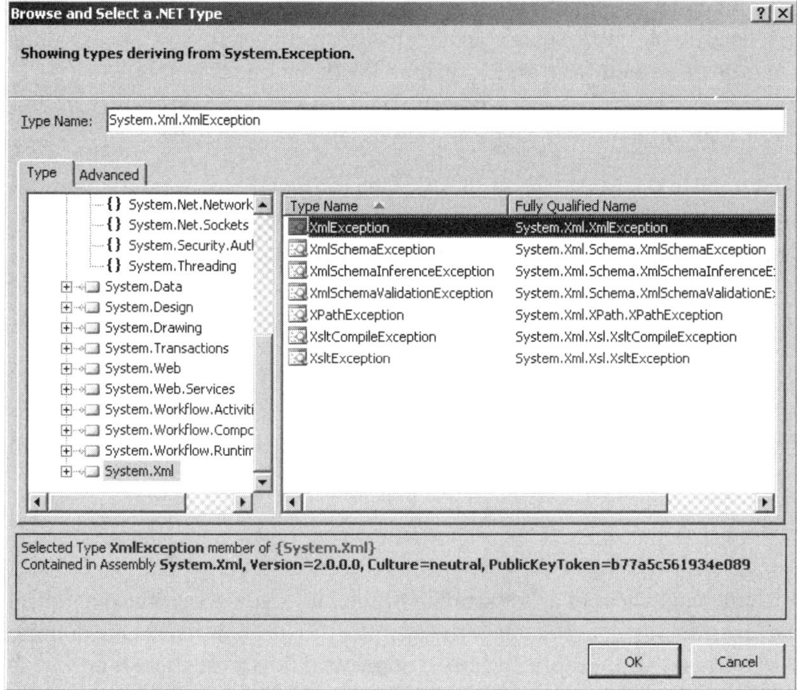

Figure 9-6. *This dialog box indicates which type of exception is handled by our FaultHandler activity.*

Other than this one case, I recommend that you read on and understand the benefits of imperative fault handling—it's a little more work but well worth it for the extra value, as you'll see.

Imperative Fault Handling

Imperative fault handling, as I alluded to earlier, is a little more involved than simple declarative handling. However, it gives us a lot more control and a lot more capability to manipulate our handler process and to be specific with how we process our faults.

Imperative fault handling makes use of one new property of the FaultHandler activity: the `Fault` property. The `Fault` property allows us to create a property that will be used to store the object representing the exception that was thrown by our workflow. With that, we can then handle our exception however we need to, typically within a Code activity. When the exception is thrown, we will have access to the entire `Exception` object through the variable referenced in the `Fault` property.

To make this work, follow these steps:

1. Repeat steps 1–3 from the previous section.
2. Right-click on the FaultHandler activity and select Promote Bindable Properties from the context menu.

3. Take a look in your code-behind file and you'll see that a new dependency property, named `<Fault_Handler_Activity_Name>_Fault1`, has been created for you. For example, if your fault handler is named `faultArgExcep`, then the dependency property will be called `faultArgExcep_Fault1`. The new property will have a type of `System.Exception`. If you choose to, you could make the type for this variable more specific.

4. You'll still need to fill in the `FaultType` property to tell the workflow runtime which type of error this particular handler is taking care of. For this example, you can type in **System.Exception**.

That's it. If your workflow ever triggers this handler, your dependency property will store a reference to the exception that was thrown. You can drop a Code activity onto the canvas, reference the dependency property, and do with it whatever you need to do in order to handle this error. The main benefit is that you have a lot more information about the error available to you. To harp on logging again—placing some of this information (stack trace, source, etc.) into your logging is going to make errors much easier to troubleshoot.

Local Scope

So far, we've looked at fault handling at what is essentially the global level. We've created handlers for faults that bubble up, unhandled, to the top of the chain—the workflow itself. One definite problem with this is that when you are capturing errors at the workflow level, there is no way to continue the workflow after the error has been handled. Faults caught at the workflow level always immediately precede the termination of the workflow. This is obviously less than desirable.

So, what can we do about it? Fortunately, there is an option. Faults can also be handled at the level of any composite activity, so the Parallel, Repeater, Sequence, and While activities (just to name a few) can all handle faults at a more granular level.

Handling the errors at the level of a composite activity is exactly the same experience as we saw at the global level. The only thing that is different is how you access the fault handler design canvas for a specific composite activity—simply right-click on the activity itself and select View Fault Handlers from the context menu. That's it. The rest is identical to what I described earlier.

■ **Tip** With the scope issues discussed in this section in mind, I recommend that you make judicious use of some of the composite activities that ship with WF. Certainly the Parallel, IfElse, and While activities have their place by performing a specific function in addition to being composite activities. There is, however, the Sequence activity, which can be used when you are executing activities serially but still need to be able to handle faults locally.

If an error is not explicitly handled at a local scope, it will bubble up to the global handler to attempt to be handled there. If the global handler does not take care of the error, the workflow will error out with unpredictable results—including potentially leaving your documents or tasks in unknown states.

Fault Handling Summary

So now we have a pretty good idea of how we go about handling faults in our workflows. The only thing that I'd like to conclude this section with is a brief discussion of how you *should* handle errors in your SharePoint workflows:

- As I alluded to previously, you should always log the error. Whether this is with code or a logging activity is entirely up to you. I'll just leave the recommendation at this: log it somewhere.
- Local, local, local. Whenever possible, handle your faults as locally as possible.
- Always, *always* provide a catchall fault handler at the workflow level. Add a FaultHandler activity at the workflow level and configure it to catch exceptions of type `System.Exception`. If it does nothing else, log the error details somewhere.
- If tasks were already assigned, you should go back and either delete them or flag them as inactive. Specific details around this would be dependent on your particular business requirements, but it wouldn't do much good, and could potentially be very confusing, if participants had tasks assigned to them for a workflow that had errored out.

■ **Caution** If you are going to undo changes in your workflow because of an error, you should understand how workflows process operations in batches and do some experimentation with your particular situation. Go back and read the section "Workflow Processing" earlier in this chapter before proceeding too far down this road. Specifically when your workflow will commit operations to the database is unique to every workflow. Keep this in mind as you plan your fault handling.

Canceling Workflows

Canceling workflows is similar in many ways to fault handling in our workflows. If fault handlers are the `catch` block, then cancellation handlers are the `finally` block. Workflows can be canceled in a few ways and for any number of reasons:

- By unhandled exceptions
- By an administrator in the UI
- Explicitly based on a condition within the workflow through the use of a Terminate activity

The cancellation handler allows us to perform any processing that needs to occur before the workflow actually shuts down. One thing that is important to note is that *there is no way to stop the cancellation of a workflow once it has been initiated by any means.*

So, if we can't stop the cancellation of a workflow, what can we do? The answer is just about anything else. Off the top of my head, the following comes to mind:

- Notify a document owner that the workflow has been canceled.
- Notify participants that the workflow has been canceled.

- Just like with fault handling, if tasks were already assigned, you should go back and either delete them or flag them as inactive.
- Again just like fault handlers, log the cancellation.

Caution The caution at the end of the section "Fault Handling" applies equally as much to cancellation handlers as well. Go back and reread it. You'll be glad that you did.

So, with all of that out of the way, how do we actually catch a workflow cancellation event and respond to it? As I said when I started this section, it is similar to fault handling. To work with the cancellation handler for the whole workflow, click on the middle tab at the bottom of the Designer canvas (and shown earlier in Figure 9-4). This will reveal another canvas used specifically for handling workflow cancellations.

Also, composite activities can also contain specific, local cancellation handlers. This local cancellation handler will be called if one of their child activities is canceled or is executing when the workflow is canceled. Access this via a similar mechanism to the fault handler—right-click on the activity and select View Cancel Handler.

One thing to note about cancellation handlers is that they may not exactly execute as you would expect. If you place a cancellation handler globally on the entire workflow, it would be logical to assume that it would fire any time the workflow is canceled—for any reason. Unfortunately, this is not the case. Because cancellation can be handled locally, only the composite activities that have children executing at the time the error is thrown or the workflow otherwise canceled will have their cancellation handlers triggered. So, in the case of the global cancellation handlers, this will only be triggered if the whole workflow is canceled—typically by an administrator via the user interface.

In other cases, in order to get multiple activities executing simultaneously, you need to be using the Parallel activity. If one branch of the Parallel activity causes the workflow to be canceled—for example, by throwing an unhandled error—the other branch(es) of the Parallel activity will be notified that the workflow is being canceled. Individual composite activities within those other branches will also have their cancellation handlers triggered. However, the Parallel activity itself and the workflow as a whole will not have their cancellation handlers triggered.

It's all a bit happenstance and highly dependent on execution order, timing, and which activities are executing at the time the cancellation is triggered. While you can generally plan out your cancellation handlers pretty well, there will be an experimentation aspect to it to see how things execute in your environment.

Note For an example of the variable nature of cancellation handlers, in a nod to Mr. Heisenberg, I could consistently produce different results just by alternating between running my test workflow in the debugger or outside the debugger. As I said, this all highly dependent on exactly what is happening at the moment the cancellation is triggered. Your mileage may vary.

Tools Comparison

In Chapters 4, 5, and 6, we work with the two development tools for building workflows in Office 2007—the SharePoint Designer and Visual Studio. Each tool is good and serves a specific audience and purpose. To help you get a handle on where and when to use each tool, take a look at Table 9-1. This information is reproduced from the WSS v3 SDK and is available online at `http://msdn2.microsoft.com/en-us/library/ms461944.aspx`. It is reproduced here with the express permission of Bill Gates (well, no, not really, but I know a guy named Bill and he said it would be OK... does that count?).

Table 9-1. *Differences Between SharePoint Designer and Visual Studio for Workflow Development. Taken from the WSS v3 SDK, See Previously Cited URL.*

Visual Studio 2005 Designer for Windows Workflow Foundation	Office SharePoint Designer 2007
Can write workflows for Microsoft Windows SharePoint Services (version 3).	Can write workflows for Microsoft Windows SharePoint Services (version 3).
Code-behind file enables developer to write custom Microsoft Visual C# or Microsoft Visual Basic .NET code to express business logic.	No code behind; workflow rules file declaratively encapsulates business logic instead.
Generates workflow markup file.	Generates workflow markup file.
Workflow is authored as a template, which can be associated with multiple sites and lists.	Workflow is authored against and data-bound to specific list at design time.
Workflow markup file, or markup and code-behind files, compiled into workflow assembly.	Workflow markup, workflow rules, and supporting file are stored, uncompiled, in a specific document library on the site.
Workflow template must be associated with each list on which it is to be available.	Association happens when the workflow is authored against the specific list; no later association is necessary or possible.
Workflow template can be associated with a site content type.	Cannot author workflows against content types.
Can use any forms technology. For example, Microsoft ASP.NET 2.0 forms for Microsoft Windows SharePoint Services (version 3) workflows.	Automatically generates Microsoft ASP.NET 2.0 forms, which you can then customize.
Can include workflow modifications.	Workflow modifications are not available.
Can author custom activities for inclusion in workflows.	Must use activities provided.
Package workflow assembly and workflow definition as a SharePoint Feature, and deploy to the site.	Automatically handles deployment to specific list.
Can use initiation form to gather information from the user when they start the workflow.	Can use initiation form to gather information from the user when they start the workflow.

Table 9-1. *Differences Between SharePoint Designer and Visual Studio for Workflow Development. Taken from the WSS v3 SDK, See Previously Cited URL.*

Visual Studio 2005 Designer for Windows Workflow Foundation	Office SharePoint Designer 2007
Can use custom forms for users to interact with tasks in Microsoft Windows SharePoint Services (version 3).	Can use custom forms for users to interact with SharePoint tasks.
Visual Studio debugging available.	No step-by-step debugging available.
Can author both sequential and state workflows.	Can author only sequential workflows.

* *Taken from the WSS v3 SDK, available online at* `http://msdn2.microsoft.com/en-us/library/ms461944.aspx`

Integrating Office 2003

The experience of working with the Office 2007 client applications and the Office 2007 server applications—specifically Workflow in our case—is phenomenal. The level of integration and interaction is exceptional.

But let's face it—not everyone will upgrade all of their client applications to the 2007 versions immediately. This is understandable. Upgrading thousands of users' desktops is not an operation to be taken lightly—especially when the change is as significant as the change from Office 2003 to Office 2007. Microsoft and their partners are making a valiant effort to streamline this and help however they can, but it is nonetheless a daunting task.

So, does this mean that we can't take advantage of the server-side benefits and improvements in the Office 2007 System until the client side is updated? Absolutely not. As we explored earlier in the book, users of previous Office versions can still play in the SharePoint 2007/Workflow playground. They just don't get all the bells and whistles.

To help alleviate some of their feelings of being second-class citizens, we'll burn a few cycles here exploring how the experience for Office 2003 users can be made a bit better.

■ **Note** I'm only going to be focusing on the Office 2003 client here. You could probably take some of this material and make it work in Office XP and maybe even Office 2000, but I'm not going to be looking at either of those here.

Before we get started solving the problem, let's make sure we all understand exactly what it is we're trying to accomplish. From my perspective, the elements lacking in Office 2003 related to workflow are the following:

- Notification of pending workflow tasks for the current document
- The ability to interact with workflow tasks from the client
- The ability to initiate a workflow from the client applications

There are some other elements, but these are the biggies. Of these three, the first is the one that will break all kinds of new ground for us. The other two are just extensions of the core required for the first one, so we're just going to tackle the first item here. I'll leave you to tackle the other two as a homework assignment.

■ **Note** If you'd like to explore the other two or other aspects of integrating Office 2003, please visit `www.kcdholdings.com`. I'll get around to posting more information there eventually and would love to hear any ideas you have.

Getting Started

The overall architecture of the solution is going to make heavy use of Visual Studio Tools for Office (VSTO) and custom task panes. If you are not familiar with programming task panes in Office 2003, it's OK; you can pick most of it up as you go. It wouldn't hurt, however, to do some brushing up. I'll list some good VSTO resources on my web site: `www.kcdholdings.com`.

■ **Note** In addition to limiting this to Office 2003, I am going to limit it further to just Word. There is no technical reason for this—it's just that to cover all of the major Office 2003 applications would entail a book unto itself. With very little work, you should be able to easily convert the solution presented here to work with any of the Office 2003 applications that support task panes. Similarly, with a little work, you could make this work for the Office 2007 clients if you do not have the Forms Server available in your environment—i.e., you only have WSS installed.

In order to continue with the rest of this section, you'll need a slightly different environment than what we have been working with so far. Although you can have Word 2003 and Word 2007 on the same machine, the potential for cross-contamination is too much for something so far out on the edge. If something is going wrong while I'm developing, I don't want a whole lot of extraneous variables thrown into the mix while I'm trying to debug. I'm going to do all of my development on a separate virtual machine and just use my SharePoint 2007 virtual machine as a server that I'll connect to remotely. If you'd like to mirror this environment, here's how I have it set up:

- *VM #1—SharePoint 2007 Server*: Nothing special here—I'm using the same VM image I've done the rest of the development on throughout the book. I created a new site and a new document library to work with this section just to keep things separate. I also cranked the memory down to 900MB of RAM. It's low for SharePoint and slows things down a bit, but I need to run two virtual machines for this exercise, so I need some memory for the other. If you have a SharePoint 2007 server available somewhere in your test environment, you can skip this one and allocate more memory to VM #2.

- *VM #2—Office 2003 development machine*: This is a new virtual machine created with the following specs:
  - Virtual machine configured with 600MB of RAM (or as much as you can allocate).
  - Windows XP, SP2 with all updates and security fixes.
  - Visual Studio 2005 (install this before Office so you get the option for .NET Programmability Support when you install Office).
  - Office 2003—Word plus the common Office files only. Make sure that you install .NET Programmability Support.
  - Visual Studio Tools for Office 2005 (VSTO).

Now that we have our environment ready to go, we can get started. At a high level, there are only ten steps to the whole process:

1. Write a web service to operate on the SharePoint server.
2. Create a new VSTO document and assembly pair.
3. Create a file share on the SharePoint server.
4. Publish the VSTO solution to the file share.
5. Create a SharePoint site and document library to test the solution with.
6. Move the VSTO document into the `Forms` folder of the document library.
7. Switch the template used by the document library.
8. Set security.
9. Test.
10. Celebrate.

Easy as pie, right? We'll obviously go into a little more detail on most of those steps. I do have a whole book to fill out here and I wouldn't want you to feel ripped off... so let's go. As in the rest of the book, I'm not going to hold your hand and walk you through each and every step. I'm assuming you don't need that level of support. If you do, stop by my web site and I'll help as much as I can.

■ **Note** There's a fair amount of code to this solution—and I stripped it down to about the bare minimum. If you don't want to type it all in (to borrow from Truman Capote—*that's not coding, that's just typing*), you can download all of the code from my web site: `www.kcdholdings.com`.

Step 1: Write a Web Service

This is the code that will execute on the SharePoint server. Because the SharePoint object model is not available remotely, we need some way of accessing it from the client—web services to the rescue.

For the main flow of the book here, I'll assume that you are an experienced developer and comfortable creating web services in a SharePoint environment and understand some of the quirks that go with that territory. If you're not comfortable with that task, see the sidebar "It Shouldn't Be This Hard." If you're following along at home, just make sure that you name your web service **WFTask** so that the code we write later will work.

There is only one method for this web service; the code is shown in Listing 9-2. You'll also need to add a reference to the `Microsoft.Sharepoint.dll` and add `using` statements for `Microsoft.SharePoint`, `Microsoft.SharePoint.Utilities`, `Microsoft.SharePoint.Workflow`, and `System.Xml`.

Listing 9-2. *The Custom Web Service to Retrieve Workflow Task Information*

```
[WebMethod]
public XmlDocument GetWFTasks(string sSiteURL, string sDocLibName, ➥
 string sFolder, string sDocName,string sUser)
{
    string sTaskName = string.Empty;
    string sTaskURL = string.Empty;
    XmlDocument xDoc = new XmlDocument();
    XmlElement xElem = null;
    XmlText xText = null;
    XmlNode xNode = null;
   SPSite site = new SPSite(sSiteURL);
   SPWeb web = site.OpenWeb();
   SPDocumentLibrary doclib = (SPDocumentLibrary)web.Lists[sDocLibName];
   SPListItem item = null;
   foreach (SPListItem itemTemp in doclib.Items)
   {
       if (sFolder == string.Empty)
       {
           if (itemTemp.File.Name.ToLower() == sDocName.ToLower())
           {
               item = itemTemp;
               break;
           }
       }
       else
       {
           if ((itemTemp.Folder.Name == sFolder)
               && (itemTemp.File.Name.ToLower() == sDocName.ToLower())
               )
```

```
                {
                    item = itemTemp;
                    break;
                }
            }
        }
        string sTaskAssignedTo = string.Empty;
        for (int i = 0; i < item.Workflows.Count; i++)
        {
            SPWorkflow wf = item.Workflows[i];
            if (!wf.IsCompleted)
            {
                wf.TaskFilter = new SPWorkflowFilter(SPWorkflowState.Running,➥
                    SPWorkflowState.None);
                for (int j = 0; j < wf.Tasks.Count; j++)
                {
                    SPWorkflowTask task = item.Workflows[i].Tasks[j];
                    sTaskAssignedTo = task["AssignedTo"].ToString();
                    sTaskAssignedTo = sTaskAssignedTo.Substring(➥
                        sTaskAssignedTo.IndexOf('#') + 1);
                    if (sUser.ToLower() == sTaskAssignedTo.ToLower())
                    {
                        sTaskName = task.DisplayName;

                        sTaskURL = sSiteURL.TrimEnd('/') + "/Lists/" + ➥
                            wf.TaskList.Title + "/DispForm.aspx?zID=" ➥
                            + task.ID.ToString();
                        break;
                    }
                }
            }
        }
        xNode = xDoc.CreateNode(XmlNodeType.XmlDeclaration, string.Empty, ➥
            string.Empty);
        xDoc.AppendChild(xNode);
        xElem = xDoc.CreateElement("WorkFlowTask");
        xDoc.AppendChild(xElem);
        xElem = xDoc.CreateElement("TaskName");
        xText = xDoc.CreateTextNode(sTaskName);
        xElem.AppendChild(xText);
        xDoc.ChildNodes.Item(1).AppendChild(xElem);
        xElem = xDoc.CreateElement("TaskURL");
        xText = xDoc.CreateTextNode(sTaskURL);
        xElem.AppendChild(xText);
        xDoc.ChildNodes.Item(1).AppendChild(xElem);
        return xDoc;
    }
```

Line numbers are included for reference only. This code looks like it does an awful lot, but really it's pretty straightforward. Starting from the top of Listing 9-2:

- Lines 4 through 13 set up some variables, which we'll use later.
- Lines 14 through 34 get a reference to the document the user is working with, whether it exists in the root of the document library or in a folder/subfolder, and stores it in the `item` variable.
- Line 36 begins a loop through all of the workflows running on `item`.
- Line 39 ensures that we don't do any processing against workflows that are closed already.
- Line 41 applies a filter against the workflow tasks to limit it to only those that are currently in a running state.
- Line 42 begins a loop through the filtered workflow tasks.
- Lines 45 and 46 check the name of the user the task is assigned to so that we can limit further processing to only tasks assigned to the current user (passed in as a parameter) in line 47.
- Lines 57 through 68 build our XML document to return the workflow task information.

That is really the heart of our solution. The rest of the work we need to do is preparing to call that web service and then reacting to its return value.

That's all of the code we need for the web service so you can go ahead and compile and deploy. If you need a refresher on the steps, see the sidebar "It Shouldn't Be This Hard."

IT SHOULDN'T BE THIS HARD

So, just a little editorializing there, but it's true—creating web services in the SharePoint environment should not be as hard as it is. There are a bunch of moving parts and lots of steps to go through. I'm sure there's a reason, and I'm sure it makes perfect sense, but it still doesn't change the facts. Creating a web service in a SharePoint environment is more difficult than creating a "regular" web service. It's not impossible, honestly, not even that hard, despite what I said. It's just harder than it should be. There's no good way around it, though, so we just learn to live with it. (One potential way around it is to create your web services on a separate virtual server on the same box as your SharePoint server. You can add references to the SharePoint DLLs and access the object model that way. Just make sure that this separate virtual server is running with the same application pool account as your SharePoint virtual server and things will work OK. The only drawback is that I've seen some strange permission problems and that you lose the SharePoint context this way. Depending on what you're doing, this may be an option. Try it and see how it works for you.)

Anyway, enough whining. To create a web service within the SharePoint environment, maintaining the SharePoint context, you need to do the following:

1. Create a regular ASP.Net Web Service project with Location set to File System.
2. Add a new class library project to the web service solution.
3. Add references to the `Microsoft.Sharepoint` and `System.Web.Services` assemblies.

4. Move the Service.cs file from the web service project to the class library solution and delete the Class1.cs file.

5. Add the custom WebMethod code to the Service.cs file.

6. Strong-name the class library project.

7. Build the class library project and deploy it to the GAC.

8. Open the Service.asmx file (rename it if you'd like something more descriptive).

9. Remove the CodeBehind attribute from the page directive.

10. Modify the Class attribute to read Class="*<class_project_name>*, *<assembly_strong_name>*". You can retrieve the strong name for your assembly using the Reflector tool we discussed back in Chapter 7.

11. Copy your ASMX file to Program Files\Common Files\Microsoft Shared\web server extensions\12\TEMPLATE\LAYOUTS.

12. From a Visual Studio command prompt, run the following command: disco.exe http://*<server_name>*/_layouts/Service.asmx. Make sure that you change the name of the ASMX file to whatever you called yours. This will generate static .disco and .wsdl files for you.

13. Open the .disco and .wsdl files in Visual Studio and replace the XML processing directive (<?xml version="1.0" encoding="utf-8"?>) at the top of each with the code shown here:

```
<%@ Page Language="C#" Inherits="System.Web.UI.Page"%>
<%@ Assembly Name="Microsoft.SharePoint, Version=12.0.0.0, Culture=neutral,➥
 PublicKeyToken=71e9bce111e9429c" %>
<%@ Import Namespace="Microsoft.SharePoint.Utilities" %>
<%@ Import Namespace="Microsoft.SharePoint" %>
<% Response.ContentType = "text/xml"; %>
```

14. Near the bottom of the .wsdl file, replace the entire <soap:address element with the following: <soap:address location=<% SPEncode.WriteHtmlEncodeWithQuote(Response, SPWeb.OriginalBaseUrl(Request), '"'); %> />.

15. In the .disco file, replace the entire <contractRef and <soap:address elements with this code:

```
<contractRef ref=<% SPEncode.WriteHtmlEncodeWithQuote(Response, SPWeb.➥
OriginalBaseUrl(Request) + "?wsdl", '"'); %>  docRef=<% SPEncode.CCC
WriteHtmlEncodeWithQuote(Response, SPWeb.OriginalBaseUrl(Request), '"'); %>  ➥
xmlns="http://schemas.xmlsoap.org/disco/scl/" />
<soap address=<% SPEncode.WriteHtmlEncodeWithQuote(Response, SPWeb.➥
OriginalBaseUrl(Request), '"'); %>  xmlns:q1="http://tempuri.org/" binding=➥
"q1:HelloWorld" xmlns="http://schemas.xmlsoap.org/disco/soap/" />
```

16. Rename the .disco file to <service_name>disco.aspx, for example Service1disco.aspx.

17. Rename the .wsdl file to <service_name> wsdl.aspx, for example Service1 wsdl.aspx.

18. Copy the ASMX, DISCO, and WSDL files to Local_Drive:\Program Files\Common Files\Microsoft Shared\Web Server Extensions\12\ISAPI.

Step 2: Create the VSTO Solution

The next thing we need to do is create our solution. This is all pretty typical Visual Studio stuff; just make sure that you select Word Template as the project type and choose to create a new document when the VSTO Project wizard prompts you. Name the document anything you like, but if you're following along, I'm calling the document `WFTaskDocument`.

After Visual Studio whirs and pops for a few seconds, the project will be created with a Word template file open right inside Visual Studio. Everybody all together now... *oh, that is so cool.*

Starting with an overview, our code is going to perform the following steps:

1. Collect the information we need about the current document and the document library it resides in—site URL, document library name, document name, folders.
2. Call the custom web service we created in step 1, passing in the values we collected in the previous step.
3. Receive XML from the web service.
4. Parse the returned XML to retrieve the information we need: the name of the task and the URL to display it.
5. If the XML indicates a task assigned to the current user, create an action pane and display the information as well as a link to the task form.

Unfortunately, the code to handle this is not as straightforward as you would hope. Steps 2 through 5 are pretty run-of-the-mill, but step 1—collecting the information—is a little harder than it should be. What we end up doing is a lot of string parsing to get the values we need. Not pretty, but certainly functional.

■ Note This code worked for as many different permutations I could think of to throw at it. However, it is certainly possible that your situation could introduce a combination of site, document library, folder, and document names that will break this logic. In that case, you'll just need to adjust the string parsing as appropriate.

Before we begin, you'll need to add a reference to the web service we created in step 1. For the code to work, name your web service proxy **WFTaskService**. Now, open the `ThisDocument.cs` file in Code view and you'll see the default `ThisDocument_Startup` and `ThisDocument_Shutdown` methods. For our solution, we're going to make use of the startup procedure.

Taking things in order, Listing 9-3 shows the variable declarations we need to place at the top of our class. We'll use these variables to store the values we need to pass to the web service. The last two variables will be used once we have retrieved our task information from the web service.

Listing 9-3. *Variable Declarations for Our Class*

```
string sSiteURL = string.Empty;
string sDocLibName = string.Empty;
string sDocName = string.Empty;
string sFolders = string.Empty;
string sTaskName = string.Empty;
string sTaskURL = string.Empty;
```

Listing 9-4 shows the contents to add to the `ThisDocument_Startup`. It's pretty straightforward—basically just a few method calls. We'll be adding those in just a bit.

Listing 9-4. *Code Called When We Open Our VSTO Document*

```
if (GetValues())
{
     XmlNode xNode = CheckForWFTasks();
     if (GetValuesFromXML(xNode))
     {
          ShowTaskPane();
     }
}
```

The first method, `GetValues`, is going to do all of our string manipulation and parsing in order to retrieve the information we need to pass over to the web service. Unfortunately, to retrieve this, we need to do some gyrations. As I said before, it ain't pretty, but we have to work with what we're given and it gets the job done. In this case, what we're given to work with is a few pieces of information about the document library the document came from (including an indicator as to whether it actually came from one at all) and then the name and path of our document. That's about it. So, we do a little parsing and all is right with the world. Listing 9-5 shows the full contents of the `GetValues` method. As always, line numbers are for reference only and here's a breakdown of what is going on:

- Line 9 is the first interesting code; it checks whether we're getting the document from a document library by checking if we're connected to a shared workspace. If we're not, there's no reason to continue—there's no way it has any workflow tasks assigned to it; we just skip ahead to line 45 and we're done. Otherwise, we continue.

- Line 11 checks whether or not the document library contains folders. If it does, we need to look for a match between the folder name (which is actually the full folder hierarchy, such as ParentFolder/ChildFolder/GrandchildFolder/, etc.) and the full path to our document. If we find a match, we know the name of the folder our document is in. If the document library does not contain folders, our document cannot possibly be in a folder, so we don't need to retrieve the folder path—we skip ahead to line 36.

- Lines 13 through 20 loop through all of the folders in the document library checking to see if our filename contains the folder path. If it doesn't, our temporary string variable remains empty and so lines 22 through 26 will execute and figure out the name of the document library we're in. If we do find a match, line 29 determines the name of our document library.

- Once we know the name of the document library, we can assume that everything in front of that is the URL for the site, so line 31 does that parsing.
- Now that we have the name of our document, the name of the document library and the URL for the site, the only thing that can remain in the full name of our document is the folder structure. Lines 32, 33, and 34 remove the known elements from the full name, and so the only thing remaining is the folder path.
- Line 36 will only execute if the document library does not contain folders. In this case, lines 38 and 39 do some basic parsing and then lines 40 and 41 figure out the name of our document library and the site URL, respectively, by doing some more string manipulation.
- Line 47 only executes if we're not coming from a document library, so it can just return `false`.
- Lines 50 through 53 simply catch any errors and return `false`, signifying that we shouldn't continue with any processing. This is certainly an area that could stand some improvement.

Listing 9-5. *GetValues—Functional, but Not Pretty*

```
1       private bool GetValues()
2       {
3           string sTemp = string.Empty;
4           string sFullName = string.Empty;
5           try
6           {
7               sFullName = this.FullName;
8               sDocName = this.Name;
9               if (this.SharedWorkspace.Connected)
10              {
11                  if (this.SharedWorkspace.Folders.Count > 1)
12                  {
13                      for (int i = 1; i <= this.SharedWorkspace.Folders.Count;➥
                            i++)
14                      {
15                          if (sFullName.IndexOf(SharedWorkspace.Folders[i].➥
                            FolderName) > -1)
16                          {
17                              sTemp = this.SharedWorkspace.Folders[i].➥
                                FolderName;
18                              break;
19                          }
20                      }
21                      if (sTemp == string.Empty)
22                      {
```

```
                    sTemp = sFullName.Replace(sDocName, String.Empty);
                    sTemp = sTemp.TrimEnd('/');
                    sDocLibName = sTemp.Substring(sTemp.LastIndexOf("/")➥
                         + 1);
                }
                else
                {
                    sDocLibName = sTemp.Substring(0, sTemp.IndexOf('/'));
                }
                 sSiteURL = this.FullName.Substring(0, this.FullName.➥
                          IndexOf(sDocLibName));
                 sFolders = sTemp.Replace(sDocLibName, string.Empty);
                sFolders = sFolders.Replace(sDocName, string.Empty);
                sFolders = sFolders.Replace(sSiteURL, string.Empty);
            }
            else
            {
                sTemp = sFullName.Replace(sDocName, String.Empty);
                sTemp = sTemp.TrimEnd('/');
                sDocLibName = sTemp.Substring(sTemp.LastIndexOf("/") + 1);
                     sSiteURL = this.FullName.Substring(0, this.FullName.➥
            IndexOf(sDocLibName));
            }
            return true;
        }
        else
        {
            return false;
        }
    }
    catch (Exception ex)
    {
        return false;
    }
}
```

The next method called from our startup method is CheckForWFTasks. This method, shown in its entirety in Listing 9-6, is pretty simple. It is basically just the call to the web service we created earlier. It returns an XMLNode that contains any task information.

Listing 9-6. *Calling the Web Service and Passing Back the XML*

```
private XmlNode CheckForWFTasks()
{
     WFTaskService.WFTask wft = new WFTaskService.WFTask();
     wft.Credentials = System.Net.CredentialCache.DefaultNetworkCredentials;
     XmlNode xNode = wft.GetWFTasks(sSiteURL, sDocLibName, sFolders, sDocName);
     return xNode;
}
```

Next up is the method to parse the XML and set the values into the variables we created way back in Listing 9-3. Before we show this code, let's take a look at the XML we'll be getting back. There's really only two pieces of information we need here—the name of the task and the URL for the task form—so it's pretty simple. Take a look at Listing 9-7 to see what it looks like.

Listing 9-7. *An Example of the XML We'll Get Back from Our Web Service*

```
<WorkFlowTask>
 <TaskName>Task 1</TaskName>
  <TaskURL>http://mossrtm/o2003/Lists/Tasks/DispForm.aspx?ID=4</TaskURL>
</WorkFlowTask>
```

Now let's parse that out and assign the values back into our variables. Listing 9-8 shows the GetValuesFromXML method referenced in our startup method. Again, there's not much to this method, either; a couple of SelectSingleNode calls and we're pretty well done with this method.

Listing 9-8. *Parsing Out the Retrieved XML to Get Our Task Information*

```
private bool GetValuesFromXML(XmlNode xNode)
{
     try
     {
         sTaskName = xNode.SelectSingleNode("/TaskName/text()").Value;
         sTaskURL = xNode.SelectSingleNode("/TaskURL/text()").Value;
         if ((sTaskName != string.Empty)
             && (sTaskURL != string.Empty)
             )
         {
             return true;
         }
         else
         {
             return false;
         }
     }
     catch (Exception ex)
     {
         return false;
     }
}
```

The error handling here is pretty sparse (OK, really it's nonexistent) but it works fine. If there are no tasks for the current document, an error will be thrown in one of the SelectSingleNode statements, and our catch statement will grab it and just return false. You can add whatever more robust error handling you need. Notice, too, that this method does double-duty. Not only does it populate the variables we need with the task information, it also returns a Boolean value so we know whether or not to show the task pane.

If we got valid values from the GetValuesFromXML method, the last thing we need to do is show the task pane with the workflow task information. While this can certainly be made nicer looking by using user controls and the visual design environment in Visual Studio, my main goal here is to highlight the functionality, so we're just going to create a very rudimentary task pane. You can gussy up your task pane any way you need to when you're building your production system. For now, the code in Listing 9-9 does the trick. It creates a button and a label, and creates an event handler for the button to launch a browser and open the task form for the workflow task. That's all we need for now.

Listing 9-9. *Our Task Pane*

```
private void ShowTaskPane()
{
     Label lblTaskName = new Label();
     lblTaskName.Text = sTaskName;
     Button btn = new Button();
     btn.BackColor = Color.Silver;
     btn.Text = "View Workflow Task";
     btn.Click += new System.EventHandler(btn_Click);
     this.ActionsPane.Controls.Add(lblTaskName);
     this.ActionsPane.Controls.Add(btn);
}

private void btn_Click(object sender, System.EventArgs e)
{
     System.Diagnostics.Process.Start(sTaskURL);
}
```

That's all there is for this step. Go ahead and compile your solution.

Step 3: Create the File Share

No rocket science here—just a simple file share. It makes things easier to put it on your SharePoint server but it could go anywhere on your network—as long as it is accessible. One important thing is that anyone who will be using this solution will need at least Read access to this share so that they can get at the VSTO assembly. The account we use in the next step to publish our VSTO solution will need Write access as well. Your network security policies will dictate exactly how you make that happen.

For this exercise, I'll call the share *VSTOApps*.

Step 4: Publish the Solution

With our assembly built and our file share created, we can go ahead and publish. Before doing so, we need to configure the publishing process just a little. In the Properties window for your project, on the Publish tab uncheck the box that says Automatically Increment Revision With Each Release. We don't need it for our development and testing, and it just makes our deployment share cumbersome and bloated.

With that out of the way, it's time to publish our masterpiece. Right-click on the project name in the Solution Explorer and select Publish from the context menu. Specify the UNC path to the file share you created in step 3. In my case, the path looks like this: `\\mossrtm\VSTOApps`. Click Finish and wait. If the gods are smiling down upon your endeavors, publishing will be successful and you can move on.

The last part of publishing is to move the assembly DLL from the subdirectory the publishing wizard kindly created for you and paste it right into the root of the file share. The subdirectory will be named for the name of your project and the version of the assembly—something like `WordTemplate4_1.0.0.0`. Simply drag the file from there and drop it directly into the root of the share.

Step 5: Create Site and Document Library

There's nothing special about this step—you can even skip it if you already have a site and document library you can work with in a sandbox environment that won't impact or be impacted by other users.

For my environment, I created a site called *O2003* and a document library named *O2003a*. Notice the nice and confusing naming I give everything.

Step 6: Move VSTO Document

In this step, we're going to take the Word template document we published to our file share and move it into our document library. We're not going to do a regular file upload, though. We're going to do this through Windows Explorer because we need to get to the `Forms` folder of the document library.

The easiest way to do this is, from the SharePoint server itself, to open the document library in a browser and then click into Explorer view. Open the `Forms` folder in Explorer view. Copy the Word template you created (in my case, it's called `WFTaskDocument.dot`) *from the file share* and paste it into the document library's `Forms` folder (which you have open in Explorer view).

■ **Caution** Make sure that you are copying the template file from the file share that you published to and not the project folder on your development machine. Part of the work performed by the Publish wizard is to create and configure the application's manifest. If you take the copy from your project folder, it will not have this manifest information.

Step 7: Switch New Document Template

Next we need to tell SharePoint to use this new template for all new documents in this document library. Go into the Advanced Settings page for the document library and change the entry for the Document Template setting to point to our new template file. In my example, this means that I change the value to `O2003a/Forms/WFTaskDocument.dot`. Your settings may be different, but basically the value should be `<name of document library>/Forms/<Name of template file>`.

Step 8: Set Security

Setting security for VSTO applications is a black art. Experienced practitioners move in the shadows and rarely mingle with mere mortals.

OK, so it's not really that bad. Getting your Code Access Security (CAS) set properly, though, is a fairly detailed process and one that will be different for every environment. There are plenty of white papers that cover the gory details and your organization should already have your guidelines in place (right?).

So, with that cop-out firmly set in place, what I'll cover here is setting up CAS for our development environment. What that means is that we basically leave all of the doors wide open. After you have this set up and configured, I'll ask that you kindly tear this page out of your book and burn it. That way, your organization's security team has no way of knowing that I told you to do this.

Thanks.

To get started, you'll need to fire up a command prompt on your client machine—not the SharePoint server, unless it is also your client machine. Remember, CAS is concerned with determining what our code can do, and our code executes within Word on the client machine. Yes, that means that if you were to deploy this into production, you'd need to configure CAS on each and every client. There are ways to make that less painful—Google "Code Access Security Group Policy" and you'll be headed down the right road.

Now, back in our command prompt (I told you this was a black art). Navigate to the `\WINDOWS\Microsoft.NET\Framework\v2.0.50727` folder and then type the two commands shown in Listing 9-10, replacing `<file_share_path>` with the path of your file share and `<url_for_doclib>` with the correct URL for your customized document library. The asterisk at the end of each URL entry is important—it means "everything in this location." This avoids having to explicitly name each DLL and document.

Listing 9-10. *Configuring CAS for Our Development Environment*

```
caspol -m -ag LocalIntranet_Zone -url "file://<file_share_path>\*" FullTrust -n ➥
"VSTO Assemblies"
caspol -m -ag LocalIntranet_Zone -url "<url_for_doclib>/*" FullTrust -n "VSTO ➥
Documents"
```

Listing 9-10 contains two separate commands; you'll need to hit Enter and run each one individually. After hitting Enter, you will be prompted to confirm that you really want to change the security policy. Go ahead and confirm that you do and then wait a second or two for the heart-warming confirmation that you've "Added union code group with '-url' membership condition to the Machine level. Success."

Step 9: Test

Well, that's it. Now comes the big moment—time for the rubber to meet the road. Fire up a browser and navigate to your document library. Click the New button and confirm that you really want to open this file from the server.

Wait a few seconds for Word to open your new document and bask in the glory of... nothing. Remember, if this is a new document it is not associated with a document library so there is no possibility of it having any workflow tasks yet. Most of our code doesn't execute yet. What you should have open on your screen is a regular old Word document.

Type some startlingly brilliant prose and save the document back into the document library. Close down Word and refresh your browser window. Click on your new document again and open it in Word. Get ready now, because... still nothing.

Our code executed this time but we still don't see anything. We need to initiate a workflow on the new document and assign ourselves a task. Close Word again and go back to the browser. Initiate a workflow for the new document—the default Approval workflow will work nicely—and make sure that you list yourself (whatever account you're logged in with) as approver. After the workflow kicks off, go back to the document library and try opening the document again.

It seems that the third time is a charm—now we have something. As shown in Figure 9-7, our task pane shows up this time and has the information on our workflow task. If we click the button, the task form will open inside a browser.

Go ahead and try it.

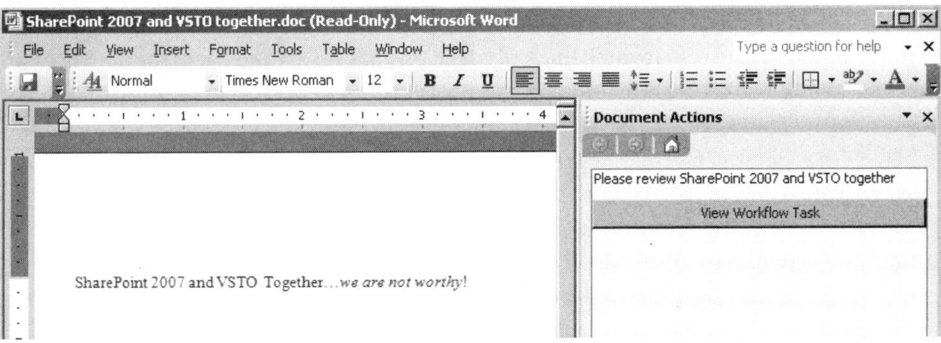

Figure 9-7. *Office 2007 workflow tasks in Office 2003. How sweet it is...*

Step 10: Celebrate

I can hear Kool & the Gang wafting over the cubicle walls already. Congratulations, you've successfully integrated Word 2003 with the Office 2007 Workflow engine.

Wrapping Up

The information presented here barely scratches the surface of the possibilities. As I said at the beginning, there are three primary classifications of the possible functionality:

- Notification of pending workflow tasks for the current document
- The ability to interact with workflow tasks from the client
- The ability to initiate a workflow from the client applications

We only covered the first, as the rest are just variations on that theme. To support each, all you need to do is create a new web service to return the appropriate information and modify the UI generated in the task pane.

From those three core pieces of functionality, there are many, many places you can take this to. Off the top of my head, the following is just a partial list of where you could go from here:

- Enable users to initiate workflows available in the document library that their document is stored in.
- Enable Forms Server integration so users can directly interact with their workflow from the client applications.
- Embed the Workflow Designer into a task pane to allow advanced users to create ad hoc workflows from within Office 2003. With a little additional work, this one could be rolled into Office 2007 as well.
- Integrate the ASPX task form directly into the task pane rather than launching an external browser session. This could come close to mimicking the Forms Server without requiring Forms Server.
- Build the task pane with a user control. This will give you better control over the UI so you can make the task pane look nicer.
- Add a new button to allow the user to refresh the workflow task information on demand.

There is more, I'm sure, that you'll think of based on your needs and background. My main goal here was to show that the functionality was possible and to get you thinking. If you'd like to explore this further, please stop by my web site—`www.kcdholdings.com`. I'll post some musings on this and other topics as often as my copious spare time allows.

■ **Caution** One warning on this solution: *it is far from perfect* as it currently stands. As I said in the beginning of this chapter, my main goal is to push the envelope a bit and get you thinking of how you can get the most out of workflows in Office 2007. This section certainly does that, but there are a lot of moving parts and you will need to touch every client's machine to install the VSTO runtime and the various other prerequisites. I think, however, that this is still easier than upgrading all of your clients to Office 2007 in one fell swoop. One other issue that will rear its ugly head is the fact that this will only work for document libraries that you have attached the VSTO solution to. If you are seriously exploring this option for a production environment, you are going to want to look into Features and content types in SharePoint 2007. Google them or pick up a good book on SharePoint 2007 (Scot Hillier's books—also from Apress—are always a good choice) and you should find everything you need. These approaches won't change the core of how the functionality is delivered; they will only impact the way in which you deploy everything to SharePoint.

Picking On People—The InfoPath Contact Picker and the ASPX People Editor

If you were paying attention as you explored the out-of-the-box workflows, you'd have noticed that they contain a pretty nifty interface for indicating the participants in your workflow. In InfoPath forms, it looks like Figure 9-8. In ASPX forms, it is similar, but looks like Figure 9-9.

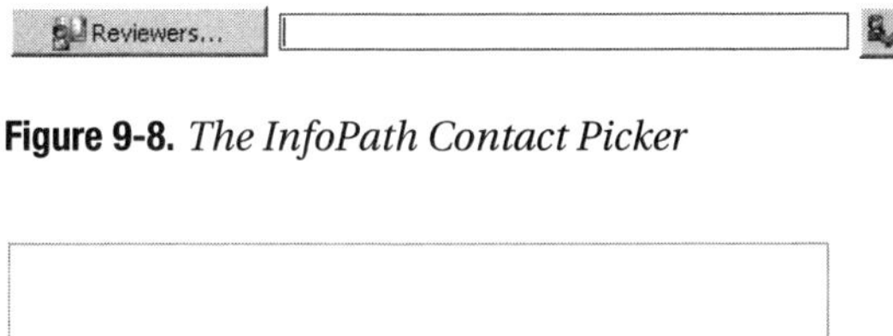

Figure 9-8. *The InfoPath Contact Picker*

Figure 9-9. *The ASPX People Editor*

In each case, you get the same functionality, though the UI is slightly different. Each control allows you to browse or search for users and to validate the users entered. This validation can occur against any of the following:

- SharePoint users and groups
- Active Directory (or other LDAP server) users and groups
- Local machine users and groups

Figure 9-10 shows the lookup interface for ASPX pages. The InfoPath rendition is similar.

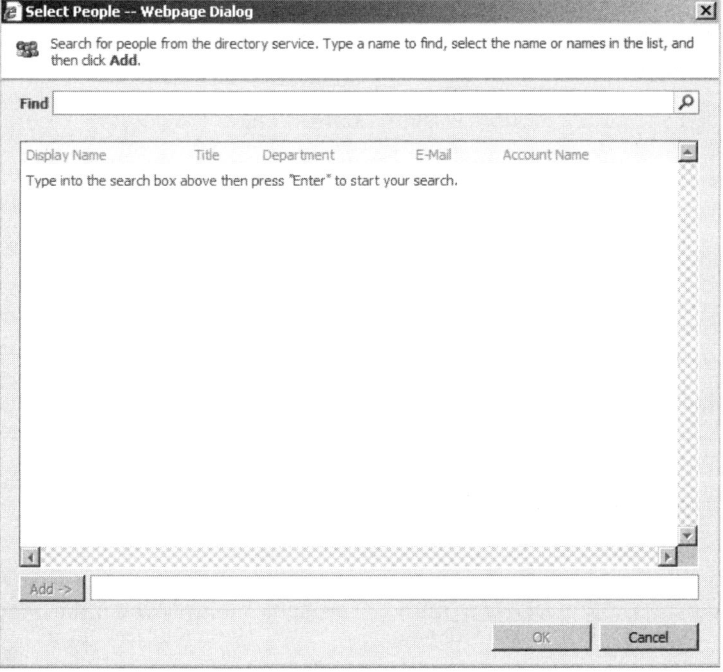

Figure 9-10. *The user lookup interface from the ASPX version of the People Editor*

Always trying to be the bearer of good news, I'm happy to let you know that this same control is available to you for use in your custom workflows. In InfoPath, it is called the Contact Picker control. In ASPX it is known as the People Editor. Two names, same great functionality.

Let's take a look at how you can make use of these controls in your custom workflows—first for InfoPath forms.

InfoPath Contact Picker

The InfoPath Contact Picker is an ActiveX control that ships as part of MOSS. As mentioned earlier, it encapsulates all of the functionality you need to specify users for various roles within your workflow and validates those users before the form is submitted.

Using the InfoPath Contact Picker is pretty simple. At a high level, you need to

1. Add the control to the InfoPath toolbar.
2. Add an instance of the control to your form and configure it for use.
3. Write some code to grab data sent to the form by SharePoint to be used by the control.

We'll cover these steps in a bit more detail in the following sections.

Adding the Control to the InfoPath Toolbar

Here's the first task we need to make the Contact Selector control available to add to our InfoPath forms:

1. In InfoPath 2007, click the Add or Remove Custom Controls link at the bottom of the Controls pane.
2. Click the Add button.
3. Select the option for ActiveX Controls.
4. Select Contact Selector and click Next.
5. Select the option to not include a `.cab` file and click Next.
6. For the Binding Property, select Value and click Next.
7. For the Data Type options, select Field or Group (Any Data Type) from the drop-down near the top and click Finish.
8. Click Close and OK to exit the wizard.

The Contact Picker control is now available in the list of available controls under the "Custom" section.

Adding and Configuring an Instance of the Control

Adding the control to the form is no different from any other InfoPath control—just drag it out and drop it where you need it. Configuring the control for use in our workflow forms is a little more involved but not too bad:

1. Double-click on the control you dropped onto your form.
2. On the Data tab, give the control a meaningful name—perhaps something clever like **Approvers**.
3. On the General, Display, Size, and Advanced tabs, customize the look of the control to your needs.

If you click the Items tab, you'll see information about binding the control and the schema required for the control. We'll cover this in the next few steps.

Each contact entered into the control at runtime is going to produce a single XML node that adheres to the schema shown in Listing 9-11. Most of the nodes in this XML are pretty self-explanatory. Only the `AccountType` node may be a little unclear but is really pretty easy. The `AccountType` holds a value indicating whether this is a user or a group. That's it!

Listing 9-11. *The Schema Required for Contacts in Our Contact Selector Control*

```
<person>
    <DisplayName> </DisplayName>
    <AccountId> </AccountId>
    <AccountType> </AccountType>
</person>
```

To configure our control to make use of this schema, we need to do some work with data sources, covered in the next few steps.

1. From the Design Tasks pane in InfoPath, select Data Source.
2. Underneath the (default) myFields entry should be an entry with the same name as our Contact Selector control. In my case, it is simply called Approvers.
3. From the drop-down menu for Approvers, select the Add option to add a new field or group.
4. In the resulting dialog box, configure the new field as follows and then click OK:
    - Name: person
    - Type: Group
    - Repeating: (checked)

5. Back in the Data source pane, click the new person group you just added and add a new field to it, configured as follows:
   - Name: DisplayName
   - Type: Field (element)
   - DataType: Text (string)
   - Repeating: (checked)
6. Add another field to the person group as follows:
   - Name: AccountId
   - Type: Field (element)
   - DataType: Text (string)
   - Repeating: (checked)
7. Add the final field to the person group:
   - Name: AccountType
   - Type: Field (element)
   - DataType: Text (string)
   - Repeating: (checked)

Our control is now configured to handle contact data. You'll have noticed, I'm sure, that the data source information we added matches the schema presented earlier.

The last piece we need to do for this section is to add a secondary data source to our InfoPath form. When our form is rendered, this channel will be used to pass useful information from the SharePoint workflow host to our form. The primary piece of information is the URL of the site that the workflow is running within—this allows our form to know which site to validate users against. Other information includes

- `isStartWorkflow`: A Boolean flag that indicates whether the form is an initiation form
- `isRunAtServer`: A Boolean value that indicates whether the form is being opened from the server
- `provideAllFields`: Another Boolean value that indicates whether the form is used as either an initiation form or an association form for a workflow that starts automatically

We need to create a simple XML file so that we have something to work with when we add the data source. It's a pretty small file, so just fire up Notepad and add the contents of Listing 9-12. Save the file as `ContactsDataSource.XML`. Looking at Listing 9-12, you'll notice that we have supplied values for the three Boolean fields. This is not setting defaults—it is only to indicate that these are Boolean fields.

Listing 9-12. *The Contents of the File We'll Use to Establish Our Secondary Data Source*

```
<Context
     isStartWorkflow="true"
     isRunAtServer="true"
```

```
        provideAllFields="true"
        siteURL=""
    />
```

Note If you remember back in Chapter 7, this is the same process we went through to establish the secondary data source for our workflow task forms with the `ItemMetadata.xml` file.

Now that we have this XML file, we just need to add it as a data source within InfoPath.

1. In the DataSource pane, click Manage Data Connections and then Add.
2. Choose the Create a New Connection to Receive Data option and then click Next.
3. Select the option to receive data from an XML document and click Next.
4. Browse to and select the `ContactsDatasSource.xml` file we created earlier and click Next.
5. Choose the option to include the data as a resource file in the form template and click Next.
6. Make sure that the Automatically Retrieve Data When Form Is Opened box is checked, and then click Finish and Close.

Note You will not need the `ContactsDatasSource.xml` file anymore. Keep it with your solution's source files in case you need to rebuild things later, but you do not need to distribute it with your form.

That's it. Our InfoPath form is now configured to display and use the Contact Picker control. In addition, we've configured it to receive the information passed to it by SharePoint when the form is displayed. The rest of the process involves writing code within our workflow to handle inbound and outbound contacts data. We'll cover that in the next section.

Writing Code to Handle Data

The process that occurs as part of the handoff from SharePoint to our workflow in this scenario is similar to what happens with other Workflow forms and we generally handle it in a similar fashion. There are a few little quirks, as you'll see when we walk through the process.

As before, the information is handed to our workflow as XML. Also as before, we need to grab the XML and parse it to get to the information we need. For our initiation form, the data is stored within the `WorkflowProperties.InitiationData` property of the OnWorkflowActivated activity. Also, just as before, the information contained within the `InitiationData` property is *all* of the form data—we need to go in and parse out the contact information—we'll get to that in just a minute.

For workflow modification forms, the form data is passed to our workflow and is stored in the `ContextData` property of both the EnableWorkflowModification and OnWorkflowModified activities. Once again, we need to write some code to parse out the contact information—we'll get to that in a minute, too.

For workflow task forms, things are a little different—one of those quirks I mentioned. In this case, the data is passed as a hash table as opposed to XML.

In the case of data coming in as XML—for the initiation and modification forms—we are dealing with serialized XML so we can take the same route we used in Chapter 7 with the `xsd.exe` utility to generate a class that maps our XML data into properties. You can flip back to Chapter 7 to see details on making this work (it's right around Listing 7-4), but at a high level, the process is as follows:

1. Save your InfoPath form schema files.
2. Use the XSD utility to generate a class file from the `myschema.xsd` file.
3. Add the generated class to your workflow project.
4. Use code similar to Listing 9-13 to access the data.

Listing 9-13. *Accessing the First Contact's Information from Our Approvers Control*

```
XmlSerializer ser = new XmlSerializer(typeof(MyFields));
xmlTextReader rdr = new XmlTextReader(new StringReader(workflowProperties.➥
InitiationData));
MyFields fields = ser.Deserialize(rdr);
string sPersonName = fields.Approvers[0].DisplayName;
string sLoginName = fields Approvers[0].AccountId;
string sContactType = fields.Approvers[0].AccountType;
```

Remember that when we added the Contact Picker control to our InfoPath form, we named it Approvers—hence the reference to an `Approvers` object in the code in Listing 9-13. Along the same lines, the name of our primary `DataSource` in InfoPath was `MyFields` so that becomes the name of our class from the XSD utility and the type of our `fields` object in Listing 9-13.

The last piece we need to fit in here is the task form. Remember that this one is handled slightly differently—data is passed to our workflow as a hash table instead of as XML. We handle it in a similar fashion, though.

For task forms, we create a hash table object and populate it with the `TaskProperties.ExtendedProperties` property of the activity that triggered the display of the task form (CreateTask, DeleteTask, UpdateTask, or CompleteTask). We also make use of a utility class that Microsoft provides for us in the `Microsoft.Office.Workflow.Utility` namespace. Listing 9-14 shows how we accomplish this task (no pun intended) by using the `ToContact` method of the utility class `Contact`.

Listing 9-14. *Accessing Task Form Data in Our Workflow*

```
Contacts[] approvers = Contact.ToContacts(taskProperties.ExtendedProperties ➥
["Approvers"].ToString());
```

We can now use the Contact class's methods and properties to work with our contact information. Table 9-2 provides information on some of these members.

Table 9-2. *Members of the Contact Class*

Member	Type	Notes
DisplayName	Property	Returns the name for the contact that is typically shown in the UI
EmailAddress	Property	Returns the email address for the contact
LoginName	Property	Returns the name the contact uses to log into the network, in the format Domain\LoginName
ToContacts	Method	The method we used in Listing 9-14 to convert the hash table to an array of Contacts objects

So there you have it—everything you ever wanted to know about the InfoPath Contact Picker but were afraid to ask. Next up—duplicating the functionality in ASPX forms.

ASPX People Editor

The functionality delivered by the ASPX People Editor is identical to that provided by the InfoPath Contact Picker. Naturally, however, the means of achieving that functionality is quite different. In this section we'll delve into the mysteries of the ASP.NET version of this dark magic.

The process of working with this control is similar to the process we used for InfoPath:

1. Add the control to the page and configure it as necessary.
2. Write some code to grab data sent to the form by SharePoint to be used by the control.

Adding and Configuring an Instance of the Control

First things first—the ASPX People Editor is encapsulated within a server control contained within the Microsoft.SharePoint.WebControls namespace (within the Microsoft.SharePoint assembly). So, in order to release this little nugget, we need to add the line shown in Listing 9-15 to the top of our ASPX page.

Listing 9-15. *Setting Things Up to Access the People Editor Functionality*

```
<%@ Register Tagprefix="wssawc" Namespace="Microsoft.SharePoint.WebControls" ➥
Assembly="Microsoft.SharePoint, Version=12.0.0.0, Culture=neutral, ➥
PublicKeyToken=71e9bce111e9429c" %>
```

Next up is adding the code to actually render the control onto the page. Like other server controls, there are a handful of properties that we can set to configure our instance of the control as we need to. First, adding the code in Listing 9-16 will render a basic version of the control. After you've pondered that for about the two seconds it will take to understand what is going on, you can take a look at Table 9-3, which spells out the properties available to configure the control.

Some of the information presented in Table 9-3 is inherited from a base EntityEditor class, but I'll cover it as though it were all directly in PeopleEditor.

Listing 9-16. *The ASPX People Editor—Sample Code from the MOSS SDK*

```
<wssuc:InputFormControl LabelText="Approvers:" runat="server">
     <Template_Control>
          <wssawc:PeopleEditor
               AllowEmpty="false"
               id="Reviewers"
               runat="server"
               SelectionSet="User,SecGroup,SPGroup"
               width='300px'/>
        </Template_Control>
</wssuc:InputFormControl>
```

■ **Note** For information on other building blocks for our ASPX forms, including information on the InputFormControl and Template_Control tags, see the next section in this chapter.

Table 9-3. *Some of the More Useful Properties of the ASPX People Editor*

Property	Description
Accounts	An array list of the validated accounts entered into the control
AllowEmpty	A Boolean indicating whether the control requires a value
AllowTypeIn	A Boolean that indicates whether users can type their own values to be validated or whether they are required to select from the attached directory
CommaSeparatedAccounts	A string containing the validated accounts entered into the control, separated by commas (duh)
CssClass	Allows you to modify the presentation of the control
MaximumEntities	Allows you to limit how many names are entered into the control
MultiSelect	Indicates that users can enter more than one contact
PlaceButtonUnderEntityEditor	Denotes that you want to have the button to validate names or use the address book show up underneath the entry text box
PrincipalSource	Allows you to specify which directory names are validated against
SharePointGroup	Allows you to limit available options for contacts to members of a specific SharePoint group

There are a bunch more properties for things like specifying the images for the buttons and the text of the buttons, but I listed some of the key ones in Table 9-3. They give you an idea of what is possible with this control.

Writing Code to Handle Data

So now that we know all about adding the control to our page and configuring it, how do we actually work with the content it collects? Unfortunately, as with most things about the ASPX forms in our workflows, it is quite a bit more involved than with the InfoPath forms. Read on, MacDuff, but you'll find yourself sorely missing InfoPath before too long.

Note I've previously mentioned the MOSS SDK Microsoft has published. I strongly recommend that you download that and study the CollectFeedbackWorkflow example. I'll cover a lot of what you need to know here, but there is just a ton of information available. If you can't find it via Google (unlikely), check `www.kcdholdings.com`. I'll post a link to it once the final version is published.

While it would certainly be possible to reinvent this wheel, there is no reason to do so. The SDK has 90 percent of what you need to solve this problem. All of the code and explanatory material I'm covering in this section is taken directly from the SDK—code examples intact; scintillating, explanatory prose from my own review; and analysis of the samples in the SDK. Spend a little time with it—you'll wonder how you ever lived without it.

The first piece of the CollectFeedbackWorkflow sample that you're going to want to get really cozy with is the `WFDataPages` class from the `CollectFeedbackSampleAspxPages` project. It contains all of the utility routines for getting ASPX form data—including the `PeopleEditor` information—into and out of the forms and moving it back and forth to our workflow. There is also the `FormData.cs` file, which actually contains three distinct classes—`Contacts`, `FormData`, and `Helper`. We saw these pieces earlier (in Chapter 7 where we worked with the templates I created) but didn't go into the elements of the FormData file that we're going to cover here. You can crack open the original file or the templates I made from them to see the inner workings—I'll just cover the various pieces of these two files here and how they are used.

Note It looks like the samples from the SDK are only going to be available in C#. VB .NET (and naturally all of the Eiffel.NET developers out there) are going to have some translating to do. Sorry, folks, I'm just the messenger.

Table 9-4 lists the useful parts of the SDK classes, along with some descriptions, circles, and arrows and a paragraph on the back of each one explaining what each one is to be used as evidence against us (every technical book worth its salt has to have at least one Arlo Guthrie reference—there's mine).

Table 9-4. *Useful Elements from the SDK's Utility Classes*

Class	Element	Description
`Contacts`	`ContactList`	A public property to access the list of contacts stored in a private `System.Collections.GenericList` variable.
`Contacts`	`AddContact`	Not typically used directly. Front-ended by an `AddContact` method of the `FormData` class.
`FormData`	`Reviewers`	A public property that returns an instance of the `Contacts` class.
`FormData`	`GetReviewers`	Returns a string array representation of the `Contact.ContactList` property.
`FormData`	`AddContact`	Front-end to the `Contacts.AddContact` method. Before calling this underlying method, ensures that the property contains a properly instantiated `Contacts` object.
`Helper`	`DeserializeFormData`	Casts the passed in XML string to a `FormData` object and returns it to the calling routine.
`WFDataPages`	`PopulatePageFromXml`	Responsible for deserializing the XML representation of a Workflow form and populating values into global variables.
`WFDataPages`	`SerializeFormToString`	Does the exact opposite of the `PopulatePagesFromXml`—takes existing Workflow Form data, converts it to an XML string, and returns it to the caller.

With those utilities doing most of the heavy lifting, the basic process for the ASPX forms is pretty straightforward.

1. Add the control to your ASPX form—something similar to Listing 9-16 earlier.

2. When the form is loaded, check whether we are creating new or modifying existing data. If the former, we don't need to do anything. If the latter, we need to add code to retrieve the existing data and populate the form. The SDKs handle this by deserializing the `AssociationData` (or `InitiationData`) properties from our workflow, parsing out the contact information, and populating the `CommaSeparatedAccounts` property of our `PeopleEditor`. The relevant portion of this code (from the `PopulatePageFromXml` method) is shown in Listing 9-17.

3. When the form is submitted, we need to store the information from the People Editor in the appropriate property of our workflow—either `AssociationData` or `InitiationData`. The SDKs accomplish that with this line from the `BtnOK_Click` event handler: `m_assocTemplate.AssociationData = SerializeFormToString(FormType.Association);`. The `SerializeFormToString` method is defined in the `WFDataPages` class. It is responsible for storing all of our form's data—the People Editor information just comes along for the ride. The relevant portions of the `SerializeFormToString` method are shown in Listing 9-18.

Listing 9-17. *Grabbing People Editor Data from the AssociationData or InitiationData Properties of Our Workflow*

```
string[] reviewers = formdata.GetReviewers();
string commaSepAccts = "";
foreach (string reviewer in reviewers)
{
commaSepAccts += reviewer;
commaSepAccts += ",";
}
Reviewers.CommaSeparatedAccounts = commaSepAccts;
```

Listing 9-18. *Storing Our People Editor Data with the Rest of Our Form Values*

```
foreach (Microsoft.SharePoint.WebControls.PickerEntity person in Reviewers.➥
ResolvedEntities)
{
    data.AddContact(person.Key);
}
```

That about covers the important aspects—adding the control and adding code to move data in and out. While there is a lot more to a complete solution around this, you need to take a look at the CollectFeedbackWorkflow sample from the SDKs. It covers everything. I'm not going to sit here and regurgitate it all back to you. I'll just point you to the source. If you have any questions, feel free to ping me.

As if all of this weren't cool enough, because the ASPX People Editor control is nothing more than a server control; it is available for use with other components of our solutions as well—like web parts. See the sidebar "The Flying Purple People Picker" for more information.

THE FLYING PURPLE PEOPLE PICKER

See, there's this song from the late '50s by Sheb Wooley about a flying, purple...oh never mind.

The important thing to know is that we can get all of the functionality described in this section for the ASPX People Editor anywhere we need it. For example, add the code here to a web part and add the line `pedt.RenderControl(writer)` to your web part's `Render` method and *whammo*—instant, full-blown People Editor functionality.

```
PeopleEditor pedt;
protected override void CreateChildControls()
{
    pedt = new PeopleEditor();
    this.Controls.Add(pedt);
    base.CreateChildControls();
}
```

You can set all of the same properties as specified in Table 9-3. When the control is posted back to the server, the data will be available in the `Accounts` or `CommaSeparatedAccounts` property. All in all, not too shabby for eight lines of code...

Building with Blocks—The Makings of an ASPX Form

Microsoft provides a number of components that we can utilize to streamline the process of building our ASPX forms and make them look like they fit in with the rest of the site. These components act as building blocks that can help us jump-start our form's interface. As an added benefit, they will make use of the standard Microsoft styles and so remain fully synchronized with Cascading Style Sheet (CSS) changes you make for the rest of the site.

If you take a look in the `\Program Files\Common Files\Microsoft Shared\web server extensions\12\TEMPLATE\CONTROLTEMPLATES` folder, you will see a bunch of user controls. From the 40-plus provided, we are interested in three:

- `InputFormSection.ascx`
- `InputFormControl.ascx`
- `ButtonSection.ascx`

These three user controls give us the ability to quickly add user interface constructs to our ASPX workflow forms. They're the same constructs Microsoft uses elsewhere in SharePoint, so by default we already look like we fit in. Before we take a look at how they work, let's first show a completed form so you can see what the whole picture looks like before we start dissecting it to see how it ticks. Figure 9-11 shows an association form from the Collect Feedback sample that ships with the SDKs. Take a quick look at it, and then refer back to it as we step through its constituent parts.

Customize Feedback Workflow : Shared Documents
Use this page to customize this instance of Feedback Workflow.
Workflow Tasks
Specify how tasks are routed to participants and whether to allow tasks to be delegated or if participants can request changes be made to the document prior to finishing their tasks.
Assign tasks to:
All participants simultaneously (parallel)
One participant at a time (serial)
Default Workflow Start Values
Specify the default values that this workflow will use when it is started. You can opt to lock the list of participants so that it cannot be changed by the person starting the workflow.
Type the names of people you want to participate when this workflow is started. Add names in the order in which you want the tasks assigned (for serial workflows).
Reviewers:
Type a message to include with your request:
OK
Cancel

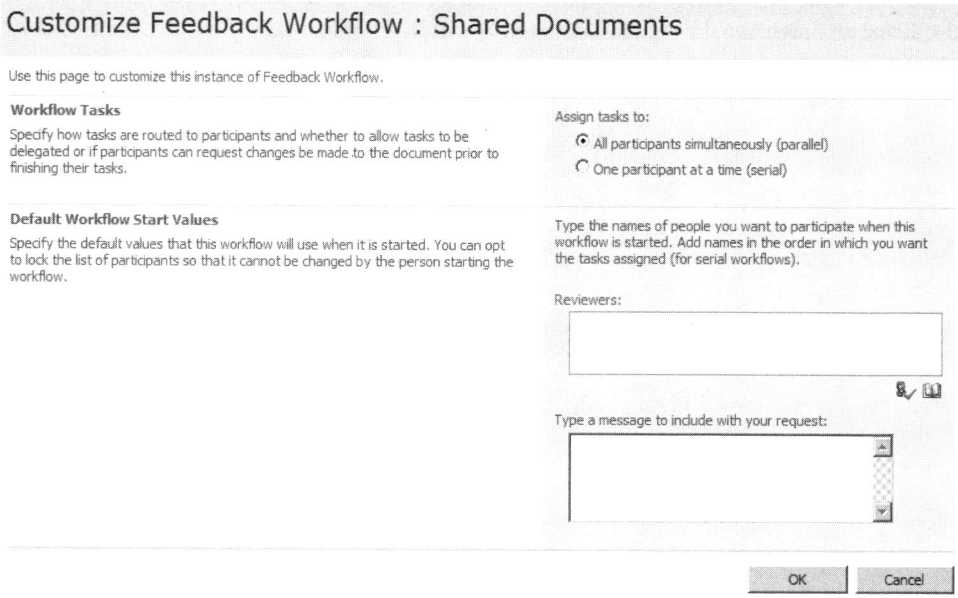

Figure 9-11. *A sample association form from the workflow SDKs*

The first control to look at is the InputFormSection. InputFormSection does just what you would expect considering its name—it renders the HTML to create a visual section on our form. In Figure 9-12, the thin gray lines running the width of the screen indicate the boundaries of each section and are rendered via the InputFormSection control. Properties of the control can be used to customize its appearance and to provide some instructions to the user. The following list provides details on the properties of the InputFormSection control and how they are used. Those four properties aside, the InputFormSection control does very little else. To get value from it, you need to add other controls to it—as we'll see next.

- `Title`: This string property displays the header for the form section. The text you enter here is styled with the `ms-standardheader` CSS class.
  - Interface rendered:

    Workflow Tasks.

  - and:

    Default Workflow Start Values

- `Description`: Another string property. This one is displayed underneath the title and provides instructions to the user. The text you enter here is styled with the `ms-descriptiontext` and `ms-inputformdescription` CSS classes.
  - Interface rendered:

    Specify how tasks are routed to participants and whether to allow tasks to be delegated or if participants can request changes be made to the document prior to finishing their tasks.

- `Collapsible`: A Boolean property that indicates whether the form section can be collapsed to show just the title. Defaults to `false`. If set to `true`, a small plus/minus indicator is shown to the left of the title. If set to `false`, displays the title as shown earlier for the `Title` property.
  - Interface rendered for `true`:

    ⊟ **Workflow Tasks.**

- `Collapsed`:This Boolean property indicates whether a section is shown as collapsed or expanded. Defaults to `false`.
  - Interface rendered for `false`:

    ⊟ **Workflow Tasks.**
    Specify how tasks are routed to participants and whether to allow tasks to be delegated or if participants can request changes be made to the document prior to finishing their tasks.
    Assign tasks to:
    ◉ All participants simultaneously (parallel)
    ○ One participant at a time (serial)

- Interface rendered for `true`:

- `Padding`: A Boolean property that indicates whether or not extra space is added at the bottom of the form section. Can be used to make complex forms look less *busy*. Defaults to `false`.
    - Interface rendered for `false`:

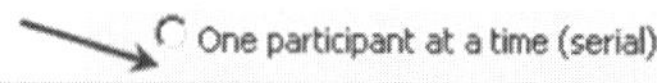

    - Interface rendered for `true`:

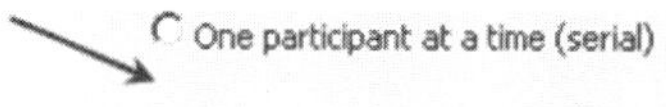

■ **Caution** The data types for each of the properties are indicated in this list. However, when you enter them in your markup, they are all treated as strings. The user control attempts to convert them to the proper data type but it *will* throw an error if it can't convert them properly. So, for example, while there is nothing that will stop you from entering **x** where a Boolean value is expected, you will get a big ugly error page when the form is rendered. Double-check your values!

The full markup to define and display an InputFormSection is shown in Listing 9-19, which is taken from the SDK Collect Feedback sample. It includes both the InputFormSection and the InputFormControl, which is next up in our discussion. Again, this name is pretty descriptive of the function it serves.

Listing 9-19. *The Full Markup to Define a Form Section (Taken from the MOSS SDK Collect Feedback Sample)*

```
<wssuc:InputFormSection Title="Workflow Tasks." Description=➥
"Specify how tasks are routed to participants and whether to allow tasks to ➥
be delegated or if participants can request changes be made to the document ➥
prior to finishing their tasks." runat="server" Collapsible="true" ➥
Collapsed="false" Padding="true">
     <template_inputformcontrols>
          <wssuc:InputFormControl Runat="server" LabelText="Assign tasks to:">
               <Template_Control>
                    <TABLE border=0 cellspacing=0 cellpadding=0>
```

```
                        <tr>
                            <td class="ms-authoringcontrols">
                                <asp:radiobutton runat="server" id="radParallel" ➥
                                  text="All participants simultaneously (parallel)" ➥
                                 GroupName="stage" OnClick="ParallelSettings()" ➥
                                   checked="true"/>
                            </td>
                        </tr>
                        <tr>
                            <td class="ms-authoringcontrols">
                                <asp:radiobutton runat="server" id="radSerial" ➥
                                  text="One participant at a time (serial)" ➥
                                  GroupName="stage" OnClick=➥
                                  "SerialSettings()" />
                            </td>
                        </tr>
                    </TABLE>
                </Template_Control>
            </wssuc:InputFormControl>
        </template_inputformcontrols>
</wssuc:InputFormSection>
```

Only one property is available to customize the InputFormControl itself: `LabelText`. You use that property to specify the text that will appear just above the controls rendered within the InputFormControl control (more on these in a minute). Figure 9-12 shows you how this is rendered.

This is the LabelText for the InputFormControl that contains the 2 radio buttons

RadioButton 1

Radio Button 2

Figure 9-12. *The LabelText property of the InputFormControl renders just above the controls it contains and is useful for labeling the controls.*

The secret to this little gem lies in the markup that you place within its opening and closing tags. You can place any valid HTML or ASP.NET tag in there and the control will take care of wrapping it properly to render as part of the form. For an example, see the sample code in Listing 9-19. You'll see that it has a regular HTML table and two ASP radio buttons. Nothing too fancy, but the result, as shown back in Figure 9-11, is a nice-looking label for our contained controls.

The final user control we need to look at is the ButtonSection control. As you will likely have guessed from the name, this control renders the buttons for your form. There are two properties available to customize the rendering of this control, as shown in Table 9-5.

Table 9-5. *Properties for the ButtonSection Control*

Property	Data Type	Description
ShowSectionLine	Boolean	Indicates whether or not a section line should be shown above the buttons to visually close off the sections above. Defaults to false.
BottomSpacing	Integer	Indicates the number of pixels worth of space to insert after the buttons are rendered. Useful if you have other text or markup coming after the buttons. Pretty useless if the buttons are at the bottom of your form.

Caution The data types for each of the properties are indicated in Table 9-5. However, when you enter them in your markup, they are all treated as strings. The user control attempts to convert them to the proper data type but it *will* throw an error if it can't convert them properly. So, for example, while there is nothing that will stop you from entering *x* where a Boolean value is expected, you will get a big ugly error page when the form is rendered. Double-check your values!

The last piece that we need to look at to style our ASPX forms is actually the header and introductory text that appears at the top of the page. These two elements are delivered via standard HTML and ASP.NET. Figure 9-13 shows which elements on the page I'm talking about.

Customize Feedback Workflow : Shared Documents

Use this page to customize this instance of Feedback Workflow.

Figure 9-13. *The form head elements are rendered with standard HTML and ASP.NET.*

Again, lifting code from the SDKs, Listing 9-20 shows the markup to render these elements. The two variables, strPTS and strPD, are used to hold the values that are displayed at the top of the page. strPTS is the title, and strPD is the descriptive text below it.

Listing 9-20. *Markup from the MOSS SDK Demonstrating How to Render the Form Head Elements*

```
<asp:Content ContentPlaceHolderID="PlaceHolderPageTitleInTitleArea" ➥
runat="server">
    <%
        string strPTS = "Customize " + m_workflowName;
        SPHttpUtility.HtmlEncode(strPTS, Response.Output);
    %>
    :
        <asp:HyperLink ID="hlReturn" runat="server" />
</asp:Content>
```

```
<asp:Content ContentPlaceHolderID="PlaceHolderPageImage" ➥
runat="server">
     <img src="/_layouts/images/blank.gif" width="1" height="1" alt="">
</asp:Content>
<asp:Content ContentPlaceHolderID="PlaceHolderPageDescription" ➥
runat="server">
     <%
          string strPD = "Use this page to customize this instance of " + ➥
m_workflowName + ".";
          SPHttpUtility.HtmlEncode(strPD, Response.Output);
     %>
</asp:Content>
```

If you want to customize the text displayed in either of these two sections, it is a simple matter to edit one or both of those two variables.

So that's it. Those are the major components to building an attractive UI for your ASPX forms. We covered a fair amount of material, but it's not difficult. Now that you understand how to do it, customizing your ASPX forms is just a matter of adding InputFormSections, InputFormControl sections, the specific controls your form needs inside the InputFormControl, and a ButtonSection control. You can use the various properties of the controls to customize how they are rendered on your form.

■ **Note** InfoPath forms, at least the majority of the ones SharePoint ships with in the sample workflows, are typically not styled to look like these ASPX forms. They are left pretty plain because they potentially serve double duty by being rendered into the Office 2007 client applications. There is nothing that would stop you from styling them—you would just do it strictly in InfoPath.

XAML

XAML—YAGA (XAML—"Yet Another Geeky Acronym").

Sigh. Yes, folks, in our already acronym-choked world, we have another to add—XAML, pronounced "zammel"). XAML stands for Extensible Application Markup Language, and why it's not EAML goes back to someone deep in the bowels of the World Wide Web Consortium (W3C), who decided that X was a cooler letter than E and that Extensible Markup Language should be XML and not EML. Go figure.

Anyway, tangents about the death of the English language aside, just what the heck is XAML and why do we care in our Office Workflow world?

The answer is that we do and we don't. We care, because it is an underlying technology within Workflow and it is always good to know as much as you can about your toolkit; we don't care because, in Office at least, we are not going to make use of it. I will, however, provide a very (very!) brief overview of XAML here just so you know what it is and you can impress your peers at cocktail parties.

Note The reason that we won't be using XAML is that the SharePoint Designer takes care of this for us. We'll get into a little more on this soon; just keep it in mind.

So, first of all, what exactly is XAML? We need to answer this question before we can go into how it is used in WF workflows and then why we *won't* use it in our Office workflows—at least not directly. So, XAML is a purely declarative (no-code) style of defining a workflow in the form of a valid XML file. Put another way, we set up our workflow in XAML by building constructs (activities, etc.) described entirely in XML. At runtime, the workflow compiler converts this declarative markup into an in-memory workflow object and executes it.

The benefits to this include

- XAML files are both human-readable and machine-readable.
- Because they are XML files, XAML files can easily be manipulated by the wealth of XML tools available from both Microsoft and other vendors. This means that we can write (or buy) tools that will generate XAML for us or manipulate existing XAML.

There, that second benefit points to why we won't be exposed to much XAML in our Office workflows. The SharePoint Designer is one of those tools that can both create and edit XAML. While it is possible to view the XAML generated by SPD and manipulate it outside of SPD if you wanted to, SPD nicely insulates us from all of this.

Note If you want to look at the XAML generated by SPD you'll actually be looking for a file with an `.xoml` extension. Why Microsoft changed one letter is beyond me. And, yes, when you're talking about this file created by SPD, it is pronounced "zommel" instead of "zammel."

Now you know what XAML is and why we won't be using it much. To wrap up this brief discussion on XAML, let's take a look at some sample XAML markup. Listing 9-21 shows a very basic "Hello Workflow" example created as pure XAML.

Listing 9-21. *A "Hello Workflow" Example Created Entirely in XAML*

```
<SequentialWorkflowActivity
   xmlns="http://schemas.microsoft.com/winfx/2006/xaml/workflow"
   xmlns:xaml="http://schemas.microsoft.com/winfx/2006/xaml"
   xaml:Class="HelloWorkflow" >

   <CodeActivity ExecuteCode="HelloWorkflow" />

   <xaml:Code>
      <![CDATA[
      private void HelloWorkflow(object sender, EventArgs e)
```

```
    {
       Console.WriteLine("Hello Workflow");
    }
    ]]>
  </xaml:Code>

</SequentialWorkflowActivity>
```

The code and markup shown in Listing 9-21 is pretty straightforward—it contains a single Code activity that executes the method defined within the CDATA section to write to the console. Not particularly useful, especially from an Office point of view, but it gives you a sampling of what XAML looks like. You can get as crazy as you'd like to with it.

That's it. We'll end our discussion of XAML right there. We haven't touched on any details but I just wanted to give you an overview—and even then just one that applies to XAML's use in Workflow. XAML is a very large part of the .NET Framework 3.0 and there are tons of other uses for it besides Workflow. If you're interested, just Google "XAML" and be prepared to spend the next several hours reading all about it.

■ **Note** For you purists out there, yes, XAML is, at its core, simply a schema for defining objects and their properties in a purely declarative XML format. XAML is a large part of the Windows Presentation Foundation (nee Avalon) where it provides a separation between the user interface and the application logic. Its use as part of Workflow may seem a little strange but if you separate XAML as a schema from its heritage of defining user interface objects, you'll see that it makes perfect sense. XAML in WF is used to define and describe workflow objects. That's a perfect use of the technology.

Hiding Documents During Workflow Processing

I flip-flop on this one. On the one hand, I would expect that keeping users from seeing documents until any workflows finish processing should be the default—especially for workflows that start automatically when a document is created or modified. On the other hand, though, I can easily think of situation where you would not want this to happen. So I guess Microsoft took the right road by not making it the default. All we need now is a means to hide documents when we have to.

Fortunately, it's pretty easy. We take advantage of the security-trimming features of SharePoint (which don't show things that a user doesn't have access to) and use those features to hide our documents until we're ready to show them.

First, we need to hide the documents. At the beginning of your workflow, add a Code activity and add the code from Listing 9-22. This code will do two things:

- Stop the document from inheriting its permissions from its containing document library—this automatically causes the current user to be assigned as an administrator on the document.
- Assign the specific approvers as administrators (or whatever access level you need to give them) to the per-item permission set for the current document.

Listing 9-22. *Hiding Documents from Users Not Involved in the Workflow*

```
SPListItem item = this.workflowProperties.Item;
item.BreakRoleInheritance(false);

SPUser user = this.workflowProperties.Web.CurrentUser;
SPRoleAssignment assignment = new SPRoleAssignment(user);
SPRoleDefinitionBindingCollection binding = new ➥
SPRoleDefinitionBindingCollection();
binding.Add(workflowProperties.Web.RoleDefinitions.GetByType➥
(SPRoleType.Administrator));
assignment.ImportRoleDefinitionBindings(binding);
item.RoleAssignments.Add(assignment);

//repeat code similar to the following for each user involved in your workflow.
SPRoleAssignment assignment2 = new SPRoleAssignment➥
(@"KCDHoldings\User1", "user1@kcdholdings.com", "User1", "");
SPRoleDefinitionBindingCollection binding2 = new ➥
SPRoleDefinitionBindingCollection();
binding2.Add(workflowProperties.Web.RoleDefinitions.GetByType➥
(SPRoleType.Contributor));
assignment2.ImportRoleDefinitionBindings(binding2);
item.RoleAssignments.Add(assignment2);
```

In Listing 9-22 we break the permission inheritance and then add specific permissions for two users—the current user and then the ever-present "User1." In your workflow, you would likely want to add permissions for every user who will play a role in your workflow. You can get this list of users easily from the Contact Selector (or People Editor) control—see the information earlier in this chapter. Notice that you can specify different permissions for each user added to the permission set—we gave the current user administrative access but User1 contributor access.

The last thing we need to do is reset the permissions once the workflow is done so that it is again available according to the permissions of its containing document library. Two lines of code will take care of this for us. Add another Code activity to the end of your workflow and add the code from Listing 9-23 to it.

Listing 9-23. *Granting Access to the Document Again*

```
SPListItem item = this.workflowProperties.Item;
item.ResetRoleInheritance();
```

Bang. Done. By setting the per-item permissions for the document, we have hidden it from users who are not involved in the workflow. Once we reset those permissions to inherit from the document library, the document automagically appears for all users who should have access.

Before you say anything, yes, the Approval default workflow does exactly this for you if you choose—as shown in Figure 9-14, which was taken from the association form for the Approval workflow. One drawback, however, is that it requires content approval be turned on in the document library. Our code will work regardless of the content approval setting on the list or document library.

Post-completion Workflow Activities

Specify the actions you want to occur after the workflow has been successfully completed.

After the workflow is completed:

☐ Update the approval status (use this workflow to control content approval)

Figure 9-14. *The default Approval setting allows you to hide documents until they are approved, but it requires content approval be turned on in the document library.*

Custom Conditions and Actions for SPD

Way back in Chapter 5, we wrote a custom activity that removes macros from Office 2007 documents. In Chapter 6 we made use of that activity in our workflow. The workflow we created was done in Visual Studio and we could easily add the custom activity to the toolbar. But what about workflows created using the SharePoint Designer? Wouldn't it be nice if we could add custom actions and conditions to meet our business needs?

Fortunately, you can—easily.

Custom Actions

We'll start with a custom action. There's not a lot to this, beyond writing a custom activity—which we covered in Chapter 5. There are a few things to keep in mind. I'll blow through most of the activity stuff pretty quickly here and focus instead on the things that are specific to custom actions. The custom activity we're going to build here will allow workflow builders using the SharePoint Designer to determine a working date (Monday through Friday) a certain period of time from the date the action runs. It is similar to the default Add Time to Date action that ships with the SharePoint Designer, but goes one step further by returning the nearest working day.

To begin with, create a new activity, derived from SequenceActivity. If you're following along at home, for my sample, I called my namespace `WorkDayDate` and my class is called `GetWorkDayDate`. Add three dependency properties using the Workflow Code Snippet:

- `WorkingDayDate`: type = `DateTime`
- `AddValue`: type = `int`
- `Unit`: type = `string`

■ Note The dependency properties are the secret sauce here. They're what make the whole thing work by making our properties available outside our activity. If you read a lot of the Microsoft documentation, they will often call these *promoted properties*.

Just like any other activity, this one needs an `Execute` method. The code I used for mine is shown in Listing 9-24.

Listing 9-24. *Calculating a Valid Working Day for Our Custom Action*

```
protected override ActivityExecutionStatus Execute(ActivityExecutionContext ➥
executionContext)
{
     DateTime dt = DateTime.Now;
     switch (this.Unit)
     {
         case "days":
             dt = dt.AddDays(this.AddValue);
             break;
         case "months":
             dt = dt.AddMonths(this.AddValue);
             break;
         case "years":
             dt = dt.AddYears(this.AddValue);
             break;
         default:
             break;
     }
     if (dt.DayOfWeek == DayOfWeek.Saturday)
     {
         WorkingDayDate = dt.AddDays(-1);
     }
     if (dt.DayOfWeek == DayOfWeek.Sunday)
     {
         WorkingDayDate = dt.AddDays(+1);
     }
     return ActivityExecutionStatus.Closed;
}
```

All this code does is add the appropriate number of days/weeks/months to `Now` (whenever the activity executes) and then modifies the result to be a weekday. In a real production system, you'd need to worry about holidays, too. It's nothing fancy, but it makes the Kessel run in less than 12 parsecs, so we'll just go with it. Strong-name your assembly, compile it, add it to the GAC, and it's time to move on.

Now we can get down to the details of making this activity into an action. There are only five steps to this:

1. Open the `web.config` file for your virtual server.

2. Add the assembly to the `authorizedTypes` list (down near the bottom of the `web.config`): `<authorizedType Assembly="WorkDayDate, Version=1.0.0.0, Culture=neutral, PublicKeyToken=16837ed8463a28fd" Namespace="WorkDayDate" TypeName="*" Authorized="True" />`. Except for the last attribute being `Authorized` instead of `Safe`, this entry is identical to the `SafeControls` entry we use for web parts.

3. Save and close the `web.config` file.

4. Create a new file named `WorkDayDate.actions` in the `\Program Files\Common Files\Microsoft Shared\web server extensions\12\TEMPLATE\1033\Workflow` folder and paste the code from Listing 9-25 into it. This code sets up our activity to be accessible in SPD and configures how it is displayed to developers. Most of Listing 9-25 is pretty straightforward. Microsoft provides a lot of functionality for us in the form of the default Designer types for our actions and some other interesting tidbits. See the sidebar "Action Heroes" for more information.

5. Reset IIS.

Listing 9-25. *The Contents of Our Custom WorkDayDate.actions File*

```
<?xml version="1.0" encoding="utf-8" ?>
<WorkflowInfo Language="en-us">
     <Actions Sequential="then" Parallel="and">
          <Action Name="Get Working Day Due Date" ➥
               ClassName="AWLookup.GetWorkDayDueDate" ➥
               Assembly="AWLookup, Version=1.0.0.0, ➥
               Culture=neutral, PublicKeyToken=16837ed8463a28fd" ➥
               AppliesTo="all"  Category="Custom" >
               <RuleDesigner Sentence="Get Nearest Working Day %1 %2 ➥
                    from current date (store in %3)">
                    <FieldBind Field="Span" DesignerType="Integer" Text="number"➥
                          Id="1"/>
                    <FieldBind Id="2" Field="SpanType" DesignerType="Operator" ➥
                         OperatorTypeFrom="DropDownMenu" Text="timeframe">
                         <Option Name="days" Value="days" />
                         <Option Name="months" Value="months" />
                         <Option Name="years" Value="years" />
                    </FieldBind>
                    <FieldBind Field="WorkingDayDueDate" Text="WorkingDayDueDate"➥
                          Id="3" DesignerType="parameterNames" />
               </RuleDesigner>
              <Parameters>
                   <Parameter Name="Span" Type="System.Double, ➥
                        mscorlib" Direction="In" />
                   <Parameter Name="SpanType" Type="System.String, ➥
                        mscorlib" Direction="In" InitialValue="days" />
                   <Parameter Name="WorkingDayDueDate"  ➥
                        Type="System.DateTime, mscorlib" Direction="Out" />
               </Parameters>
          </Action>
     </Actions>
</WorkflowInfo>
```

Mission accomplished. Launch the SharePoint Designer and create a new workflow. Our WorkDayDate action will be available on the Custom Actions list. Add it to your workflow and you'll see the fruits of your labor in action—as shown in Figure 9-15.

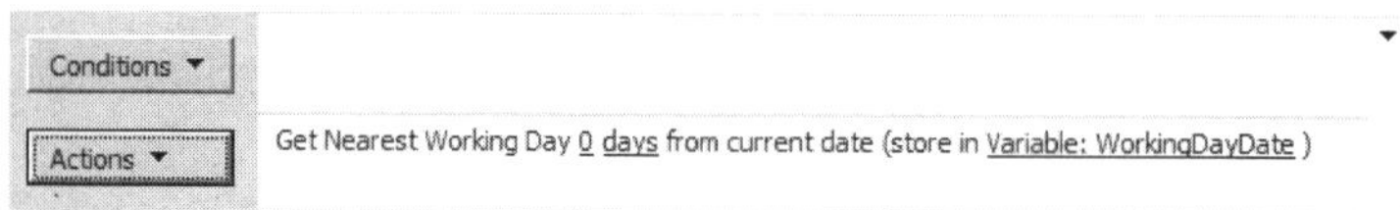

Figure 9-15. *Our custom action in the SharePoint Designer*

ACTION HEROES

The functionality available to us to customize and support our custom actions is pretty good. Microsoft allows us to specify

- What type of SharePoint entity our action can be used against via the `AppliesTo` attribute of the `Action` tag. Valid values are `doclib`, `list`, or `all`.
- Whether the parameter is supplying data to the action or receiving data from the action via the `Direction` attribute of the `Parameter` tag. A value of `In` indicates that the information is passed from the workflow to the activity assembly. A value of `Out`, then, indicates the reverse—the workflow receives the value from the action assembly. A third option, `Optional`, specifies that the `In` parameter is not required.
- The category that our custom action will be displayed in within SharePoint Designer via the `Category` attribute of the `Action` tag.
- We can set an initial value for a given parameter by adding the `InitialValue` attribute on the `Parameter` tag and supplying a value.
- There are a number of options available to us via the `DesignerType` attribute of the `FieldBind` tag to customize the interface presented to the workflow builder to allow them to enter values:
    - `FieldNames`: Retrieves the column names from the list the workflow is attached to.
    - `Date`: Presents a calendar to select a date.
    - `Person`: Presents an interface to allow you to select one or more people from the SharePoint site containing the list, the email address book, a workflow lookup, or the user who created the workflow payload.
    - `Integer`: Limits input to a number value.
    - `Email`: Presents an interface to supply typical email fields.
    - `Survey`: Presents an interface that allows our action to launch the Custom Task tool.
    - `SinglePerson`: Similar to `Person`, but limits choice to only one user.
    - `ParameterNames`: Presents an interface that shows existing variables in a drop-down, and also an option for creating a new variable.
    - `WritableFieldNames`: Shows a drop-down similar to `fieldNames`, but choices are limited to only those fields to which the workflow builder can write new values.
    - `UpdateListItem`: Presents an interface allowing the workflow builder to commit changes to a list item.

- `CreateListItem`: Presents an interface allowing the workflow builder to create a new item in a specified list.
- `ChooseListItem`: Presents a drop-down list of all lists on the site in a pop-up box. Once a list is selected, the interface to choose a specific list item is presented.
- `ListNames`: Presents a drop-down of all lists on the site.
- `ChooseDoclibItem`: Similar to `ChooseListItem`, except limited to only document libraries.
- `TextArea`: Presents an interface in which the workflow builder can type free text.
- `StringBuilder`: Presents an interface that allows the workflow builder to enter a larger amount of textual content and then stores that content in a variable.
- `Dropdown`: Allows you to present a list of choices to the workflow builder.

Finally, there are a few specialty parameters that you can make use of to pass information into your assembly:

- A parameter of `<Parameter Name="__Context" Type="Microsoft.SharePoint.WorkflowActions.WorkflowContext, Microsoft.SharePoint.WorkflowActions" />` will allow your assembly to access the current context of the workflow instance.
- A parameter of `<Parameter Name="__ListId" Type="System.String, mscorlib" Direction="In" />` will pass the GUID of the current list in to your assembly.
- A parameter of `<Parameter Name="__ListItem" Type="System.Int32, mscorlib" Direction="In" />` will pass the integer ID of the current item within its parent list.

Custom Conditions

A condition is used to determine which steps of our workflow will execute. As we discussed in Chapter 4, the SharePoint Designer ships with a number of default conditions that will be sufficient in many situations. However, we can add our own if the defaults do not fit the bill.

Adding a custom condition is pretty much as easy as the custom action. A custom condition is simply a class that contains one or more public, static methods. There is nothing that would stop the class from containing other things as well, like, perhaps, our custom action that we just created. The static method called by the SharePoint Designer to evaluate our condition must return a Boolean value. In order to demonstrate this functionality, we can either create a new class library or simply add the static method to our custom action assembly. The benefit to this latter option right now is that part of our configuration will then already be done—the entry in the `web.config` file will be exactly the same as what we entered for the custom action. In the interest of time, I am going to choose the latter route and add my condition method to my custom action assembly.

The entire contents of my condition method are shown in Listing 9-26. Obviously this is extremely simple—I always return `true`. In your custom condition, you can perform whatever actions you need to in order to determine your return value. Calling web services, instantiating and using other objects, interacting with the SharePoint object model—these are all fair game for your condition.

Listing 9-26. *A Simple Condition Method but Complete Nonetheless*

```
public static bool ReturnTrue()
{
     return true;
}
```

■ **Caution** A condition is nothing more than a method that returns a Boolean value, but it *must* be declared as `static` because the class will not be instantiated—the method will be called directly.

As before, we need to register our condition assembly as an `authorizedType` in our `web.config`. The entry for this will follow exactly the same model as the entry for our custom action. We also need to register our condition with WSS. Again, we do this in a very similar manner—adding more text to our `.actions` file. The options for parameters and fields are the same as for the action, with one notable exception—any fields passed in to our method must be declared parameters of the method we wrote. So, for example, if we wanted to pass in the name of the current user, we would need to code our condition method to accept a string parameter. This makes a certain amount of sense—if we're going to declare a parameter, our method is going to have to be able to accept it.

My sample code for the `.actions` file is shown in Listing 9-27. This code would go right above the opening `<Actions>` element but below the `<WorkflowInfo>` element. The end result is shown in Figure 9-16.

Listing 9-27. *Adding a Custom Condition to the .actions File*

```
<Conditions>
     <Condition Name="AlwaysTrue"
          FunctionName="ReturnTrue"
          ClassName="WorkDayDate.GetWorkDayDate"
          Assembly="WorkDayDate, Version=1.0.0.0, Culture=neutral, ➥
     PublicKeyToken=16837ed8463a28fd"
          AppliesTo="list"
          UsesCurrentItem="true">
               <RuleDesigner Sentence="True">
               </RuleDesigner>
               <Parameters>
               </Parameters>
      </Condition>
</Conditions>
```

Figure 9-16. *Our custom condition in SPD. This step will always execute.*

Activity Verbs

Activity verbs are the options that show up on the context menu when we right-click on the activity inside the Workflow Designer of Visual Studio. The default context menu contains a number of useful elements. Figure 9-17 shows a few samples of these context menus. You can see that the menu options are different, depending on which type of activity they are attached to. From left to right, the activities are Sequence, Parallel, and Code. The options on each menu are a combination of standard items from the root ActivityDesigner type; others are added to a specific subtype, for example, CompositeActivityDesigner or ParallelActivityDesigner.

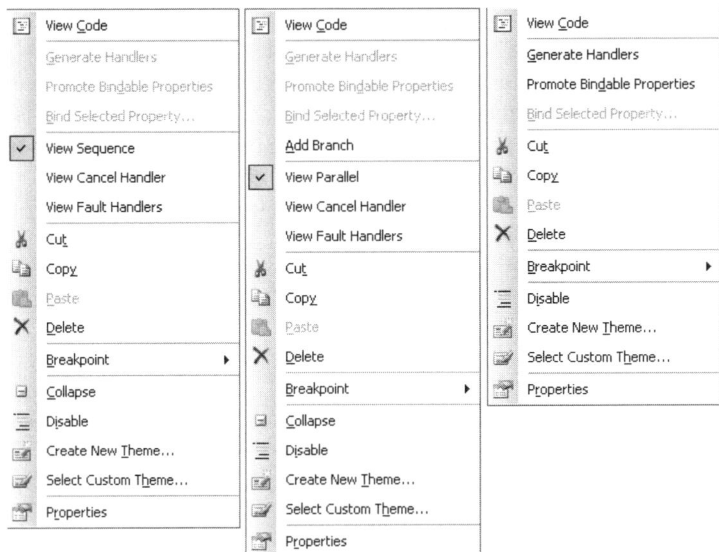

Figure 9-17. *Context menus from three different activities—each with common options and options specific to that activity*

Wouldn't it be nice if we could add our own options for our custom activity? As you've probably guessed, we can, and it's easy. As alluded to earlier, the custom verbs are added via the activity's Designer class, which we covered in detail back in Chapter 5.

I'll walk through a sample here to add a Help verb to the context menu of the MacroStripper custom activity we built back in Chapter 5. When selected, it will display a simple message box with information that will be handy to people using our activity.

The first thing we need to do is add the item to the context menu. The `System.Workflow.ComponentModel.Design` namespace contains a class called `ActivityDesignerVerb`, which is what we need to work with. We need to create a new instance of this class, set a few properties, and then add it to the Designer class's `Verbs` collection (stored in the `Verbs` property).

Before we can do that we'll need to create a global variable in our Designer class that will store our new ActivityDesignerVerb: `ActivityDesignerVerb helpVerb;` will do the trick.

Now we can actually create the `ActivityDesignerVerb` object and add it to the `Verbs` collection. The perfect place to do this is in the `Initialize` method, which we've already overridden in the MacroStripper activity we created in Chapter 5. The code in Listing 9-28 shows the full method. The parameters of the `Add` method are pretty straightforward, except perhaps the second one—the DesignerVerbGroup. All this does is specify where in the context menu our new item is added. The options are Actions, Edit, General, Misc, Options, or View. Again, they just determine where on the menu we are placed.

Listing 9-28. *Creating and Adding Our New Verb to the Context Menu*

```
protected override void Initialize(Activity activity)
{
          helpVerb = new ActivityDesignerVerb(this, DesignerVerbGroup.Edit, ➥
"Help", new EventHandler(ShowHelpHandler));
           Verbs.Add(helpVerb);
}
```

With our new verb added to the menu, the only thing left to do is to write the handler that is referenced in Listing 9-28. The code you add to this method will obviously do whatever it is you need your verb to do. In our case, that is just displaying a message box. The only thing even marginally tricky about this is the method signature itself: `private void ShowHelpHandler (object sender, EventArgs e)`. From there, add whatever code you need to within that event handler.

Build your project, add or update the GAC as necessary, reset IIS if you updated the GAC, and then create a new workflow project to try it out. If today is your lucky day, you'll end up with something similar to Figure 9-18.

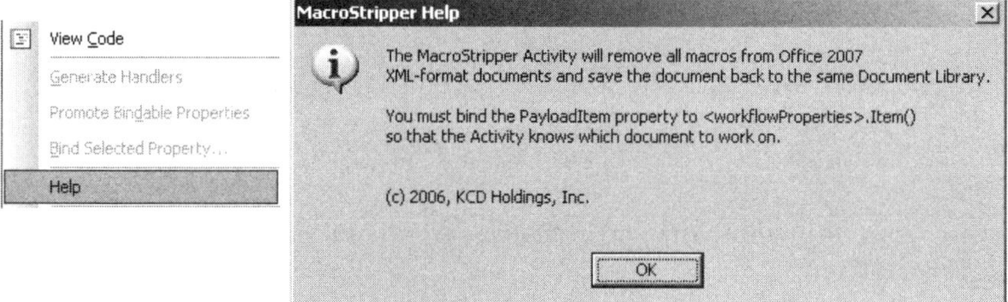

Figure 9-18. *Our custom verb in action*

■ **Tip** The Designer class is only reloaded after you shut down and relaunch Visual Studio. Even just closing your solution and reopening it won't do the trick. It's frustrating, but not too hard to work around.

If your verb is dependent on a property of the underlying activity—for example, if it should only be enabled when the activity is enabled—you can override the OnActivityChanged event and add some code similar to Listing 9-29.

Listing 9-29. *Keeping Our Verb in Synch with the Underlying Activity*

```
protected override void OnActivityChanged(ActivityChangedEventArgs e)
{
    base.OnActivityChanged(e);
    customVerbObject.Enabled = this.Activity.Enabled;
}
```

This example was pretty basic, but it covered all of the important parts. To create other verbs, all you would need to do is to change the text displayed on the context menu and change the code executed in the custom handler to do whatever you need it to do. Here are a few ideas that come immediately to my mind for how you could use this functionality:

- For a composite activity, the ability to set properties on all of its children could conceivably be of use.
- If your activity is particularly complex, or contains a property that is dependent on external values, you could launch a wizard from your verb to walk the workflow builder through your configuration.
- Programmatically add child activities to a custom composite activity.

Overall, it is likely that you won't use activity verbs too often. Just remember that they are a weapon in your arsenal and use them when it would be appropriate.

Workflow Reports

Workflow reports in SharePoint are a bit light (hmmm...I wonder if they give Nobel Prizes for understatements?). Other than some usefulness during debugging, or other troubleshooting, they're not very useful. Let's take a look and then you can decide for yourself.

Using a document library as an example (lists work the same way), you get to the Workflow Reports page through Document Library Settings. From there, click the Workflow Settings link under the Permissions and Management heading. The Workflow Settings page gives you three choices; we're naturally interested here in the View Workflow Reports link, so go ahead and click it.

The next screen, shown in Figure 9-19, shows the two reports available to us for each workflow that has an association with our document library. The two reports available are the Activity Duration Report and the Cancellation & Error Report. I'd show you examples except that I just can't bring myself to do it; it's too painful. Take a look for yourself and you'll see what I mean.

I have to tell you. There is absolutely *nothing* I like more than looking at a report that has wonderfully sexy GUIDs in the first three columns and ends with a three-mile-wide column of raw XML; if that doesn't make you sit up and pay attention, I don't know what will.

Seriously, though, I understand that this is just raw data. I know that it is XML (even though it is targeted at Excel). I know that I can transform it any way I need to, or else dump it into a SQL database and report against it from there. I know all of that. My comment then is then, *don't call them reports.* Perhaps I'm splitting hairs—perhaps it is just a matter of semantics—but by calling something a *report* you set a certain expectation level, and this just doesn't meet it.

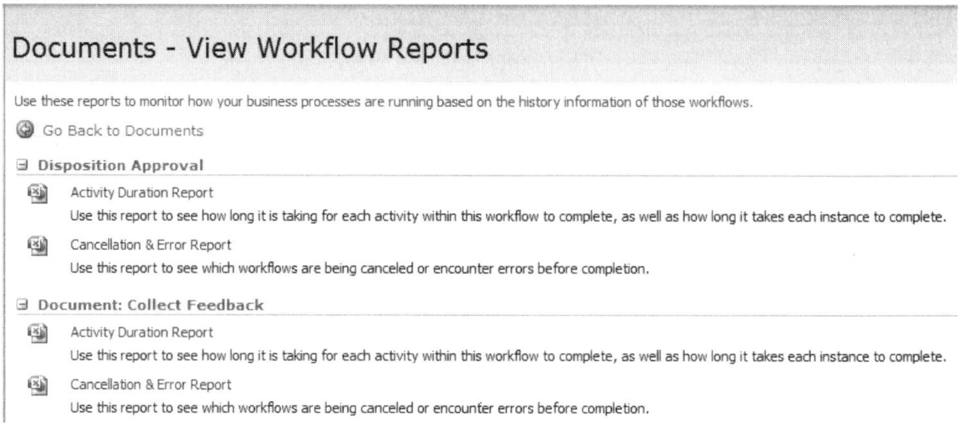

Documents - View Workflow Reports

Use these reports to monitor how your business processes are running based on the history information of those workflows.

Go Back to Documents

Disposition Approval

Activity Duration Report

Use this report to see how long it is taking for each activity within this workflow to complete, as well as how long it takes each instance to complete.

Cancellation & Error Report

Use this report to see which workflows are being canceled or encounter errors before completion.

Document: Collect Feedback

Activity Duration Report

Use this report to see how long it is taking for each activity within this workflow to complete, as well as how long it takes each instance to complete.

Cancellation & Error Report

Use this report to see which workflows are being canceled or encounter errors before completion.

Figure 9-19. *The Workflow Reports screen*

So, take a look. One thing you *can't* say is that there isn't enough information here. Like I said, though, other than some use in debugging or other troubleshooting, I don't see that these reports provide much value.

Sorry.

Odds and Sods

Here are a handful of things important to know that didn't fit in anywhere else:

- This may be common sense, but the *Onxxx* activities that ship with SharePoint are not global listeners. They can only respond to events triggered by other SharePoint activities. So, for example, placing an OnTaskCreated activity in your workflow will not cause the activity to fire when *any* task is created. It only fires when a task is created by a CreateTask activity. Furthermore, it will only fire if the CreateTask activity and the OnTaskCreated activity have the same `CorrelationToken`. For information on `CorrelationTokens`, see Chapter 6.

- A potential problem that I expect a lot of people to trip over is an issue of documents being checked out (either manually by a user or by another workflow process) when the workflow attempts to update them. In this case, the workflow will throw an exception that you will need to handle. Imagine this scenario: a parallel workflow assigns tasks to two different people. One of the people opens the payload document and checks it out. The other person merely opens the document for viewing. The second person reviews the document and marks their task as complete. If the workflow process attempts to write any values back to the document library item (for example to update a column) while the first person still has the document checked out, the workflow will fail unless you explicitly check to see whether the document is checked out before you attempt to update it. So, the take-away from this is to check whether you can write to an item before you attempt to do so. Also, before you do write back to a list, check the item out.

■ Note This may seem somewhat farfetched until you think about the fact that a list or document library can have more than one workflow flagged to start automatically when an item is created or modified. That increases the chances of things tripping over each other. Also, toss in the fact that human workflows are inherently long-running processes and the possibilities increase even further. My advice is just to keep it in mind and use good defensive programming techniques to mitigate the risk.

- Another potential land mine is related to task properties. We previously looked at various incarnations of task property objects—for example, the `TaskProperties` and `BeforeProperties` or `AfterProperties` properties of the various task activities. Keep in mind that these are only snapshots in time. They do not synchronize with the underlying task.

Summary

We've covered lots of ground in this chapter—too much to try to recap here at the end. If you've read this chapter you likely hit upon one or two things that were of value. I hope the rest at least made you think about your workflows differently.

The only thing left at this point is to point you at the object model for Workflow. Looking at that should round out the picture of what is possible. We're going to take a look at the object model in the next chapter.

CHAPTER 10

The Workflow Object Model

Well, here we are at Chapter 10. I said in Chapter 2 that if you felt a pathological need to skip a chapter it should be that one. For Chapter 10, I'll say that if you ever have insomnia and are looking for some dry reading material to put you fast asleep, you should pick up this chapter. Let's face it, a bunch of object descriptions isn't exactly best-seller material. It's reference material, folks; necessary, like a dictionary, but not Stephen King.

The first thing we need to understand about the Workflow Object Model is why we would ever use it. Chances are, you won't need to directly manipulate your workflow environment too often. However, when you do, your only option will be the Object Model. Specifically what you'll be looking to do will depend on your situation, but here are some likely candidates for direct Object Model manipulation:

- Manipulating workflows and tasks from an external application
- Customizing data extraction for reporting or other purposes
- Writing advanced workflows to manipulate workflow aspects of the SharePoint system, including perhaps modifying one workflow as a result of another

My advice would be not to try to read this chapter straight through. I've found that the best way to learn a new object model is to peruse the classes several times. Try first to get a feel for what is possible—don't get bogged down in all of the details. Skim through the chapter—look at the classes and some of the properties or methods. Once you know what is possible, IntelliSense or a quick MSDN search (or even a quick run back to this chapter) can fill in the details you need for implementation. As you use the Object Model more and more, you'll become familiar with the aspects that you use all of the time. Make subsequent passes through this chapter periodically as you work more and more with Workflow. Various bits and pieces will start to make more sense once you have a broader base of experience.

Primary Objects

Everything begins with the `Microsoft.Sharepoint.Workflow` namespace. This is the primary namespace containing all of our objects and is part of `Microsoft.Sharepoint.dll`. I'm not going to pad out the book by listing each and every object, interface, and enumeration in the namespace and then each and every property and method within each object. I'll just cover the main ones that you are more likely to use. If you need information on one of the remaining elements, you can fire up the Object Browser in Visual Studio or peruse the SDK.

■ **Note** I likely can't say this enough: this chapter does not contain every member of every class. I cover the highlights—the stuff you are more likely to use. For a deep-dive into all methods, properties, enumerations, and so forth for each and every class, see the SDK reference material.

SPWorkflow

This class represents a workflow instance. It could be an instance that is currently running or one that completed running (either successfully or resulting in some type of error). The properties and methods of the class give you access to information about the instance as well as the ability to manipulate the instance. Table 10-1 lists the important properties of this class.

Table 10-1. *Properties of the SPWorkflow Class*

Property	Data Type	Description
`HistoryList`	`SPList`	Read-only. Returns the `SPList` object that contains the history entries for this workflow instance. There is also a similar `HistoryListId` property that returns the GUID for the history list that is also read-only.
`InstanceId`	`GUID`	Read-only. Returns the unique identifier for this workflow instance.
`InternalState`	`SPWorkflowState`	Read-only. Returns the current state of the workflow instance. See the `SPWorkflowState` object for details on this enumeration.
`IsCompleted`	`bool`	Read-only. Returns an indicator as to whether the workflow instance has finished processing. You could also get this information from the `InternalState` property, although this property returns `true` for any `InternalState` value that indicates the workflow is no longer running, i.e., `Cancelled`, `Completed`, `Expired`, `FatalError`, `Orphaned`, or `Terminated`.
`IsLocked`	`bool`	Read-only. Returns an indicator as to whether this workflow instance is locked. You could also get this information by interrogating the `InternalState` property and looking for a value of `SPWorkflowState.Locked`.
`ItemGuid`	`GUID`	Read-only. Returns the unique identifier for the `SPListitem` or `SPWeb` to which this instance is attached.

Table 10-1. *Properties of the SPWorkflow Class*

Property	Data Type	Description
`ListId`	`GUID`	Read-only. Returns the unique identifier for the `SPList` to which this instance is attached.
`ParentAssociation`	`SPWorkflowAssociation`	Read-only. Holds a reference to the `SPWorkflow` association object for this instance. Provides access to all of the information related to the association between this workflow and its parent list.
`ParentItem`	`SPListItem`	Read-only. Returns an `SPListItem` object that is the item that this instance of the workflow is attached to.
`ParentList`	`SPList`	Read-only. Returns an `SPList` object that is the list this workflow instance is associated with.
`ParentWeb`	`SPWeb`	Read-only. Returns an `SPWeb` object that is the `SPWeb` that this workflow instance is executing within.
`SiteId`	`GUID`	Read-only. Returns a unique identifier for the site collection that this workflow instance is executing within.
`TaskList`	`SPList`	Read-only. Returns the `SPList` object that contains the task entries for this workflow instance. There is also a similar `TaskListId` property that returns the GUID for the task list that is also read-only.
`Tasks`	`SPWorkflowTaskCollection`	Read-only. Returns an object that contains the collection of tasks associated with this workflow instance.
`WebId`	`GUID`	Read-only. Returns a unique identifier for the web that this workflow instance is executing within.

There are also a few methods, but only one that you will likely use from the `SPWorkflow` class. It is described in Table 10-2.

Table 10-2. *The Useful Method from the SPWorkflow Class*

Method Name	Description
`CreateHistoryEvent`	Allows you to programmatically write entries to the history list for this instance. You can specify an event ID, the history outcome, a description, and various other elements in the parameters.

Sample Code

To see this object in action, take a look at Listing 10-1. It contains code that could be placed inside a workflow to log some pertinent details about the workflow to its own history list.

Listing 10-1. *Working with SPWorkflow Properties in C#*

```
//"workflowProperties" is an object of type SPWorkflowActivationProperties
SPWorkflow spw = new SPWorkflow(workflowProperties.Item, ➥
workflowProperties.WorkflowId);
StringBuilder sbLogInfo = new StringBuilder();
sbLogInfo.AppendFormat("Date Created: {0}", spw.Created.ToLongDateString());
sbLogInfo.AppendFormat("Instance ID: {0}", spw.InstanceId.ToString());
sbLogInfo.AppendFormat("Payload Item ID: {0}", spw.ItemGuid.ToString());
sbLogInfo.AppendFormat("List ID: {0}", spw.ListId.ToString());
sbLogInfo.AppendFormat("Web ID: {0}", spw.WebId);
spw.CreateHistoryEvent(0, null,workflowProperties.OriginatorUser, ➥
"Workflow Information", sbLogInfo.ToString(), string.Empty);
```

SPWorkflowCollection

This class represents… drum roll please… a collection of `SPWorkflow` objects. Go figure. There are two ways to instantiate an `SPWorkflowCollection` object:

- By accessing the `Workflows` property of an `SPListItem` object. This property returns an `SPWorkflowCollection` object containing all workflows for the particular list item.
- By creating a new collection and passing in parameters to specify which workflows you want.

There is no way to filter the first method—you just get all of the workflows that have run or are running on the `SPListItem`. The second method has four overrides that allow you to specify different content for the resulting `SPWorkflowCollection`:

- `public SPWorkflowCollection (SPList list)`: Specifying an `SPList` as the parameter will return a collection of all workflows associated with that list.
- `public SPWorkflowCollection (SPListItem item)`: Specifying an `SPListItem` as the parameter will return all of the workflows that have run or are running on the `SPListItem`.
- `public SPWorkflowCollection (SPList list, Guid associationId)`: Specifying an `SPList` and a GUID for the particular association that you are interested in will return a collection of all workflow instances based on that association within the specified list.
- `public SPWorkflowCollection (SPListItem item, SPWorkflowState inclusiveFilterStates, SPWorkflowState exclusiveFilterStates)`: This final override allows you to specify the particular list item to retrieve workflows from as well as a set of filters to narrow down the workflows returned based on the `SPWorkflowState` specified as either included or excluded. For more information on filters, please see the `SPWorkflowFilter` class later in this chapter.

Once you have created or retrieved your `SPWorkflowCollection` object, there are a number of properties and one method that you can use. The major properties are described in Table 10-3 and the method is described in Table 10-4.

Table 10-3. *The Major Properties of the SPWorkflowCollection Class*

Property Data Type	Description	
`Count`	`int`	Returns the total number of items in the collection
`Item[int]`	`SPWorkflow`	Returns the `SPWorkflow` object at the specified integer position from the collection
`Item[GUID]`	`SPWorkflow`	Returns the `SPWorkflow` object with the specified unique identifier from the collection

Table 10-4. *Major Method of the SPWorkflowCollection Class*

Method Name	Parameters	Description
`GetInstanceIds`	None	Returns a collection of the unique identifiers for each `SPWorkflow` object in the collection

Sample Code

The code shown in Listing 10-2 shows an example of working with the `SPWorkflowCollection` class. It grabs all of the workflow instances currently running on the `SPListItem` object represented by `<List_Item_Object>`, and iterates through them.

Listing 10-2. *Working with SPWorkflowCollection in C#*

```
SPWorkflowCollection spc = new ➥
SPWorkflowCollection(<List_Item_Object>,SPWorkflowState.Running,➥
SPWorkflowState.None);
for (int i=0;i<spc.Count;i++)
{
     SPWorkflow spw = spc[i];
     // do something with workflow instance
}
```

SPWorkflowFilter

The `SPWorkflowFilter` class allows you to limit the workflows returned as part of a collection based on certain criteria. By itself, it does very little, but used as a parameter to various other class methods it allows for fine-tuning of the returned results. There are no useful methods in this class and only three properties, as detailed in Table 10-5.

Table 10-5. *Useful Properties from the SPWorkflowFilter Class*

Property	Data Type	Description
AssignedTo	SPWorkflowAssignedToFilter	Useful for filtering tasks by the person or group they are assigned to. Values for this enumeration are CurrentUserandGroups, meaning the filter encompasses the current user and any applicable groups they belong to), or None, which means the filter does not restrict based on user.
InclusiveFilterStates	SPWorkflowState	Specifies which SPWorkflowStates to allow through the filter.
ExclusiveFilterStates	SPWorkflowState	Specifies which SPWorkflowStates to block.

Sample Code

Listing 10-3 is adapted from the web service we wrote in Chapter 9 to integrate Office 2003 with our Office 2007 workflows. It creates a workflow filter, applies it to a workflow instance, and then iterates through the filtered task collection.

Listing 10-3. *Filtering Tasks*

```
SPWorkflowFilter fltr = new SPWorkflowFilter();
fltr.InclusiveFilterStates = SPWorkflowState.Running;
fltr.ExclusiveFilterStates = SPWorkflowState.None;
for (int i = 0; i < item.Workflows.Count; i++)
{
     SPWorkflow wf = item.Workflows[i];
     if (!wf.IsCompleted)
     {
          wf.TaskFilter = fltr;
          for (int j = 0; j < wf.Tasks.Count; j++)
          {
               //do something with each task in the collection
          }
     }
}
```

SPWorkflowActivationProperties

This class is another one that does not have any useful methods. The properties, however, are quite useful (see Table 10-6). In general, this class provides access to information about the state of a workflow when it is activated, or started, upon a particular list item.

It is possible that you haven't realized this, but we have seen this class in action multiple times throughout the book—the `workflowProperties` object we've been using frequently is of type `SPWorkflowActivationProperties`.

Table 10-6. *Properties of the SPWorkflowActivationProperties Class*

Property	Data Type	Description
`AssociationData`	`string`	Read-only. Stores the serialized data from the workflow's association form as an XML string.
`HistoryList`	`SPList`	Read-only. Returns an `SPList` object that represents the history list associated with this instance of the workflow.
`HistoryListId`	`GUID`	Read-only. Returns the unique identifier of the history list associated with this instance of the workflow.
`HistoryListUrl`	`string`	Read-only. Returns the fully qualified URL of the history list associated with this instance of the workflow.
`InitiationData`	`string`	Read-only. Stores the serialized data from the workflow's initiation form as an XML string.
`Item`	`SPListItem`	Read-only. Returns an `SPListItem` object that represents the item this instance of the workflow is running on.
`ItemId`	`int`	Read-only. Returns an integer that represents the payload item within its parent list's `Items` collection.
`ItemUrl`	`string`	Read-only. Returns the fully qualified URL for the list item this instance of the workflow is running on.
`List`	`SPList`	Read-only. Returns an `SPList` object representing the list that contains the item that this instance of the workflow is running on.
`ListId`	`GUID`	Read-only. Returns the unique identifier for the list that contains the item that this instance of the workflow is running on.
`ListUrl`	`string`	Read-only. Returns the fully qualified URL for the list that contains the item that this instance of the workflow is running on.
`Originator`	`string`	Read-only. Returns the name of the user who initiated this instance of the workflow.
`OriginatorEmail`	`string`	Read-only. Returns the email address of the user who initiated this instance of the workflow.
`Site`	`SPSite`	Read-only. Returns an `SPSite` object that represents the site collection that contains the item that this instance of the workflow is running on.
`SiteId`	`GUID`	Read-only. Returns the unique identifier for the site collection that contains the item that this instance of the workflow is running on.
`SiteUrl`	`string`	Read-only. Returns the fully qualified URL for the site collection that contains the item that this instance of the workflow is running on.

Table 10-6. *Properties of the SPWorkflowActivationProperties Class (Continued)*

Property	Data Type	Description
`TaskList`	`SPList`	Read-only. Returns an `SPList` object that represents the task list associated with this instance of the workflow.
`TaskListId`	`GUID`	Read-only. Returns the unique identifier of the task list associated with this instance of the workflow.
`TaskListUrl`	`string`	Read-only. Returns the fully qualified URL of the task list associated with this instance of the workflow.
`TemplateName`	string	Read-only. Returns the name of the workflow template on which the current instance is based.
`Web`	`SPWeb`	Read-only. Returns an `SPWeb` object that represents the web that contains the item that this instance of the workflow is running on.
`WebId`	`GUID`	Read-only. Returns the unique identifier for the web that contains the item that this instance of the workflow is running on.
`WebUrl`	`string`	Read-only. Returns the fully qualified URL for the web that contains the item that this instance of the workflow is running on.
`Workflow`	`SPWorkflow`	Read-only. Returns an `SPWorkflow` object that represents the current workflow instance to which this object belongs.
`WorkflowId`	`GUID`	Read-only. Returns the unique identifier for the current instance of the workflow.

Sample Code

An example of using the properties of this object is shown in Listing 10-4. It simply sets the To address of a `SendEMailActivity` object to the email address of the person who kicked off the workflow.

Listing 10-4. *Working with SPWorkflowActivationProperties in C#*

```
sendEmailActivity1.To = this.workflowProperties.OriginatorEmail;
```

SPWorkflowAssociation

The `SPWorkflowAssociation` class provides access to information and functionality related to the association between a workflow template and a particular list or content type. Table 10-7 provides details on the more useful methods of this class.

Table 10-7. *Methods of the SPWorkflowAssociation Class*

Method	Return Type	Description
`SetHistoryList`	None	This method allows you to specify which SharePoint list will record the history entries for this workflow instance.
`SetTaskList`	None	This method allows you to specify which SharePoint list will store the task entries for this workflow instance.

The `SPWorkflowAssociation` class has a multitude of properties to store the information pertaining to a specific association. Table 10-8 lists the important properties likely to be used by developers.

Table 10-8. *Some Useful Properties of the SPWorkflowAssociation Class*

Property	Data Type	Description
`AllowManual`	`bool`	Read/write. Indicates whether or not the instance of the workflow can be started manually by a user.
`AssociationData`	`string`	Stores the serialized data from the workflow's association form as an XML string.
`AutoStartChange`	`bool`	Read/write. Indicates whether or not the workflow instance is automatically started whenever the attached item is modified.
`AutoStartCreate`	`bool`	Read/write. Indicates whether or not the workflow instance is automatically started whenever a new item is created.
`BaseTemplate`	`SPWorkflowTemplate`	Read-only. Returns the template on which the current association is based.
`Created`	`DateTime`	Read-only. Returns the date and time that the association was created.
`Description`	`string`	Read/write. Contains a description of the specific association instance.
`HistoryListId`	`GUID`	Read/write. Contains the unique identifier for the list that stores the history entries for this association.
`HistoryListTitle`	`string`	Stores the name of the history list for this association.
`Id`	`GUID`	Read-only. Stores the unique identifier for this association.
`InstantiationUrl`	`string`	Read-only. Returns the URL of the association's initiation form, as specified in the `workflow.xml` file.
`LockItem`	`bool`	Read/write. Controls whether the association is locked. Locked associations cannot have any new instances started on them.

Table 10-8. *Some Useful Properties of the SPWorkflowAssociation Class (Continued)*

Property	Data Type	Description
ModificationUrl	string	Read-only. Returns the URL of the association's modification form, as specified in the workflow.xml file.
Modified	DateTime	Read-only. Returns the date and time that the association was last changed.
Name	string	Read/write. Stores the name assigned to this association.
ParentContentType	SPContentType	Read-only. Returns an SPContentType object representing the content type this association is related to.
ParentList	SPList	Read-only. Returns an SPList object representing the list this association is connected to.
ParentSite	SPSite	Read-only. Returns an SPSite object representing the site collection that contains this association.
ParentWeb	SPWeb	Read-only. Returns an SPWeb object representing the web that contains this association.
SiteId	GUID	Read-only. Returns the unique identifier of the site that contains this association.
StatusUrl	string	Read-only. Stores the URL of the association's status page, as specified in the workflow.xml file.
TaskListId	GUID	Read/write. Contains the unique identifier for the list that stores the task entries for this association.
TaskListTitle	string	Read/write. Stores the name of the task list for this association
WebId	GUID	Read-only. Returns the unique ID of the web that contains this association.

Sample Code

Listing 10-5 shows how to programmatically set the association so that a user can start it manually through the user interface and then save those changes. Note that <List> represents a valid SPList object, and this code assumes that a valid association GUID is passed in on the QueryString.

Listing 10-5. *Setting an Association to Allow Manual Startup*

```
Guid g = new Guid(Request.QueryString["TemplateID"]);
SPWorkflowAssociation assoc = <List>.WorkflowAssociations[g];
if (assoc != null)
{
     assoc.AllowManual = true;
     <List>.UpdateWorkflowAssociation(assoc);
}
```

SPWorkflowManager

The `SPWorkflowManager` class is likely the second-most important class in the whole SharePoint Workflow Object Model—coming in only behind the `SPWorkflow` class. As a developer, you're likely going to spend a fair amount of time in this class if you do any custom workflow programming, beyond just creating activities and workflows in the Designer.

The `SPWorkflowManager` class does just what its name implies—it allows you to programmatically manage workflows. Although there are only a handful of methods and properties available in this class, they are all powerful. Table 10-9 shows the one property for this class and Table 10-10 shows the useful methods.

Table 10-9. *The Property Available in the SPWorkflowManager Class*

Property	Data Type	Description
`ShuttingDown`	`bool`	Read-only. Returns a value to indicate whether or not the Workflow Manager is shutting down.

Table 10-10. *The Methods of the SPWorkflowManager Class*

Method	Return Type	Description
`CountWorkflowAssociations`	`int`	This method will return the number of associations a specific `SPWorkflowTemplate` has within an `SPSite`. You specify the `SPWorkflowTemplate` and the `SPSite` as parameters.
`GetItemActiveWorkflows`	`SPWorkflowCollection`	This method returns a collection of the workflows that are currently active for the list item passed in as a parameter.
`GetItemTasks`	`SPWorkflowTaskCollection`	This method returns a collection of the current tasks for a list item specified as a parameter.
`GetItemWorkflows`	`SPWorkflowCollection`	This method returns a collection of all of the workflows that are associated with the specified list item.

Table 10-10. *The Methods of the SPWorkflowManager Class (Continued)*

Method	Return Type	Description
`GetWorkflowTasks`	`SPWorkflowTaskCollection`	This method returns the tasks associated with the specified list item and workflow instance.
`ModifyWorkflow`	`void`	Allows you to update a currently running workflow.
`RemoveWorkflowFromListItem`	`void`	This method disassociates a workflow, specified as a parameter, from a list so that it is no longer available to be started on items within that list.
`StartWorkflow`	`SPWorkflow`	This method initiates a workflow and returns a new `SPWorkflow` object representing the newly initiated instance.

Sample Code

Listing 10-6 shows how to start a new workflow instance using the `SPWorkflowManager` object. Each item in angle brackets (`<SPSite>`, `<SPListItem>`, etc.) represent valid object of each specified type. The last parameter, `<string>`, represents the serialized data from the initiation form.

Listing 10-6. *Starting a New Workflow Instance*

```
SPWorkflowmanager mngr = <SPSite>.WorkflowManager;
SPWorkflow myNewWorkflow = mngr.StartWorkflow(<SPListItem>, ➥
<SPWorkflowAssociation>, <string>);
```

SPWorkflowState

This enumeration is used to indicate the current condition of a given workflow. It is returned by various properties and also used by the `SPWorkflowFilter` class to fine-tune the results returned by a method. Table 10-11 shows the potential values of the `SPWorkflowState` enumeration.

Table 10-11. *Values of the SPWorkflowState Enumeration*

Value	Description
`All`	This state will never be returned by a property but is instead used to indicate all possible states when setting a filter.
`Cancelled`	Workflow has been canceled in one of three ways: manually by a user, programmatically, or due to a certain condition set within the workflow itself.
`Completed`	Workflow has completed normal processing.
`Expired`	Should never be returned from a property. Internal use only.
`Expiring`	Should never be returned from a property. Internal use only.

Table 10-11. *Values of the SPWorkflowState Enumeration*

Value	Description
`Faulting`	Workflow has encountered an error.
`HasNewEvents`	Should never be returned from a property. Internal use only.
`Locked`	Workflow is valid but no new instances can be started.
`None`	This state will never be returned by a property but is instead used to indicate no states for a filter.
`NotStarted`	Workflow association has been created but the instance of the workflow has not begun processing.
`Orphaned`	Should never be returned from a property. Internal use only.
`Running`	Workflow is currently executing normally.
`Suspended`	Workflow has been put on hold.
`Terminated`	Workflow was manually stopped by an administrator.

Examples of this enumeration being used in code are provided in various places throughout the samples in this chapter.

SPWorkflowTask

`SPWorkflowTask` is a very thin wrapper around the `SPListItem`. It adds a handful of pieces of new functionality to make it "workflow-ready." As the name implies, `SPWorkflowTask` is a representation of a workflow task that has been or will be assigned to a participant. Table 10-12 lists the two useful methods for this object, and Table 10-13 lists the two new properties.

Table 10-12. *Methods of the SPWorkflowtask Class*

Method	Return Type	Description
`AlterTask`	`bool`	This method makes the alteration to the workflow specified in the parameters and returns a Boolean value indicating whether or not the change was made successfully.
`GetExtendedPropertiesAsHashtable`	`Hashtable`	Returns a set of key/value pairs representing the extended properties for the specified task from the `SPListItem` specified in the parameters.

Table 10-13. *The Single Workflow-Specific Property of the SPWorkflowTask Class*

Property	Data Type	Description
`WorkflowId`	`GUID`	Read-only. Returns the unique identifier for the workflow that owns the current task.

SPWorkflowTaskProperties

The SPWorkflowTaskProperties class is responsible for storing the specific details about a particular task. This is another class we've seen before, perhaps without knowing it. All of the task properties objects we've dealt with—taskProperties, afterProperties, beforeProperties, etc.—are of this type.

There are no particularly useful methods defined in this class; however, there are a number of properties. These are detailed in Table 10-14.

Table 10-14. *Properties of the SPWorkflowTaskProperties Class*

Property	Data Type	Description
AssignedTo	string	Read/write. The name of the user to whom the task has been or will be assigned.
Description	string	Read/write. The description of the task provided by the workflow originator.
DueDate	DateTime	Read/write. Stores the date that the task is due.
EMailBody	string	Read/write. The text of the email sent to the user the task is assigned to informing them of their task.
ExtendedProperties	Hashtable	Read-only. Returns the extended properties for the task as a set of key/value pairs.
HasCustomEMailBody	bool	Read/write. True if the email body has been changed from the default, otherwise false.
OnBehalfEmail	string	Read/write. The email address of the user the task is sent for.
OnBehalfReason	string	Read/write. The reason the email is sent by a different user.
PercentComplete	float	Read/write. Indicates the progress made on finishing the task.
SendEmailNotification	bool	Read/write. A flag to indicate whether or not this task is configured to send notifications via email.
StartDate	DateTime	Read/write. The date that the task is configured to begin.
Title	string	Read/write. The name of the task.

Sample Code

We've seen code using this class throughout many of our examples. Any workflow that uses the CreateTask activity is going to make use of an instance of this type.

SPWorkflowTemplate

SPWorkflowTemplate represents a workflow template deployed to a site. It contains properties and methods to retrieve or set information about the template and the default values set on it.

Typically, these default values can be overridden by an administrator when they associate the template with a list. Table 10-15 shows the properties of `SPWorkflowTemplate`. There are no overly useful methods for this class.

Table 10-15. *Properties of the SPWorkflowTemplate Class Likely to Be Used by Developers*

Property	Data Type	Description
`AllowManual`	`bool`	Read/write. Indicates whether or not the instances of the template can be started manually by a user.
`AssociationData`	`string`	Stores the serialized data from the template's association form as an XML string.
`AssociationUrl`	`string`	Read-only. URL to the template's association form. Specified in `workflow.xml`.
`AutoStartChange`	`bool`	Read/write. Indicates whether or not the workflow instance is automatically started whenever the attached item is modified.
`AutoStartCreate`	`bool`	Read/write. Indicates whether or not an instance based on this template is automatically started whenever a new item is created.
`Description`	`string`	Read/write. Contains a description of the template.
`Id`	`GUID`	Read-only. Stores the unique identifier for this template.
`InstantiationUrl`	`string`	Read-only. URL to the template's initiation form. Specified in `workflow.xml`.
`IsDeclarative`	`bool`	Read-only. Indicates whether this workflow was created in code (`false`) or via XAML (`true`). Useful for identifying workflows built with the SharePoint Designer.
`ModificationUrl`	`string`	Read-only. URL to the instance's modification form. Specified in `workflow.xml`.
`Name`	`string`	Read/write. Stores the name assigned to this template
`StatusUrl`	`string`	Read-only. URL to the status page for the template. Specified in `workflow.xml`.

SPWorkflowHistoryEventType

Entries written to the history list for a workflow can specify an event type. This helps to categorize the events in the history list and also helps administrators (or developers doing debugging) classify the type of event being recorded in a standard format. The entry description can then simply record the pertinent information for that particular entry.

The members available within the `SPWorkflowHistoryEventType` enumeration are shown in Table 10-16.

Table 10-16. *SPWorkflowHistoryEventType Enumeration Members*

Member	Description
`None`	Should perhaps be listed as *Other* instead of *None*. Signifies that this entry is essentially uncategorized.
`TaskCompleted`	The entry is marking the completion of a task.
`TaskCreated`	The entry signifies a new task being successfully created.
`TaskDeleted`	The entry for a task being deleted.
`TaskModified`	The entry for a task being modified.
`TaskRolledBack`	The entry for a task being rolled back to a previous state.
`WorkflowCancelled`	The entry for a workflow that has been canceled.
`WorkflowComment`	The entry represents a comment on the workflow—not tied to a particular event.
`WorkflowCompleted`	The workflow has completed, but does not indicate success or failure.
`WorkflowDeleted`	The entry for when a workflow is deleted.
`WorkflowError`	The entry to denote an error in workflow processing. The description parameter should specify error details.
`WorkflowStarted`	The entry for a new instance of a workflow being initiated.

Workflow Throughout the Object Model

The objects we've covered so far represent the major objects from the `Microsoft.Sharepoint.Workflow` namespace. Workflow, however, is baked into SharePoint all across the board. For this reason, there are workflow aspects to various other objects throughout the SharePoint object model. Again, this section will provide information only on the major elements.

- A new `Workflows` property has been added to the `SPListItem` class. This property returns an `SPWorkflowCollection` object containing all of the workflows that are running or have run on the particular list item.
- The `SPList` class has gained two new methods (`AddWorkflowAssociation` and `RemoveWorkflowAssociation`) that allow you to programmatically manage the collection of workflows available to items in a given list.
- `SPContentType` also has an `AddWorkflowAssociation` and a `RemoveWorkflowAssociation` method to allow you to manage the collection of workflows available to items based on a particular content type.
- `SPContentType` also contains an overridden method (`UpdateWorkflowAssociationsOnChildren`) that allows you to push new or modified workflow associations down to other content types that are derived from the given content type. The various overrides of this method allow you to control what gets pushed down and under what conditions.

- SPContentType has a WorkflowAssociations property, which returns an SPContentTypeWorkflowAssociationCollection object of all workflow associations currently available for the given content type.
- SPList contains an UpdateWorkflowAssociation method, which allows us to programmatically change the details of a workflow association.
- SPList contains a DefaultApprovalWorkflowId property, which contains the GUID of the default Approval workflow for the particular list. This property value can be changed programmatically if you need to change the default Approval workflow for a particular list.
- SPSite now contains a WorkflowManager property, which returns an SPWorkflowManager object.
- SPWeb now has a property (WorkflowTemplates), which returns an SPWorkflowTemplateCollection object allowing you to manipulate the workflow templates available on a given site.

There is a little bit more Workflow *stuff* sprinkled elsewhere in the Object Model. This only covers the aspects you are most likely to use. Think of finding the rest as a geeky sort of "Where's Waldo?" game.

MOSS

So far, everything we've covered in this chapter is straight out of WSS, so it is available in both WSS and MOSS. MOSS, as a product built on WSS, naturally extends the WSS workflow capabilities to meet its own needs and provide some additional value. I'll cover the major differences from an object model perspective in this section.

Workflow Web Service

MOSS exposes a web service to allow for the manipulation of certain aspects of its Workflows from an external system. In this release only a handful of methods are available in this web service. They are detailed in Table 10-17.

Table 10-17. *The Methods in the Workflow Web Service Available with MOSS*

Method	Description
AlterToDo	This method allows you to programmatically change a task.
GetTemplatesForItem	This method returns an XmlNode containing information about the workflow templates available for the specified item.
GetToDosForItem	This method returns an XmlNode containing information about the tasks available for the specified item.
GetWorkflowDataForItem	This method returns an XmlNode containing workflow information about the item.

Table 10-17. *The Methods in the Workflow Web Service Available with MOSS (Continued)*

Method	Description
`GetWorkflowTaskData`	This method returns an `XmlNode` containing information about the task information on the item.
`StartWorkflow`	This method is the web service equivalent of the `SPWorkflowManager` `StartWorkflow` method.

Extensions to the Core Object Model

MOSS also includes a `WSSTask` class within the `Microsoft.Office.Workflow` namespace that exposes a number of extensions to the default WSS workflow tasks. Table 10-18 provides information on the properties available in this class.

Table 10-18. *Properties Exposed in the MOSS Object Model That Extend WSS*

Property	Data Type	Description
`DeleteOnComplete`	`bool`	Read/write. Indicates whether or not the particular task should be removed from the system once it has been marked as complete.
`IsChangeAllowed`	`bool`	Read/write. Indicates whether or not the particular task can be modified.
`IsTaskCompleted`	`bool`	Read/write. Indicates whether or not the particular task is finished.
`OnTaskCancelled`	`delegate`	Read/write. Allows a developer to specify an event to be called when a task is canceled.
`OnTaskDeleted`	`delegate`	Read/write. Allows a developer to specify an event to be called when a task is deleted.

Summary

This chapter is loaded with raw information. I included some code samples for most of the major classes to let you see a bit of the Object Model in action. There is no way to summarize concisely all of the information presented in this chapter—and as I said at the beginning, I only cover the major elements of the Object Model here.

Take your time; peruse the chapter a few times. Each time you do, something new will catch your eye. If you can come away with a good sense of what is possible, you'll be a big step ahead of most other Office Workflow developers. You can always look up the details.

APPENDIX

Frequently Asked Questions

Well, OK, you caught me. If this is all new material and the first publishing of the book, who exactly is asking these questions so "frequently"? I suppose I could claim that we set up focus groups and did thousands of interviews across the world, but the truth of the matter is that I just plain made them up. These questions represent what I would ask about this technology and what I assume the rest of you will be asking too. The goal is to help you find the material you are looking for when perhaps you don't quite know what the question is that you're asking or don't know the terminology to use to ask the question.

The FAQs in this section are broken down into a few sections:

- *Introductory and General*: Covers material generally from the first two chapters. Also includes some overview material from other parts of the book.
- *Development*: Covers common development tasks (duh).
- *Administration*: Quiz time. You have to guess what this section covers...

Again, the goal of this appendix is to help you locate material elsewhere in the book. If you're new to Workflow or Office 2007, you should be able to find the material you need more easily here than in a regular index (which requires that you know the proper terminology). Once you've become familiar with the technology, you can likely tear these pages out and make fancy origami cranes out of them.

Introduction and General Questions

What is workflow?

For a dictionary definition, see the "Introducing Workflow" section in Chapter 1. For examples of different types of workflow, including noncomputerized workflows, see the same section.

What role does a computer play in workflow?

Computers are process controllers and automaters (I think I just made up a word). For details see the "Introducing Workflow" section in Chapter 1.

How does workflow relate to business process management, business process automation, or <*insert_fancy_new_term_here*>?

Really, they're the same thing. See the sidebar "A Workflow by Any Other Name..." in Chapter 1.

I've heard that Office 2007 supports human-centric workflows. What does that mean?

Human-centric and machine-centric workflows are discussed in the "Workflow Scenarios" section of Chapter 1.

If Workflow is new to Office 2007, how did people get anything done before?

Boy, you really need to back away from the Kool-Aid station. Workflow is not a new concept and, believe it or not, people got work done before Microsoft entered their lives. See the section "*Workflowasaurus*: Workflow in the Pre–Office 2007 Mesozoic" in Chapter 1.

What is a sequential workflow? What is a state machine?

Both of these questions are covered in Chapter 1, with examples and pictures. We explore them further in Chapter 6 when we build one of each.

What is Windows Workflow Foundation and why should I care?

Windows Workflow Foundation (WF) is described in Chapter 1. You should care because I said so... (hmmm, that never works on my kids, either). OK, you should care because WF forms the foundation for all Office workflows.

Just about every presentation I've seen on Windows Workflow Foundation uses a puzzle-piece diagram to explain all of the pieces. Why don't you?

See Figure 1-6 in the "Windows Workflow Foundation Architecture" section of Chapter 1.

What is the airspeed velocity of an unladen swallow?

African or European?

Where does SharePoint fit into Workflow in Office 2007?

The components of Workflow in the Office 2007 System are covered in various places throughout this book. For a general overview, see the section on the Office 2007 servers in Chapter 1. For details on working with the new version of SharePoint in a Workflow scenario, see, well, the whole rest of the book.

What are some examples of scenarios for Office workflows?

See the top-10 list at the end of Chapter 1 for a quick synopsis. There are also other examples littered throughout that chapter and the rest of the book as well.

Workflow is part of the Office 2007 System. What does that mean? Is it a server or what? How do the Office client applications fit into the picture?

The Office server and client pieces of the 2007 Microsoft Office System are covered in the last third of Chapter 1.

I've heard a lot about something called content types in SharePoint 2007. How does that relate to Workflow?

Content types are discussed in Chapter 1.

Does Microsoft provide any default workflows that I can look at to get an idea of how this all works?

Yes, take a look at the beginning of Chapter 3, the section "The Out-of-the-Box Workflows."

How do I install and configure my Workflow environment?

Installation and configuration are covered in Chapter 2. Unfold the origami cranes you made from the pages and take a look.

Development Questions

What is the SharePoint Designer?

The SharePoint Designer is the preferred client for SharePoint modifications (including Workflow) that do not involve writing code. See Chapter 4 for details.

Where did FrontPage go?

FrontPage is now called the SharePoint Designer. See Chapter 4 for details.

Do all custom workflows need to be developed by a developer using Visual Studio?

No, see Chapter 4 for information on the SharePoint Designer. Also, see Chapter 9 for a brief discussion of XAML.

I've heard that the SharePoint Designer uses conditions and actions to build workflows. What the heck are they?

The SharePoint Designer is covered in Chapter 4; I included listings of the out-of-the-box conditions and actions. Chapter 9 discusses the process of creating new conditions and actions.

Can SharePoint Designer–built workflows support conditional branching?

Yep. See Chapter 4.

Can SharePoint Designer–built workflows support custom forms?

Yep. See Chapter 4.

Can SharePoint Designer–built workflows be deployed to more than one list?

No, at least not out of the box. See Chapter 4.

Can SharePoint Designer–built workflows define variables, look up values from external sources, make potato fritters?

Yes, yes, no. See Chapter 4.

The SharePoint Designer supports a number of actions and conditions out of the box. Can I add my own?

Naturally. See Chapter 9.

What is an activity? What is a simple activity? What is a composite activity?

All things activity are covered in Chapter 5.

Can I build my own activity and have it operate just like Microsoft's?

Yes—we walk through building both a simple and a composite activity in Chapter 5.

I typically only see references to *activities*; I don't often see references to *simple* and *composite* activities.

There are differences between the two. We look at them in Chapter 5.

What are some examples of activities?

The full list of WF and SharePoint activities are provided in Chapter 5. There are also examples of other activities you and your friends can build.

How do I deploy my activities so I can use them in multiple workflows?

Activity deployment is covered in Chapter 5.

Are all WF activities usable in SharePoint workflows?

No. Most are, but there is an important caveat about officially supported activities in Chapter 5.

Why on earth would I ever write a custom activity?

You may never need to; it depends on your situation. See the sidebar "Why Write Custom Activities?" in Chapter 5.

I want to build an activity but I'd like to make it look and act differently when it is used inside Visual Studio. Can I?

Absolutely—we do exactly this in Chapter 5. Look for information on the `Theme`, `ToolboxItem`, and `Designer` classes.

I want to build an activity but don't need it to look or act differently in Visual Studio—the default functionality is fine. Can I?

Yes. This is easier than the previous question and, again, we cover it in Chapter 5.

How can I make sure that the person building a workflow using my activity supplies all of the required values?

See the information on the `Validator` class in Chapter 5.

My custom activity can only contain/cannot contain certain other activities. Can I do this?

Again, yes. See Chapter 5.

I've heard that Microsoft Office now supports XML-based file formats. What does this mean to us as workflow developers?

Good, you've crawled out from under that rock. While the new file formats are not directly related to workflow, they do open up a whole world of possibilities. We look at one of these possibilities in detail in Chapter 5 and briefly discuss some other capabilities.

How is Visual Studio extended to facilitate workflow development?

There are a number of important elements installed with the Workflow Extensions for Visual Studio. We use them extensively in Chapters 5, 6, 7, and 8. There are also a number of Code Snippets available for building workflows. Some of these are installed with the Workflow Extensions, and some are available with the Office 2007 Open XML Snippets. We use those in Chapter 5.

What is the Workflow Designer?

This construct is part of the Workflow Extensions and is used as a graphical environment for building workflows. It is very similar to the BizTalk Orchestration Designer. We make use of it in Chapters 5, 6, 7, and 8.

If I'm building a workflow and need to get information on the payload item that my workflow is running on, how do I accomplish that?

See the information on the `WorkflowProperties` object in Table 6-1.

How do I make new activities available in the Toolbox within Visual Studio?

See the sidebar "Managing Activities in the Toolbox" in Chapter 6.

If there are multiple instances of my workflow running, each on different payloads, how does the workflow engine keep them all straight?

See the information on correlation tokens in Chapter 6.

How do I deploy a workflow?

It's different, depending on whether you are deploying for development and test or for production. Both options are covered in Chapter 6.

Where does InfoPath fit into all of this?

InfoPath is discussed heavily in Chapter 7. It also crops up in various other chapters that reference the user experience in our workflows.

I've seen references to Workflow forms but don't really understand them. What do they do?

Before we actually build our custom Workflow form in Chapter 7, we spend some time on what the various types of forms are used for.

How can I integrate my forms into the Office 2007 client applications if I'm only using WSS?

While technically the answer is that you can't—this is MOSS-only territory—you can get a semblance of the same functionality by looking at Chapter 9. You'll find a section on integrating Office 2003 clients with our workflows. You could follow a similar approach for WSS-only environments with Office 2007.

Is there anything special about the way in which our workflows are processed?

Yes. (A resounding *Yes.*) There is a very important section that you should read in Chapter 9 that covers workflow processing. It's kind of buried, but is important nonetheless.

■ **Note** Hopefully, if you're just skimming this page as you build origami out of it, this note will catch your eye. Read the section in Chapter 9 on workflow processing. You'll be glad you did.

How does the Forms Server know which form to render as part of our workflow?

See the information in Chapter 7 on deploying workflows, specifically the `workflow.xml` file. Also, take a peek at the sidebar "Ode on an InfoPath URN."

Once we build our forms, how are they actually rendered into the browser?

See the sidebar "So Just How Are Our Forms Rendered Anyway?" in Chapter 7 for information.

What are Workflow rules and why do I care?

See Chapter 8. You don't have to care.

How is a Workflow rule related to an activity condition?

Also covered in Chapter 8.

Can I maintain a common set of rules outside of my workflows?

Yes. This is the functionality we explore in Chapter 8.

Can I version and audit rules?

Again, yes, we cover this in Chapter 8.

How do I build rules?

See Chapter 8.

What is chaining?

Chaining is a very simple concept, but also one likely to make your head explode as you explore its power and potential for complexity. Get out the duct tape and plastic sheeting and flip to Chapter 8.

How about rulesets? What are they?

The answer is pretty obvious, once you know it. Flip to Chapter 8.

Is any part of my Office 2007 Workflow available from a mobile device?

Parts are, yes. See Chapter 9.

All of this material is pretty dry, but what does dehydration have to do with my workflows?

Besides being an opportunity for a bad pun, dehydration is an architectural concept key to performance and reliability of WF. See Chapter 9.

How do I handle errors in my workflow?

See Chapter 9.

How do I debug my workflows?

See Chapter 9.

There are elements of the SharePoint user interface that allow my workflow to be canceled by an administrator. How can I make sure that my workflow handles this event?

See Chapter 9, specifically the section "Canceling Workflows."

We've worked with two different tools for building workflows: the SharePoint Designer and Visual Studio. How do I know which tool I should use?

Table 9-1 shows a comparison of the two approaches that I pilfered from the WSS SDK. It will help.

All of this workflow stuff is pretty neat and I can see the value, but we use Office 2003. How can I still get some value without the same level of client interaction?

See the section of Chapter 9 that covers integration with Office 2003. It is not a complete picture and it does not approach the same level of integration that you get with Office 2007, but it's a good start and provides a good foundation on which you could build to suit your needs.

Some of the default Workflow forms have constructs that allow me to validate users against my user store. How can I get that same functionality in my custom forms?

Microsoft really helped us out here. See the section "Picking on People—The InfoPath Contact Picker and the ASPX People Editor" in Chapter 9 for details.

What if I want my forms to look like the rest of my SharePoint application? How can I do that?

See the section "Building with Blocks—the Makings of an ASPX Form" in Chapter 9.

What is XAML? Is it just a typo—did you really mean XML?

No, XAML stands for Extensible Application Markup Language. It is really part of Windows Presentation Foundation (nee *Avalon*) but is used for our workflows as well. See the section on XAML near the end of Chapter 9 for details.

I really don't need your stupid book to learn about Workflow. All I need is an object model. Why do you have all of this inane banter and dumb fluff? Just show me the object model.

OK, see Chapter 10.

The code examples in the book are good, but I was really hoping for more. How do I know how to use some of the capabilities that aren't touched on elsewhere in the scenarios?

There are more short code samples throughout Chapter 10 that deal directly with specific objects and methods within the SharePoint Workflow Object Model.

Administration Questions

What does a workflow administrator do?

First of all, Office workflows support a stratification of administrative functionality into two potential roles. See the section "The Cast of *Ben-Hur*" in Chapter 1 for details.

How do I add a workflow to a list or document library so it is available for my users?

The process to accomplish this task will be slightly different for every workflow. However, a good example is shown in Chapter 3. It covers associating one of the out-of-the-box workflows with a document library. Chapters 6 and 7 also associate a workflow with a document library—in this case, a custom workflow. Finally, Chapter 4 covers the process via the SharePoint Designer, which is a significantly different process from every other method.

How do I check the status of a currently running workflow?

Each workflow provides a Status screen. See the section "The Document Owner's Experience" in Chapter 3 for information.

How do I check what happened on workflows that have finished processing (either successfully or with an error)?

Viewing workflow reports is covered in Chapter 9.

Once I have uploaded a document, how do I start a workflow on it?

There are a number of ways this can happen, for example:

- From the SharePoint site
- From the Office 2007 client applications
- Automatically, based on conditions
- Manually

The examples in Chapters 3 through 8 all walk through the process in slightly different ways. Take a look at those chapters for more information.

Do all of my Workflow participants need to be in my Active Directory?

No. See the "Permutations = Power" section of Chapter 3 for more information.

Where are tasks assigned by my workflows stored?

This is covered throughout the book, but perhaps the best walkthrough is in Table 3-1.

Where is information about the processing of my workflow stored?

The short answer is *history lists*. The long answer is that this is covered throughout the book, but you'll find a good walkthrough in Table 3-1.

How do I delete a workflow from a list or document library?

See the sidebar "Removing a Workflow" in Chapter 3.

Having workflow tasks in SharePoint is great, but that means people have to go looking for them. Is there any way to have it show up somewhere else that puts it right in their faces?

Thanks for lobbing up that softball; yes, synchronizing with Outlook is discussed in Chapter 3, and with mobile devices in Chapter 9.

How do users initiate a workflow on a document or other list item manually?

See the section "The Document Owner's Experience" in Chapter 3. While this section discusses the experience for documents, it is no different for any type of list item.

Can tasks be reassigned by the user they are initially given to?

Yes, the out-of-the-box workflows support this Feature (called workflow *modifications*). See "The Workflow Participant's Experience" in Chapter 3.

How does Workflow integrate with the Office 2007 client applications?

See the various experience walkthroughs and the "Permutations = Power" section in Chapter 3 for descriptions and screenshots.

All of the examples in the book deal with concrete examples. How can I apply them to my specific situation?

This one I'm going to answer right here because there really isn't anywhere else in the book that it is covered. Yes, you're right—these examples may not fit your situation. However, I'm a firm believer in the *teach a person to fish* approach to training. I don't know the specific details of your scenario so I can't answer here. What I can do, however, is expose you to the wealth of possibilities and tools available to you and teach you how to use them. It's up to you, then, to take that and apply it to your situation. You are a good student, Grasshopper; now it is time for you to go out into the world.

Glossary

A lot of new terms are introduced throughout this book, as there would be with any new technology. While you're learning about Workflow in Office 2007, it may be helpful to peruse this glossary periodically. It will help as you're making your way through the book by serving as a refresher of the material you've covered and an introduction to what is yet to come. Once you're a Workflow guru, you can also tear these pages out, write cryptic messages on them, and toss them over the cubicle wall at your neighbor. Make sure you're chanting like a Gregorian monk while you do so. Your legendary status will only grow.

action

The work performed in a workflow built with the SharePoint Designer.

activity

A discrete unit of functionality used to build a workflow. Send Email, Create Task, and Write to Log are all examples of activities.

administrator

The person responsible for establishing and maintaining the environment in which the workflows operate. Can be broken down into *server administrator* and *site administrator*.

association

A relationship between a Workflow template and list or document library that makes the workflow available to items within that list or document library.

builder

This role is tasked with creating new workflows. Typically this person would be using Visual Studio (the Workflow Designer) to build compiled workflows. See *designer*.

business process automation

Another term for workflow.

business process management

Another term for workflow.

composite activity

An activity that contains other activities. It controls the processing of those child activities and/or does some processing before or after the child activities. See *simple activity*.

condition

The circumstances that indicate whether or not a step of a SharePoint Designer Workflow should execute.

condition

A construct within Visual Studio–built workflows that returns a Boolean result to indicate a course of action within the workflow.

content type

A new feature in SharePoint that serves as a means of centralizing the definition of a cohesive unit of information and its associated metadata into a single manageable and deployable unit.

correlation token

The construct used to keep individual instances of a workflow separate, ensuring that activities operate on the proper instance and data is connected to the proper instance.

dehydration

The process of persisting our workflow to disk and removing it from memory for performance benefits. See *rehydration*.

dependency property

A special type of property on an activity that allows the workflow builder to assign values that will not exist until runtime.

designer

Another name for someone who creates workflows. Typically, this person would be using SharePoint Designer to create declarative (no code) workflows as opposed to Visual Studio. See *builder*.

event

In a state machine workflow, an occurrence that is responsible for invoking the transition of our workflow from one state to another.

feature

A package of SharePoint functionality that can be developed, deployed, managed, and activated as a unit.

host

An executable process that serves as the interface between the workflow engine and workflow participants. The host provides common mechanisms for all WF workflows to provide core services. For Office workflows, SharePoint is our host.

human-centric workflow

People are the primary participants and completers of tasks. See *machine-centric workflow.* This type of workflow is the primary focus of Workflow in Office 2007. Human participants play critical roles in the process.

initiation

The process of launching a workflow on a specific list item or document. Workflows must be associated with the list or document library first. See *association.*

initiator

The person who originates or kicks off a workflow. Typically, this will be the owner or author of the document or list item, but it doesn't have to be. Anyone with sufficient privileges can start a workflow on an item. Also referred to as *originator.*

instance

An individual occurrence of a workflow running on a given list item or document. Also known as *workflow instance.*

lookups

See *workflow lookups.*

machine-centric workflow

Computers are the primary participants and completers of tasks. See *human-centric workflow.* This type of workflow is not the primary focus of Workflow in Office 2007. There is, however, nothing that stops WF from implementing a machine-centric process.

MOSS (Microsoft Office SharePoint Server)

The next version of SharePoint Portal Server—and no, it does not gather on rolling stones.

originator

See *initiator.*

participant

The person who receives the tasks of a workflow and completes them.

payload

The document or other piece of content that a workflow is assigned to. For example, in an instance of an Approval workflow, the document that a reviewer must approve or reject is called the payload.

rehydration

The process of reading our workflow information from its persisted state on disk and re-creating its representation in memory exactly the same as if it had never been persisted. See *dehydration.*

rules

A set of conditions evaluated at runtime to determine how a workflow should execute.

ruleset

A collection of rules applied as a unit. Within a ruleset, rules can be assigned priorities, reevaluation conditions, dependencies, and so forth.

sequential workflow

A style of workflow in which the process moves via a prescribed path from beginning to end. Often depicted as a flowchart. Compare to *state machine workflow.*

server administrator

The role responsible for installing workflows on a server or farm so that they are available for use.

simple activity

An activity that does a single task. See *composite activity.*

site administrator

The role responsible for creating a workflow association.

state

In a state machine workflow, a condition that represents the current status of our process.

state machine workflow

A style of workflow in which there is no prescribed path to follow through the process. The process is completed as a result of events triggering transitions from one status to another. Compare to *sequential workflow.*

steps

A portion of a workflow built with the SharePoint Designer. Each *step* of a workflow is composed of conditions and actions that dictate when and what it does.

Windows Workflow Foundation

Part of the .NET Framework 3.0, it is responsible for providing the core services necessary for running all Windows workflows.

workflow

The process that defines and controls the completion of one or more tasks in order to bring about the realization of an identified goal.

workflow instance

See *instance.*

workflow lookups

In SharePoint Designer's workflows, a means of retrieving data from external sources to use within the workflow without writing code.

Workflow template

The SharePoint feature deployed to the server that defines the forms and assemblies used by the workflow. Templates cannot be accessed directly other than to create an *association*.

XAML (Extensible Application Markup Language)

An XML dialect for describing objects and all of their members entirely in XML. Programs can then read and parse this XML and then create the objects as part of the application.

Index

A

E

F

G

J–K

L

P

R

U

X–Z

eBookshop

ASP Today

Apress®
THE EXPERT'S VOICE™